Soviet Global Strategy

Soviet Global Strategy

* * *

William R. Kintner

* * *

Sponsored by
American Security Council Foundation
A National Security Policy Paper

* * *

HERO BOOKS
Fairfax, Virginia

Printed and bound in the USA

HERO BOOKS
10392 Democracy Lane
Fairfax, Virginia 22030
703-591-3674

Table of Contents

Foreword

Bill Kintner's book SOVIET GLOBAL STRATEGY will bury forever Winston Churchill's assertion that "I cannot forecast to you the action of Russia. It is a riddle wrapped in a mystery, inside an enigma." Instead, Soviet programmatic statements from Lenin to Gorbachev matched by Soviet actions and Soviet military programs from support of terrorism to the search for mastery in space reveal an expansive strategy far more frightening than that set forth by Hitler in MEIN KAMPF. Bill's analysis and insight into the Soviets and their long-term strategy for world domination is chilling reading. Too often, particularly today in the era of Soviet "glasnost", men who formulate policies and opinions in our government and media either will not or cannot understand the Soviet global thrust.

From the beginning in 1917, with the victorious Bolsheviks, the Soviet Union has pursued a continuing policy to subvert free democratic societies and the virtues that make them great. That pursuit has not wavered in 70 years. At the core of this Soviet ideology for world domination is the Marxist-Leninist dogma which will not allow the country to make any radical changes in those ideological tenets. No matter how much Mr. Gorbachev says he is creating "openness" within the Soviet system and that through this action he is bringing about much needed change, there can be no real change without repudiation of the original doctrinal plan devised by the Soviets in 1917. There can be no real peaceful co-existence with the "bourgeois" world without the repudiation.

Ambassador Kintner has done a remarkable job of outlining in precise detail the global challenges of the Soviets and why all free democratic nations must be concerned with them. I sincerely hope that our policy makers study this work and glean from it a true understanding of the long-term Soviet goals and how they are affecting and will continue to affect the world and all mankind.

Ambassador Clare Boothe Luce

ix

Acknowledgements

During the many years of gathering and organizing the vast amount of material presented in this book I was both a professor at the University of Pennsylvania and president of the Foreign Policy Research Institute. I retired from the latter position in February 1982. I owe a real debt to the Institute and the many people associated with it.

During the initial years, Dr. Nimrod Novik served as coordinator of the study, currently he is a special assistant to Shimon Peres in Israel. Dr. Shaheen Ayubi helped with the initial survey of the eastern Mediterranean region. Lyushen Shen, who obtained a doctorate at the University of Pennsylvania in 1981 read the manuscript and was most helpful in eliminating historical errors and in dealing with Chinese-English spelling.

Several chapters for the Asian area were initially contributed by Richard Porth, Kenneth Hillas, and Roy Kim. Hillas was a doctoral candidate at the University of Pennsylvania before entering the U.S. Foreign Service in 1980. Dr. Roy Kim is a professor at Drexel University and is a leading scholar on Northeastern Asia. Richard Porth, also a doctoral candidate at the University of Pennsylvania was an invaluable assistant. Ivan Volgyes of the University of Nebraska-Lincoln has made some extremely useful comments for this study.

Parts of the manuscript benefited from the criticism and suggestions of Dr. Robert Zimmerman, a foremost expert on Southeast Asia, who was a member of my staff in Bangkok. Ambassador Robert Strausz-Hupé, while Distinguished Diplomat in Residence at the Foreign Policy Research Institute, and Lord Morrice St. Brides, also a Distinguished Diplomat in Residence at the FPRI, gave me invaluable suggestions.

My understanding of Soviet strategy has been enhanced by my association with Richard B. Foster, Director, Strategic Studies Center, SRI International, Arlington, Virginia. While a student at Georgetown University, Dr. Stefan Possony opened my mind to strategic vistas. Dr. Nils H. Wessell, Director of the FPRI and Dr. Richard E. Bissell, while managing editor of

ORBIS gave me sound counsel. Ori Even-Tov and Edward Shorr, members of the FPRI staff, made important suggestions concerning Soviet strategy. Michelle Wallace, Bradley Hahn, and Lynne Smith have also been helpful in many ways.

Alan Luxemberg and Charles Purrenhage have aided me editorially, Michael Dorfman and Ronald Burton, a Ph.D. candidate at the University Political Science Department was most helpful. David E. Colton rendered invaluable service in the final production of the manuscript.

Numerous individuals have helped with the voluminous typing required to get this manuscript to press and run versions through the xerox machine. These include Carmena Pyfrom, Millie Gioffre, Josephine Fabrizio, Keith Halterman, Donna Hill, Sandy Baily, Dottie Stephens, and the indefatigables Dorothy Greenwood and Ghristina B. Chen. For the final polishing phase I owe thanks to Marla Chazin, Tracey Brown, and Kay Gatsby. To all of the above I amy deeply indebted.

During the summer of 1984, I was a resident in Boston, Virginia at the American Security Council helping to write "A Forward Strategy for America." This current work benefited greatly from numerous meetings with co-authors, visiting scholars, and experts conversant with Soviet policy and practices.

Faith C. Halterman was especially helpful in the final preparation of this manuscript for publication.

It is my privilege to have this book published under the auspices of the American Security Council Foundation.

Needless to say, the views presented in this work are soley my own. Likewise, the author is responsible for all errors in judgment and omission.

William R. Kintner
University of Pennsylvania
July 1 1987

Introduction

Much of my adult life has been devoted to exploring the challenge to free societies created by the Bolshevik party as designed by Vladimir Lenin. Lenin devised a new kind of organization, ostensibly a political party but in actuality an unique structure built on a military model for the purpose of seizing, maintaining, and extending power. Much of my study of the Soviet system took place while I was associated with the Foreign Policy Research Institute (FPRI) in several capacities, including president.

In 1973 I became U.S. Ambassador to Thailand and during my stay in Bangkok I developed an open relationship with my Soviet ambassadorial colleague, Boris I. Illychev. The size of the Soviet mission to the Royal Kingdom of Thailand—second only to our own—impressed me, especially since the actual business between the Soviet Union and Thailand could have been handled by two or three people. My role in Thailand led me to explore the larger issues of American and Soviet undertakings in the adjacent Indian Ocean region.

After returning from Thailand in April 1975, at the request of Secretary of State Kissinger, I undertook a study of U.S. policy interests in the Asian-Pacific area. This examination of U.S. interest analyzed the aims and policies of the People's Republic of China, The Soviet Union, Japan, and many other countries touched by the Indian and Pacific Oceans. The study was supported by the Bureau of Intelligence and Research of the State Department. I consulted with many leading U.S. scholars focusing on Asia before the study was completed.

My prior studies of Soviet foreign policy and my recent experience in Asia convinced me that the Soviet role in Asia was of growing importance to the future of the United States. When I rejoined the Foreign Policy Research Institute in January 1976 it became apparent that much time and study was needed to make a definitive appraisal of Soviet strategy toward Asia. During the ensuing period, while with the FPRI, I organized and supervised a long-term team research effort designed to monitor Soviet activity in the principal regions of Asia as well as along the maritime approaches to the vast Eurasian land mass. By the 1980's it had become increasingly clear that Soviet strategy had become truly global in scope and that one could not grasp the implications of Soviet operations in any region without relating them to Soviet activities elsewhere. This realization led to a shift in the focus of this study from Asia to the globe at large. This shift then added several years to the research and writing task.

By the beginning of the 1980's, the Soviets had acquired the military power to support imposition of totalitarian regimes far from the USSR. Their strategy for doing so is the subject of this work. The enormous and carefully orchestrated Soviet activity in every region of the globe led me to conclude that the Soviets are seeking global hegemony.

This book outlines and addresses the total threat which Soviet Communism presents to democracy and political freedom around the globe. The first three chapters trace the development of Soviet strategy. Chapter IV summarizes the Soviet record of intrusion and expansion into every region of the world, with particular emphasis placed on the last decade. From this record the general parameters of Soviet strategy are then deduced in Chapter V. The final chapter forecasts Soviet strategic options for the rest of this century—which may prove to be the most crucial years of this tumultuous century.

During the writing of this work I have traveled through most areas of the world to discuss the matters presented herein with officials and scholars of many nations. My travels included many trips to Europe and the Soviet Union as well as several trips to Southeast and Northeast Asia, Latin America, and the Caribbean. I have also visited the People's Republic of China, Southern Africa, the Middle East, and India.

The most disturbing conclusion of this study is that as long as Soviet leaders such as General Secretary Gorbachev and his successors are guided by the pernicious concepts of Marxism-Leninism the Soviet bid for world hegemony will continue, and an armed truce will characterize relations between the Soviet Union and the United States and its free world allies.

Fortunately this realistic appraisal is being increasingly recognized and made public. For example, on March 22, 1987 the *New York Times* published an Op Ed article written by important Soviet dissidents living in the West and which asserted that

"What Westerners fail to understand is that if the Soviet leaders were really intent on radical change, they would have to begin by discarding the ruling ideology.

Ideology is that hard core of the Soviet system that does not allow the country to deviate too far for too long; unless the central ideological tenets were to be challenged, long-term Soviet strategy would remain imprisoned by its assumptions.

As long as there is no doctrinal possibility of peace with the "class enemy," how can there be genuine peaceful co-existence with the "bourgeois" world? Nor is peaceful co-existence inside the Soviet Union any more likely."

On April 3, 1987 the *Washington Post* published a piece by one of its editors, Stephen S. Rosenfeld, entitled: "Gorbachev: A Leninist Still." Mr. Rosenfeld states:

> "Gorbachev says that he wants to get back to Lenin, leader of the 1917 Russian Revolution. This goes along with an analysis blaming Stalin, who came to power at the end of the 1920s, for the flaws that are now being officially spotlighted, including the dragging economy and the self-serving bureaucracy. But Lenin installed the style of top-down single-party rule, enforced by terror, that produced not just the failings of the economy and bureaucracy but also the immense atrocities that were committed against the Soviet people in Lenin's and Stalin's times alike."

Charles Krauthammer wrote about "Gorbachev's Iron Smile" in the *Washington Post* on April 24, 1987. He concluded:

> "Stalin was, to borrow a prophetic phrase from a 19th-century Russian revolutionary, Genghis Khan with a telegraph. Gorbachev is Khrushchev with a tailor. Why is Gorbachev so readily extenuated by the leaders of the leading democracy? Because there is nothing that Western publics hunger for more than a communist with a human face. So when the smile reveals iron teeth, it is best to pretend we do not see them. Or better still, to argue that they cannot be there."

It is my hope that his book will enhance Western understanding of the Soviet system and the total threat it presents to freedom everywhere.

William R. Kintner

CHAPTER I

The Roots of Soviet Strategy

A nation's strategy springs from many roots. The roots of Soviet strategy can be traced to two broad sources—the legacy of Russia under the imperial rule of the Czars and the philosophical and operational elements imposed on Russian life after the Bolshevik revolution. Soviet grand strategy for changing the world balance of power in Moscow's favor is deeply related to Soviet military doctrine. Military doctrine is developed by the Communist Party USSR, taking into account factors such as the status of revolutionary forces, the aggressive nature of the "Imperialists" led by the United States and the types of wars and conflicts in the modern era and their class context. Doctrine so developed provides:

> a system of guiding views and directions of a state on the character of wars in given specific historical conditions, the determination of the military tasks of the state, the armed forces and the principles of their structuring, and also the methods and forms of solving all these tasks, including the armed struggle, which flow from the goals of war and the socioeconomic and military-technical possibilities of the country.[1]

Thus, Soviet military doctrine sets the political course of the Communist Party and the Soviet state in the military sphere and dictates the role of Soviet military power in support of other elements of Soviet grand strategy. Doctrine, though formed "with the help of military science and . . . based on its conclusions,"[2] constitutes a "single system of views and directions free from private views and evaluations," while "in military science various and even contradictory points of view do have a place, with various presentations and hypotheses."[3]

Military strategists of the Soviet Union—in research institutes as well as in the armed forces—operate under the control and guidance of the Com-

1

munist Party. Military doctrine stems from the party decisions, and military strategy must be consistent with approved doctrine.

Thus, discussions of doctrine, strategy, military science, and military art are found throughout Soviet strategic studies in which such terms have assumed definite meanings and are not used interchangeably. For the purposes of this study the term "strategy" will be consistently used in the western sense to indicate "the science and art of conducting a campaign by the combination and employment of means on a broad scale for gaining advantage in war.*"

Soviet grand strategy is, ultimately, a fusion of military power, presence or action with diplomacy, ideological propaganda, misinformation, cultural exchanges, and scientific breakthroughs in which the fusion is so complete that the "hardware" and "software" elements of Soviet strategy are difficult to separate. Yet, finally, it is *force,* issuing from military power, that is the indispensable element in Soviet global strategy. "What counts," Lenin once wrote, "is to be the strongest."[4] According to Jean-Francois Revel:

> Force functions at two levels in Moscow's Imperial Advance, the highest and the lowest, the two ends of the strategic are: First it functions as a means of overall strategic pressure to enable communism's homeland to win without war by imposing its will on big and middle-sized powers, where will to resist is paralyzed or suspended by their awareness of Soviet military superiority or parity. Second, pure force is used to crush the weak in no-risk operations.[5]

The Soviet leaders, however, are aware of a cardinal lesson of history that no country can enforce its will by military power alone. Hence Soviet military power operates within the framework of a grand strategy which patiently employs intrigue, infiltration, terrorism, subversion, deception, and propaganda to explore and exploit the human weakness of its opponents.

The historical roots of present Soviet strategy are important for several reasons. First, the historical dimension influences present-day Soviet strategic thinking. Second, Soviet strategic thinkers pay far more attention to the lessons of the past than do their western counterparts. Finally, there are many parallels in the manner in which the Czars extended the Imperial Russian Empire and the way their Soviet successors are expanding today's Soviet Empire.

The Czarist Roots

The Czarist regime was despotic and expansionist. The *knout,* a knotted whip, was its principal tool of rule. Secret police were developed to keep track of politically rebellious subjects. The Czar was an absolute monarch,

---

* Funk and Wagnalls New Encyclopedia, 1983, vol. 24, p. 377.
The "art of employing all elements of the power of a nation or nations to accomplish the objectives of a nation or an alliance in peace or war."

whose power was limited only by the fundamental laws of the empire. One such law was that the Empire could not be partitioned but must be passed entirely to a Czar's descendent in order of primogenitor. The Duma, the principal legislative assembly in Czarist Russia, had no real power until 1905. Its members were elected by a complicated process so manipulated as to secure an overwhelming preponderance for the wealthy, especially the landed classes, and for representatives of the Russian as opposed to the subject peoples.

A secret police, armed with inquisitorial and arbitrary powers, has always existed in autocratic, Czarist Russia. Its activity was directed mainly to the discovery of political offenses, frequently leading to reigns of terror.

From 1238 to 1462 much of present-day Russia came under Mongol or Tartar dominations. The invaders built for themselves a capital, called Sarai, on the lower Volga. Mongol rule frequently caused much devastation and suffering. The people were forced to pay a fixed and heavy tribute.

The Mongol rule left a lasting mark on the Russian psyche. It destroyed nascent forces of self-government. It kept Russia hundreds of years behind the countries of Western Europe. The brutality of the Mongol rule established a precedent followed by subsequent Russian autocrats. Most notorious was Ivan the Terrible who resorted to torture, exile, and execution to repress rebellious subjects.

Eventually the "Golden Horde" began to break up into independent and mutually hostile Khanates and the subjugated Moscow princes were able to free themselves from Tartar control. They began to carry out what became their traditional policy of expanding and consolidating their dominions over their less powerful neighbors.

Thus, the forefathers of the Czars of Muscovy were schooled in Tartar methods of political coercion and, not surprisingly, their ideas of government resembled those of the Tartar Khans. Russia, which had lived for centuries under the Mongol yoke, never experienced the Renaissance, the Reformation, or the Enlightenment. There was no separation of church and state, the Russian Church being a tool of the state or Caesar-Papism.

The Czarist armies became the instrument of Soviet expansion as well as enforcers of Czarist rule which rested on police control and violence. After the fall of Constantinople to the Ottoman Turks in 1453, the Russian Orthodox Church considered Moscow to be the "Third Rome." The two-headed eagle of Byzantium was incorporated into the Moscovite coat of arms.

The expansion of the Czarist Empire was phenomenal. It became the largest contiguous land empire ever created. It was guided by a vision of pan-Slavism within the geopolitical setting of the Eurasian land mass. The dynamics of such expansion extended even across the Pacific into Alaska. However, Russian conquests in North America were relinquished with the sale of Alaska to the United States in 1867.

Most of the institutions and practices of the modern Soviet Union have been modeled after their Czarist predecessors. The Soviets, operating in the traditions of the Czars, continued to expand both their ambitions and the geopolitical frame of Soviet strategy. Though Lenin's Bolshevik Party did introduce philosophical, ideological and militaristic innovations that gave new twists to Soviet strategy, Soviet strategy ultimately issues from historic traditions of that vast empire now called the Soviet Union. This tradition includes centuries of calculated, methodical Russian expansionism under the Czars followed by almost seventy years of phenomenal growth in power and influence under their Soviet successors. Thus, while many aspects of current Soviet strategy can be traced to Lenin and his Bolshevik cohorts, the roots of Soviet policy are found in Czarist-Soviet sources.

The continuity between Czarist expansionist strategy and that of the Soviets can be clearly seen in the Russian conquest of Central Asia in the 18th and 19th centuries. In July 1868 a senior British army officer and Orientalist, Sir Henry Rawlinson, submitted to the India Office in London a memorandum on the "Central Asian Question". Rawlinson was keenly aware of Russia's skill in pursuing Central Asian expansion with utmost caution and sensitivity: "Although steadfastly making progress year by year—whether from accident or design is immaterial—she has never placed her foot beyond that point from which she could, if required, conveniently, withdraw it." In a brilliant summary, Rawlinson portrayed Russia's approach to India as like an army besieging a fortress. She had, he observed, laid a first "line of observation" along the Orenburg-Irtysh line, and was prepared to take up a next "line of demonstration" from Krasnovodsk along the Oxus River to the Pamir plateau, with obvious plans toward seizing the third parallel, running from Herat to Kabul and Kandahar. "Established upon such a line, her position would indeed be formidable . . . and all forces of Asia would be inadequate to expel her."[6]

Past Russian advances into Central Asia are culminating in the current Soviet invasion of Afghanistan—which, however long and costly the conquest will eventually be incorporated into the Soviet Empire. In Afghanistan the Soviets are continuing to build their empire on the proven foundation of annexation on historical grounds.

During the Czarist period the Russian armies crushed their weak opponents in a methodical series of operations. In the Soviet period, after the decline of the Western empires and in a political climate in which open empire-building is no longer feasible, new rituals have been developed to legitimize Soviet conquests. A communist minority will ostensibly seize the reins of government and then call for Soviet military assistance to crush internal resistance. This trick was first unveiled in Georgia in 1918 when the Bolshevik party received a paltry share of the vote in free elections. Moscow's puppets called for help from the Red Army and after years of bloody fighting Georgia was annexed into the Soviet Empire.

The Soviets moved into Kabul in December 1979 after assassinating their own protégé, Amin, whom they had double-crossed some months before. Their new puppet, Karmel, was not even in the country when "his" cry for Soviet help was made. The Soviet device of having the "legal" government call in the Red Army is advantageous to the Soviet Union. Since the Soviet-backed Afghan government is by international law the legal government (although detested by most of the Afghans) the West cannot aid the Afghan freedom fighters effectively without going to war against Afghanistan.

These examples illustrate the continuity as well as the difference between Czarist and Soviet strategy. Many of the instruments and tactics employed by the Czars and the commissars are the same. The Soviets have proven adept in applying Lenin's Marxism in their strategy:

> The more powerful can be vanquished only by exerting the utmost effort, and by the most thorough, careful, attentive, skillful, and obligatory use of any, even the smallest, rift between the enemies, any conflict of interests among the bourgeoisie of the various countries and among the various groups or types of bourgeoisie within the various countries, and also by taking advantage of any, even the smallest, opportunity of winning a mass ally, even though this ally is temporary, vacillating, unstable, unreliable and conditional. Those who do not understand this reveal a failure to understand even the smallest grain of Marxism, of modern scientific socialism is general.[7]

Perhaps the greatest difference between Czarist and Soviet strategy is the fact that while Czarist strategy was limited to Eurasia, Soviet strategy is global in scope. The roots of such Soviet strategy are our next focus.

The Soviet Roots

Geography

By "geography" we refer to the physical characteristics of a territorial area. The impact of this territorial area on strategy is a function of its size, its location relative to other countries, its topography and climate, and the distribution of its population and raw materials. These factors combine to determine the political power exercised by a state in international politics. Geography has influenced Russian-and-now-Soviet security needs, strategy, and ambitions.

The growth of the first Russian Empire and now of the Soviet Empire, must be seen in historical and geo-political terms. At the beginning of the 20th century, Sir Alfred Mackinder warned of the potential growth of a single world empire arising from the heartland of the Eurasian continent.

The combinations of power in this system "are likely to rotate around the pivot state which is likely to be great, but with limited mobility as compared to the surrounding marginal and insular powers." The pivotal, or heartland, area is the "northern part and interior of Eurasia," which extends from the "Arctic Coast down to the central deserts, and has its limits at the broad isthmus between the Baltic and Black Seas."[8] This heartland area roughly corresponds to the region controlled by the Soviet Union west of the Urals.

The Eurasian land mass, coupled with Africa, possesses unmatched self-sufficiency and a dominant strategic position over the Western Hemisphere. Recognizing this, another famous geo-politician, Nicholas Spykman, argued that American foreign policy should be directed at maintaining the political separation of the hemispheres by assuring the independence of the states in the coastal areas, or rimlands, of Eastern Hemisphere continents. If the Soviet Union were able to gain control over the rimlands, it would dominate Eurasia and gain hegemony over the decisive portion of global territory, people, and resources.[9]

The Soviets, apparently acting on this kind of analysis, have sought to increase their influence in rimland areas through the creation of global naval forces. This effort required the Soviet Union to transform itself from a purely continental land power into a seapower as well. Comparable transformations have occurred or have been attempted in the past. Historically, whenever a land-based power also mastered the sea, it could easily defeat a primarily sea-based opponent. This is demonstrated in the bitter rivalry between Rome and Carthage in which Rome added mastery of the sea to its dominance on land and overwhelmed Carthage in the Third Punic War. More recently, the inability of Napoleon to wrest control of the seas from Britain after the battle of Trafalgar led to his eventual defeat at Waterloo. This is a classic case of a land-based power failing because it could not master the sea. The architect of growing Soviet naval power, Admiral Sergei Gorshkov, has criticized Napoleon for his preoccupation with land operations at the neglect of the naval theater. Specifically Gorshkov wrote: The actual causes of the success of the English consisted primarily in that one-sidedness of the strategy of Napoleon which stemmed from his fondness for operations in land theaters and a misreading of the role of the fleet, neglect of its possibilities in a war and hence an inability to use it in a struggle against a maritime opponent, as was England at that time."[10]

While the Soviets may recognize the geo-political significance of Spykman's analysis, they are also keenly aware of two developments which have complemented Spykman's geographic focus as the basis for strategic superiority: space flight and nuclear weaponry. In a time of war, nuclear weaponry and the development of ICBM technology could overcome the advantages of the heartland complex, which are defensive depth and possession of resources. A strategic nuclear exchange could suppress industrial activity and access to natural resources in the heartland more effectively than could an occupying army. Conversely, if the heartland complex were capable of deterring a nuclear attack by possession of equal or superior nuclear systems, its then corresponding influence over its non-nuclear or nuclear-inferior rimland neighbors would be correspondingly greater.

It is for this latter reason that the Soviet strategic rocket forces are organized differently than the U.S. nuclear arsenal. Because of the geo-political ramifications of nuclear weapons deployed in and targetted against rimland areas, Soviet planners do not delineate between theater nuclear weaponry and intercontinental missiles. The SS-20 and the variable range SS-11 are considered by the Soviets as strategic weaponry. When examined in the context of geopolitical considerations of rimland suppression, the logic of Soviet deployment of intermediate range SS-20 missiles in Asia and Europe and the refusal to remove them becomes clear.

The history of warfare shows that a superior maritime power can contain a continental nation, but if a continental power hopes to defeat a maritime power, it must first gain mastery of the sea. The Soviet leaders seem to have learned this lesson and will continue to press for mastery of the oceans as an essential element of their strategy.

Russian Nationalism

The Soviet Union, the world's largest multinational empire, was created initially by the driving force of Russian nationalism. Presently, the Russians comprise less than half of the Soviet population, yet they are the dominant element. The Russians are a proud, talented, and chauvinistic people who seek (and believe they deserve) to be considered the leading country in the world hierarchy of nation-states. Russian nationalism has become a power-ful driving force of Soviet strategy.

Philosophical Materialism

This philosophical doctrine assumes that all existence is resolvable into matter or into an attribute of matter. Anti-religious materialism, the official dogma of the Soviet state, rejects all theological beliefs and organized religions.

As the 1985 CPSU Draft Program puts it:

"the party denounces attempts to use religion to the detriment of the interests of society and the individual. The correct path for overcoming religious prejudices is people's enhanced labor and public activeness, their enlightenment, and the creation and dissemination of new Soviet rituals."

I obtained this description from the FBI's—SOV—85-208, 28 October 1985, Vol. III No. 208 supp 007, p. 20. This draft with some modifications was approved by the CPSU Congress in February, 1986.

Dialectical materialism as developed by Marx and endorsed by Lenin presents a total view of the world. Matter is the sole objective source of all human knowledge. Everything in this world is made of matter. The unity of the world, however, does not prevent it from being in a constant state of flux occurring in space and time. The world, therefore, simultaneously reflects the unity, and the struggle, of opposites. This is the essence of the dialectical process and may be summarized by this equation: thesis clashes with antithesis to produce synthesis. Because this synthesis in time becomes a new thesis on a higher level, the dialectical process of the "negation of negation" never ends. Paradoxically, the communist thinkers believe this process will come to an end with the establishment of pure communist societies, which logically is inconsistent with the dialectical process. The dialectical process includes abrupt "qualitative changes." In fact, at certain points of accumulation all quantitative changes are dialectically transformed into qualitative changes. For example, when water is heated, its temperature rises. But when the temperature has reached the boiling point, the water turns to steam, a qualitative change.

Since people are an integral part of this material world, it follows that the same "laws" have underlaid their behavior throughout history. This aspect of Marxist philosophy is called historical materialism. According to it, people's consciousness is merely a reflection of the material world around them, and the mode of material production shapes their political and social life. The mode of material production and the ensuing production relations form the "base" of every human society. The base determines and influences everything else that belongs to a given society: politics, religion, philosophy, norms of behavior, and spiritual values. These are called the "superstructure." Changes in the base lead to changes in entire societies. Just as in the physical world, the accumulation of quantitative changes results in qualitative changes—for example, revolutions. When analyzed dialectically, the communists believe that the unity and diversity of historical process demonstrate that the mainspring of history is class struggle.

Andrei Gromyko, as a member of the Politburo of the Communist Party Central Committee and Minister of Foreign Affairs of the U.S.S.R., wrote as recently as May 1984:

> Peaceful coexistence is a specific form of socialism's class struggle against capitalism. This struggle is going on and will continue in the field of economics, politics and, of course, ideology, because the world outlook and the class goals of the two social systems are opposite and irreconcilable.[11]

In Communist Ideology

The paramountcy of the class struggle is the core of communist ideology and establishes the overreaching goal of Soviet strategy.

The driving force behind Soviet strategy is the Marxist-Leninist ideology which argues for the destruction of capitalism. In the now classic work, *Imperialism, the Highest State of Capitalism*, published in 1916, Lenin explained how "capitalist" colonial countries had used exploited overseas possessions to escape the inherent contradictions of their economic systems. Therefore, the ultimate destruction of the capitalist system could be achieved by removing these colonies from the capitalist system. This gave rise to the concept of "national wars of liberation." Lenin's analysis of military and revolutionary experience began to be implemented when the Bolsheviks seized power.

Though Lenin proclaimed a built-in mechanism for the failure of capitalism, he recognized that Marxist theory was valid only under ideal conditions. Therefore, he urged that the international Communist movement undermine capitalist societies by using methods that would expedite the inevitable socialist victory. The promotion of "national wars of liberation" is one such method. Lenin's impatience led to the conception and creation of the Bolshevik party to accelerate his anticipated collapse of capitalism.

The Soviet commitment to the destruction of capitalism is not purely ritualistic and *proforma*. The Soviet leadership has rarely passed an opportunity to undermine capitalism. Soviet leadership has repeatedly made explicit that they shall not renounce their Marxist-Leninist goals. Soviet Foreign Minister Andrei Gromyko has stated:

> In its international activity, as in all its activity for revolutionary transformation—the foundations of which were laid by V. I. Lenin—the CPSU is guided by Lenin's behest, relying on the rich legacy of his thoughts and deeds and creatively developing this legacy as it applies to the emerging world situation. [12]

In Violence

The communist doctrine of revolutionary warfare accepts as given the necessity of violence in overthrowing the bourgeoisie either through armed uprising or war. As Lenin put it "not a single problem of the class struggle has ever been solved in history except by violence." Although the Soviets believe it is theoretically possible for a communist revolution to succeed using peaceful means exclusively, they regard this as an unlikely possibility.

For the Soviets, all violent means of struggle are acceptable:

> Non-peaceful means of struggle include not only insurrection . . . civil war, guerilla action, the coercive though not necessarily armed seizure of various state institutions, mass media, factories and so forth. [13]

The approval and praise of violence runs as a red thread in all communist writings dealing with the quest for political power. (The author's book, *The Front is Everywhere* [14] cites numerous communist sources extolling violence as an indispensable arm of the Bolshevik movement.)

The Soviet penchant for violence manifests itself in "wars of national liberation," in Soviet support, assistance and training of terrorist groups, and in the slaughter of dissidents within the Soviet Union, such as Stalin's war against the Kulaks in which millions of Soviet peasants suffered deaths. The Soviets have also employed assassinations to murder impor-

tant individuals who have attempted to escape from their clutches; the
KGB's killing of Trotsky in Mexico City on Stalin's orders is a classic
example. Soviet complicity, via Bulgaria, in their attempted assassination
of the Pope is widely suspected even if unprovable.

In Subversion

Lenin always employed a campaign of subversion to soften up an opponent so that minimal violence would be required at the moment of conquest.[15] There are many types of subversive activities, including
indoctrination, agitation and propaganda, psychological warfare, bribery,
disinformation and misinformation, infiltration into opposing intelligence
services, forgeries, and a host of other active measures. Examples of Soviet
subversive activities will be presented subsequently.

In Deception

The English language has no word to express adequately the complex of
duplicity the Soviet Union has developed to deceive, confuse, and disori-
ent the leaders of the free world. However, the Soviets *do* have such a
term—in Russian, *maskirovka*. It sums up all the meanings of deception
and more. According to Soviet reference works, *maskirovka* includes such
activities as camouflage, concealment, deception, trickery, oral and
printed disinformation, and more. Stalin described the value of deception
in Soviet strategy and diplomacy as follows:

> With a diplomat words *must* diverge from acts—what kind of diplomat would he
> otherwise be? Words are one thing and acts something different. Good words are masks
> for bad deeds. A sincere diplomat would equal dry water, wooden iron.[16]

Elements of deception directly involved in Soviet strategic activities
include: violations of treaties signed by Soviets; concealment of intentions
in the development and deployment of weapons systems; disinformation
ploys designed to mask real political actions; semantic warfare; and propaganda campaigns aimed at evoking desired reactions from free world
peoples and governments.[17] Specific instances of Soviet deceptions will be
discussed in Chapter 3.

Covert Intelligence, Counter-Intelligence and Coercion

The Soviet organ of state security, the KGB, has its roots in the secret
police employed by the Czar. The KGB plays a dominant, pervasive role in
the Soviet Union's power hierarchy. Some Western observers treat the
KGB as a discrete institution whose independence at any given moment is
more or less tightly controlled by the Politburo. This view of the KGB
distorts the reality of the Soviet system. The KGB is the core of the

coercive power by which a Kremlin clique exploits, rules, and wars against its own people, and seeks to eliminate all opposition abroad. The KGB is an embodiment of Soviet power—"an administrative-political organ actively participating in the realization of all the functions of the Soviet State," as the Soviets themselves officially describe it. It "carries out the line of the Central Committee of the Party and of the Soviet State."

The KGB is practically the heart of Soviet leadership. It does not merely protect the one-party regime—as its well-known "sword and shield"—but permeates every institution of society and colors all of Soviet life. No Soviet citizen can achieve and maintain influence or privilege without submitting to, cooperating with, and defending the KGB.

The KGB is the coercive arm of the Soviet state. It is also the organ of espionage and subversion abroad. Suppose the FBI to be increased in size a hundredfold, to be given large-scale military units to command, and to be above-and-outside all law—this new FBI would approximate the KGB inside the Soviet Union. Likewise, increase the CIA two hundred fold—give it full power to do anything it might get away with to undermine and destabilize hostile foreign governments and a rough picture of the foreign arm of the KGB would emerge. (Occasionally KGB agents are caught red-handed and deported.) These two arms of the KGB are the enemy of the Soviet people as well as of free men everywhere.

It was indeed fitting that Yuri Andropov, for 15 years head of the KGB, should have become, for a while, head of the Soviet state—for the KGB is the ultimate expression of the method and character of the Soviet state. In a book detailing the role of Sir William Stephenson, (World War II British security agent), in exploiting the Gouzenko defection, we are told concerning the KGB that:

> Andropov had used history's largest political power to claim the Soviet Party's top job. His enormous bureaucracy was calculated by foreign experts to number 40,000 clerks to service 90,000 supervisory and administrative staff behind 1,500,000 KGB informers, officials, and agents executing the KGB's primary task—internal control. For external operations, there were known to be 250,000 KGB operatives in embassy, legation, consular, trade, and airline functions, or in foreign employ. These were minimum CIA and SIS estimates. They conveyed a sense of Andropov's awesome powers, but also a measure of his anxieties about internal unity. The emphasis was on the KGB's role of killing dissent within Soviet borders, a reaffirmation of Stalin's old obsessive fears of a revolt that, once it began, would look for Fourth Arm help from abroad.[18]

In Semantic Manipulation

During his revolutionary struggle against the Czar, Lenin frequently lamented being forced to use "this cursed Aesopian language" in order to conceal his plans from the Czar's secret police. The manipulation of language and the distortion of meaning has since become one of the prime elements of Soviet strategy. As Stalin put it "the most important weapon in my arsenal is the dictionary." While examples of Soviet semantic manipulation will be presented below, here attention is directed to two important exposures of this devious element in the Soviet strategic arsenal. The first is *A Lexicon of Marxist-Leninist Semantics,* edited by Raymond S. Sleeper, published by Western Goals, 1983; and the second is Ilya Zemtsov's *Lexicon of Soviet Political Terms,* published by Hero Books in 1984.

Although the authors expose Soviet semantics differently, both books are extremely useful. Sleeper's book is a compilation of Soviet sources. For example, he cites:

PROPAGANDA, bourgeois
. . . In our work we must reckon with the fact that bourgeois lies and slander still find a fertile soil among unstable persons. This calls for a stirring up of our ideological work in all possible directions, and for a fight against the noxious, putrifying influence of bourgeois propaganda which employs the most diverse and crafty forms and methods of drumming into everybody, daily and hourly, the different 'good' sides and achievements of the capitalist society and the beauties of the so-called 'free world.'
Aid to Political Self Education (Moscow), Dec. 1958.

PROPAGANDA, communist, truthfulness of
The truthfulness of our propaganda springs from its genuinely scientific character and its party spirit. Our party has never concealed and does not conceal its real aims— the struggles for the workers' interests and for communism which it is consistently waging. . . . Our propaganda gives people a true picture of reality, explaining it from working-class positions, from the only correct class positions.
V. Stepakov, "The Leninist Ideological Legacy and Party Propaganda," *Kommunist* (Moscow), 1965, No. 16.

Zemtsov, in contrast, defines each term, explains it and then cites Soviet sources confirming his explanation. Thus Zemtsov defines *propaganda* as "The organized dissemination of Communist ideology for the purpose of indoctrinating the masses in the Communist world view. He explains "The Soviet system is extolled as having no equal in the world. The Party is billed as a perfect expression of the solidarity of the interests of the leadership and the masses." He then presents these examples.

"Open meetings held by Communists in district schools have met with impressive results. Their aim has been to spread *propaganda* about the Soviet way of life among senior pupils." (*Agitator,* No. 4, 1984, p. 48)

"Imperialist *propaganda* lies in the fact that the influence of atheism on religious families is still weak." (*Agitator,* No. 4, 1984, p. 57)

Power

The persistent Bolshevik, and now Soviet, goal has always been power— the maintenance of power once acquired and a constant effort to extend power over additional subjects and territories. This priority for power also has Czarist roots. As materialists, the Soviets know that military forces are the sine qua non of power and, from the beginnings of the U.S.S.R., their largest allocation of resources has always gone to the military sector. Their war-oriented command economy has been geared to the production of military hardware and has always neglected consumer needs. Despite the Nazi seizure of much of their industry, the Soviets were able to supply 90% of the equipment needed by the Red Army in World War II. This was possible because of the large-scale investment in heavy industry under the leadership of Stalin after he seized sole power in the Kremlin in 1929. The initial industrial build-up to support Soviet armed forces continued and expanded after World War II. The growth in the Soviet military-industrial complex during the sixties was generally ignored by the West, which was preoccupied with protesting America's involvement in the Indo-China war.

The Chinese were among the first to assert that the vast Soviet military forces were made possible by the Soviet war economy.

> The entire Soviet economy has taken a peculiar form of war economy. With stress laid on 'an economy which can guarantee the waging of war by either nuclear fragmentation means of conventional weapons,' the new tsars all along have given arms expansion and war preparation top priority and have geared even more manpower, material resources and money to military objectives steadily intensifying the militarization of the national economy. Military spending has spiralled year after year. The proportion of military outlay in the national income also has registered a yearly increase. It was about 13 percent in 1960 and 19.6 percent in 1974. As far as the proportion is concerned, the Soviet Union has not only surpassed the pre-war Hitlerite Germany (19 percent), but also greatly outstripped U.S. imperialism at the time of its wars of aggression to Korea (15 percent) and in Vietnam (10 percent). According to obviously doctored official Soviet statistics, national income is said to be about 66 percent that of the United States, but actual military spending tops the United States by 20 percent.[19]

Moscow's commitment to military spending and achievement of across-the-board military superiority is not diminishing. Instead of leveling off or declining in a context of lowered rates of economic growth, Soviet defense spending continues to increase. As weapons became more complicated and the race for mastery of space intensified, the Soviet Union adopted as a fundamental policy the promotion of science and technology. This program was to provide the primary means of overcoming stagnation in their economy and of achieving superiority in military forces over those of the West. Yuri Andropov discussed these aims in his first major address after taking power:

> If we really want to advance the introduction of new technology and new work methods, it is necessary for the central economic management bodies, the Academy of Sciences, the State Committee for Science and Technology, and the relevant Ministries not merely to popularize them but to identify and eliminate the actual difficulties that hamper scientific and technical progress. The alliance of science and production should be promoted by planning methods and by the system of material incentives. It is necessary to create a situation in which those who boldly introduce new technology do not find themselves at a disadvantage.[20]

The Soviet Science/Technology policy has been implemented in various ways. First, there was a major increase in the allocation of resources in the so-called science budget. Also, there was a much greater effort in science education. Goals for the lower grades through high school were established for the production of scientifically and mathematically trained high school graduates. Finally, there was a major increase in military Research, Development Technology and Engineering activities. The RDT&E budget is currently doubling about every 10 years—a 7–8 percent per year annual growth rate compared with a 2–3 percent growth rate of the overall military budget (which doubles every 15–20 years). The strategic use of the weapons systems generated by this Soviet technological surge will be discussed in Chapter 2.

On no one issue has there been greater division within the United States than on the nature of the threat from the Soviet Union. Perhaps if the American people would examine seriously the roots of Soviet strategy as described above they might better understand the current situation. The Kremlin obviously has a strategy for conquest, which it takes seriously. The Soviet governing mechanisms, based on a military model, are organized to implement this strategy.

The Soviet Strategic Command Structure

People are accustomed to think of the leading personalities of a self-proclaimed revolutionary government exclusively as politicians, but it is probably more accurate to think of them as political soldiers. Lenin is the example of the successful military revolutionist. Up to 1917 Lenin prepared to command a revolution. The timing, the selection of objectives, and the actual command of the Bolshevik revolution were Lenin's. "Lenin devoted special attention to the task of elaborating the Marxist views on war," his official Soviet biography informs us. "He studied and analyzed from the materialist point of view the best of what had been produced by the bourgeois military science. He had a high opinion of the works of that outstanding military thinker of the nineteenth century, Clausewitz."[21]

From Lenin's own pen we read, "No Social-Democrat at all familiar with history, who studied Engels, the great expert on the matter, ever doubted the importance of military knowledge, the tremendous importance of military technique as an instrument in the hands of the masses of the people for deciding the issue of great historical conflicts."[22] It was also Lenin who wrote that the revolutionary task is "to give the masses military leadership as necessary in civil war as in any other war.[23]

> For Lenin, military organization was the best model: "Let us take a modern army," said Lenin. "Here is a good example of organization. This organization is good simply because it is flexible, because it knows how to impart a single will to millions of people . . . that is what you call organization, when in the name of one object, inspired by a single will, millions of people change the form of their intercourse and their action, the place and methods of their activity, their weapons and arms, in accordance with the changing circumstances and demands of the struggle.[24]

In Goethe's insightful words, "Everything remains true to its origins." The military basis upon which Lenin founded the fledgling Soviet state is evident today in the militarized command structure of the Soviet Union.

Soviet decision-making is distinguished from decision-making in the free world by its centralization and secrecy. Whereas in the free world numerous interest groups compete for power and influence, in the Soviet Union such competition is generally non-existent. Any political competition that exists occurs within the Party, preceding and during a struggle for power.

Similarly, economic competition is, for all practical purposes, non-existent. The CPSU controls all means of production and therefore allocates the country's economic resources as it sees fit. The Soviets call this the "dictatorship of the proletariat," but it is in fact the dictatorship of the elite of the Communist Party, the so-called *nomenklatura*. This elite within an elite enjoys all the privileges of power. Indeed it owns the Soviet Union and runs it accordingly.

At the apex of the CPSU is the Politburo of the Central Committee. Although the size of the Politburo varies, it typically includes some dozen full members and half-dozen candidate members.

No one achieves Politburo status without the help of strong patrons both personal and institutional. For example:

> Gorbachev's rise as the youngest-ever secretary of the party has been a classic example of these maneuvers. Before 1978, Gorbachev was secretary of the Stavropol Territory—a small resort area of mineral baths for the Soviet elite in the Caucuses mountains of Georgia, Stalin's birthplace. There Gorbachev had an opportunity to cultivate the friendship of visiting party leaders and to supply them with choice fresh fruits and vegetables and wines, sometimes flown to wintry Moscow, luxuries unavailable to other Soviet citizens. During the 1960s and 1970s, Gorbachev had two patrons in Moscow: M. Suslov, the embittered brilliant chief ideologue of the party, and F. Kulakov. Both earlier had held the Stavropol post—Kulakov immediately before Gorbachev.[25]

Gorbachev was brought to Moscow in November 1978 to fill the post vacated by Kulakov's sudden death. He was named secretary of the Central Committee and a candidate member of the all-powerful Politburo of the party in 1979. By 1985 Gorbachev reached the top and quickly consolidated his position by inserting his own men into the Politburo and dropping his most powerful rival, Grigory V. Romanov, from that same body.

The Politburo does not vote on issues, but instead reaches decisions by consensus. The Soviet decision-making process is conducted in secret, as is the case in military commands. Although Soviet leaders are eager to use free world political pluralism to affect decision-making by their free world counterparts, they regard influence in their own country as unacceptable. According to a prominent Soviet journalist, "A decision can be prepared more objectively and more scientifically if it is protected from the general public, which could influence it in one direction or another. It is more convenient for us like that."[26]

Of central importance to the Soviet decision-making process is the Committee for State Security (KGB). This preeminent Soviet intelligence agency prepares daily summaries of current events for the Politburo along with regular forecasts of world developments. Besides gathering intelligence through, e.g., listening posts such as the strategically situated Soviet embassy in Washington, D.C., it undertakes covert operations overseas and is responsible for maintaining the control of the Communist Party at home. Under the leadership of the late Yuri Andropov, who subsequently became the General Secretary of the Communist Party, it created a new directorate "especially to harrass, intimidate, and ultimately eliminate nonconformists" within the Soviet Union.[27]

Toward the Future

Ever since the triumph of the Bolshevik Revolution, Soviet communism has represented a threat to the survival of free democracies. "While capitalism and socialism exist side by side, they cannot live in peace," Lenin declared in 1920. "One or the other will ultimately triumph—the last obsequies will be observed either for the Soviet republic or for world capitalism."[28] Lenin's renunciation of the possibility of peace with the democratic states, his uncompromising objective of total communist victory, continues to guide Soviet policy to this day. "Imperialism will not collapse by itself, automatically," Brezhnev revealed in 1970. "Active and determined action by all the revolutionary forces is needed to overthrow it."[29]

If one looks at the roots of Soviet strategy and the record of Soviet performance since the 1917 Bolshevik revolution, future Soviet strategy (barring some unexpected transformations in the Soviet system) is reasonably predictable. A large part of that strategy was outlined in the work *Fundamentals of Scientific Communism*[30] written by B. G. Afanasyev. In the introduction to this work all the troubles of the world are laid at the door of Capitalism which has "pushed the contrast between poverty and riches to the limit, raised war, colonial plunder, and racism to the rank of official policy, and wasted countless material resources and labor unproductively for the benefit of a tiny handful of monopolists . . .", etc. The capitalist-imperialist system must be replaced, says Afanasyev, and he then enunciates the theory of Scientific Communism as follows: "It is the science of the ways and means of overthrowing capitalism, of the ways and laws of building the new communist society and the economic, social, and cultural conditions for the all around development of Man; it is the science of communist society as a complex social organism; and it is the science of the deliberate, purposeful control of social processes in the interest of Man." Afanasyev goes on to define Leninism as a "thoroughly international doctrine; it is the Marxism of this, the twentieth century, Marxism of the modern age."

The objective of global communist victory continues to guide Soviet strategy to this day. A particularly blunt statement of this goal is the following:

> What is right is right: indeed, Communists are not willing to make fundamental concessions and are not about to repudiate their belief in the ultimate universal triumph of communism; they do indeed consider coexistence as something that will not last forever, but only until the day that capitalism ceases to exist. . . . It is, therefore, just as absurd to demand the Communists issue a guarantee that capitalism will be preserved as it would be to seek assurances that the earth will stop its movement around the sun.[31]

But the Soviets are keenly aware that capitalism will not collapse by itself. Hence they persistently pursue a sinister strategy in their campaign of imperial conquest.

NOTES

1. S. W. Kozlov, *The Officer's Hand Book* (Moscow: Voyenizdat, 1971) p. 73.
2. *Ibid*, p. 291.
3. *Ibid*, p. 294.
4. Cited in Revel Jean, Francois, *How Democracies Perish* (Doubleday and Co., Inc., Garden City, NY,), p. 75.
5. *Ibid*, pp. 96–97.
6. Hauner, Milan, *Seizing the Third Parallel: Geopolitics and the Soviet Advance Into Central Asia*, Orbis, Spring, 1985, pp. 5–6.
7. Lenin, *Collected Works*, Vol. 31, pp. 70–71.
8. MacKinder, Alfred, "The Round World and the Winning of Peace," *Foreign Policy*, Vol. 21, No. 4, July 1973, p. 601.
9. Spykman, Nicholas J., *American Strategy in World Politics*.
9a. S. G. Gotshkov, Seapower of the State, Annapolis: Naval Institute Press, 1979 (1st Soviet Edition, 1976).
10. Colonel V. Rutlov, "The Military-Economic Might of the Socialist Countries: A Factor of the Security of Peoples," *Kommunist*, No. 23, December 1974, Voreyherrykh, p. 19.
11. Gromyko, Andrei, "A Lenin's Peace Policy," Moscow Newsweekly, No. 16, 1984, p. 5.
12. Gromyko, Andrei, "Leninist Foreign Policy in a Contemporary World, *Soviet Press*, No. 81 *4, April 1981, p. 119.
13. K. Zazadov, *Leninism and Contemporary Problems of the Transition from Capitalism to Socialism* (Moscow, Progress Publishers, 1976) p. 193.
14. See William R. Kintner, *The Front is Everywhere* (Lanham, MD: University Press of America, 1984), p. 7.
15. See Beilensom, Lawrence W., *Power Through Subversion* (Public Affairs Press, Washington, D.C., 1972).
16. MASKIROVKA V SOVREMMENNOM BOYU (Camouflage in Modern Combat)
    Author: M. I. Tolochkov
    Publisher: Izdatel'stvo DOSAAF
    Place and year of publication: Moscow, 1975
17. Arms Control and Disarmament Agency, *Arms Control: U.S. Objectives, Negotiating Efforts, Problems of Soviet Noncompliance*, January 1984, p. 325.
18. Stevenson, William, *Intrepid's Last Case* (Villard Books, New York 1983).
19. Socialist-Imperialism Intensifies all Around Armament Expansion and War Preparations, *Peking Review*, No. 22, May 11, 1974, p. 24.

20. Address of Yuri Andropov, General Secretary of the CPSU Central Committee to Plenary Meeting of the CPSU Central Committee, November 22, 1983, *PRAVDA,* November 23, 1982.
21. *Lenin,* a biography prepared by the Marx-Lenin Institute, Moscow, p. 103.
22. *Selected Works III,* p. 315.
23. *Ibid,* p. 312.
24. *Selected Works VI,* p. 182.
25. Sanders, Sol W., Communist Party Elders Dictate From Grave. *Detroit News,* April 4, 1985.
26. Aleksandr Bovin, in Dagens Nyheter (Stockholm), February 27, 1983, in *Foreign Broadcast Information Service: Daily Report: Soviet Union* (Hereafter FBIS:SOV), March 4, 1983, p. R10.
27. John Barron, *KGB Today: The Hidden Hand* (NY: Reader's Digest Press, 1983) pp. 446, 451.
28. V. I. Lenin, *On Peaceful Coexistence* (Moscow: Progress Publishers, 1971), p. 68.
29. L. I. Brezhnev, *Following Lenin's Course* (Moscow: Progress Publishers, 1972), p. 296.
30. Published in English by Progress Publishers, first printing 1967, second printing from revised Russian edition 1977, p. 12.
31. *The World Socialist System and Anti-Communism,* trans. A. Bratov (Moscow: Progress Publishers, 1972), pp. 189–90.

CHAPTER II

The Evolution of Soviet Military Strategy and the Growth of Soviet Military Power

Strategy and tactics for advancing the communist cause were originally developed by Marx, Engels, and Lenin. All three were profound students of war and revolution. Consequently, communist strategy evolved, in part, as a synthesis of insights gained from the French revolution and the revolutionary uprisings that took place in Europe in the 19th century. It also derived from the rich czarist political-military heritage, as well as from Solviet military experience gained in the 1917–1920 Civil War and World War II.

For the Soviet Union, force, used or threatened, has been and no doubt will continue to be the pre-eminent factor in international politics. Particularly in conflicts and disputes involving the United States, Soviet decision-makers will make their moves with acute sensitivity to global power relations. The Soviets are conducting their affairs with an increasing truculence that stems from the military preponderance they have achieved at various points of conflict. Their organization and mastery of subversive warfare within the non-communist world enables them to effectively utilize the leverage of growing military ascendency.

In his introduction to the 1984 Department of Defense publication, *Soviet Military Power*, Secretary of Defense Casper W. Weinberger stated:

The USSR has greatly increased its offensive military capability and has significantly enhanced its ability to conduct military operations worldwide.

The Soviet build-up is made possible by a national policy that has consistently made military material production its highest economic priority.

Underlying Soviet military power is a vast and complex industrial, mobilization and logistics support system designed to focus the resources of the Soviet State on the capability to wage war. For decades, Soviet industry has manufactured a broad spectrum of weaponry and military support equipment in staggering quantities—production levels achieved by extremely large investments of money, raw materials and manpower. Moreover, the Soviet leadership places the highest priority on the utilization of science and technology for military purposes, and this, together with exploitation of Western technology, has sharply eroded the qualitative edge that the West had used to balance the Soviet lead in numbers of weapons and men.

Secretary Weinberger's 1985 and 1986 editions of this authoritative publication reinforce this analysis. By dint of prodigious efforts, the Soviet Union has fielded the most powerful military machine ever created in time of peace, and is ready to fight and determined to win at every level of conflict. By the use of military threats in tandem with a vast subversive network, the Soviets are attempting to defeat the United States and achieve global domination without war. Conflict is correctly viewed as a whole, as a total state, in which only functional distinctions, not essential ones, are made among components, even between peace and war.

Preparations for conventional war and general war, it should be noted, are not mutually exclusive. While a great many studies of the military challenge of communism quite rightly stress the need for a greater American and allied capability for fighting "conventional" war, not all of these investigations point out the intimate interrelationship between total war, quasi-peace, and intermediate ranges of conflict. Discussions of hypothetical land wars in the NATO area often fail to factor in the size and quality of our strategic nuclear retaliatory force. Comprehension of both limited forms of conflict and of total war are essential to strategic planning in the nuclear age.

There are almost no parallels between the whole or any parts of Soviet strategy and the strategy pursued by the United States. American strategic thought posits a dichotomy between war and peace—the Soviets see a continuum, i.e., no difference. The United States has no peacetime strategy with which to confront Soviet expansionism involving diplomacy, economic power, psychological operations and a military threat.

The development of U.S. nuclear strategy has failed to take into account the policies, capabilities, and history of Soviet strategic thought. U.S. commitment to nuclear offense with neglect of strategic defense was characterized by Walter Lippman as:

the perfect fulfillment of all wishful thinking on military matters: here is war that requires no national effort, no draft, no training, no discipline, but only money and engineering know-how of which we have plenty. Here is the panacea which allows us to be the greatest military power on earth without investing time, energy, sweat, blood and tears and—as compared with the cost of a great army, navy and air force—not even much money.[1]

In contrast, the Soviet leadership promotes and supports continuous preparation for war. One should recall Stalin's well-known speech on February 9, 1946, when he blamed World War II on the "Imperialist" powers and overlooked that his signing of the notorious Nazi-Soviet pact in 1939 was one of the instrumental causes of the conflict.

The Soviet leaders believe and act as if they are at war with us. As Stalin put it in *Problems of Leninism*, the Bolshevik seizure of power "jeopardized the very existence of world capitalism as a whole.[2] The initial weakness of the newly born Soviet Union, however, imposed on the Kremlin leaders a policy of gaining time to build its strength, which they called "peaceful coexistence." Peaceful coexistence, reiterated by Khruschchev in 1956, was and is a tactic designed to enhance the cause of communism, not the status quo. The industrialization of the Soviet Union, which Stalin began, was undertaken to build up the military power of the state and not to improve the standard of living of the Soviet people. Stalin's industrial base supplied 90 percent of the war material used by the Soviet Union in World War II. After Stalin's death in 1953, the Kremlin leaders started talking about the eventual socialist encirclement of capitalism. By that time the Soviet Union had recovered from its wartime devastation, had built a hydrogen bomb, and was on its way to becoming the world's leading producer of military hardware. The subsequent growth in the Soviet military-industrial complex during the sixties was generally ignored by the West. The seventies were a period of rapid Soviet military growth and of equally rapid decline in U.S. military power. The Soviet military build-up, which has continued relentlessly for more than two decades, is not a response to Western arms procurement, but instead is a result of internal imperatives, far in excess of any realistic security needs. The "planned" Soviet economy succeeds entirely only in its military goals, often bringing new weapons systems to the deployment stage in the third and fourth years of the procurement cycle. In the view of the Soviet leaders, a continuous favorable shift in the balance of power is necessary if their strategic goals, as enunciated by Lenin and Brezhnev, are to be achieved: "The successful implementation of the Peace Program is conditioned by the existing balance of world forces and continued orderly changes in this balance in favor of socialism."[3]

"The reality of this Soviet military build-up was generally accepted in the West consequent to the Soviet invasion of Afghanistan. However, despite incontrovertible evidence that Moscow remains determined to pay any cost to obtain across-the-board military superiority, there is still no solid consensus within the United States and among its allies as to how to cope with burgeoning Soviet military power and its pervasive influence in many parts of the world. Thus a little more than half way through the Reagan Defense Program, designed to restore military equilibrium between the U.S. and its allies, the United States House of Representatives practically put the program in reverse. The U.S. will spend less on its defenses in 1987 than it did in 1985. The House has cut FY 1987's military spending to $286 billion, $18 billion less than that authorized by Congress. Cuts of this scale will reduce the readiness of United States fighting forces. The Navy's plan for a modern 600-ship fleet will be jeopardized. President Reagan's SDI will be severely crimped. Although the President asked $5.34 billion for the SDI for 1987, the House approved only $3.1 billion. Pork barrel aspects of the defense budget were untouched. Lawmakers voted to keep open the B-1 bomber production line beyond the 100 bombers the Air Force says it needs so that production line jobs would not be touched. The mindless way in which these cuts were made does not speak well for this democracy's ability to meet the long term Soviet threat.

Soviet Military Evolution

Soviet military strategies thoroughly examined various nuclear weapons systems before making a choice. During the period of American nuclear monopoly, the Soviets deliberately ridiculed the significance of nuclear weapons. While chafing under American nuclear superiority, they pursued a cautious strategy. However, as the Soviets gained equivalence in nuclear weapons with the United States, their public recognition of the global importance of nuclear weapons drastically changed.

The basic guidelines for Soviet policy were probably agreed upon in the late fifties at the time of the publication of the *Penkovsky Papers*.[4] Their strategic appraisal was revealed with the publication of Marshal V.D. Sokolovskii's book, *Soviet Military Strategy*.[5]

By 1968, Moscow's primary security goal was to achieve a strategic nuclear force capable of neutralizing America's extended deterrent; that is, to remove the American nuclear umbrella from protecting U.S. allies on the rimlands of Eurasia. The sustained build-up of Soviet strategic forces has already been extensively detailed by many analysts, including the author of this work. Yet Soviet skills in combining the extensive support of wars of "national liberation" with advancing arms control negotiations continues to promote U.S. neglect of its own strategic nuclear posture. This neglect has been frequently overlooked both by academic and by government analysts. The U.S. strategic program reached a plateau in 1967 at the height of U.S. involvement in the Vietnam War at which time the U.S. was investing approximately $30 billion dollars per year in futile conflict. The Soviets were backing Hanoi with a much smaller figure, about a billion dollars annually, while quietly establishing superiority in strategic nuclear weapons as a first priority. When the first SALT accord was signed in 1972, the Soviets had surpassed the United States in numbers of both land and sea-based ballistic missiles. The primary reason for the Soviet lead in strategic weapons was that the U.S. had simply lagged in maintaining its initial nuclear advantage.

The second Soviet military priority was to achieve greater superiority (tactical-nuclear and conventional) in Europe, East Asia, and in the Middle East/Persian Gulf area. This goal, in general has been achieved.

The third Soviet priority during the early 1970s was the long-term development of a global naval and air power projection capability. Under the leadership of Admiral Gorshkov, they succeeded in creating a modern blue-water navy capable of projecting Soviet military power globally. Additionally, the Soviets wanted to develop external intervention forces which have now been deployed in Africa, Southeast Asia, the Caribbean, and Afghanistan. The strategic aim of this program, not yet fully realized, is to separate the United States and its allies while creating Soviet capabilities to intervene anywhere on their periphery.

A fourth Soviet priority was to develop space-based aggressive systems, designed to defend Soviet military capability on land and sea. These systems, such as "Killer" satellites (laser beam satellite destroyers), are not intended solely as defensive measures, as is the planned U.S. SDI system, but complement the offensive components of Soviet military strategy.

These Soviet priorities establish guidelines for development of both violent and nonviolent means of conflict. The Soviets have developed military capabilities along the entire force continuum: anti-satellite weapons, intercontinental bombers, tactical aircraft, tanks, chemical and biological weapons, naval forces of V-STOL carriers, submarines, and special weapons for insurgents and terrorists. They have also developed a range of nonviolent tactics designed to destabilize and to disintegrate the social structure of their opponents. Using these tactics, the Soviets hope to win the global conflict without open warfare. These nonviolent tactics include disinformation, terrorism, subversion, penetration of intelligence agencies, agitation, propaganda, trade offers, espionage, peace offensives, and forgeries. The combination of violent and nonviolent forms of conflict gives the Kremlin an edge over their Western opponents who still fail to grasp the nature of the new frontiers of war.

Principles of Soviet Strategic Design

Soviet strategy is dynamic and complex. Before discussing the basic principles in Soviet strategic design it may be useful to redefine three related concepts: goals, policy and strategy.

Goals establish the ultimate objective of a nation's foreign and security policy. Cato defined, e.g., the goal of Rome toward Carthage—total destruction. This corresponds to Lenin's dictate that "capitalism" must be destroyed. Several sub-goals, or stepping stones, may have to be reached before the ultimate goal of world socialism can be attained. Thus, before the Soviet Union can ultimately destroy "capitalism," it must isolate the West from Third World resources and induce political divisiveness in the western alliance headed by the United States.

Policy determines the basic approach toward the attainment of goals. During World War II, the goals of the United States were to defeat both Germany and Japan; but as a matter of policy, the U.S. gave first priority to the defeat of Nazi Germany. A policy choice facing the Soviet Union is whether to attempt to defeat the United States during the window of opportunity between now and the late 1980s (by then the U.S. may have restored a measure of military equilibrium between the superpowers) or to pursue a more cautious policy and await unexpected opportunities.

Strategy is the conceptual design of actions, maneuvers and processes by which a nation moves toward a given goal within the framework of a chosen policy. Strategy has been defined as "the science and art of employing the political, economic, psychological, and military means of a nation to advance its policies." Soviet strategy has always stressed subterfuge and deception as necessary aspects of international policy. As a closed, totalitarian society, the Soviet Union has many operational advantages over Western opponents. Secret preparations undertaken with the aim of achieving victory with a minimum of belligerence have been characteristic of Soviet strategic planning. Soviet strategy mandates constant testing and probing of the enemy's weak points, analysis of his overall capability, as well as the location and avoidance of his chief strengths, Lenin expressed the concept in this fashion:

> The more powerful enemy can be conquered only by exerting the utmost effort, and by necessarily, thoroughly, carefully, attentively and skillfully taking advantage of every, even the smallest, "rift" among the enemies, of every antagonism of interests, among the bourgeoisie within the various countries. . . . Those who do not understand this, do not understand even a particle of Marxism or of scientific, modern socialism in general.[6]

There are many components of Soviet strategy—military, political, subversive, economic, and deceptive. In Lenin's view, every form of conflict must be mastered:

> Unless we master all means of warfare, we may suffer grave and even decisive defeat if changes in position of the other classes that do not depend on us bring to the forefront forms of activity in which we are particularly weak. If, however, we master all means of warfare, we shall certainly be victorious, because we represent the interests of the really foremost and really revolutionary class. . . .[7]

Lenin also observed that "a revolutionary army and a revolutionary government are two institutions equally necessary for the success of the uprising and for the consolidation of its results."

The military trail to global power is as clearly blazed in Communist minds now as it was in Lenin's. Lenin still remains the prophet and architect of Soviet strategy, as his heirs attest in every important statement they make.

Given the interrelationships between goals, policy, and strategy, the following principles dominating Soviet strategy can be discerned:

1. The overriding Soviet goal is the destruction of "capitalism." Implicit in this goal is the attainment of global hegemony. Unless the last vestiges of private enterprise and self-determination are removed, the human desire for personal freedom will continuously threaten the Communist system of total state control.

2. Soviet strategy is designed to operate along both temporal and spatial dimensions. There is no compulsion to gain victory within any set time period. Communists describe their "war for the overthrow of the international bourgeoisie" as "a war which is a hundred more times more difficult and complicated than the most stubborn of ordinary wars between states."

Communist strategy, ever opportunistic, can and will change in accordance with both local and global factors.

3. From the beginning, design of Soviet strategy has been global and universal in scope even though initially restrained by inadequate means. From the Kremlin perspective, the greater the areas of struggle, the greater the prospects for victory.

4. Regardless of the ebb and flow of continuing struggle, the first imperative of Soviet strategy will necessarily remain the protection of the "core," the Soviet Union, its periphery, and its ruling regime. The security of the ruling clique, the chief internal security task of the KGB, is a matter of topmost concern of Soviet leadership and is the chief task of the KGB. In fact some of their operations abroad are motivated as much by the need to remove presumed or real threats to their internal rule as by the desire to expand the frontiers of "Soviet socialism." Any opposition to their sole grip on internal power concerns Soviet leaders as much as "capitalist" subversion, harassment, and "spasm" counterattacks. The insecurity of the Soviet political elite, which at times borders on paranoia, stems more from the immediate concern of preserving their personal power than from external threats. The leaders in Moscow are defended from their own proletariat, which they theoretically represent, as well as from external threats.

5. Any and all appropriate instruments and weapons are employed in waging the campaign toward the achievement of the Communist goal.

6. For the Soviets, offense remains the principal strategical concept. A campaign which is entered into without the idea of taking the offensive to achieve victory is doomed to failure. The Soviets clearly understand this basic strategic truth.

On the eve of the Bolshevik seizure of power Lenin cited Marx to this effect: "Act with the greatest determination, and on the offensive. The defensive is the death of every armed rising, it is lost before it measures itself with its enemies. Surprise your antagonists while their forces are scattering."

Soviet offensive strategy covers a wide range of possibilities. These include the acquisition of nuclear weapons, which intrinsically imply the threat of a surprise nuclear attack and are described at great length in official Soviet works: (Sokolovsky) Soviet *Military Strategy,* previously cited. The design characteristics of Soviet nuclear weapons are such as to support a strategy calling for a surprise nuclear attack. This threat imposes an additional burden on U.S. and Western security programs.

7. The Soviets can also employ a defensive stance when it is to their advantage. As a rule, a defensive posture remains the optimal strategy for the side with less force, or for a stronger power whose force is not fully mobilized. The object of such a strategy is simply to prevent the enemy from achieving his anticipated goals. In a campaign of long duration, as the present struggle for world hegemony promises to be, defensive strategy calls for a series of tactical offensives so as to weaken the stronger power bit by bit.

8. Deception has always been a crucial element of an effective strategy. The Soviets are masters of deception.

9. In Soviet strategy, the mix of instruments and weapons varies over time and with the ebb and flow of the conflict. Until the Soviet industrial base was adequately developed, strategic efforts were based less on hardware, than on softer approaches. However, strategic instruments always were, and are, combined together in an orchestrated conflict.

10. Until the death of Stalin, the Soviets were concerned about the "capitalist" encirclement" of the USSR. As Soviet power grew, Soviet territorial goals widened. Nevertheless, the Soviet Union constantly declares its need for security against perceived threats of subversion, harassment, and "spasm" counterattacks by "capitalist" adversaries—even in the territories they have secured to "protect" the central Soviet homeland.

11. Eventually, the Soviets believe, the "capitalist" enemy must be defeated on his home ground by subversion, strangulation (resource denial), and military force. The Soviets still hold the strategic view that an imperialist attack against the Soviet Union may occur in the dying days of "capitalism." Consequently, they claim there is no contradiction between preparations for defense against this worst-case contingency and a consistent "peace" policy.

12. The advent of nuclear weapons introduced a major material factor into the struggle requiring the Soviets to seek dominance in the nuclear sphere. The Soviets also seek comparable dominance in space.

13. The Sino-Soviet split has introduced a major obstacle into the conduct of Soviet strategy. Geopolitical and policy schisms between China and the USSR did not originate with the split. Stalin continued to attempt to establish buffers against the Chinese threat even after Mao had gained power. The Sino-Soviet struggle is far from over despite occasional Soviet moves to moderate it.

14. As the Soviet Union grew more powerful, it prevented the possibility of encirclement (containment), sought a dominant position on the Eurasian land mass, and began positioning itself globally to deny the industrialized

countries access to indispensable energy and mineral resources. This phase now in force, first required the development of maritime and air power to advance their military reach far beyond Soviet frontiers. The extension of Soviet global power and influence via political-psychological-military intrusion into bases in strategically located countries is setting the stage for what may prove to be the crucial phase of the Soviet campaign for world hegemony. The outcome may be determined by whether the Soviet Union, a land-based continental power, can achieve sea power dominance over the United States.

The Organization of Soviet Military Forces

Soviet armed forces are organized differently than those of the United States. The Soviet Army is the largest and the dominant component of the Soviet armed forces. The other components are the Strategic Rocket Forces, PVO (Aerospace defense forces), the navy and air forces. In addition, there are several hundred thousand men in KGB units (Committee of State Security) and MUD troops (Ministry of Internal Affairs). Soviet law makes these units part of the Soviet armed forces, although they are under joint KGB/MUD command.

While Soviet strategic-nuclear, tactical-nuclear, and conventional theater forces guard the homeland from external attack, other elements of the arsenal support the forward extension of Soviet power and influence. In recent years, Soviet leaders have put less emphasis on the role of Soviet armed forces in the defense of the homeland and have focused more on their role in support of an expansionist foreign policy utilizing "wars of national liberation."

In 1965, Marshal A.A. Grechko noted that "the external function of the Soviet state and its armed forces and that of other socialist countries and their armies have now been enriched with new content."[9]

A Soviet civilian analyst has described the new approach more starkly. Current requirements are not for defensive or piecemeal action, as was necessarily the case in the past, but "of carrying out a total offensive against imperialism and world capitalism as a whole in order to do away with them."[10] In particular, Soviet strategists believe that significant political utility flows from superiority in strategic nuclear warfare. In all editions of *Soviet Military Strategy,* Marshal Sokolovskii declared:

> The basic weapon for the execution of primary war missions on land, sea, and air is the nuclear weapon, and consequently this is of first importance in the development and organization of the armed forces. The colossal destructive power of this weapon and the ability to deliver nuclear strikes over any distance now permit the accomplishment of strategic missions and the attainment of strategic war aims, not by the successive destruction of enemy armed forces on the battlefield and the capture of his

territory, but by simultaneous action against the most vulnerable targets in the whole of enemy territory and against major formations of his armed forces.[11]

It is this very weapon that now determines the direction in which the armed forces are organized and developed and how the future war will be waged. The accelerated introduction of [the nuclear weapon] into all branches of the armed forces has radically changed their quality; it has increased their firepower and combat potential, changed the role and purpose of conventional weapons, and necessitated the supply of more technical equipment to the armed forces and improvements in their organizational structure. It requires the use of basically new methods of combat. The firepower of all branches of the armed forces is now based on nuclear weapons. The main task, now, in organizing and developing armed forces, both in peace and war, is to be superior to the enemy in nuclear weapons and the technique of their employment. It should be noted here that, at the present time, *in gaining superiority in nuclear weapons,* their quality and the technique for their employment are more important than their number.[12]

The Soviets have become more circumspect in publicizing the central thrust of their nuclear-age strategy. Yet the compelling logic of Solkolovskii's analysis still dominates Soviet overall strategy.

The Soviet Approach Toward Nuclear War

With the advent of nuclear weapons as the dominant material factor of the contemporary era, it was necessary for the Soviets to design their strategic policy, keeping within an integrated conceptual framework based on Marxist-Leninist doctrine. The full development of a Soviet strategy for the nuclear and revolutionary age was in all probability achieved late in the 1950s. In line with the Marxist doctrine of the dominance of material factors, the core of Soviet strategy was designed around a central quest for nuclear advantage. Soviet strategists quickly realized that achievement of nuclear superiority would free conventional forces, particularly naval, for offensive support of wide-ranging Soviet political and psychological maneuvers.

As their nuclear arsenal grew, Soviet ability to win a nuclear war became a central theme. The chief of Soviet strategic forces, Marshal N.I. Krylov declared in 1960:

The imperialist ideologists are trying to pull the vigilance of the world's people by having recourse to propaganda devices to the effect that there will be no victors in a future nuclear war. These false affirmations contradict all of the objective laws of history. Victory in war will be on the side of world socialism.[13]

The Soviets now regard strategic nuclear forces as the indispensable foundation of their strategy. In July 1981, the former Soviet armed forces chief of staff, Marshal Nikolai Ogarkov, indicated that the Soviet Union had begun a build-up of strategic nuclear forces to counter U.S. attempts to gain military superiority. Ogarkov stated: "Special attention is being given to those forces and weapons that ensure the highest degree of the might of the Army and Navy." And that, "The first component of this might . . . is the strategic nuclear forces, which serve as the basic factor to deter an aggressor."[14]

By the time of the first Reagan Administration, the Soviets enjoyed an advantage in strategic nuclear forces. A report by the U.S. General Accounting Office in August 1981 stated:

> the large, sustained Soviet program to enhance its strategic nuclear capabilities has, by many measures, succeeded in altering the strategic nuclear balance.[15]

The Reagan Administration has sought to restore the nuclear balance. The Soviets are determined to make any U.S. attempt to regain parity in strategic nuclear weaponry as difficult as possible. It is now apparent that once the Soviet Union achieved nuclear parity, its strategy grew more aggressive. If they attain a significant strategic nuclear advantage over the U.S., they are quite likely to become even more adventurous.

Soviet Space Strategy

The use of space for military purposes is increasingly linked with strategic nuclear capabilities. According to Secretary of Defense Weinberger,

> A serious threat is posed by the USSR's increasing use of space for military purposes. The majority of Soviet space programs have been specifically designed to support terrestial military operations. However, the long-term development of an anti-satellite system has extended Soviet military use of space from support operations to a direct space warfare capability. The relative scope of the overall military program is demonstrated by a launch rate that is four-to-five times that of the United States, and by an annual payload weight placed into orbit, 660,000 pounds—ten times that of the United States.[16]

Potentially surpassing nuclear weaponry as a revolutionary force in geopolitics is the emergence of manned space flight. Since the early 1960s the Soviets have recognized the importance of space as the absolute "high ground." Soviet doctrine at the time called for the extension of the "combined arms" concept into space, through the use of active offensive and defensive systems. Unlike the "space spectaculars" of the American media, Soviet space efforts focused on geo-political and military considerations. The Soviets began a measured deployment of a series of manned orbital space systems in an effort to create an orbiting "Kosmograd." Improvements in Soviet technology have been directly translated into increased efforts toward space mastery.

One such item is Cosmos 1603, the largest spy satellite ever placed in orbit. Highly maneuverable, and weighing as much as a small school bus, it is able to occasionally elude the global radar trackers of the North American Aerospace Defense Command. Cosmos 1603 may have other functions beyond spying.[17]

The political significance of Soviet domination of space would be to wed the terrestrial geopolitical domination of the heartland with the high frontier of space. Control of space access is the absolute manifestation of geopolitical control, and the Soviet Union has made tremendous efforts to secure space for its advantage.

1986 has been a disastrous year for the United States space program. The destruction of Challenger and its seven manned crew on January 28, 1986 was an accident that did not have to happen. The shuttle disaster report was highly critical of NASA. Subsequently the U.S. experienced a failure in the launching of an important satellite by its Titan rocket. The next U.S. shuttle flight has been postponed for at least two years. Meanwhile, the less spectacular but more persistent Soviet program is putting the Soviets in a position of commanding the military high frontier.

In the wake of the Challenger shuttle disaster, the Soviet Union holds an "almost frightening" lead over the United States in space experience, according to the new edition of Jane's Spaceflight Directory. The American program has fallen 10 years behind the efforts of the Soviet Union in the practical utilization of space, by the estimate of Jane's, a British publisher that specializes in military and transportation cataloguing and analysis. Many aerospace experts in the U.S. contend, however, that although Soviet experience with long-duration space flight has been greater, the American space systems and its overall space program remain superior despite the current setbacks. "The Soviets are so far ahead of the U.S. in space experience that they are almost out of sight," said Reginald Turnill, the editor of the 453-page directory. He cited the delay of the shuttle program because of the Challenger explosion as evidence of his point along with general estimates that a U.S. space station might not be practical until the mid-1990's.

Meanwhile in the United States months after the Challenger explosion, major activity at the once bustling space port, Cape Canaveral, had come to a virtual halt. Crucial projects have been canceled, hundreds of engineers and workers have lost their jobs, and those that remain have been wrenched by doubts about what lies ahead. Unless the U.S. makes a major, determined effort in space Soviet dominance of earth's high frontiers will be inevitable with enormous negative consequences to the United States' strategic balance vis-a-vis the Soviet Union.

The Soviet view of nuclear war, including space systems, is radically different from that of the United States. It is based on the goal of destroying the opposition's forces and on the ability to carry on a war to insure the survival of the Soviet Union. For the Soviets, this aspect of their strategy is a primary characteristic of deterrence. Steps in the Soviet strategic program are listed below.

• A first strike counterforce capability, particularly the SS-18 with accurate MIRVs has been developed.

- A second strike counterforce capability, primarily in submarine forces with new long-range missiles has been developed.
- A large scale program of improvement of both the land-based ICBMs and IRBMs, (now called INF) is being conducted; these forces are gaining in both survivability and accuracy.
- An ABM system is being developed and the capability of the Moscow complex increased. This system includes the Krasnoyask ABM target acquisition radar system, an all-altitude air defense system with increasing capability of "look-down, shoot-down" long-range interceptors and AWACS.
- An extensive C³I system (command, control, communications and intelligence) including thousands of protected, hardened command sites for key leadership is in place.
- An extensive civil defense program, for both population and industry has been developed. A large scale ASW program to attempt to reduce the threat of the U.S. SLBM retaliatory force is being supported.

All these forces are centrally coordinated by a combined arms command team. The Soviet program calls for intelligence reconnaissance, surveillance, communications, and space denial missions in space. Such extensive preparations utilizing ASAT systems are continuing.

To meet the comprehensive and sophisticated Soviet nuclear threat, the United States has begun to modernize all three branches of the United States strategic triad as well as taking other measures to reduce Soviet hopes for quick nuclear victory. Secretary of Defense Weinberger warns that as "the Soviet Union has acquired a margin of nuclear superiority in most important categories . . . We must strengthen our nuclear force posture as quickly as possible."[18]

The Soviet advantages at the top end of the military spectrum open up the possibility of destroying "capitalism" without war. This goal is sought by Soviet leaders because they can never be secure as long as there are strong nations committed to the idea of human freedom. Motivated by their "perception" of continuing threats and of the impossibility of the convergence of the capitalist and socialist systems, they are increasingly militarized. The Soviet goal of winning without war requires a sufficient margin of Soviet strategic and conventional military superiority to deter a U.S. and/or allied response to Soviet initiatives at a lower level of violence. The Soviets have already achieved general strategic and conventional superiority (except for maritime power) around the frontiers of the Soviet empire. The Soviet leaders appear confident that the risk of U.S. escalation to a major test of arms has been sharply reduced.

Soviet Conventional-Theater Forces

In his foreword to the authoritative, NATO and Warsaw Pact Force comparisons, NATO Secretary-General Joseph M.A.H. Luns stated in 1982 that:

> The numerical balance of forces has moved slowly but steadily in favor of the Warsaw Pact over the past two decades. During this period, the members of the North Atlantic alliance have lost much of the technological edge which permitted NATO to reply on the view that quality could compensate for quantity. It is clear that this trend is dangerous.[19]

For purposes of military planning, the Soviets have divided Eurasia into three theaters: Western, Southern and Far Eastern. Each of these theaters includes a large number of military "districts" defined so as to expedite the detailed organization of military forces.

The Western Theater

The Western Theater, encompassing all of Europe, contains those nations that possess a substantial portion of the world's wealth, technology, industrial capacity, and military power. This area is the focal point of all Soviet security planning.

Soviet forces positioned for operations against NATO continue to be given the highest priority in receiving the newest and most capable systems. Since 1981 the Soviets have produced 4,500 tanks, including the T-80, which are deployed to forces opposite NATO. At the same time, they have introduced new ground-attack aircraft and armored fighting vehicles. In this theater, Soviet forces are fully prepared to wage nuclear, conventional, chemical, and biological warfare. As a NATO study points out: "This strengthening of forces is intended to enable the Soviets to achieve their political/military objectives as rapidly as possible with the most modern and capable theater forces, either through intimidation or direct military action."[20] Out of a total of over 190 active Soviet divisions, 94 are located opposite the central and northern regions of NATO. Some 20 allied divisions oppose these Soviet forces.

The Southern Theater

The Southern Theater encompasses Southwest Asia and the Arabian Peninsula. In this theater, Turkey, Syria, Iraq, Iran, and Afghanistan are of particular importance because of their proximity to the Soviet border and their location near Persian Gulf Oil Reserves. Eventually the Soviets would like to link up these countries with their Eastern European "allies" into a security belt frontier stretching from the Baltic Sea to the Indian Ocean. Some 20 Soviet divisions are located in the Transcaucasus and North Caucasus Military District and could be committed against Turkey or southwest Asia. After more than seven years in Afghanistan, the Soviets find themselves embroiled in a brutal counterinsurgency campaign. Moscow has not yet either won control of the Afghan countryside or installed a regime whose influence extends more than a few miles from major population centers. However, current Soviet levels of commitment and combat losses are acceptable to Moscow. The Soviets will take as much time as necessary to subdue that country.

Despite many difficulties and troop morale problems, the war in Afghanistan provides a testing ground for Soviet weapons and tactics.

> It further provides the Soviet Army with a pool of battle-tested officers, non-commissioned officers, and soldiers. The Soviets will continue to maintain their presence in Afghanistan to keep the Afghan regime under Soviet control. They will use Afghanistan to extend their own zone of security, as a potential staging area for power projection to South and Southwest Asia, and to intimidate the regional states.[21]

Far Eastern Theater

The Far Eastern Theater encompasses China, Japan, Korea, and Southeast Asia. The Soviets' political goals in these areas are:

- To improve relations with the PRC at the expense of US/PRC ties (or to neutralize any PRC threat to the Soviet Union);
- To seek to prevent Japan from increasing its contribution to Western security;
- To unify Korea under communist rule; and to expand Soviet influence in Southeast Asia.

In the event of war, "the Soviets would strive to control western and northeastern China, to preclude Japanese participation in a war in Asia and to defeat U.S. and South Korean forces in Korea."[22]

In the Far East, as elsewhere, the Soviet leadership sees its growing military power as a key means of accomplishing political, economic, and military objectives. At present, Soviet military forces in the Far East are second only to those forces deployed in opposition to NATO forces in size, modernization, and capability.

Soviet forces in the Far East have been substantially expanded and improved since 1969. They are now capable of large-scale offensive and defensive operations. During the past 15 years, the number of Soviet divisions opposite China have more than doubled, the number of tactical, fixed-wing aircraft have more than tripled, and the USSR has also managed to place more than 100 SS-20's within a few miles of striking distance of the Far Eastern capitals. Although the Soviet build-up in the Far East was largely triggered by the Sino-Soviet rift in the 1960s, it expanded significantly after Hanoi's conquest of Saigon and subsequent Soviet access to Cam Ranh Bay.

Soviet military deployment in East Asia has been consistent with their belief that any enemy, or potential combination of enemies, can be intimidated without a shot being fired, if the Soviets are perceived to have military superiority. This is in keeping with a growing Soviet inclination to rely on its military power to achieve political goals.

Between their achievement of strategic nuclear superiority and their conventional/tactical nuclear ground/air superiority in each of their Eurasian military theaters, the Soviets have, for all intents and purposes, immunized themselves from any external military attack into their territorial base. One element lacking if the Soviet Union was to be a force to be reckoned with anywhere on the globe was a power projection capability (primarily naval) that could serve Soviet interests in every continent and ocean. The advent of strategic-nuclear "parity," along with a concomitant weakening of the U.S.-led alliance system, has enabled the Soviet Union to overcome what it had once preceived as a land-locked encirclement and to challenge U.S. forward positions in Eurasia and elsewhere in the globe.

The Emergence of the Soviet Union As a Global Naval Power

For three decades after World War II, the United States dominated the oceans to an extent previously unmatched. U.S. supremacy in this arena is now vigorously contested by the Soviet Union.

The Russian quest for sea power can be traced back to Peter the Great. Westerners tend to overlook the fact that Czarist Russia was a considerable naval power from the end of the 18th century.

There was a long ebb tide in Russian naval fortunes during the closing years of the Czarist era and throughout the early Soviet period. The Soviet Navy's primary mission until the end of World War II was coastal defense and support of the army. The ships built in this period were appropriate to this mission. Gradually, as the cold war ensued, Soviet naval ambition expanded.

Some observers attribute the determined Soviet drive toward global naval power to the Soviet "humiliation" in the 1962 Cuban Missile Crisis. Others argue that:

> . . . it is more likely that the decision to construct a modern *surface* fleet was taken about 1956, shortly after Gorshkov's appointment to head the Navy and probably in response to the changing U.S. naval threat and the 1956 "humiliation" at Suez. Additional evidence for this may be found in the submarine and destroyer conversion programs of the later 1950s, in which a dozen submarines and about ten destroyers were provided with antiship missile launchers.[23]

The Soviet empire is the only modern international power created by the expansion of forces into contiguous land areas. All other European empires—the Spanish, the Portuguese, the British, the French, and the Japanese—were made possible by naval power. While navies and shipping played a small role in the development of the Czarist Empire and its Soviet successor, the Soviet navy has become a unique instrument in the current Soviet bid for global preeminence. Ultimate world domination can be established only if Soviet command of the seas is added to strategic nuclear superiority.

It is well to note that navies have in modern times been the instruments of the relatively few countries that were building large over-the-water colonial empires and which were heavily involved in world trade—neither of which attributes were characteristic of the Soviet Union. It would seem likely that the Soviet acquisition of a powerful naval arms is a sign of things to come.

The man largely responsible for the Soviet naval build-up, Admiral Sergei Gorshkov, was appointed Chief of the Soviet Navy in 1956. The present Soviet Navy reflects his vision, will, bureaucratic skills, strategic and tactical genius, and perseverance. Admiral Gorshkov deserves recognition as the world's foremost contemporary naval officer. The design characteristics of the Soviet Navy, the resources allocated to it, and its expected role in peace and war, all issued from Gorshkov's assessments in the context of increasing Soviet technological-industrial capabilities. The decisions relating to Soviet naval developments were also affected by such factors as historical experience, geo-strategic and political considerations. Historically, Russia has been a land power, with access to the oceans channelled through enclosed seas and narrow passages, controlled by other countries. The distances between the widely separated seas surrounding the Soviet Union forced it to maintain separate, non-mutually supporting fleets. Admiral Gorshkov has made no secret of the fact that the Soviet Navy has grown beyond the needs of Soviet defense and is, in fact, seeking global mastery of the sea.[24]

If, in a crisis, the U.S. sea communications and supply lines can be cut off, then the Soviet Union can potentially dominate all countries beyond the American land reach. Soviet naval seapower is the instrument used to obtain this objective in war. Seapower consists of three components: 1) "the fleet" (all naval forces including surface fighting ships); 2) "naval strategic positions"; and 3) the combination of geographic position and the ability of the fleet to operate from a base or bases located at or within the naval strategic position. Bases provide support and maintenance facilities, communications with the homeland, and control of the intermediate sea areas. A ship uses up its strength with every day of operation away from a base in terms of fuel, supplies, and difficulty of repairs or essential maintenance. Personnel endurance also decreases with the length of time that a crew is at sea. Some of the support available at a base can be provided by logistic ships or by logistic airlift, but some cannot. So the nearness of a fleet to its base of operation is an index of its effectiveness within its area of operation. Some writers give the impression that opposing bases somehow neutralize each other, but a base is only a springboard for forces which may, of course, be used against another base. A base has no offensive power in and of itself. Thus sea power is the product of the quality of naval forces and the availability and adequacy of base facilities in a given operational area.

The more effective the ships in the fleet and the more strategic the location of supporting bases, the greater the seapower.

Although frequent attempts are made to predict the relative combat capabilities of opposing naval forces, war is the only true test. Both the Soviet and U.S. navies play a role, albeit an imprecise one, in the present international order characterized by tension, confrontation, and political conflict between the superpowers in an age of strategic deterrence. In peace-time situations, there is no real control of the sea; if both forces are present, they simply neutralize each other. Shipping continues without harassment. Such a situation is generally the case in most of the world's oceans at the present time.

In order to realize his vision of Soviet naval power, Admiral Gorshkov redirected the trends of Soviet ship building toward the development of a missile-armed fleet of small craft (Komar and OSA classes of frigates and corvettes) and submarines to defend the Soviet Union from possible Western aggression, particularly from U.S. carrier attack. In order to provide shore-based protection, as well as anti-ship capabilities, several hundred medium range bombers were transferred to Soviet naval aviation. By the late 1950s, the Soviets were also beginning the production of the Kynda class cruisers (4,500–6,000 tons), armed with eight launchers for SS-N-3 Shaddock missiles (with a range of 300 miles with target acquisition by aircraft, submarine, or other surface ships). The production of the Kyndas allowed the Soviet Union to out-range all allied airships, except aircraft carriers, as Gorshkov attempted to counter U.S. platform superiority with different types of vessels, rather than competing in a category of overwhelming U.S. superiority.[25]

Meanwhile, specific U.S. naval advantages had to be overcome. The Soviet response to the launching of the first U.S. ballistic-missile submarine, the *George Washington,* in 1960 was to begin production of classes of anti-submarine warfare (ASW) ships. ASW ships such as the gas turbine propelled *Kashin* class destroyer were placed into operational service by the early 1960s, followed at the end of the decade by the first two Moskva class helicopter cruisers. By the beginning of the seventies, Soviet ship building reflected more than just a quest for defensive naval capabilities. The production of the *Kresta* I/II class cruisers, each armed with an array of surface-to-surface and surface-to-air missiles, as well as ASW helicopters, indicated that the Soviets were interested in expanding the global reach of their navy.

The *Kresta* II units changed the main weaponry of the cruiser from the long-range SS-N-3 to eight launchers for the SS-N-14 ASW missile (with a range of 25 miles), reflecting a shift of submarine and selective sea control.[26] By 1970 the Soviets were also producing the *Krivak* class of destroyers, ton-for-ton the most heavily armed and most effective destroyer afloat. These vessels are armed with 4 tubes for SS-N-14 ASW missiles, 2 reloadable launchers for SAN-4 short-range surface-to-air missiles, anti-submarine rockets and torpedo tubes.[27] These trends were continued with the 1973 appearance of the new *Kara* class cruisers, the world's largest combatant with gas turbine engines. These cruisers are more heavily armed than similar classes of ships possessed by Western navies, with armaments comparable to the *Kresta* II, with the addition of 2 launchers for short-range anti-aircraft missiles.[28]

By the 1980s, Moscow had deployed 2 out of 4 (and possibly 5) planned *Kiev* class aircraft carriers. As of 1981, the *Kiev* (1977–1978) was deployed with the Northern fleet and the *Minsk* was deployed in the Far East. The *Kharkov* was commissioned in 1982 and the *Novorossisk* in 1983. A fifth unit, the *Kursk,* may be under construction. The relatively small size (40,000 tons) and armaments of these Soviet carriers indicate that they have limited ASW and anti-air warfare capabilities for fleet operations, rather than a long-range air warfare capability, or for long-range air strikes against shore targets (the type of mission usually associated with the much larger U.S. attack carriers). When accompanied by *Kirov* or *Kara* class cruisers and their missile-configured escorts, these ships would be used to neutralize hostile attack by aircraft and submarines.

Further trends towards producing classes of ships for overseas operations were indicated by the commissioning of the 40,000 ton logistical support vessel *Berezina* and the deployment of the new assault landing ship *Ivan Rogov.* U.S. analysts reported that the Soviet Union is in the process of building a 50,000-plus ton nuclear-powered aircraft carrier (in a far northern shipyard at Severodvinsk),[29] possibly to be followed by three more. This would be the largest such ship built for the Soviet Navy, and would further expand its potential for deployments to distant seas.

The Soviet Union is also working hard to move ahead in underseas warfare. In November 1980, the Pentagon announced that the Soviet Union had launched the Typhoon, the world's largest submarine, a nuclear-powered missile-firing boat twice the size of the biggest American submarine. The Soviets launched several new classes of submarine in 1980. One class, the *Alpha,* is the fastest and deepest diving vessel in the world.[30] This vessel can dive more than three thousand feet and can move underwater at 50 miles an hour. The Alpha's hull is made of extra-strong titanium, which because it is non-magnetic, eliminates a major means of detection by overhead patrol planes. While the U.S. did not launch a single submarine in 1980, the Soviets developed many technological firsts in submarines.

In January 1981, U.S. Navy officials announced that the Soviet Union had launched a new submarine carrying cruise missiles that would make U.S. aircraft carriers more vulnerable than they are now. The jumbo submarine, code-named *Oscar,* is almost twice the size of the largest U.S. attack submarine now at sea and is of the third class of submarines capable of launching cruise missiles while submerged. The forerunners to this design technology, the *Charlie* and *Papa* classes, were fitted with the SS-N-7 missile system having an effective range of over 30 nautical miles. Prior to 1968, all Soviet submarines fitted with aerodynamic missile systems had to surface in order to launch SS-N-3 with nuclear capabilities. Now attack submarines, such as the *Oscar,* utilize speed, quietness, and diving depth to approach surface ships and destroy them before being detected. Several *Oscars* could surround a U.S. aircraft carrier and, while submerged, simultaneously launch cruise missiles against it.

Current Soviet naval emphasis appears to focus on qualitative improvements. The ships coming out of the modern Soviet shipyards are innovative, versatile, and increasingly able to operate globally.

The Soviet Merchant Marine and Auxiliary Forces

For the past 20 years, the Soviets have been building up one of the world's largest merchant marine fleets. These vessels can and do support the Soviet navy, but also can be used to challenge the economic interests of the United States and its allies. According to a Tass Dispatch:

> The gross displacement of the Soviet merchant fleet including transport and fishing vessels, has reached 17 million 848 thousand 923 tons. The Soviet Union has a fleet of 7,000 ships. The number of steamships has significantly declined this year over last year. They are now giving way to motorships and turbe-gas ships. The overall displacement is constantly growing: The first tanker capable of carrying 150,000 tons of oil has gone into regular service and a series of ore carriers with a displacement of more than 60,000 tons each has been started.
>
> The passenger fleet is also growing. Its basis is formed by modern liners like the Alexander Pushkin capable of carrying 700 passengers. The Soviet Union's passenger lines carry about 40 million people annually.
>
> In the course of the current 5-year economic plan period (1971–1975), the Soviet fleet is to receive ships with an overall displacement of about five million. Most of them will be built at Soviet shipyards, but some will come from the German Democratic Republic, Poland, France, Finland and other countries. The Soviet Union operates services on 50 international lines.[31]

The Soviets can carry on most of their foreign trade and military and economic assistance programs in their own ships. Only about five percent of U.S. trade is conducted from its own flag ships.

As of 1983, there were over 7,000 Soviet merchant vessels. A recent report states that the Soviet fleet "features a large number of ultramodern transport ships, cargo freighters, and smaller specialized craft, as well as an uncommon number of passenger ships. The Soviet merchant marine is thus one of the few fleets capable of effectively pursuing both commercial and military objectives."[32] The Soviet merchant marine is, therefore, truly a component of Soviet sea power and plays an important role in supplying and maintaining widely scattered units of the Soviet navy. For example, 70% of the fuel used by Soviet combat ships is provided by Soviet merchant marine ships. Fishing trawlers and research vessels serve reconnaissance and intelligence collection functions well.

The Soviet Union is now focusing on the production of roll-on-roll-off vessels. Such craft "have great loading and unloading capability and are suited for use in small and poorly equipped ports—which makes them valuable for traffic with the Third World."[33]

The Soviet merchant marine now has 45 roll-on-roll-off ships in service. Logistical direct support of Soviet naval forces come from 85 replenishment ships. With the introduction of the 40,000 ton fleet oiler, *Berezina,* Soviet ships are no longer confined to anchorages for refueling. It is expected that more of these modern logistics ships will enter the Soviet fleet in the 1980s.

The West, and particularly the United States, has neglected the merchant shipping needed to support naval operations in time of war. In contrast, "the Soviet Union has a unified, quickly mobilizable apparatus at its disposal, and many Soviet freighters have electronic gear far in excess of "commercial" needs. Morever, according to American sources, Soviet naval officers are regularly assigned to merchant ships in order to become acquainted with Western ports.[34]

The Soviet Union has also become a world leader in deep sea fishing. They now operate in almost all the fishing areas of the world including off Alaska and both coasts of the Continental United States. The Soviets possess about 4,000 ocean-going craft and some 15,000 smaller coastal craft. On an annual basis only Japan exceeds, or even approximates, the Soviet fishing catch. Needless to say, the Soviet fishing fleet is under highly centralized governmental control.

In oceanography the Soviets also have a very extensive research fleet which also serves as an intelligence arm for both naval and commercial fleet activities. The U.S. currently has almost no equivalent of the 150 or so modern Soviet research ships.

In 1970 Norman Polmar wrote that a final factor measuring maritime power is centralized direction and coordination:

This the Soviet Union has done to a high degree, beginning with Admiral Gorshkov, who also is a Deputy Minister of Defense and member of the Central Committee of the Communist Party. Naval officers regularly serve with non-naval fleets; merchant tankers are employed as matter of course to refuel warships; the Ministry of Shipbuilding is responsible for building all ships: naval, merchant fishing, research, and inland transport; the Ministry of Fishing Economy maintains a central information center, with virtually real-time representation of the location of Soviet fishing flotillas and their catches (with the computer-display also showing the status of ships in ports, and so forth), and radio-telephone communications with the various flotillas at sea.[35]

There are varying opinions about the extent of the Soviet naval challenge and its implications for the security of the United States and its allies. The comparative effectiveness of the U.S. and Soviet navies for a wide range of peacetime and wartime activities cannot be measured with any degree of precision.[36] Differences in mission, ship design, and building programs all make this difficult to do.

Actual numbers of men, ships, and aircraft can be misleading. Admiral Gorshkov has written of the limitations of simple numerical or qualitative comparisons:

> The qualitative transformations which have taken place in naval forces have also changed the approach to evaluating the relative might of navies and their combat groupings: We have had to cease comparing the number of warships of one type or another and their total displacement (or the number of guns in a salvo or the weight of this salvo), and turn to a more complex, but also more correct appraisal of the striking and defensive power of ships, based on a mathematical analysis of their capabilities and qualitative characteristics.[37]

In a June 1975 interview, Admiral Elmo R. Zumwalt, Ret., former Chief of Naval Operations, U.S. Navy, said that Admiral Sergei G. Gorshkov had transformed the Soviet navy from a few pitiful coastal boats to a first-class fighting force, challenging American naval supremacy throughout the world. "The trends are going against us," Zumwalt said. He predicted Gorshkov will continue to enlarge the Soviet navy and obtain land bases for it around the world.[38]

After President Reagan assumed office in 1981 and John F. Lehman became Secretary of the Navy, the U.S. began a determined effort to regain naval superiority. Yet the momentum of Soviet shipbuilding gives them the edge in new ship construction. Congressional opposition to the U.S. naval build-up program surfaced in the 1985 congressional debate over the Defense Budget. Only time will tell if the American people have the will and staying power to rebuff the Soviet bid for naval superiority.

Soviet naval construction over the past twenty years indicates a key role for the Soviet navy in the extension of Soviet global reach and reflect a long-term offensive orientation in Soviet global strategy. As Admiral Gorshkov presciently observed in his *The Sea Power of the State,* "Establishing the conditions for gaining sea control has always required lengthy periods of time and the execution of a series of measures while still at peace."[39]

Soviet Air Power

Another factor which must be included in estimates of Soviet global reach is Soviet airpower in all of its many forms. The massive Soviet airlift to Ethiopia in 1977–78 revealed a formidable capacity to transport large numbers of troops and weapons to any area in Africa, the Middle East, or Asia. Toward the end of November 1977, exceptionally heavy air traffic was observed from the Soviet Union to Addis Ababa, Ethiopia, Aden at the Southern tip of the Arabian peninsula and Maputo in Mozambique. While part of the purpose of this airlift was to deliver military supplies to Ethiopia it was also a massive exercise in air logistics. Many of the planes did not carry cargo. By this exercise, the Soviets demonstrated that they could easily move into Libya, Mozambique, Angola, and elsewhere in Africa.

They have adequate ground crews and communications in place and are now capable of moving several divisions of combat troops to critical locations on very short notice. In addition, during the airlift exercise, the Soviets did not seek diplomatic approval for flying through any country's air space.

During some six months of this stepped-up air lift the Soviets delivered almost 100,000 tons of military hardware and ferried some 45,000 troops around Africa. For the latter task, the Soviets appropriated at least a quarter of the civilian transport capabilities of their Warsaw Pact allies. The Soviets have flown a large number of logistical support flights from Tashkent to Hanoi either directly or via Bombay. The Soviet deployment of troops (8–10 divisions, numbering some 95,000 men) into Afghanistan in December 1979 was another demonstration of the impressive Soviet airlift capability.

In addition to tremendous airlift capabilities, the Soviets have deployed air reconnaissance aircraft from bases in Cuba, East and West Africa, Aden, Ethiopia, Vietnam and Vladivostok. This, of course, facilitates their naval activity. Furthermore, Soviet long-range backfire bombers are capable of executing extended reconnaissance and air strike missions over vast reaches of the global ocean. The combined Soviet air and naval air arm is larger than that of the United States. Qualitatively most Soviet aircraft are equivalent to those possessed by the United States. Jane's Defense Weekly has reposted that "the new Soviet SU-27 fighter plane has narrowed the technological gap in aircraft." The Soviets have likewise acquired by exercises and actual operations the requisite experience to operate globally. In 1974, for example, they sent long-range aircraft into the Indian Ocean, over-flying Pakistan, to participate in a coordinated exercise with the Soviet navy.

The Cutting Edge: Expanding Soviet Global Reach

The Soviet fleet and related air power have become the cutting edge in the increasingly assertive Soviet grand strategy. These forces, particularly the Soviet navy and supporting merchant marine, enabled the Soviet Union to link up politically with strategically significant countries bordering the sea routes between Europe and Northeast Asia as well as within the Caribbean Basin. It should be noted that political "influence" and "links" generally precede base acquisition, but are then reinforced by actual presence.

For the Soviets to gain an advanced position on the rimlands of the Afro-Eurasian land mass they have had to make progress on both land and sea. The Soviets have acquired bases through a variety of mutually supporting operations. Once access to a new base is obtained, the influence generated by the increasingly visible Soviet civilian fishing, whaling, merchant, and oceanographical ships are also elements for expanding Soviet maritime positions. The Soviets have developed an innovative logistical infrastructure for the Soviet fleet—a chain of supply points, deep-sea mooring buoys, and fleet anchorages—along the key maritime transit areas between European Russian ports and Vladivostok. At the same time, for both the Soviet and U.S. navies, bases for their fleets continue to remain an important component of their combat readiness. Consequently, despite ingenious logistical innovations, the problems of base acquisition and utilization remains an important facet of contemporary naval art.

Over the past several years, while elements of the American overseas base system have been closing down (Diego Garcia has been an exception), Soviet overseas operations have witnessed a proliferation of "facilities," including deep-sea mooring buoys, fleet anchorages and ports-of-call suitable for resupply, which give the Soviet fleet considerable operational flexibility, particularly in the Indian Ocean. Due to the informal, and even secret, nature of Soviet agreements with host nations to allow Moscow access to their facilities, the Soviet Union has been able to condemn the West for its "bases policy" (Subic Bay, Diego Garcia), while claiming that it has none.

Soviet enforced discipline also increases their flexibility, Soviet warships are generally smaller than those in the U.S. Navy. Likewise, their crew complements are smaller with less consumption of ship stores all around. As they employ helicopters along with STOL (short take-off and landing) and VTOL (vertical take-off and landing) aircraft on their carriers, they do not need to consume fuel for high speed steaming to generate wind on carrier flight decks. The Soviets have no comparable need for liberty ashore for their crew because of better discipline and lower expectations (their able bodied seamen are conscripts). Hence, the Soviets have smaller logistical support needs for their powerful, missile-armed ships.

A dramatic expansion of Soviet naval and related air power base along with Moscow's deployment of substantial naval forces in the North Sea, the Baltic, the Mediterranean, the Caribbean, the South Atlantic, the Indian Ocean, the Sea of Japan, and the Western Pacific matches the *British base system* at the height of the empire. On March 20, 1984, the Pentagon reported that a Soviet helicopter carrier, the *Leningrad,* and an advanced guided-missile destroyer, the *Udaloy,* steamed toward Cuba to show concern over the Caribbean. A Pentagon spokesman said, "It shows the importance the Soviet Union places on the region. We consider it a major movement."[40]

Soviet projections in the Atlantic, Indian, and Pacific Ocean areas are operationalized through a strategy of "acquisition and denial." Such a strategy attempts to deny the West and the PRC access to strategic assets (air and naval bases, logistical facilities or military staging areas, etc.), while attempting to acquire such facilties for the USSR. The access to such facilities is usually preceded by:

- Initial penetration—through the establishment of diplomatic relations, the extension of economic and military aid, reciprocal cultural and trade agreements, fishing agreements;
- Establishment of a "presence"—technical and military advisors, diplomatic personnel, port-of-call visits by the navy, development of local harbors,
- Friendship treaties
- Tacit agreements whereby the USSR is allowed to utilize a host country's strategic base facilities as long as the relationship proves to be mutually advantageous.

The USSR has promoted a variety of pro-Soviet activities. These include: support of pro-Soviet coup d'etats; extended trade, aid, and arms to left-of-center governments; supply of material support to aid allies in their inter-regional disputes; and dispatch of high-level delegations to allied countries, which elevate the host government's prestige. Such tactics, normal in expansionist power behavior, should be clearly understood.

In January 1987, President Reagan issued National Security Strategy of the United States, which interalia stated:

> The most significant threat to U.S. security and national interests is the global challenge posed by the Soviet Union. . . .
> Internationally, the Soviets have continued to assist groups waging so-called wars of "national liberation," sponsor with arms and military training international terrorist groups, promote and exploit regional instabilities and conduct an aggressive and illegal war in Afghanistan. In numerous other places around the globe, Soviet advisors and combat troops have also engaged in conduct in violation of international agreements.
> The Soviets have undertaken an unprecedented military buildup that poses a continuing threat to the United States and our allies. The Soviet leadership clearly attaches the greatest importance to its military strength, which has been the most significant source of the USSR's influence on the international scene. For decades the Soviet Union has allocated a disproportionate percentage of national income to the buildup of its military forces. It now has a uniformed military of more than five million (excluding more than one million border guards and other security forces). It is estimated that military expenditures currently absorb 15–17 percent of the total Soviet GNP.
> Soviet military power permits Moscow to provide a strong defense of the homeland while facilitating direct and indirect participation in regional conflicts beyond Soviet borders. Furthermore, Soviet military resources increasingly are used to influence and broker the policies of other countries and to promote instability.

Soviet strategy is fundamentally aggressive in nature. The Soviet Union has clearly followed an expansionist foreign policy. According to Milovan Djilas, "What our five senses tell us is that, whether with brute force or without, Soviet hegemony has gradually been expanding in all parts of the world."[41]

As long as the Soviet Union retains its present ideology and political structure, it will continue to pose a serious threat to the security of the United States and its allies. This threat has grown as Soviet military power has grown. From Lenin to Brezhnev to Andropov to Chernenko to Gorbachev, the aims of Soviet policy have widened and extended geographically commensurate with Soviet military expansion.

A frightening example of Soviet military development was the 1986 revelation that high-powered Soviet ground-to-space microwaves have disabled U.S. reconnaissance satellites on more than one occasion, a space-war breakthrough causing deep concern among intelligence officials. The danger was foreseen in a prophetic 1980 report to President Reagan warning that the U.S. could be "completely blinded" by the mid-1980's.[42]

Gorbachev is pressing rapidly ahead with the Soviet's own war-in-space program under cover of an attempted U.S. satellite black-out. Simultaneously, Gorbachev is propogating a world-wide fear of "Star Wars" to pressure the President to kill SDI. This masterful combination of accelerated technological advance with highly-focused psychological warfare reflects Gorbachev's Machiavellian skills.

Obviously, in the Soviet process of gradual extension of power and influence around the world, the violent and non-violent instruments are fused into a carefully designed program of intrusion and infiltration. The operational conduct of Soviet strategy will be the focus of the next chapter.

NOTES

1. Johnson, James T. "Ground for Nuclear Optimism," a review of *The Evolution of Nuclear Strategy* (Studies in International Security: 20) By Lawrence Freedman, New York, St. Martin's Press, 1983, (London, The International Institute for Strategic Studies, 1981), in *Freedom At Issue*, May–June 1983, No. 72, p. 10.
2. Stalin, Joseph, *Problems of Leninism*, Foreign Languages Publishing House, Moscow, 1940, P. 20.
3. *PRAVDA*, June 5, 1974, in *Current Digest of the Soviet Press*, July 3, 1974, p. 14.
4. See Oleg Penkovsky, *The Penkovsky Papers*, translated by Peter Deriablin in Garden City, NY, Doubleday, 1965; Colonel Penkovsky was shot as a spy by the Soviet Union on May 16, 1963, for his exposure of Soviet nuclear programs during the late 1950s.
5. Sokolovskii, V.D. *Marshal of the Soviet Union*, translated by Herbert S. Dinezster, Leon Gouze, Thomas W. Wolfe, A Rand Corporation Study, published by Prentice Hall, 1963.
6. Lenin, V.I., *"Left Wing" Communism*, edited by Saul N. Siberman, Englewood Cliffs, New Jersey, Prentice Hall, 1972, p. 76.
7. *Essentials of Lenin*, Volume 2, Westport, CT, Hyperion, 1973, p. 609.
8. Lenin, *Selected Works*, International Publishers, New York, 1943, Vol. 8, pp. 296–7.
8.A "Constitution and Program of the Communist Party of America", 1921, p. 16
8.B Lenin, Selected Works, 12 Volumes, New York, International Publishers prepared and translated in Moscow by the Marx-Engels-Lenin Institute, VI, p. 291.
9. "The Leading Role of the CPSU in Building the Army of a Developed Socialist Society," *"Voprosy Isstorii KPSS"* (Questions of History of the CPSU), No. 5, May 1974, and *Vooruzhennye sily sovestskovo gosudarstva*, (Armed Forces of the Soviet State), Moscow, Voenizdat, 1975, p. 127.
10. N. Lebedev, "The USSR's Effort to Restructure International Relations," *International Affairs*, No. 1, January 1976, p. 3
11. Sokolovskii, *op.cit.*, p. 335.
12. *Ibid.* emphasis supplied.

13. *New York Times,* September 12, 1960.
14. *Washington Post,* July 1, 1981, p. 1.
15. *New York Times,* August 6, 1981, p.A-9.
16. *Soviet Military Power,* Department of Defense, U.S. Government Printing Office, Washington, D.C. 1983.
17. Weeks, Albert, "What is Their Spy-N-Sky Trying to do?" *The Washington Times,* January 24, 1985, Section B1.
18. Annual Report to the Congress, Casper W. Weinberger, Secretary of Defense, FY1984, p. 34.
19. *Soviet Military Power,* 1983, *op.cit.,* pp. 6–7.
20. *Ibid.,* p. 33.
21. *Ibid.,* p. 50.
22. *Ibid.,* p. 35.
23. Norman Polmar, *Soviet Naval Power—Challenge for the 1970s,* Crane, Russia & Co., Inc., New York, 1974, p. 41.
24. *PRAVDA,* July 27, 1981.
25. Elmo R. Zumwalt, Jr., "Gorshkov and His Navy," *Orbis,* Fall 1980, p. 501.
26. *Understanding Soviet Naval Developments,* (Office of the Chief of Naval Operations, Department of the Navy, Government Printing Office, Washington, D.C.; January 1981), p. 30.
27. *Ibid.,* p. 30.
28. *Ibid.,* p. 30.
29. *New York Times,* December 19, 1979.
30. Toth, R.C., *Philadelphia Inquirer,* November 11, 1980, p. 38.
31. TASS in English 1313 GMT 25 Apr. 75, From FBIS Report of a Moscow Broadcast.
32. Dedial, Gorg, "The Soviets' Merchant Marine," in the Neue Zurich Zeitung, *World Press Review,* March 1981, p. 51.
33. *Ibid.*
34. *Ibid.*
35. Polmar, *op.cit.,* pp. 105–106.
36. Two books that address this problem are Robert A. Kilmarx, "Soviet United States Naval Balance," Center for Strategic and International Studies, 1975 and Norman Polmar, "Soviet-Naval Power: Challenge for the 1970s," Crane, Russia & Co., Inc., New York, 1974.
   An unclassified study, "Strategic Forecast: U.S. Navy in the year 2000 Phase 1, Critical Issues and Future Naval Missions, prepared by the Strategic Studies Center, Stanford Research Institute, addresses this issue in depth. (1983)
37. Gorshkov, "Navies in War and in Peace," pt. 1, *loc.cit.,* February 1972.
38. *Op.cit.*
39. Gorshkov, S.J., *The Sea Power of the State,* (Annapolis, MD, Naval Institute Press, 1976), p. 246.
39.A. *National Review,* Dec 31 1985, p. 11
40. *The Philadelphia Inquirer,* March 21, 1984, p. D-1.
41. Urban, George, "A Conversation With Milovan Djilas", *Encounter,* December 1979, p. 36.
42. Rowland Evans and Robert Novak, "Blinded Satellites" The Washington Post, Oct. 29, 1986, A-19.

CHAPTER III
Soviet Grand Strategy

The integration of all elements of Soviet power into a single operational complex is known as grand strategy.

The non-military components of Soviet strategy are as old as history, but these have been skillfully combined and refined by Soviet strategists and operators to a level never before realized. In this sense they are new and, unfortunately, poorly understood by most Western leaders. In a previous book* the author described the fusion of military and non-military aspects of Soviet strategy. Fundamentally, non-military means of conflict are used to subvert a target society so that it can be taken over without open warfare. Non-military methods include psychological warfare, disinformation, agitation, anti-military subversion, negotiations, and intimidation. These activities are as highly organized and as centralized as their military counterparts.

Although the military and non-military components of Soviet strategy mutually reinforce and support each other, the most active element of the Soviet expansionist forces are the trained professional cadres, who captain the communist parties and fronts and who mobilize Soviet support in both the industrialized and Third World countries.

Lenin preferred subversion to military conflict in his plan for communist world domination. He never advocated commencing a war that would jeopardize communist control of the Soviet Union. While the constant aim of Soviet strategy is subversion, the more powerful the Soviet military becomes, the more aggressive its political actions.

---

*See book on communist political warfare by Kintner, William R. and Kornfedder, Joseph R. *The New Frontier of War,* Henry Regnery Company, Chicago, 1962. Kornfedder studied at the Lenin School under Stalin and organized the Communist Party of Colombia and of Venezuela before defecting in the mid-thirties.

The Correlation of Forces

The Soviets act more aggressively when they perceive "the world correlation of forces" moving in their favor. Thus, the four-year period following the capture of Saigon in 1975 was one of the most expansionist in their history. At the beginning of this period the Soviets moved into Angola, then into Ethiopia, and finally into Afghanistan in 1979. They perceived, correctly, that the United States was almost paralyzed by its traumatic defeat in Vietnam. Generally the Soviets move against weakness and are reluctant to move against strength. In the first four years of the Reagan Administration they did not gain ground anywhere and suffered setbacks in Poland and Grenada.

The author was told in 1978 by a Soviet scholar that a detailed study of global, regional, and local "force relations" (resembling earlier studies by the "real-politik" school), was being conducted by the USSR Academy of Science. According to the scholar, the study assessed the likelihood of certain international developments on the basis of a correlation of relevant forces. To this end, the "power potential" of a country was assessed using objective criteria (e.g., natural resources) modified by the subjective factor of intentions—i.e., assumed policy objectives. Power potentials were compared with those of relevant countries. Thus, for example, even in the absence of U.S. troops in Korea, a north-south conflict was determined to be unlikely following a "correlation of forces" analysis. Soviet strategy begins with an assessment of the "correlation of forces" between the Soviet Union and its opponents. The importance Soviet leaders assign to such analysis of relative strengths in making foreign policy is repeatedly stressed in their writings.

> The sphere of international relations remains an arena of tense struggle between the two world systems, socialism and capitalism.
>
> In these conditions the correlation of forces as a major factor for the development of international relations acquires particular importance, for this correlation is indispensible both for the elaboration of long-term foreign policy strategy and for the state's practical activity in international affairs.[1]

Determination of the "correlation of forces" identifies which states can influence others to their advantage. While Soviet planners regard military power as the primary source of influence, economic and technological considerations, relations with allies, ideological factors, and political motivation are also vital for such assessments.

Soviet power and influence have increased tremendously since World War II. Soviet tactics may also have changed, but the urge for expansion and the relentless waging of a "struggle between systems" have not. Flexibility of tactics varies with specific regions and objectives. Concentration of efforts in a geographic area is dependent on the assessment of the balance or "correlation of forces" in that locale. Soviet leaders increasingly claim that the global correlation of forces has shifted in favor of the Soviet Union and predict that this shift has become irreversible.

Even with this favorable assessment, Soviet leaders see the active struggle to promote further change in the world "correlation of forces" as a major task facing all members of the Socialist camp. At the bottom of this struggle is the Soviet effort to gain and maintain military superiority over the United States.

While recognizing the complexity of world politics, Soviet leaders hold that military strength decides position in the world. The inclination in the West to oppose strong defensive postures, and the belief of some Western analysts that military potential no longer is the foundation of influence contributes to the Soviet perception of the superiority of their position.

To obscure the role of military strength in Soviet planning, Soviet leaders suggest that the "correlation of forces" can not and should not be restricted to an analysis of global military balances. They contend that their studies analyze "strictly the *correlation of class forces in the worldwide system of international relations.*"[2]

Despite such camouflage, the Soviet Union actually assesses "correlation of forces" by the criterion of military capacity, which is dependently interrelated with geography, population, industrial potential, technological expertise, and political motivation.

Combining Revolutionary Nuclear Strategy

The Bolshevik Party, created by Lenin, was adept at every aspect of subversive activity. The revolutionary goal of Bolshevism channeled the party into a conspiracy organized along military lines. Lenin acknowledged that the heart of the Communist Party was conspiratorial organization. "Conspiracy," he said, "is so essential a condition of an organization of this kind that all other conditions (the number and selection of members, their functions, etc.) must be made to conform with it."[3]

The Soviet record since 1917 reveals that the entire machinery of Soviet communism works toward conquest by force, and is military in method and purpose. The Third World Congress proclaimed in 1921: "The organization of the Party must be adapted to the conditions and to the goal of its activity. . . . To conquer the bourgeoisie and to wrest the power from its hands is . . . its determining and guiding role."[4] It is of the "greatest importance," this same congress exhorted, "that the directing body of the Communist Party should be guided in its entire activity by the revolutionary requirements."[5] In 1935, Stalin told the Seventh World Congress of the Communist International: "The victory of the proletariat never comes by itself. It has to be prepared for and won. And only a strong proletarian (Communist) revolutionary party can prepare for and win victory."[6]

The Soviets relied on revolutionary tools to subvert other countries after World War II, with the exception of the Baltic States and the countries of Eastern Europe. These countries were seized by the Red Army and made part of the Soviet empire.

The Soviet acquisition of nuclear weapons in the 1950s led them to explore how to adhere to principles of conquest while avoiding a nuclear exchange. At the same time, the Soviets launched a massive program to achieve strategic superiority. The primary architect of this innovative program was Nikita Krushchev. The outlines of this masterful strategy were revealed to the West in 1961 by Anatoly Golitsyn, a KGB career officer with access to the government's most secret files concerning foreign policy and political military strategy.[7]

Golitsyn, increasingly disillusioned with the Machiavellian practices of the Soviet regime, concluded that the only practical way to fight the regime was from abroad. Golitsyn was able to do this effectively with his inside knowledge of the KGB. Adoption of the new and aggressive long-range communist policy precipitated Golitsyn's break with the regime. He felt that the necessity of warning the West of the new dimensions of the Soviet threat justified his abandoning his country and accepting the personal sacrifices involved. His final deliberate break with the regime came after lengthy self-examination.

The new Soviet strategy which Golitsyn described a quarter of a century ago has been pursued by the Soviets ever since. The key to this new strategy has been the increased emphasis on "active measures." This term describes Soviet activities designed to infiltrate, mislead, and weaken Western societies. Disinformation, media corruption, formation of fronts, campus seminars, and peace movements undermining Western resolve, have all been included in the Soviet panoply of tricks. Such "active measures" called for a variety of indirect assaults: Soviet-supported "wars of national liberation" throughout the Third World; a campaign of international terrorism; the promotion of antiwar, antinuclear, and neutralist movements of middle class and intellectual groups in the West; penetration of Western parliamentary institutions under the banner of "peaceful coexistence" through coalitions with socialists, social democrats, and left-of-center Roman Catholic parties. These "active measures" are accompanied by a flood of disinformation designed to deceive and lull the West into believing that the communist camp is riven with dissension, weak, and desperate for accommodation.

This new strategy was aimed at two distinct but complementary groups—industrialized democracies and countries of the Third World. The United States, Britain, France, West Germany and Japan were marked as the "main enemies" of the Soviet Union and the Communist bloc. The immediate aim of the new general strategy was to "destabilize" these main enemies, weaken their alliances and isolate them, from each other and from the Third World.

The KGB was given an enhanced role in the new Soviet strategy. The KGB along with the national security and intelligence services of the entire Soviet bloc would henceforth collaborate in the new task of advancing the Soviet camp's long-range political and military strategy. The KGB's main objective was to assist in achieving Soviet strategic objectives. The KGB made imaginative use of agents in the ranks of the main enemies to deceive the West about the true aims of the new strategy. A new department was created in the KGB to plan and direct the concealment of the bloc's swing to a Leninist strategy adapted to the imperatives of the nuclear age.

Golitsyn defined the communist strategy of disinformation as the name "for secret operations and activities which are conducted by the entire Communist Bloc or by a number of its members in accordance with a consistent design or a strategic plan to create favorable conditions for long range communist grand policies and strategies and to contribute to the success of these policies and strategies. The essence of such operations is an active misrepresentation of the true communist principal goals and strategies in order to accomplish them by influencing and inducing their western adversaries to contribute, albeit unwittingly, to the accomplishment of their objectives. Such active misrepresentation is performed by the concealment of true information and by the calculated distortion and dissemination of false information sometimes detrimental to themselves and contradictory to their own propaganda. The communist components involved include the party, the assets of its Security and Intelligence services, the controlled political opposition."[8]

The Main Enemies: The Industrialized Democracies

Soviet strategy regarding the industrialized democracies is directed toward a number of discreet but interrelated goals. The primary focus is to split the United States from its allies. Second, the Soviet Union has sought to weaken the Western will by a combination of intimidation tactics and sustained peace campaigns marked by passionate appeals for disarmament and arms control. Third, the Soviet Union has sought to undermine the economic wellbeing of its opponents while simultaneously seeking to beg, borrow, or steal advanced technology. Fourth, the Soviet Union has aided and abetted terrorist actions designed to destabilize Western societies. These complimentary strategies are sustained by a massive campaign of subversion utilizing a relentless outpouring of propaganda.

Alliance Splitting

Under Krushchev, the Soviet Union tried to split the Western alliance with threats and by creating crises. These tactics only spurred Western unity. Krushchev's successors abandoned his policy and instead stressed a softer approach. As Brezhnev told a gathering of European Communist Parties in 1967:

> What does this experience teach us? Specifically, it teaches that the situation of "cold war" and the confrontation of military blocs, the atmosphere of military threats, seriously hinder the functioning of the revolutionary, democratic forces. In the bourgeois countries in a situation of international tension reactionary elements become active, the military clique raises its head, and anti-democratic trends and anti-communism in general are intensified. Conversely, in a situation of reduced international tension the needle of the political barometer shifts to the left.[9]

Despite the 1968 Soviet invasion of Czechoslavakia, the seeds of detente began to blossom during the latter Nixon-Kissinger years. In the mid-1970's the Soviet Union began to deploy a new intermediate range missile, the SS-20, against targets in Western Europe. This development alarmed European leaders, who felt that under the terms of strategic parity between the United States and the Soviet Union a Soviet advantage at the theater nuclear level could not be allowed. Accordingly, these European leaders, notably Chancellor Helmut Schmidt of West Germany, insisted that NATO (meaning U.S.) should deploy intermediate range missiles. In December, 1979, NATO adopted the two-track decision, pledging to seek an arms control agreement that would make U.S. deployments unnecessary, but failing that, to proceed with deployment beginning in December, 1983.

After the NATO decision was taken, European opposition to the prospective deployments rapidly grew, and political parties that had initially endorsed the decision began to waver.

The Soviets launched a massive political and psychological campaign to encourage a split between Western Europe and the United States. "In the postwar period," wrote an influential Soviet commentor in 1980, "West Europe has spent too long . . . in a strange 'looking glass land' where its whole policy has mirrored American policy . . . everything the United States regarded as being to its own advantage has ultimately turned into tragedy for West Europe. . . . It is time for West Europe to get out of the political 'looking glass land' before it is too late."[10]

Despite a huge outlay of money and men, the Soviets lost this round. They walked out of the Geneva INF talks in December 1983, when U.S. missile deployments began on schedule. After stating that they would not resume arms control negotiation unless the US missiles were removed, the Soviets did agree to resume talks in Geneva in March 1985 without conditions.

Peace and Arms Control

Central to Moscow's plan to change the world balance of power in its favor is the manipulation of "peace forces" in the free world, since these political groups inhibit the ability of free world governments to respond to the Soviet Union's military buildup. A Soviet specialist on nuclear arms wrote on the eve of the first SALT negotiations that the Soviet Union should base its diplomacy on the erosion of the American position resulting from domestic political pressures.

> Disarmament . . . can be achieved only as a result of the most active pressure on their governments by the revolutionary forces in the imperialist countries in conjunction with a flexible and principled policy by the socialist camp. Any other notion of the paths for achieving disarmament is an illusion.[11]

In 1983, the same author wrote in *Military History Journal*, the monthly organ of the Soviet Ministry of Defense, that the Soviet Armed Forces and free world peace movements are effectively united in one giant "front" against free world governments.[12]

More than 70 pro-Soviet communist parties throughout the world are political warfare legions. International and local front organizations, dominated by pro-Soviet communists, are employed by the Soviets to influence many political groups. These organizations are not overtly pro-Soviet, and are designed to attract support from a broad political spectrum. The largest and most important of these front organizations are the World Peace Council (WPC), with affiliates in over 130 countries, the World Federation of Trade Unions, the World Federation of Democratic Youth, and the Women's International Democratic Federation.

The Soviet Union's peace propaganda has the dual aim of disarming its enemies while justifying its own military machine. The advent of nuclear weapons has made peace the most important single demand of communist political warfare. It is the thread which ties together Soviet nuclear rockets, Soviet schemes for general disarmament, and communist support of wars of national "liberation for the purpose of freeing people from the 'imperialists'."

"The opening of a profound dialogue with the antiwar movements in the free world is a prime task of the peace movement in socialist countries," B. Sarkadi Nagy, the General Secretary of the All-Hungarian Peace Council, has explained. "This can be facilitated substantially by such a respected international organization as the World Peace Council (WPC)."[13]

WPC activities in the United States had been coordinated by the U.S. Communist Party (CPUSA), but in 1979 two of the CPUSA's members established the U.S. Peace Council as a WPC affiliate. Subsequently, WPC-related activities in the United States increased materially.

Nevertheless, the close public association between the WPC and the international communist movement has tended to undermine the credibility of the WPC and its affiliates. Indeed, even Nagy, while disputing the idea that the WPC is a Moscow "puppet organization" nevertheless cannot avoid acknowledging that "the socialist countries fully share the aims of the WPC."[14]

It is nothing new for aggressor governments to mask their real intentions by professing a love of peace. It is new, however, for a government to engage in permanent peace drives. Such permanent peace drives make sense only if a government considers itself permanently at war with the world around it.

It is paradoxical that the Soviet Union, the professed world champion of peace, should build the world's largest and most powerful nuclear missile force. Soviet power and influence have increased since the ICBM joined the Soviet arsenal. The fear of war in the free world has increased, and the resolution of the free world has declined as the number and power of Soviet missiles have grown.

Past and present Soviet peace drives differ in that the present peace campaigns are no longer defensive—they are designed to gain time through aggressive political warfare, to keep the West off-balance and to gain technological-military supremacy over the United States. We live in a twilight period between peace and war. This undeclared armistice, which the West may mistake as peace, could last a decade or even longer, depending on the situation within the Soviet Union under its new leadership, possible splits among the Western powers, and erosion of the will to survive in Western countries.

The Soviets perceive the peace movements, particularly the present nuclear freeze program, as an unparalleled opportunity for influence. Thus, Georgii Arbatov, head of the USSR's USA and Canada Institute and a leading Kremlin expert regarding U.S.-Soviet relations, wrote in the October 1982 issue of the USA Journal:

> . . . this choice (against nuclear weapons) must not be made only by governments, but also by people—the millions and millions of people whose future and fate are at issue. All indications are that this fact is increasingly getting through to the broadest circles of the world public. Does the anti-nuclear movement which has developed in Europe and America in 1981–82 not testify to this?[15]

Such Soviet propaganda efforts are strictly for external consumption, for within the USSR itself, efforts are directed toward keeping the Soviet people from developing any sort of pacifism. Thus the CPSU Draft Program (1985 stated:

> An important task of the party's ideological education work is military patriotic education, the formation of readiness to defend the socialist fatherland and to give it all one's efforts and, if necessary, one's life too.[16]

As long as the Communists rule the Soviet Union, the danger of war with the United States will remain. Hence the Soviets feel the need to prepare their people for it. But the Soviets are also waging an adroit game of political warfare against the United States. From this perspective, the Geneva talks, the freeze movements, and U.S. congressional debate over the defense budget are all part of the same psychological conflict. In the Geneva arms control talks, the Soviets hope to enhance their strategic advantage and create a perception of overall nuclear superiority which will allow them to practice coercive diplomacy.

The highly organized Soviet "peace campaign" has used the WPC and its affiliates and other front organizations and communist parties to organize demonstrations and conferences against militarily strengthening NATO. The Soviets have employed the fronts to support a variety of well-meaning religious groups, antinuclear movements, pacifists, environmentalists, youth groups, and others such as "Women Strike for Peace." Similar groups are not permitted to operate in the USSR and Eastern Europe.

Moscow made a determined effort to mobilize mass demonstrations, civil disobedience, and violence in Western Europe as part of its strenuous campaign to curb the deployment of U.S. INF missiles in Europe. It sought to stress anti-US themes in the "peace campaign" while deflecting world attention from Soviet military programs and expenditures against potential enemies.

Obviously Soviet military power places a powerful tool into the hands of Soviet leaders and diplomats. The massive Soviet campaign against the deployment of U.S. missiles in Western Europe failed, but their 1985 return to arms control talks in Geneva only means that the Soviets will exploit the peace issue many times again in the future.

The Soviet "peace" game should be quite obvious. They seek to portray a possible nuclear war as the sole evil confronting humanity. A former Soviet intellectual, Vladimir Bukovsky, who became a professor of psychology at Stanford University tackles this pivotal issue head-on:

> The truth of the matter is that a great number of people have already accepted the primacy of physical survival over traditional values, over human rights and dignity. And that is exactly what the Soviets were counting on when they launched their massive campaign of "struggle for peace" in 1980 under the slogan: 'The people have the power to preserve peace—their prime right.'
>
> Confronted with the absolute value of the survival of mankind, people have been required to sacrifice their other rights—and have been willing to do so, particularly when they have been skillfully reminded of the potential holocaust caused by artificially created international "tension."[17]

The author of the above, wrote an article for Commentary in 1982 which began:

> The "struggle for peace" has always been a cornerstone of Soviet foreign policy. Indeed, the Soviet Union itself rose out of the ashes of World War I under the banner of "Peace to the People! Power to the Soviets!" Probably from the very first, Bolshevik ideologists were aware of how powerful a weapon for them the universal craving for peace would be—how gullible and irrational people could be whenever they were offered the slightest temptation to believe that peace was at hand.[18]

The article concluded:

> Peace has never been preserved by a hysterical desire to survive at any price. Nor has it ever been promoted by catchy phrases and cheap slogans. There are 400 million people in the East whose freedom was stolen from them and whose existence is miserable. It so happens that peace is impossible while they remain enslaved, and only with them (not with their executioners) should you work to secure real peace in our world.[19]

Gorbachev's persistent effort to make arms control the central focus of the unrelenting Soviet "peace" campaign finally began to pay off.

The most significant foreign policy shift in the second Reagan administration has been the move from an initial apparent indifference toward the significance of the role of arms control in U.S.-Soviet relations to a 1986 momentum that arms control might be the door to a more stable world.

Both before and after the 1986 Reykjavik Summit Meeting Soviet opposition to President Reagan's SDI program became the controversial centerpiece of U.S.-Soviet Arms Control Negotiations.

The SDI, or Star Wars, represents the first real challenge to the most ominous strategic development of the decade; a growing Soviet nuclear first-strike capability combined with its own "Red Shield," a ballistic-missile-defense system covering the entire USSR. While Star Wars remains largely theory, with experimental testing, Red Shield is an emerging operational reality.

President Reagan has now fully endorsed serious arms control negotiations with the Soviet Union. Mikhail Gorbachev has been playing a skillful game in seeking the support of the world for his arms control proposals and actions.

But what does Gorbachev really want? In a "Letter to Gorbachev" which appeared in the New York Times Magazine Oct. 26, 1986, Craig R. Whitney wrote: "you're not going to be any easier to deal with than any of your predecessors." As to Soviet Arms Control policy, "it's full of new initiatives, but skeptics here wonder what the real aim is. Do you really want to reduce expenditures on arms so you can build up your domestic economy, or do you just want to get us to let our guard down while you strengthen the K.G.B. and your military-industrial complex even more?" Whitney, who from 1977 to 1980 served as a correspondent in the New York Times Moscow Bureau implicitly answered this question in his open letter when he told Gorbachev about "the still unresolved legacy of Stalinism that pervades so many levels of Soviet society, particularly the level at which the K.G.B. and the police can still control what people can say and read and think even in the privacy of their own homes. As long as that is the way you run your society, no democratically elected leader can trust you, which is one reason President Reagan is so wary of making deals with you."

Terrorism: A Central Soviet Tool

Another avenue of Soviet attack against the West involves terrorist movements. The Soviet Communists have a long history of supporting terrorism to create fear and uncertainty, which undermine existing governments and facilitate their takeover. This is part of Communist philosophy. Terrorism has long been an accepted tool of Communist revolution. In 1848 Karl Marx wrote: "Only one means exists to shorten the bloody death pangs of the old society and the birth pangs of the new society, to simplify and concentrate them. Revolutionary terrorism,[20]. Soviet intensification of terrorism was set in motion by the Tri-Continental Conference, held in Havana in January 1966. Within a few months, "the first important network of guerrilla training camps was set up around Havana, and it was in these camps, Europeans came for their first guerrilla training."[21]

The Soviet role in international terrorism has been deliberately obscured in the West. Because Lenin opposed uncoordinated terrorism of individual anarchists, the erroneous conclusion has been drawn that the Soviets look askance at political terrorism. Such a conclusion does a disservice to the sophisticated nature of Soviet strategic doctrine. Lenin always favored organized political terrorism to enhance the progress of the Bolshevik Party. During the 1905 Revolution Lenin wrote:

> I see with horror, real horror, that we have been talking of bombs for more than half a year and not one single one has been made. . . . Give every company short and simple bomb formulae. . . . They must begin their military training immediately in direct connection with practical fighting actions. Some will immediately kill a spy or blow up a police station; others will organize an attack on a bank, in order to confiscate funds for the uprising. . . .[22]

Faithful to this Leninist heritage, the Soviet KGB supervises a large-scale terrorist training activity. Terrorists are trained in the Soviet Union and Eastern Europe as well as in Cuba, Libya and other cooperative countries. Patrice Lumumba Friendship University, which indoctrinates Third World students, is the *alma mater* of Carlos, the Venezuelan terrorist who led the seizure of an OPEC meeting in 1975.

In addition to training, the Soviet Union provides weaponry and financial support to a variety of terrorist organizations.

> The heart of the Russians' strategy is to provide the terrorist network with the goods and services necessary to undermine the industrialized democracies of the West. . . . As Italy's Red Brigades have made clear, the ultimate objective is "the supreme symbol of multinational imperialism," the United States.[23]

In practice, terrorists have been useful to the Soviet Union in undermining an opponent's public safety and government stability. Terrorists of varied ideological persuasions have been trained and indoctrinated in Soviet schools including Lumumba University and Sanprobal, the Soviet Academy of Military Training, near Simferopol on the Black Sea. Associated camps with Soviet trained instructors have been established in Cuba, North Korea, Lebanon, Syria, Iraq, South Yemen, Algeria, and North Vietnam. Arms and ammunition have also been sent via proxies to groups such as the IRA, PLO, Red Brigade, Baader Meinhof, and similar organizations in Africa and South America. According to Ray S. Cline and Yonah Alexander:

> In the 1970's terrorism, whether backed directly or indirectly by the Soviet Union or independently initiated, appeared to have become an indispensable tactical and strate-

gic tool in the Soviet struggles for power and influence within and among nations. In relying on this instrument, Moscow seems to aim, in the 1980's, at achieving strategic ends in circumstances where the use of conventional armed forces is deemed inappropriate, ineffective, too risky or too difficult.[24]

Terrorism can be used both defensively and offensively. Lenin murdered the Czarist family and eliminated much of the Russian governing establishment so that the remainder would submit to communist rule. The Soviets have benefited from other terrorist acts. The Stern Gang forced the British to give up their mandate over Palestine, and Cypriot terrorists led them to abandon control of Cyprus. No one has ever tried a sustained offensive campaign of terrorism against a communist regime. During the 1950's and 1960's France used strong countermeasures against the rebellious Algerians, but the Nationalist terrorism eventually weakened French determination to remain as well as intimidating the native opposition to the revolution.

Global television has enormously enhanced the power of terrorism by erecting an immense stage for mounting and magnifying their demands. This was convincingly demonstrated by American TV coverage of the 39 hostages captured and held prisoners in Beirut by Shi'ite hijackers in June 1985.

Most of the terrorists spreading chaos and anarchy throughout the democratic world do it for their own purposes which, however, almost always fit in with the Soviet campaign to destabilize the West.

Yuri V. Andropov, who headed the KGB for 15 years before he became Secretary General of the CPUSSR, made that sinister organization the most aggressive terrorist machine the world has ever seen. The expansion of terrorism during this period resulted in terrorist atrocities in many European countries. A spring 1983 situation report of the Security and Intelligence Foundation[25] has highlighted these developments. In Italy the most spectacular feats were the kidnapping and murder of former Prime Minister Aldo Moro in the spring of 1978, and the abduction in Verona in December, 1981 of Brigadier General James L. Dozier of the United States Army, a senior officer on the staff of the NATO headquarters in that city.

Terrorism erupted in the West German Republic out of much of the same convulsion which seized the Italian radicals. There finally emerged the organization of the Red Army Faction, known as the Baader-Meinhof Gang, after two of its founders, Andreas Baader and Ulrike Meinhof. In 1977, West German terrorism was at crescendo. The director of the West German Employers Association, Hanna-Martin Schleyer, was kidnapped and murdered when the huge ransom demanded for his release was not forthcoming.

France, too, has been the theater of many brazen acts of terrorism. In 1982, in Paris, the American *charge d'affaires* narrowly escaped assassination in the street. Earlier in the year a U.S. military attache was killed in the city, and the bombing of a Jewish synagogue was another outrage.

Given the character of these destructive happenings, the debate over the complicity of the Soviet bloc in the instigation and support of terrorism and insurgency, whether directly or through surrogates, evades reality. Paul B. Henze, a member of the National Security Council during the Carter administration, put Soviet involvement into proper perspective in an essay in the *Atlantic Community Quarterly,* in its winter issue of 1981–82:

> What we know of the Soviet methods for more than 60 years, attested time and again by documents, defectors and other witnesses, leaves very little reason to expect that a government which has long used the world's most sophisticated and varied techniques of subversion in the most unprincipled manner would, at this stage in history, either forego them or permit its operations to be compromised by the creation of the kind of evidence that legal purists would find acceptable.

The outrages that have been perpetrated on U.S. personnel in Lebanon are the most heinous. Nearly three hundred U.S. marines were the victims of a 1982 truck bombing in their barracks near the Beirut airport. In April, 1983, the U.S. Embassy in Beirut was blown apart. Seventeen embassy staff members were killed, including the senior CIA officer in the Middle East. The use of the Beirut airport as a base for Shi'ite terrorist piracy was vividly demonstrated in the TWA hostage crisis in June 1985. Airport attacks in Rome and Vienna on December 27, 1985 left 18 dead including five Americans. These attacks led FBI Director William Webster to state that Americans travelling overseas can "assume . . . they are at risk because of terrorist attacks, even if there is no specific warning of danger."[26]

While the U.S. has not experienced terrorist incidents of this magnitude in the continental U.S.A., the potential is always there. The FBI has an investigative interest in more than a dozen domestic groups which advocate and practice terrorism to advance racist, anti-establishment, or pro-independence policies. Prudence dictates that we keep a sustained focus on this issue.

International terrorism supported and abetted by the Soviet Union's effort to destabilize the West by generating fear of their nuclear capabilities, may be the most crucial issue confronting the U.S. and its allies for the remainder of this century. Terrorism must be judged not from the point of view of right and left, but from that of right and wrong.

While all responsibility for recent acts of global terrorism cannot be placed on the Soviet Union, terrorist activities by a wide variety of ideological groups are important in destabilizing democratic industrial societies. The CPSU 1985 draft party program blandly asserts that "imperialism engendered the wave of terrorism that has swept through capitalist society."[27]

Almost all terrorist acts take place outside the Soviet Union and the socialist camp. Conversely, most terrorist targets are selected to advance the strategic interest of the Soviet Union.

> It is in this sense that the Leninist regime of the Soviet Union is an 'evil empire.' It is not only oppressive, and bereft of popular support, but it regards any deviation from the

'party line' of the moment as (literally) 'heresy.' The sovereignty of such a political religion is different from, and infinitely more depraved than, any traditional political tyranny.[28]

Terrorist operations in the third world have added a new variant to Soviet strategy. As Herbert Romerstein has suggested:

. . . Today a Marxist-Leninist terrorist organization can quite openly proceed through a series of evolutionary stages to become a recognized and accepted government. The process begins with a small group of individuals working to destabilize a society through assassinations and other violent acts. These are often described as pointless but in fact they have very astute purposes: intimidation of the general population; destruction of the economy by frightening off capital and skilled workers; and a demonstration to possible political opponents that these madmen will stop at nothing.[29]

This describes the process by which the communist terrorists destabilized El Salvador in the mid-1970's. They subsequently evolved into a strong unsurgency movement and forced the United States to seek to negotiate a political settlement with them in that strife-torn country. The Soviet sponsored terrorist movement is now recognized by the governments of Western Europe as a major menace. France, the Federal Republic of Germany, Belgium, and Italy plan to increase joint anti-terrorist measures. West Germany's spokesman, Peter Burnisch, stated: "It is necessary to intensify cooperation in pursuing and combatting terrorism, which is now being organized on a Europe-wide scale."[30]

The fundamental issue which state sponsored terrorism raises is how can civilized nations combat international terrorism while adhering to humane principles and practices that are the heritages of free democracies. President Reagan spoke on June 30, 1985, about the release of hostages from the TWA Flight 847:

. . . those responsible for terrorist acts throughout the world must be taken on by civilized nations; that the international community must ensure that all our airports are safe and that civil air travel is safeguarded and that the world must unite in taking decisive action against terrorists, against nations that sponsor terrorists and against nations that give terrorists a safe haven.

Translating these aims into practical results will be difficult indeed. Reprisals may have little value in negotiating with Shi'ite zealots who seek martyrdom more than life. Our predicament is heightened by the complicity of the renegade governments of Libya, Iran, and Bulgaria. But more important is the sinister role of the Soviet Union in recruiting, training, and arming terrorists. If the Soviet Union does not terminate its support for terrorism, it must be isolated diplomatically from the West and denied the benefits it seeks, from advanced technology to grain. American leadership must organize a concerted anti-terrorist program with its closest allies to include the breaking of diplomatic relations if terrorist outrages continue.

The difficulty of creating a united anti-terrorist program was demonstrated by the reluctance of the staunchest U.S. European allies to take either economic or diplomatic action against Libya in the wake of evidence that Libya assisted the terrorists who had killed 15 travelers Dec. 27, 1985 at airports in Vienna and Rome. The lack of Western cohesion in dealing with terrorists can only aid and abet the Soviet strategy of destabilization.

Terrorist Upsurge

The first half of 1986 marked not only an upsurge in terrorism but an increasing recognition that state-sponsored terrorism was becoming a permanent feature of the chaotic international scene. While the principal perpetrators of international terrorism are Libya, Syria, the PLO, North Korea, the IRA and Iran there is growing evidence that the Soviet Union supports and undergirds terrorist activity on a massive scale via training, arms, diplomatic assistance visas (false passports, fake documentation, travel arrangements and other measures).

A May 1986 issue of the respected London-based International Institute for Strategic Studies' (IISS') "Strategic Survey 1985–1986, says that its findings prove that a new awareness worldwide about the "growth industry of terrorism" now is seizing public consciousness—based, to quote the IISS, on the following facts, namely that:

> A very large body of evidence, drawn from confessions, police investigations and captured documents (not to mention captured weapons), leaves little doubt about the Soviet Union's active support to organizations which practice terrorism as a matter of policy,

> Terrorism as a phenomenon in the modern world is not going to go away. . . . Even the most sanguine hopes for 'peaceful coexistence' [between the Soviet Union and the West] offer little basis for believing that Soviet policy makers will refrain from assisting low-level violence against the West and its interests . . . particularly if this can be done without an embarrassing display of complicity.

> The United States has become a principal focus for much terrorist enterprise. . . . Almost half the total [of terrorist incidents since 1983] were directed at Americans or U.S. interests, and more Americans were killed (271) [as of January 1986], more than 40 percent of the world total, than in the whole of the preceding 15 years. Americans have been selected from amongst groups of hostages for execution by hijackers in at least three recent incidents, and they appear to be terrorists' second choice for murder, after Israelis.

While the Soviet Union does not believe in spontaneous terrorism, its support of international terrorism was explained in an article by CIA Director, William Casey. According to Casey, in 1922 Lenin gave instructions to his commissar of justice, D.T. Kursky which "legitimized terror in the new Criminal Code of the Russian Soviet Federated Socialist Republic against those who 'by agitation and propaganda assist that part of the international bourgeosie which does not recognize the equality of the communist system replacing capitalism.' Lenin wrote: 'The basic idea, I hope is clear . . . to state openly a principled and politically truthful (and not only juridically narrow) position which motivates the *essence* and *justification* of terror, its necessity and limits.

"The Court must not eliminate terror; to promise this would be self deception or deception, but the Court must justify and legalize it in principle without hypocrisy and adornment. It should be formulated as broadly as possible, since only the revolutionary legal consciousness and the revolutionary conscience will set the conditions of its actual application, which is more or less broad." (Hydra of Carnage: International Terrorism, The Witnesses Speak, D.C. Heath and Co. Lexington, MA)

Up to the present the United States and its western allies have been unwilling to confront the Soviet Union with its role in international terrorism. We close our eyes to this unpleasant issue because exposure might shatter hopes of finding an improved relation between the U.S. and the Soviet Union via arms control negotiations or cultural exchange programs.

In April 1986 Bill Buckley suggested that the time has come for the "United States to demand that the Soviet Union lay on the table its position on terrorism. How? By agreeing to cooperate in boycotts against any nations that give sanctuary to terrorists, specifically Iran, Syria and Libya.

Why not make this our precondition to a summit meeting? Summit meetings are designed to enhance the chances of peace. There is no peace for individuals so long as terrorism is tolerated. Why not stick it to the Russians and ask them to declare their policy on the matter of terrorism, and explore the question whether we can make common cause respecting petit terrorism, before we address the question of whether we can make common cause respecting terrorism on a grand-scale, nuclear, saber-rattling stage?" (Washington Post, April 29, 1986, p.A8)

As Libyan terrorist attacks against U.S. citizens mounted President Reagan made it clear that, "we are going to defend ourselves and we are certainly going to take action in the face of specific terrorist threats". (N.Y. Times, April 13, 1986, Sec. 4, p.1)

On April 14, 1986 U.S. planes from 6th fleet carriers and F-111s based in the United Kingdom hit targets near Tripoli and Benghar. President Reagan said that the raids "were a single engagement in a long battle against terrorism."

Most of America's allies appeared dismayed at the U.S. action. However, as time passed the need for an integrated, positive response to terrorism was recognized. In fact, at the May 5 meeting of the Tokyo Economic Summit, the leaders of seven major industrial nations and the representatives of the European Community issued a joint statement on international terrorism reaffirming condemnation of international terrorism in all its forms and pledging to make maximum efforts to fight the scourge of terrorism. The statement specifically named Libya as a state clearly involved in sponsoring or supporting international terrorism.

The battle against international terrorism is far from over. While there are many measures that can be taken to check this diabolical threat to international order, victory can be won only if the will to win exists.

The Soviet Subversive Arsenal .

Subversion has historically been the most active part of Soviet grand strategy, and the KGB has directed and coordinated diverse subversive activities.

To select decisive subversion as the chief Communist offensive tool, Lenin had to believe that it could win his goal—overthrow of the governments of the world. The capability of the subversive tool—like that of any weapon—depends partly on the capacity of its target to resist. A one-time subverter can concentrate on the particular strengths and weaknesses of the target government he wants to topple. For his wider subversion, Lenin also had to estimate the general vulnerability of governments to overthrow.[31]

Disinformation has become a chosen instrument and guiding force of Soviet subversion. According to a German authority:

Western societies have always been exposed, in one measure or another, to manipulative influences from beyond their borders. In bygone days, the effective access of these outside influences was limited by the relatively slow pace of communications and by the lack of central amplifiers within the societies themselves. In the modern era, the evolution of instant communications, of mass media and of the transmission of evocative pictures along with the spoken or printed word has vastly widened the vulnerability associated with the openness of democratic systems.[32]

John Barron, in his book on the KGB, describes the phenomenon as follows:

. . . The Russians define disinformation as the dissemination of false and provocative information. As practiced by the KGB, disinformation is far more complex than the definition implies. It entails the distribution of forged or fabricated documents, letters, manuscripts, and photographs; the propagation of misleading or malicious rumors and erroneous intelligence by agents, the duping of visitors to the Soviet Union; and physical acts committed for psychological effect. These techniques are used variously to influence policies of foreign governments, disrupt relations among other nations, undermine the confidence of foreign populations in their leaders and institutions, discredit individuals and groups opposed to Soviet intentions and conditions within the Soviet Union.[33]

Ladislave Bittman defected to the West after the "Prague Spring" of 1968. He had been an officer in the Czechoslovakian Secret Service since 1954, and from 1964 to 1966 served as deputy director of its department of disinformation, about which he wrote:

In 1959 a new department was established within the Soviet intelligence service—a department for disinformation. East Germany, Czechoslovakia and Hungary (and most likely Poland and Bulgaria as well) followed suit in 1963 and 1964. Czechoslavakia's department for special operations was established in February 1964, officially designated as Department Eight.[34]

The Politburo uses foreign communist parties in free world countries to influence foreign public opinion. These party leaders routinely meet with Soviet Communist Party officials to report on activities and receive advice or instructions. Through these parties, Soviet Friendship Societies, and a variety of international front organizations, the Politburo is able to influence the political climate in foreign countries, weakening opposition to its policies and creating opportunities for indigenous communist politicians.

The principal weapon of Soviet psychological warfare is disinformation as practiced by the KGB. Soviet KGB deception involves not only the transmission of false and misleading information, but also "active measures" designed to shape popular perceptions and to adversely affect Western policies.

A favorite KGB "active measure" is forgery. The number of forged documents designed to promote Soviet foreign policy interests has more than doubled since 1975–76, according to a U.S. inter-agency intelligence study.[35]

Perhaps the most notorious of these forgeries was a U.S. Army field manual 30-31B, which, among other things, asserted that the U.S. envisaged "the use of extreme leftist organizations to safeguard the interests of the United States in friendly nations where communists appear close to entering the government." The forgery gained attention in Europe following the abduction and murder of former Italian Prime Minister Aldo Moro by Red Brigades, which Soviet commentators claimed were acting under the instructions of the CIA.

A recent example is that of letters sent to athletes from twenty African and Asian countries, threatening them if they did not support the Soviet boycott of the Olympics. The letters were made to appear as if they had been sent by the Klu Klux Klan. This KGB forgery was revealed by Attorney General William French Smith in an address to the American Bar Association concerning the Communist threat in international law. Smith revealed that laboratory investigations revealed the source of the letters as the KGB.[36]

The political influence operation is another favorite tactic, which is designed "to insinuate Soviet policy views into foreign governmental, political, journalistic, business, labor, artistic, and academic circles in a nonattributable or at least seemingly unofficial manner." Because they "fall in the gray area between a legitimate exchange of ideas and an active measures of operation," these operations are extremely difficult to uncover.[37]

In addition to "active measures," conducted by the KGB, the Soviet Union also operates the most massive propaganda mechanism ever created. Gene L. Tyson studied Soviet expenditures on propaganda and he concluded that "all reasonable estimates are so huge that, even discounting for error, they provide an astounding picture of the size of the Soviet effort."[38]

According to Tyson, "Suzanne Labin, a French expert on communism, estimated in 1967 that the communist were spending about $2 billion annually and were supporting at least a half million people on propaganda outside the USSR as agents, fellow travelers, or active sympathizers."[39] Tyson also noted that,

> the position of propagandist or agitprop is a prestigious one in the Soviet apparatus, considered to be as respectable a profession as accounting or civil engineering in the United States.[40]

The 1985 Draft CPSU program by presenting a lofty description of Soviet domestic propaganda confirms Tyson's appraisal:

> The role of the *mass information and propaganda media* is being enhanced in the life of society. The CPSU will seek to ensure that they analyze in depth domestic and international life and economic and social phenomena, actively support everything new and progressive, raise topical problems which perturb people and propose ways of solving them. The press, television and radio are called to persuade people through the political clarity and purposefulness, depth of content, promptness, fully informed nature, vividness, and comprehensibility of their items. The party will continue to render active support and assistance to the press and all mass information and propaganda media.[41]

In December 1985, Mr. Gorbachev's top lieutenant for ideology and party personnel, Yegor K. Ligachev, gave a sternly orthodox definition of the tasks of radio and television.

> 'Our television and radio broadcasts must be fully and totally political,' Mr. Ligachev told a party conference of the State Committee on Television and Radio. 'Of course, that does not mean that political slogans should resound in every program. But all TV and radio programs should serve one aim—propaganda, the clarification and implementation of the policy of the party.'[42]

Both Soviet domestic and external propaganda is vitriolic, malicious, and persistently anti-American. One of its special targets has always been the CIA, with the aim of destroying the effectiveness of the primary intelligence arm of the United States.

The Soviet effort to debase language and the meaning of words that shape the political process has already been mentioned. The twisting of the word "peace" is a classic example of such semantic warfare, giving the concept a meaning fundamentally different from that understood in the west. The Soviets have, of course, always conducted a massive propaganda campaign to convince people around the world that they are the party of peace. In particular, they have attempted to portray themselves as the champions of disarmament. Indeed, in 1983, Foreign Minister Andrei Gromyko, in a major speech cited Lenin's comment that "disarmament is the ideal of Socialism" as proof of the peaceful intentions of the Soviet Union throughout its history.[43] Mr. Gromyko did not go on to recount Lenin's full remarks, which are more revealing of Soviet purposes:

Disarmament is the ideal of socialism. There will be no wars in socialist society; consequently, disarmament will be achieved. But whoever expects that socialism will be achieved *without* a social revolution and the dictatorship of the proletariat is not a socialist. Dictatorship is state power based directly on *violence*. And in the twentieth century—as in the age of civilization generally—violence means neither a fist nor a club, but *troops*. To put "disarmament" in the program is tantamount to making the general declaration: We are opposed to the use of arms. There is as little Marxism in this as there would be if we were to say: We are opposed to violence.[44]

An even more revealing expression of the Communist interpretation of peace and disarmament was published in Warsaw in 1950. The purposes of the peace movement were listed as:

(1) To deprive the enemy, i.e., the Western democratic countries, of their masses, without which no modern army can exist (revolt and revolution)

(2) To lay hands on valuable raw materials (by force or cunning)

(3) To slow down the development of armament industry (activating systematic sabotage)[45]

Aware of the attraction of democracy in the modern world, the Soviets invented the concept of a "people's democracy," in which, however, the "people" are actually denied the democratic rights available in the free world. In a book entitled *Socialist Democracy,* the head of the Soviet Political Science Association explains the difference between Soviet and free world concepts of democracy.

The question of freedom cannot be approached from an abstract point of view. To reject a class approach is to do violence to reality. Any moral assessment of the right of the state to restrict individual freedom depends entirely on the basic premises adopted. The proletariat and other working classes reject the right of the bourgeois state to limit their freedom of action in the struggle against capitalism and assert the right of the socialist state to limit freedom of action in the struggle against socialism.[46]

The Soviet concept of democracy, in other words, is the exact opposite of ours: whereas democracy in the free world protects the political rights of all, democracy in the Soviet bloc suppresses the political rights of those opposed to the Communist party.

The Soviet claim to be democratic is pure fiction both with regard to the party and with regard to state administration. The election of governing bodies, from the top of the baton of the hierarchy, the accountability of the representative of the electorate, and the deliberation of Party Congresses and of the Supreme Soviet sessions are pure formalities—intended to create the semblance of popular mandate.[47]

The Soviet leadership has transformed the Russian language into a coercive instrument. The Soviets have added semantic distortion into their arsenal of subversion. Although the rulers of the Soviet Union make every effort to subvert their adversaries by influencing free world public opinion they resolutely resist giving their own people that same power. For them, as we have seen, such influence would be "inconvenient:"

> While the political decision making process in the free world takes place as though at a circus before the eyes of a colossal number of spectators, we have a different tradition. Our decision making processes run their course without too much publicity. It is important that the people taking part in the decision making process retain maximum objectivity in their evaluation of the actual issues.
>
> Pressure from public opinion could make their approach to the problems more difficult when decisions are made in public. That is why we think that, at the present stage of development at least, it is better for these problems to be handled with as little public access as possible.[48]

Having examined the Soviet program for subverting the industrialized democracies, let us now turn to their campaign against the countries of the Third World.

The Third World Battle Ground

The Soviets have long sought to sever the industrialized democracies from markets and natural resources in the Third World. One of their most successful ploys was their hidden hand in the Egyptian-Israeli 1973 War. The end result, which the Soviets openly encouraged, was a major surge in oil prices which led to the largest capital transfer in history as well as global economic dislocations and recessions in many countries.

The Soviets refer to countries in the third world as the "liberated countries" Soviet policy toward these countries was set forth in the Draft 1985 Program of the CPSU:

> The CPSU supports the just struggle of the countries of Asia, Africa and Latin America against imperialism and the oppression of the multinational monopolies and advocates the assertion of the sovereign right to control one's own resources, the restructuring of international relations on an equal, democratic basis, the creation of a new economic order, and deliverance from the debt shackles imposed by the imperialists.[49]

The nations of the Third World, sometimes called the developing nations, have emerged as key targets for the execution of Soviet global strategy, because it offers opportunities for expansion with few constraints and low risks. A primary Soviet goal in the Third World is to deny the industrialized democracies access to critical strategic minerals and energy. High-technology defense industries are particularly vulnerable to disruptions resulting from what has been called "the resource war." Soviet strategy thus includes the possibility of gaining important holds on critical oil-rich regions and strategic mineral resources in Africa through conventional means, proxies, or local supporters. Subverting relations between developed and developing nations has been a constant Soviet strategic endeavor. Such subversions should not be viewed as isolated and expedient efforts; rather they constitute a well-integrated dimension of Soviet political and economic doctrine. The isolation of the West from its former colonies in order to weaken the economies and political structure of industrial countries was a goal explicitly stated by Lenin and reiterated by his successors.

The overall pattern of Soviet expansion is carefully designed to gain control of specific sea lines of communications (SLOCs) as well as critical sources of energy and strategic minerals. The sea lanes between the European and Asiatic provinces within the Soviet Union are important for Moscow's commercial and industrial needs, and are vital for communication and coordination between the four fleets of the Soviet Navy (Northern, Baltic, Black Sea, and Far Eastern). All of the Soviet fleets have problems of access to the open ocean. The difficulty of fleet linkages is the chief reason the Soviets seek to secure strategic lines of communication (SLOCs) between their base areas. The deployment of Eskadras, or squadrons, from the four major USSR fleets began in the Mediterranean in 1964, followed by the Indian Ocean in 1968, the Caribbean in 1969, South Atlantic and Southern African littoral in 1970, and finally the South China Sea in 1979.

The 1955 Soviet expansion from its continental base into the Mediterranean was followed by moves into Central America, Southern Africa, the Horn of Africa, Southwest Africa, and Southeast Asia (Vietnam), and the establishment of a powerful position in Northeast Asia. Except for Grenada, no Soviet gains have been reversed. The Soviet advances in the Third World since the move into Egypt in 1955 attest to their skill in waging protracted conflict against the West.

Soviet leaders have never hidden their intention to pursue revolutionary goals in the developing countries. "Obviously, peaceful coexistence does not apply to the internal processes of class and national-liberation struggle in the capitalist countries and in the colonies," Brezhnev declared in 1966. "The principle of peaceful coexistence is inapplicable to relations between the oppressors and the oppressed, between the colonizers and the victims of the colonial yoke."

Yet Moscow's policy toward the Third World has not been without complications. Initially, the Soviets clearly hoped that new Third World leaders, harboring resentments toward former colonial powers, would gravitate naturally toward communism and the Soviet bloc. Instead, however, they began to persecute indigenous communists as threats to their power. The Kremlin then faced a fundamental choice: it could support the local communist parties as the vanguard of the communist revolution, thereby alienating the revolutionary leaders in power; or it could abandon Marxist orthodoxy and support the revolutionary leaders as serving Moscow's interests, hoping that this support would eventually engender communist loyalties.

After some internal debate, Moscow chose the latter course. It reasoned that local communist parties were not as important as before, since the Soviet Union, growing in strength and influence, could replace them as the vanguard of communist revolution. For their part, the revolutionary leaders, even if not communist, could often serve Moscow's purpose by helping to tilt the balance of power in its favor. Soviet flexibility as to whom to court in the Third Wold was openly revealed in the CPSU Draft Program (1985):

> The practice of the USSR's relations with the liberated countries has shown that real grounds also exist for cooperation with young states which are travelling the *capitalist* road. There is the interest in maintaining peace, strengthening international security, and ending the arms race; there is the sharpening contradiction between the peoples' interests and the imperialist policy of diktat and expansion; and there is the young states' realization of the fact that political and economic ties with the Soviet Union promote the strengthening of their independence. (Emphasis supplied)[50].

If through such flexibility the Soviet Union changes the balance of power it induces closer alignment with Moscow on the part of Third World leaders; this closer alignment in turn furthers the tilt of power relations in the USSR's favor. If this process is not stopped at some point, it eventually becomes irreversible, and Third World leaders then have no effective choice over their future.

Soviet strategy toward the Third World employs subversion in a fundamental role, as in the case of the industrialized democracies. The violence of terrorism in the West is paralleled by "wars of national liberation" in the countries of the Third World.

Although the Soviets constantly talk of peace they believe that the wars they fight and support are just, especially the "wars of national liberation." The USSR began to encourage such wars after control of Eastern Europe was gained. Describing the Korean War, a clear case of aggression condemned by the United Nations, Nikita Krushchev wrote:

> . . . this was a war of national liberation. It was not a war of one people against another, but a class war. Workers, peasants, and intelligentsia under the leadership of the Labor Party of North Korea, which then stood and today still stands on Socialist principles, were united in battle against the capitalists. This in itself was a progressive development.[51]

Soviet aggression, no matter how blatant, automatically is transformed by the Kremlin into a "war of national liberation." Moscow feels free to encourage such wars because it risks nothing and its support of these wars is part of a design to destroy the free world state system. By promoting such conflicts, the Soviet Union hopes to strike a decisive blow against the United States and its allies.

An official of the International Department of the Soviet Central Committee has explained, that "the question of alliance with the national liberation movement . . . today . . . is a question of carrying on the *offensive* against imperialism and world capitalism as a whole in order to do away with them."[52]

The Soviets see revolutionary violence as a good in itself."The freedom of the people can be built only on the bones of the oppressors, the soil for the self-rule of the people can be fertilized only with the blood of the oppressors," Stalin wrote in 1905, a dozen years before the Bolshevik *coup d'etat*.[53]

Soviet supported "wars of national liberation" contribute to what the Soviets term the "general crisis of capitalism." A Soviet author, Colonel Konstantin Vorob'yev, analyzed the Soviet international duty in the national liberation struggle:

> In contemporary circumstances, when imperialism with all its might is striving to stop the world revolutionary process, to stifle the liberation movement of peoples of the world, the Soviet Union and other countries of the socialist community consider it their internationalist duty to give political and moral support to people defending their independence, to help these people in every possible form. This is not the imposition of one's own way of life on other people, it is a retaliatory measure to the attempts of the world bourgeois, it is aid to class brothers, to like-minded people, fighting against imperialism and striving for national and social liberation.[54]

The Third World Arena

Though some scholars debate whether the United States should focus on the East-West struggle or the North-South dialogue, the most active area of conflict between the Soviet Union and the United States and its allies is the Third World. For in reality, the issues are fused in the competition for the ultimate allegiance of the Third World. Fusion between military and non-military Soviet interests is most readily achievable in the Third World. Soviet propaganda against the U.S. finds a ready audience in most Third World countries. U.S. actions against Soviet-backed operations, for example in Central America, can be exploited by Soviet propaganda to cause internal division and dissension in the United States. A particular difficulty in U.S.–Third World relations is expressed by the ideological key word, "nonaligned." Originally a nonaligned country was one whose government remained neutral regarding the conflict between the Soviet Union and the West. But in actual practice, the "nonaligned" countries while not part of either the Western alliance or the Soviet bloc, generally favor the Soviet position on most issues relating to the Third World. The so-called "nonaligned" nations have come to dominate the debates in the United Nations General Assembly. The "nonaligned", for instance, are clearly "nonaligned" against Israel. Cuba, more closely tied to the Soviet Union than some of its East European satellites, has become a leader in the ranks of the "nonaligned."

Soviet operations against industrialized democracies and in the Third World are carefully intertwined. The Soviet-Cuban penetration into Central America can serve as an illustrative model. Central America has provided the Kremlin with a made-to-order society—complete with feudal conditions, an impoverished peasantry, a handful of rich landlords, and a fragmentary but educated middle class, that matrix of an alienated intelligentsia, always a prime source for Marxist leadership recruits.

Who can deny the poverty in Central America? Who can fail to sympathize with people suffering from malnutrition, landlessness, and hopelessness? And how easy it is for many intellectuals to be seduced by the panaceas of social reform proclaimed by communists, socialists and other utopians. Both Protestant and Catholic religious organizations have been overwhelmed by the utopian hopes which are rampant in Central America and expressed by the tiny educated minority. How easy it is for the Communist organs to heighten disaffection and stimulate agitation.

Many Congressmen who oppose the contras have overlooked the growing dissatisfaction within Nicaragua against the Sandinista regime, including the open opposition of the Catholic church.

Three former top leaders of the Sandinista revolution against Somoza wrote in the New York Times on December 13, 1985 an op. ed. entitled "Contras are on the Right Track." They spoke of the fraud being perpetuated by the Sandinistas and the growing awareness of Nicaragua's neighbors of the dangers posed by them to peace and democracy. The authors of this piece were Adolfo Calero, Arturo José Cruz and Alfonso Robelo Callejas who make up the directorate of the United Nicaraguan Opposition. All three fought in the Nicaraguan revolution. Mr. Robelo and Mr. Cruz have held high positions in the Sandinista Government.

They summed up their case as follows: The Sandinistas have failed historically because they became an instrument of foreign interests. We are not, and will never be, the instrument of a foreign power. The Nicaraguan opposition is the genuine voice of the people of Nicaragua. It does not threaten a return to Somocism. Its strength comes from tens of thousands of Nicaraguan peasants and other young people from every social class who are willing to risk their lives to fight for it—to fight for pluralism and freedom and the protection of human rights.[55]

Although American public opinion is divided as to the true nature of the Sandinista regime there is no middle ground on which both sides can agree. The wise course would be to accept the reports of those who have been directly involved in Ortega's totalitarian, Soviet Cuban-backed, repressive regime, such as Arturo Cruz. The November 1985 "Law and Intelligence Report" of the American Bar Association stated: "Within the past few months, there have been two high-ranking defections by Sandinista officials who worked in the fields of law enforcement and human rights. The defectors, Mateo Jose Guerrero, former executive director of the Nicaraguan Mission for the Promotion and Protection of Human Rights (CNP-PDH), and Alvaro Jose Baldizon Aviles, formerly chief investigator of the Special Investigations Commission of the Nicaraguan Ministry of Interior, brought with them a wealth of information about the Sandinistas' massive violations of human rights and about their deliberate attempts to conceal the truth about these violations from foreign public opinion.[56]

Again, as was the case in Vietnam, the battle for Central America will be decided by the public opinion battle in the west and particularly in the US. Despite the evidence presented by many well-informed, democratically committed Nicaraguans, who fought against Somoza and who now wish to end the Sandinista rule, intellectuals in both the United States and Western Europe still give strong verbal support to the Sandinistas. They are doubtless influenced by massive Soviet supported disinformation and propaganda campaigns. It is a remarkable fact that the some 5,000 insurgents fighting against the Duarte government in El Salvador maintain information offices in some fifty countries and quite a few throughout the United States. This is a costly effort. Where does the money come from? Such Soviet supported propaganda campaigns are characterized by the careful blending of false data with material that, may contain kernels of fact, are grossly exaggerated or otherwise modulated to fit a given Soviet objective or policy line.

The composite, explains Hans Graf Huyn, is a distorted picture that is methodically beamed at Western audiences through a variety of means, most prominent among them the Western media themselves.

"This tactic is very much in evidence today with respect to the conflict in Central America. In the Federal Republic of Germany, so-called information offices for Nicaragua, Guatemala or El Salvador regularly shower the editorial staffs of the German media with lengthy and expensive telexes extolling the Marxist-Leninist Sandinista movement, trivializing left-wing terrorism financed by Nicaragua, Cuba and Moscow in El Salvador and Costa Rica, and magnifying out of all proportion the activities of right wing "death squads" in El Salvador."[57]

Through such persuasion West European governments have been induced to provide Managua with hundreds of millions of dollars of economic assistance without which the Sandinista regime would collapse economically.

Even more bizzare is the financing of the Sandinista regime with US dollars and Japanese yen via East Berlin. In April 1985 a consortium of US and Japanese banks made a loan of half a billion dollars to the communist government of East Germany, the first Western bank loan to any East-bloc country since the Soviet invasion of Afghanistan in 1979. "The loan was made at highly favorable rates by Citibank, Bank of America, Manufacturers Hanover Trust Company and the Bank of Tokyo. A few months later, East Germany agreed to extend $54 million in credit to the communist regime in Nicaragua. As former U.S. Ambassador to France, Evan Galbraith, remarked that some Western bankers and businessmen not only will sell communists the rope that might hang them, they will do so on credit."[58]

In an attempt to persuade European and Latin American intellectuals that there was a clear and present danger to freedom in Nicaragua Max M. Kampelman, appointed by President Reagan to be the Chief U.S. Arms Negotiator for the 1985 round of Arms Control talks in Geneva spoke to a conference convened by Prime Minister Soares of Portugal in June 1984.[59]

Mr. Kampelman asserted:

> The Sandinistas proclaimed their "revolutionary internationalism" and their identification with Soviet objectives as early as 1979, at a time when the United States was providing Nicaragua with large amounts of economic assistance. The creation of a Sandinista military machine vastly superior to that of the combined other countries in the region began before there was any significant internal opposition to the Sandinistas and, indeed, while many of those now in active opposition occupied postions in that government.[60]

Kampelman then noted:

> It is no wonder that the Moscow *New Times* of last August 19 boasted of Sandinista "strategic rear" defeat of the United States. No wonder that Nicaragua's ideological status within Soviet literature is now that of a "people's democracy," a label originally used to designate the regimes of Eastern Europe immediately after the war. No wonder that a Soviet scholar recently wrote that Nicaragua is the "beginning of a new stage in the struggle on the scale of the entire continent." It is no wonder that authorized Soviet articles (*Izvestia,* January 6, 1984) make it quite clear that the next objectives are Guatemala, Honduras, and Costa Rica.[61]

Despite Mr. Kampelman's liberal background and prestigious credentials many American intellectuals seem blind to the Soviet-Cuban Sandinista game in Central America. One example, gleened from an Op-Ed in the *Philadelphia Inquirer* will suffice:

> Members of Congress will soon face the question of whether the U.S. support for terrorism can be justified in the name of security and democracy. Members of Congress need to recognize that further aid to the contras is self-defeating for the United States as well as morally repugnant. Continued contra appropriations cannot serve any legitimate foreign policy goals. In fact, they work against the administration's presumed aims of democracy and security in Central America.[62]

The author of the above article comments reminds one of the intellectual disarray described by the French philosopher Francois Reval in *How Democracies Perish.*

> "Democracy . . . is not basically structured to defend itself against outside enemies seeking its annihilation especially since the latest and most dangerous of these external enemies—communism—parades as democracy perfected. When it is in fact the absolute negative of democracy, the current and complete model of totalitarianism."

During the remainder of the eighties the Soviet strategic offensive will be increasingly waged in the Third World. This is quite different than during the Cold War period of the fifties when the main theater of conflict was located along the Iron Curtain in Central Europe.

The Soviet Union gives only lip service to the demands of many Third World countries for a New International Economic Order. Except for military equipment it has offered little tangible aid to the countries of the Third World. Yet it constantly castigates the former colonial powers and the United States as the primary source of the economic difficulties facing many Third World countries.

The Soviets pursue the goal of establishing an ideological and political connection with the Third World as an imperative of doctrine and world power, but reject the responsibility and costs of meeting the latter's claims on "equity and justice" for the Third World's share in the benefits of the world economy.[63]

Moscow seeks to blame the United States for unilaterally ending detente and causing the resumption of an unnecessary arms race. This theme has been picked up by many Third World spokesmen who argue that the United States should ignore its confrontation with the Soviet Union so as to devote more resources toward alleviating the poverty of Third World countries. Unfortunately the present conflict being generated largely by Soviet expansionist policy is largely being fought in the Third World.

How the leaders in the Kremlin appraise the global struggle in the early years of the eighties, can be seen in the summation of an April 1980 report on the world situation given by Boris N. Ponomarev, candidate member of the CPSU Politburo and Central Committee Secretary responsible for coordinating the activities of non-ruling communist parties throughout the world.

The 1970s have witnessed a new, significant advancement of the anti-imperialist movement in many areas of the world. It includes the victory of the Vietnamese people and the unification of Vietnam, the consolidation of the people's power in Laos, and the liquidation of the Pol Pot regime in Cambodia. Ethiopia, Angola and Mozambique were liberated from the fetters of imperialism. Their peoples have undertaken enormous social transformations and perform as the outposts of the socialist orientation in Africa. South Yemen plays an important role in this respect. The dictatorial regime in Nicaragua has been overthrown. The revolution in Afghanistan, the liquidation of the Shah's monarchy in Iran, and the victory of the patriots in Zimbabwe have delivered a blow to imperialism.

Not the notorious "hand of Moscow" but the inexorable objective laws of social development are moving the world revolutionary process forward.[64]

If one translates Ponomarev's perceptions of Soviet successes in the 1970s into strategic terms, it becomes clear that Soviet leaders believe that the more significant the successes of the Soviet Union and the Socialist community the deeper will become "the crisis of capitalism."

Although Soviet leaders disclaim direct responsibility for fomenting instablility around the world, they have proven themselves most adept at finding and exploiting intense regional antagonisms rooted in religious, ethnic and class animosities. Further, as this book will demonstrate, the Soviets have invested vast resources in funding and sustaining chaos and instability in furtherance of their nation's strategic goals.

The fusion of political influence issuing from Soviet military power with the subversion of their adversary's national resolve and will is the ultimate operational design of Soviet strategy. The twin prongs of military deployments and subversive action originating in Moscow are manipulated on a target country and a new Soviet outpost is established somewhere in the world. Perhaps the classic example of the success of this strategy was the U.S. concession of Angola to a Soviet-Cuban takeover in 1975. The United

States had suffered its worst diplomatic defeat in April of that year when 14 North Vietnamese divisions captured Saigon. The U.S. had lost the war in Vietnam because it did not want to win. Defeatism in Washington fed by communist propaganda, nurtured by the Jane Fondas and other communist sympathizers, produced a national trauma bordering on paralysis.

The communist faction in Angola, the MPLA, was the weakest of the three groups seeking to take over the country from the withering Portuguese rule. The Soviets, sensing the U.S. paralysis, decided to take over Angola by imposing an MPLA rule by force. The Soviet-Cuban foray into Angola could have easily been blocked. But the U.S. Congress refusal to support an inadequate covert-counter to the bold Soviet move, and the Ford-Kissinger team aware of the public morale were unwilling to consider more forceful action.

Since that dismal U.S. response, the Soviets have been emboldened to make other moves that they might once have believed too risky. What quickly followed were North Vietnam's takeover of Laos and Kampuchea, the Soviet move into Ethiopia, Cuban-Soviet aid to the Sandinistas in Nicaragua and the invasion of Afghanistan after Iranian students seized the U.S. embassy in Teheran.

The shift from low-level guerilla warfare in Vietnam to an all-out frontal assault against Saigon might well be duplicated in Central America unless the U.S. is willing to call the Soviet-Cuba hand before it is too late.

Chapter Four will trace the Soviet pattern of intrusion into the Mediterranean, the Atlantic, including the Caribbean Basin, and the Indian and Pacific Ocean sectors of the sea lines of communications linking the European and Asian frontiers of the Soviet Union. This recapitulation will reveal the ways in which the Soviets have followed the strategic script outlined by Lenin as to how to accelerate the destruction of "capitalism."

NOTES

1. Sergiyev, A. "Leninism on the Correlation of Forces as a Factor in International Relations," *International Affairs*, May, 1975.
2. *Ibid.*
3. *Lenin on Organization*, 99. From the Introduction: "Every section of the Communist International must learn how this party was formed and what organizational principles were introduced by V.I. Lenin in its formation. Toward this end the Organization Department of the Executive Committee is striving to bring to the knowledge of all the sections of the Communist International V.I. Lenin's fundamental ideas on the question of organization."
4. *Theses and Resolutions*. Third World Congress of the Communist International, 69–70.
5. *Ibid.*, 113.
6. *Seventh World Congress of the Communist International*, 39. The Seventh World Congress was held in Moscow from July 25 to August 20, 1935.
7. See, "The USSR: A Conspiracy that Calls Itself a State I," *Situation Report*, Vol. 4, No. 2. October 1984. A publication of the Security and Intelligence Foundation, Suite 1016, 1010

Vermont Ave., N.W., Washington, D.C. 20005. The Chairman of this fund is James Angleton who was for many years Chief of Counter-Intelligence CIA.

8. *Ibid.* No. 2, Part 2, November, 1985, p. 5

9. L.I. Brezhnev, *The CPSU in the Struggle for Unity of All Revolutionary and Peace Forces* (Moscow: Progress Publishers, 1975) pp. 28–29.

10. Nikolai, Portugalov, "How to Escape 'Looking Glass Land,' " *Literaturnaya gazeta,* August 6, 1980, in FBIS:SOV, August 13, 1980, p. 6.

11. Ye. Rybkin, "A Critique of Bouregeois Concepts of War and Peace," *Kommunist Vooruzhennykh Sil* (Communist of the Armed Forces), No. 18, 1968, p. 90.

12. Ye. Rybkin, "V.I. Lenin, CPSU on Imperialism as a Constant Source of Military Danger," *Voyenno-istorichesky zhurnal,* No. 4, 1983, p. 10.

13. B. Sarkadi Nagy, "The Unprecedented Scope of the Antiwar Movement," *International Affairs* (Moscow), No. 3, 1983, p. 75.

14. *Ibid.*

15. During the late Seventies, the author, as President of the Foreign Policy Research Institute, initiated a series of annual meetings held alternately in Moscow and Philadelphia with Arbotov's Institute. The staff members of the Soviet Institute of the USA and Canada are well informed, articulate and adroit.

16. FBIS-Sov 85-208, Monday, 28 October, 1985, Vol III, 208, Supp 007 Foreign Broadcast Information Service, p. 20. This program, the fourth in the entire history of the Bolshevek Party, was adopted at the February, 1986 Party Congress.

17. Los Angeles Times, January 15, 1985. Vladimir Bukovsky spent twelve years in Soviet prisons, work camps, and psychiatric hospitals before being released to the West in 1976 as a result of a public outcry. He is the author of an autobiographical book, 'To Build a Castle: My Life as a Dissenter (Viking, 1979) and, of 'Cette lancinate douleur de la Liberte: Lettres d'un resistant russe aux Occidentaux (This Stabbing Pain of Freedom: Letters of a Russian Resister to Westerners")

18. Bukovsky, Vladimir "The Peace Movement and the Soviet Union" Reprinted from commentary, 1982. The Orwell Press, 211 E 51 Street NY, NY 10022, p. 5.

19. *Ibid.,* p. 57

20. Arnold Kunzli and Karl Marx, Eine Psychographie, (Wien, Frankfurt, Zurich, Verlag, 1966) pp 703, 712, 715, in Fay S. Cline, and Yonah Alexander, *Terrorism, The Soviet Connection,* NY Crane Russak, 1984) p. 9

21. Clare Sterling in US Senate Committee on the Judiciary Subcommittee on Security and Terrorism *The Role of Cuba in International Terrorism and Subversion.* 97th Congress 2nd Sess., 1982, p. 6

22. Letter of 16 September 1905, cited in Bertram D. Wolfe, *Three Who Made a Revolution,* (NY: Dial Press, 1948), p. 372.

23. Sterling, Claire, *New York Times Magazine.*

24. Cline, Ray S. & Alexander, Yonah, *Terrorism: The Soviet Connection.* Crane, Russak, New York, 1984. p. 5,6.

25. See reference 7 for identification of this foundation.

26. The Miami Herald, Dec. 31, 1985, p.1

27. FBIS SOV 85, op.c.t., p. 5

28. Kristal, Irving, "Coping with an Evil Empire" Wall Street Journal, Dec. 18, 1985, op. ed.

29. Romersterin, Herbert, *Soviet Support for International Terrorism,* the Foundation for Democratic Education, Inc., Washington, D.C. 1981.

30. *Philadelphia Inquirer,* February 5, 1985, p. 3A.

31. Beilenson, Lawrence W., *Power Through Subversion,* Public Affairs Press, Washington, D.C. 1972, p. 13.

32. Hans Graf Huyn, Webs of Soviet Disinformation," *Strategic Review,* Fall, 1984, p. 52.

33. Barron, John "KGB, the Secret Works of Soviet Secret Agents" Reader's Digest Press, 1974

34. *Op.Cit.,* Hans Graf Huyn, p. 52.

35. U.S. Congress, House, *Soviet Covert Action (The Forgery Offensive)*, p. 86.
36. "Klan Olympic Hate Mail Said to be KGB's," *Washington Post*, August 7, 1984, p.1.
37. U.S. Congress, House, *Soviet Active Measures*, p. 60.
38. Tyson, James, L., *Target America*, Regenery Gateway, Chicago, 1981. See *Size of the Effort*, p. 10 and following.
39. *Ibid.*
40. *Ibid.*, p. 18.
41. FBIS, Sov 85, op. cit. p. 20 emphasis in text.
42. *New York Times*, Dec. 18, 1985, p. A-7
43. TASS, June 16, 1983 in FBIS:SOV, June 17, 1983, p. R9.
44. V I Lenin, *Collected Works*, (Moscow: Progress Publishers, 1964) Vol. 23, p. 95.
45. Raymond S. Sleeper, *A Lexicon of Marxist-Leninist Semantics*, Western Goals, Alexandria, Virginia, 1983, p. 205.
46. G. Shahnazarov, *Socialist Democracy*, trans. Bryan Bean (Moscow: Progress Publishers, 1974) p. 143.
47. Zemtsov, Ilya, *Lexicon of Soviet Political Terms*, Hero Books, Fairfax, Virginia, 1984, p. 76.
48. Aleksandr Bovin in Dagens Nyheter (Stockholm) February 27, 1983, in FBIS:SOV, March 4, 1983, p. R9.
49. FBIS Sov 85, op. cit., p. 25
50. *Ibid.*
51. *Ibid: Khrushchev Remembers*, trans, Strobe Talbott (Boston: Little, Brown, and Company, 1970), p. 369.
52. KN Brutents, *National Liberation Revolutions Today*, trans. Yuri Sdobnikov (Moscow: Progress Publishers, 1977), part 1, p. 16.
53. Nathan Leites, *A Study of Bolshevism* (Glencoe, IL: The Free Press, 1953), p. 358.
54. In, Scott, Harriet F. and William R. *The Soviet Art of War*, Westview Press, Boulder, Colorado, 1982. p. 255.
55. *The New York Times*, Dec. 13, 1985, p. A-35
56. American Bar Association, Steering Committee, *Law and National Security* Intelligence Report, 1985, Vol. 7, Number 11
57. Hans Graf Huyn, op.cit. p. 55
58. National Security Report, The Heritage Foundation, No. 83, Sept. 1985
59. The address by Mr. Kampelman, Chairman of the Board of Freedom House, was delivered before an international conference on Democratic Challenge in Latin America, called by Prime Minister Mario Soares of Portugal last June in Lisbon and attended by representatives of West European and Latin American Nations. Ambassador Kampelman represented the U.S. as the head of the U.S. Delegates to the Belgrade and Madrid Meetings of the Helsinki Final Act. See *Freedom at Issue*, November-December 1984. p. 12.
60. *Ibid.*
61. *Ibid.*
62. Schmid, Arthur, Associate Professor of History, Temple University, "But the U.S. Shouldn't Aid the Contras" *The Philadelphia Inquirer*, February 1, 1985, p. 15A.
63. *New York Times*, September 10, 1979.
64. Ponomarev, Boris, N. Address on 110th Anniversary of Lenin's Birth, April 21, 1980, "The Great Vital Force of Leninism," *Kommunist*, May 1980 (No. 7), p. 12.

CHAPTER IV
The Soviet Operational Record

Introduction

In reviewing the intrusion of the Soviet Union into many areas of the world, we lack access, of course, to Soviet operational files. Consequently, we can only report what is in the public record. Diplomatic agreements, meetings of top officials, naval visits, governmental statements, and reports of economic and military assistance constitute the relevant data, and though fragmentary, yield important insights into the meaning of the Soviet presence in many parts of the globe.

We will frequently support hypotheses concerning relationships between the Soviet Union and various "target states" with data on commerce, economic aid, and military aid. This is not to suggest a positive correlation between the degree of trade and aid and the level of Soviet influence—though we often find that the only reward received by the Soviets for their aid is the permission to continue giving it. The key point, however, is that the Soviet Union does not haphazardly open trade relations nor capriciously grant aid—Moscow always expects some form of quid pro quo. There were, for example, no overriding ideological justifications for the initial series of openings made to a group of Third World countries in the mid-1950s. Why should the Soviet Union have chosen Egypt, India, Indonesia, and Afghanistan out of the host of potential clients in the developing world? Simply put, these countries were of specific strategic importance to the Soviet Union. They were "targeted" countries, and the investment made by the USSR—such as military aid to Egypt, the Aswan Dam Project, the Bokara steel mill in India—evidenced the degree of commitment with which Moscow was willing to pursue its goals and the strategic/political importance of the client state.

Since we are primarily concerned with assessing Soviet-client relations, we will not discuss at length the often significant levels of interaction between the target state and other countries (specifically the U.S.). For example, although Soviet-Iranian interactions increased during the mid-1960s, they were far less significant than the political, military, and economic relations between Iran and the United States. Likewise, the investment that the U.S. made during its years of involvement in Indochina was vastly greater than that which the Soviet Union extended to Hanoi. A comparative survey of U.S. and Soviet efforts around the world would be interesting and informative, but our purpose here is to establish the strategic steps of the Soviet Union in obtaining the status accorded it in 1987 throughout the globe.

The issue which the book addresses is the Soviet strategy for a fundamental shift in global forces (the balance of power) in favor of the Soviet Union. While Soviet fleets and supporting air power have played a significant role in the expansion of Soviet influence, they have been only a part of the Soviet exploitation of conflict and chaos in advancing their strategic goals. We must trace the Soviet expansionist campaign around the globe since the Soviet Union moved out of its continental base in the mid-1950s. Only when one puts side-by-side the Soviet intrusions into the Mediterranean, the Atlantic and Pacific flanks, and ultimately into the stage of the Central Indian Ocean theater, can we visualize the massive scope of Soviet global operations.

The Mediterranean Breakout

Soviet naval policy has always been concerned with securing naval passage along the Black Sea-Vladivostok route. Soviet ships on route from Odessa to Vladivostok must first navigate passages not under Soviet control, particularly the Turkish Straits.

The Eastern Mediterranean sector provides access to major sea lanes and shorter maritime routes (via the Suez Canal and Bab al-Mandab Strait) to the pivotal oceanic regions of the Persian Gulf, the Indian Ocean, Southern Africa, Southwest Asia, and East Asia. Soviet leaders regard a strong military presence in the Mediterranean as essential to promoting their interests in these other regions. Moreover, because the Black Sea has been the well-spring of so much operational Soviet naval power, the Soviet Union has attempted to establish the principle of mare clausum there.[1] The

Soviet Union also has a vital interest in free passage from the Black Sea to the Aegean Sea.

Following the Potsdam Conference in July 1945, the Soviets fomented Communist revolution in Greece and presented a formal note to Turkey calling for an entirely new Convention dealing with the Straits. Instead of intimidation, Soviet threats and pressure produced opposite results, bringing about the advent of the "Cold War." In 1949 Washington created NATO and strengthened its Southern flank by permanently stationing the U.S. Sixth Fleet in the Mediterranean.

The Greek and Turkish entry into NATO in 1952 deeply disturbed the Kremlin. Khrushchev admitted that Moscow's Turkish policy was "to squeeze Turkey out of NATO." The Soviet Union has since tried to capitalize on the long-standing problems between Greece and Turkey over the Cyprus issue.

Greece-Turkey-Cyprus

Cyprus was detached from Turkey at the Berlin Conference of 1878 and placed under British rule. The third largest island in the Mediterranean, Cyprus is strategically located approximately 90 miles south of Turkey and some 500 miles from the Greek mainland. The population of Cyprus is about 82% Greek and 18% Turkish. The relationship between the two Cypriot communities has long been one of conflict, at times violent.

With the coming of independence in 1960, the Greek Cypriots felt that the Turkish Cypriots were granted excessive constitutional rights and powers. In January 1964, the Greek Cypriots, demanded that the constitution be amended to include a provision which would guarantee majority rule—a move strongly opposed by Turkey.

In August 1964, Greek Cypriot forces attacked and took over the heavily populated Turkish Cypriot area in northwest Cyprus. While the Western Powers sought to solve the crisis, Soviet Premier Khrushchev sent a letter to the governments of the United States, Britain, France, Greece, and Turkey denouncing the Anglo-American proposal for a NATO force which he described as ". . . a case of crude encroachment on the sovereignty, independence and freedom of the Republic of Cyprus." The Cyprus issue was no longer an exclusively Western concern.

Ten years later another confrontation occurred. On July 15, 1974, a successful coup displaced the Greek Cypriot President Makarios. Five days later the Turks invaded the island. On August 14, the Turks considerably expanded their position. With Turkish military power solidly established, the Turks called for a bi-regional solution.

The two crises over Cyprus severely exacerbated Greek-Turkish relations, not to mention the rift they caused in the Atlantic Alliance. Greece's temporary withdrawal from NATO in 1974 constituted a clear Soviet gain.

Soviet propaganda broadcasts demanded that Turkey leave NATO, abandon all "special" ties with the United States, and drop efforts to form regional alliances.[2] Interestingly since the mid-1960s, Turkish policy has tended to move away from an almost exclusive U.S. orientation towards a more flexible approach. By the 1980s, Turkey had learned to close its eyes to the steady movement of Soviet warships through the Straits. This essentially unhampered right of passage through the Straits has enabled the Soviet Union to strengthen its position in many countries on the Mediterranean.

In the face of growing domestic upheavals and frustration, a military coup took place in Turkey on September 12, 1980. General Kenan Evran and his five-man ruling National Security Committee pursued continuity in foreign policy, including membership in NATO. Domestically, the ruling Turkish Junta cracked down on leftist terrorists as well as on fundamentalist Islamic Parties. Continuing Soviet efforts to subvert Turkey and detach it from the Western Bloc seem likely. Yet the outcome of the November 1983 elections in Turkey presaged a return to democratic rule and a continued western orientation of that strategically located country.

The victory of Andreas Papandreou and his Pasok Party in the October 1981 elections in Greece was initially welcomed by Moscow. Yet the elections did not produce total Greek estrangement with NATO and the United States. Despite election vows to eliminate U.S. basing rights in Greece, Papandreou agreed on July 15, 1983 to extend U.S. naval access to Greece for another five years. Greece also assumed the Presidency of the Common Market for a six-month term. Yet Papandreou's increasingly strident criticism of the United States, NATO and the EEC in 1984 and 1985 have aroused concerns about the future East-West orientation of Greece. Political developments in Greece have created strains within the Greek-American community.

Former Senator Paul E. Tsongas, a Massachusetts Democrat of Greek ancestry, told Mr. Papandreou in March, 1985, that some of his positions were undermining the support Greece had in Congress. Mr. Tsongas told the Greek Prime Minister that if Congress becomes less supportive of Greece, the United States may ultimately side further with the Turks on such issues as their occupation of northern Cyprus.[3]

Papandreou's performance, including his public assertion that the KAL plane shot down by the Soviet Union was on a spying mission must be very pleasing to Moscow. During 1986 the Greek economy deteriorated and Papandreou's political appeal also declined.

Despite the continuing hostility between Greece and Turkey the Soviets have yet to achieve political neutralization of the Straits—the prerequisite for sustained political expansion in the Mediterranean littoral.

The methods used to promote Soviet interests with Ankara and Athens are the same employed throughout the Mediterranean. Soviet diplomacy has remained intact, yet tactically flexible. An analysis of Soviet policy towards individual littoral states will provide the necessary perspective required to understand the many-sided Soviet effort underway.

Israel

At one time the Soviets were supportive of the State of Israel to the seeming exclusion of the radical Arab world. The USSR, via Czechoslovakia, supplied Israel with the necessary arms to stand off the Arabs in the first Arab-Israeli war. The initial Soviet support of Israel was consistent with its concept of "wars of national liberation": Israel was fighting for its independence against Great Britain—still an imperialist power. In time, the Soviet perceived the neighboring Arab states, animated by their desire to shake off Western shackles and militant hostility toward Israel, as more "appropriate" objects for Soviet support.

The Soviet Union has exploited its opposition to Israel to gain entry into the nations of the Arab world, particularly the more radical ones. The Soviet Union, however, has found the existence of Israel diplomatically advantageous; it prefers to exploit the U.S.-Israeli connection as part of its campaign to eradicate Western influence from the Middle East and the Persian Gulf region. Since the Reagan-Gorbachev summit meeting of November 1985 there have been rumors of renewal of diplomatic relations between the Soviet Union and Israel. This would be a pre-condition for Soviet participation in a possible international conference convened to "settle" the Arab-Israeli conflict. Although the Soviet Union supports Israel's right to exist it has never accepted Israel's boundary claims. It still provides Israel's arch enemy. Syria, with vast quantities of arms and joins in every effort to isolate Israel diplomatically.

Egypt

Egypt, under Gamal Abdul Nasser, was to become the initial focal point of the Soviet thrust into the Mediterranean. Although Nasser had a profound aversion to communism,[4] he was unexpectedly quick to conclude Egypt's first trade agreement with the USSR in March 1954. Military aid soon followed the initial trade agreement. In September 1955, the Soviets arranged a $250 million arms agreement—the first substantial delivery of arms—between Egypt and Czechoslovakia.

Former Secretary of State John Foster Dulles, in 1955, developed the "northern tier" concept; it called for an alliance with Turkey, Iraq, and Pakistan (the Baghdad Pact, later known as CENTO) in order to prevent the Soviet Union from breaking into the oil rich Middle East. The Soviets, in turn, saw a connection with Egypt as an ideal way to leap over the hastily constructed northern tier. Egypt became the major focus of Soviet policy in the Middle East. The Soviets gained by building the Aswan Dam while the United States refused to participate in the project.[5] Soviet-Egyptian relations were quite warm between 1955 and 1958, and especially following the 1956 Suez crisis, during which Moscow supported Egypt and castigated the British-French-Israeli attack.

By June of 1967, Soviet military trade and aid involvement in Egypt was strongly entrenched. The cost of Soviet equipment delivered to Egypt between 1967 and 1971, primarily to replace that lost in the June War, has been estimated at an additional $3 billion, including aircraft, tanks, submarines, and SAM-3 missiles. Soviet commitment to Egypt also extended to military manpower, and by 1970 nearly 20,000 Russian personnel were in Egypt, assigned to missile sites. By 1973, the magnitude of the Soviet investment in military assistance to both Egypt and Syria was staggering, larger than the 1980 British or French arsenals. In terms of Soviet naval expansion, Egypt was to play a pivotal role. By December 1967, the Soviet Navy was making regular calls at Port Said and Alexandria. The following March (1968), Egypt and the USSR concluded a five-year agreement on the Soviet Navy's access to "facilities" on the Mediterranean.[6]

As the 1960s drew to a close, Soviet cooperation with Egypt was growing in every dimension. Nasser abrogated the 1967 cease-fire renewing a war of attrition between Israel and Egypt. As the war took an unfavorable turn for Egypt in the spring of 1970, the Kremlin once again had to consider rescuing its client. On January 22, 1970, President Nasser flew to the Soviet Union for a meeting with Kremlin leaders to request an air-defense system. Nasser pleaded for surface-to-air missiles and requested that Soviet experts and troops be dispatched to temporarily operate the weapons. A combined Soviet air defense and tactical air command was quickly dispatched to Egypt and placed under General Katyshkin. The Soviet Navy established itself at Alexandria and Port Said. This was an unprecedented use of Soviet military forces operating outside the Soviet Union.[7]

Nasser's death on September 28, 1970, led to an abrupt change in Soviet relations with Egypt. When Anwar Sadat quickly assumed the Presidency, Soviet-Egyptian relationships began to sour. Even though the USSR and Egypt signed a Treaty of Friendship and Cooperation in May 1971—a crafty diplomatic move, perhaps made to prevent Egypt from going to war— Soviet arms shipments to Egypt were curtailed.

On July 18, 1972, Sadat announced that Soviet experts and advisors in Egypt would be expelled and that the Egyptian Army would take over Soviet military equipment and bases.[8] Despite this Egyptian audacity, in early 1973 the Soviet Union agreed to supply Egypt with huge quantities of arms which helped Sadat to launch the October 1973 War against Israel across the Suez Canal. During the war, there was a dramatic reinforcement of the Soviet squadron in the Mediterranean (from the Black Sea and through Gibraltar). Over 100 Soviet ships had, by November, gathered in the eastern Mediterranean.

Following the war, Sadat broke with Moscow. The shuttle diplomacy of U.S. Secretary of State Kissinger bore fruit with the Sinai I and Sinai II agreements between Israel and Egypt, which laid the groundwork for Sadat's 1977 trip to Jerusalem. The U.S.-orchestrated Camp David Accords, the resultant 1979 Egyptian-Isreali Peace Treaty, and concommitant U.S. financial and military aid to Egypt—have indeed institutionalized the U.S. role in Egyptian-Israeli relations.

Moscow's huge investment in Egypt was, however, not a complete loss. The Soviets learned a great deal from their massive intervention into Egypt, as many of the combat lessons and weapons modifications implemented during the War of Attrition between Egypt and Israel were adopted by the Soviet Armed Forces. The long, close relationship that the USSR had with Egypt from 1955 until Nasser's death in 1970 was, at least, instrumental in establishing the Soviet Union as a recognized naval power in the Mediterranean and also enabled it to gain a footing in other countries in the region, especially in Syria. Sadat's assassination in October 1981 introduced new uncertainties into the region, even though his successor, President Hosni Mubarak, has pledged to continue Sadat's policies. Mubarak, however, has done little to advance the Camp David agreement, has strongly supported the PLO and in 1986 was in the process of resuming diplomatic ties with the Soviet Union. Mubarak's political position in the Arab world suffers from his heavy dependence upon the United States for economic and military aid. Domestic dissatisfaction has risen due to the rise of Moslem fundamentalism and the inability of Mubarak's government to cope with massive economic-demographic problems.

As of the close of 1986 the long-term orientation of Egypt was unpredictable

Syria

The Soviets enjoy considerable influence in Syria, although Syrian-Soviet relations have ebbed and flowed over the years. Between 1954 and 1958, the brief period of a quasi-democratic political system in Syria, a "left-leaning" alliance of Ba'athists and Communists in Damascus facilitated close ties to Moscow.

As with Egypt, the first Soviet military agreement with Syria was concluded through Czechoslovakia in February 1956. Between 1956 and the June 1967 Arab-Israeli War, arms transfers from the USSR to Syria were estimated at more than $300 million.

The February 1966 revolution, which elevated the leftist Ba'athists to power in Syria, intensified positively the course of Soviet-Syria relations. Total trade between the two countries jumped. Soviet military aid to Syria following the war and until 1970 was generous.[9] During 1970 the Syrians, through the indirect guidance of the Soviets, attempted to physically and militarily aid the PLO forces in Jordan. In September of that year the foundation of King Hussein's government was being rocked by countless terrorist and guerrilla actions conducted by the radical Palestinians.

Shaken by the discovery of an assassination plot against himself, Hussein acted against the *fedayeen*, the Palestinian guerillas, with the aim of dismembering it. To back the *fedayeen* (and the PLO in general) the Syrians, encouraged by the Soviets, on September 18, dispatched a tank force into Jordan. The following day there were about 250–300 Soviet-made Syrian tanks in Jordan. Hussein could blunt the *fedayeen* single-handedly, but the Syrians greatly complicated the matter. Hussein asked the U.S.—which, in turn, placed the Israelis on alert—for assistance, if and when necessary. With the expressed American commitment, Hussein launched an attack on Syrian armor. This, plus visible demonstration of U.S. and Israeli support, prompted the Syrians to withdraw their forces from Jordan. The Soviets obviously supported the Syria probe into Jordan, but urged a retreat when the Syrian hand was called.

In June 1976, a Syrian brigade of about 6,000 troops moved into Lebanon to restore stability in that conflict-torn country. The Syrians witnessed the alarming strength of the Lebanese left and feared their coming to power in Lebanon. Syria's Assad desired to have Lebanon be as responsive to Syrian interests as possible. Syria, then, would not tolerate either the prospect of a Maronite (Christian) partition or the emergence of a radically-oriented government in Lebanon.[10] In late 1976, at an Arab Summit meeting, an Arab peace-keeping force, consisting mainly of Syrians, was created to bring law and order back to Lebanon; the result was submission by the PLO, and by November the civil war in Lebanon temporarily ceased. It is reasonable to presume that the Soviets did not object to Syria's move. In any case, subsequent developments brought the Soviet Union, Syria, and the PLO closer together.

Syria, like Egypt, has aided the expansion of Soviet naval activity. In Syria, the Soviet Union obtained a base from which to conduct operations in the Mediterranean and, in 1980, the Soviet Union and Syria signed a Treaty of Peace and Friendship, after Iraq launched its attack against Iran. This action was notable because Syrian and Iraqi relations are antagonistic and the Soviet Union had earlier signed a similar treaty with Iraq (1972).

The highly volatile situation which erupted in Lebanon in the spring of 1981 following the deployment of Syrian surface-to-air missiles (SAMs) on Lebanese soil not only aroused fears of Syrian intentions but also raised questions about Soviet involvement in the crisis. The Soviets officially supported Syria in the positioning of the missiles in the Lebanese Bekaa Valley. President Brezhnev had asserted that the Soviet Union cannot remain indifferent to the "genocide being committed against the Palestinian people in Lebanon." Soviet Deputy Foreign Minister Korniyenko, during a 1981 visit to Damascus, emphasized the need "to defeat the Israeli arrogance." The Syrian anti-aircraft missiles stationed in Lebanon are, of course, Soviet-produced. One can assume that Moscow has had a voice in their deployment. In addition to the SAMs, nearly 7,000 Soviet technicians, officials, and KGB were stationed in Syria. Since the Soviet-Syrian

Treaty of Peace and Friendship, the Soviet Union has provided Syria with several hundred T-72 tanks. The Soviet Army Chief of Staff visited Damascus in May 1981 and met with Soviet experts there as well as with the Syrian Army Chief of Staff to discuss a "joint military plan to confront the developments arising from the missile crisis between Syria and Israel."

In mid-July 1981, a "war" broke out between Israel and PLO forces which were launching rocket and artillery attacks from positions in Southern Lebanon against border settlements in Northern Israel. Finding it increasingly difficult to penetrate into Israel, the PLO resorted to large-scale rocket and artillery attacks. Prior to the attacks the Soviet Union, via Syria and Libya, supplied the PLO with long-range Soviet 130mm artillery, T-54, T-55 tanks, and BM 21 rocket launchers capable of firing rapid salvos of rockets over 13-mile distances. In response to large-scale attacks Israel decided to launch air strikes against the PLO's logistical and command structure located within civilian areas. Casualties mounted on both sides.

The Soviets gained diplomatic ground from the Israeli June 1981 attack on an Iraqi nuclear reactor at Osirak near Baghdad. Israeli intelligence sources reported that the Osirak nuclear reactor located near Baghdad, Iraq, was designed to produce atomic bombs and that such bombs could eventually be used to threaten Israel. Several factors prompted Israel to carry out this pre-emptive bombing strike.

Since Iraq and the USSR maintain "friendly" relations, and since Iraq received most of its arms and weaponry from the Soviets, the Soviet response to the Israeli air raid insinuated U.S. provocation. The Soviet response, presented by an "authorized" TASS statement called the raid an "act of gangsterism of which the ruling circles of the U.S. are direct accomplices and in effect inspire."

In December 1981, Prime Minister Begin extended Israeli "law, jurisdiction and administration of the State" over the Golan Heights captured in the 1967 war. This move upset the U.S. and gave Syria a new diplomatic lease on life.

The fragile Israeli-PLO cease-fire was repeatedly violated by PLO artillery bombardments. Frustrated by these violations, on June 6, 1982, Israel sent 20–30,000 troops into southern Lebanon in an effort to permanently remove the PLO presence. Soviet and Syrian prestige was severely damaged when the Israelis successfully destroyed all the SAM-6 missiles and shot down 81 Soviet-made interceptors with only one plane lost. The Israelis were equally successful on the ground, repulsing Soviet made Syrian T-72 tanks with surprising ease. The PLO position south of Beirut was eliminated, but the August siege of Beirut severely strained U.S.-Israeli relations and tried the conscience of the Israeli Defence Forces.

Soviet support for the PLO and Syria was limited to polemics within the Soviet press, denouncing both the U.S. and Israel. The Soviet Union was remarkably inactive in other expressions of support, refusing either an immediate airlift to resupply Syria or a naval demonstration off Beirut.

Whether this was due to calculation or lethargy induced by succession struggles within the leadership, this lack of active Soviet participation resulted in a radical shift in PLO orientation. Forced to choose between military annihilation or evacuation, Arafat accepted an American-sponsored evacuation of PLO forces in Beirut. Supervised by a multi-national contingent of French, Italian, and U.S. troops, the PLO began its departure August 21st and finished by September 1st.

After withdrawing from Lebanon, the U.S. sent a Marine force back into the Beirut Airport area on an ostensible peacekeeping mission. Over time it became a protagonist in a bloody civil war between President Gemayel's Lebanese Army and Syrian-backed Druse and Shiite Muslim rebels. Paradoxically, the Reagan administration proposed a comprehensive settlement plan for the Middle East on September 1, 1982. Calling for the establishment of an autonomous West Bank under the political guidance of Jordan, the plan sought to actively engage King Hussein of Jordan as a Palestinian spokesman.

In the following year the U.S. prodded both Israel and Lebanon into signing a withdrawal agreement strongly opposed by Syria. In the winter of 1982–83 the Soviets came back into the play by resupplying Syria with material lost in the Lebanese war, specifically tanks, surface-to-air missiles and MiG-23 fighter aircraft. In late May 1983 the Soviets made a dramatic military move and announced the installation of SAM-5 missiles manned by Soviet personnel at the Syrian towns of Homs, Dumeir, and Shinshar.

According to Western analysts, the missiles were tied into three Soviet communications ships operating out of the Syrian port of Tartus. These ships then relayed signals to PVO-Strany regional command in the Caucusus.[11] The sites were secured by Syrian troops in conjunction with Soviet personnel, but even the Syrian Defense Minister had not been permitted within the compounds. There were also indications that the SAM-5s may have been targeted against the Turkish airbases at Erzurum and Batman. If so, these missiles could neutralize Turkish or NATO airpower in the event of a Soviet invasion of Iran. Soviet advisors were reported escorting Syrian troops in the Bekaa Valley and as far west as Beirut. The missiles are a significant addition to the region, for as they became operational they effectively shielded Syria from Israeli military reprisals. Thus, when the Syrians rejected the May 17, 1983 troop withdrawal agreement applicable to all foreign troops in Lebanon, they belatedly forced the Americans to realize that diplomatic courtship of Damascus was vital to a successful settlement.

The vulnerability of the U.S. Marine positions after the Israelis withdrew from the Chouf Mountains was tragically demonstrated by the Shiite terrorist truck bombing of October 23, 1983 which killed 241 marines. Soon after, Arafat returned to Lebanon but was forced to flee again from Tripoli in the face of attacks from Syrian supported insurgents from his own PLO ranks.

After five days of fighting in early February 1984, Shiite and Druze militiamen strongly supported by Syria wrested control of Moslem West Beirut. This led President Reagan to announce plans to withdraw the U.S. Marines deployed around the airport to U.S. Navy ships anchored off-shore. As they started to withdraw, the U.S. ships pounded militia and Syrian positions east of Beirut with heavy gunfire. Subsequently, President Reagan reaffirmed his backing of Amin Gemayel and promised to send in additional U.S. Army personnel to expedite training of the Lebanese army. Shortly thereafter Druse militiamen inflicted another major setback in the Lebanese army in the mountains southeast of Beirut. This was another severe blow against Gemayel's survival. As the contending Lebanese parties departed in March for Geneva to hold another conference on "National Reconciliation" a high-level Soviet delegation arrived in Damascus. The delegation was headed by Geidar A. Aliyev, a First Deputy Prime Minister, who was the first Politburo member to come here since a visit by Foreign Minister Andrei A. Gromyko in 1974. Presumably the Soviets reviewed events in Lebanon, the PLO split, the Iraqi-Iranian War, and made plans for the future.

While the Syrian dream of a "Greater Syria" remains strong, the incorporation of all the territory of the former French mandate of Lebanon is questionable. Assad may not want to permanently bring under Syria's control sections of the Lebanese population hostile to his own Alawite minority Moslem clan within Syria. Despite evidence of poor health, Assad's command and control of Syria was, in 1987, beyond question.

The future of Lebanon as a Syrian puppet was decided by battle. The radical Moslem-Druse forces backed by Syria and the Soviet Union clearly fought to win. The U.S., following an ambivalent policy, lost and has suffered a major diplomatic defeat. The magnitude of this defeat can be judged by a March 1984 interview given by King Hussein of Jordan and published in the *New York Times*. Hussein declared:

> The U.S. has forsaken its position as a superpower and as a moral defender of the world. I always believed values and courageous principles were an area that we (and the United States) shared. I now realize that principles mean nothing to the United States. As to the Soviet Union and any future negotiations concerning the Middle East the King stated: "The Soviets have a right to be there."[12]

Essentially, this means that a diplomatic confrontation between the Soviet Union and the United States over the future of the Middle East is inevitable. Nor can the possibility of another war be ruled out.

The Israeli troop withdrawal from Lebanon begun in 1984 and completed in mid-1985 left behind a country in anarchy with rampant sectarian fighting between Christians, Druse, Shiites, and Palestinians. It left Israel's military control roughly where it was before the Government of Prime Minister Menachem Begin mounted its full-scale thrust up to Beirut on June 6, 1982.[13]

Syria's President al-Assad's role in obtaining the release of the T.W.A. hostages from Beirut in June, 1985 clearly demonstrated Syria's dominant position in Lebanon. Subsequently, the U.S. welcomed Syrian assistance in improving the security arrangements in the Beirut airport.[14]

During 1986 the role of Syria as a major force in state-supported terrorism became evident. The Syrian attempt to blow up an Israeli aircraft taking off from London's Heathrow Airport led to Great Britain breaking diplomatic relation with Damascus.

In retrospect, the Israel invasion of Lebanon turned out to be a disaster for both Israel and the United States. With massive Soviet help Syria grows more powerful militarily while Israel struggles with war-weariness and economic crisis. The prospects for peace in that turbulent region are nowhere in sight.

The Mediterranean Persian Gulf Roller-coaster

For most of 1986 the Middle East rocked along on its customary treacherous course. The bloody Gulf war between Iraq and Iran continued. In this war the U.S. apparently leaned toward Iraq and Israel toward Iran. In the event of an Iraqi victory Israel fears that Iraq, which has fought Israel on every Arab-Israeli issue, would turn its large, battle-hardened troops against Israel. After the U.S. air strikes against Libya in April, the burgeoning Libya-Maltese alliance was strengthened. This could ultimately benefit the Soviets who would like to see Malta become the Cuba of the Mediterranean—creating an additional threat in that area.

In early July, King Hussein of Jordan shut down Yasir Arafat's PLO offices in Ammon. Hussein, who is regarded as the key to any possible Arab-Israel peace, was rebuffed by Congress' refusal to provide Jordan with arms, and his efforts to bring about reconciliation between Syria and Iraq also failed. Other peace moves were made including a visit by Prime Minister Shimon Peres to meet with King Hasson II of Morocco. Syria broke diplomatic relations with Morocco because of this meeting. President Mubarak of Egypt hailed the talks as a "good initiative." A ninety minute fruitless meeting took place in Helsinki on August 18th between Soviet and Israeli diplomats. No more talks are planned after this first Israeli-Soviet meeting since 1967.

Vice President Bush also visited the area in August on a peace exploration mission with few discernible results. His meeting with Egypt's President Mubarak focused upon the economic crises facing that country. The Soviet Union is still deeply entrenched in Syria. Turkey, keenly apprehensive about renewed Soviet endeavors to destabilize its political system, kept a wary eye over the always potentially explosive area from the Persian Gulf to the Eastern Mediterranean.

The November 1986 disclosures that the U.S. directly and via Israel had made large shipments of arms to Iran exposed a blunder of Reagan's presidency. The fact that Iranian payments for these arms may have been funneled through Swiss banks to the Contras fighting the Sandinistas in Nicaragua dismayed congressional leaders. The affair damaged U.S. credibility in Europe and dumb-founded moderate Arab leaders in the Middle East. The Soviet Union will likely be the principal beneficiary of this monumental American gaffe.

Libya

Libya, a strategically located, oil-producing Arab nation on the Mediterranean North African littoral, became an independent country in December 1951. The Soviet Union and Libya established diplomatic relations in September 1955. But Western military presence in Libya and extensive Libyan commercial contacts with the West inhibited a close Soviet-Libyan relationship. Although, in the Soviet view, British and American bases impaired its independence, nevertheless Libya was a "sovereign state."[15] The Soviet Union, under these circumstances, could merely wait for favorable developments.

The overthrow of the Idris monarchy and the establishment of a republic under Colonel Muammar Qaddafi in 1969 opened a new era in Soviet-Libyan relations. The British evacuation from bases in Libya was soon completed. By the end of 1970 the U.S. also withdrew. The Soviet Union immediately recognized the new regime in Tripoli and called the revolution in Libya a "trend of the times." Under Qaddafi, Libya has veered increasingly towards the political left. During the 1970s, for instance, Libya nationalized the holdings of major Western oil companies. Libya also extended $96 million in aid to PLO leader Yasir Arafat in 1969 and has supported other radical revolutionary movements around the world.

The Soviet Union has supported Libya's extension of aid to numerous radical movements. The Soviet Union has also become Libya's source of arms. The first shipment of Soviet arms arrived in Tripoli in July of 1970 and included tanks and artillery pieces.[16] During a May 1975 visit to Libya by Soviet Premier Kosygin, the two countries signed an arms deal, estimated at $1 billion.[17]

During the 1970s, Libyan-Soviet relations steadily improved. Although Soviet naval vessels have been calling at Libyan ports since March 1969, the USSR is not allowed to keep vessels in port for long periods of time. Support facilities for the Soviet-Mediterranean deployments, however, could be established at Benghazi and Tobruk. Moreover, Qaddafi has bought huge stocks of Soviet arms, including MIG-23, and MIG-27 jet fighters; T-62 and T- 72 tanks. The Soviet military hardware stockpiled at Tobruk is valued at some $12 billion.[18] There are about 2,000 Soviet military advisers in Libya who exercise a degree of custodianship over the arms stocks. Should a regional conflict erupt, Soviet or surrogate troops, airlifted from outside of Africa, could quickly activate the arms store.[19]

Libya has thus become a major depot for the Soviet Union, and for arms shipments to developing hot spots elsewhere in Africa.

During 1980, Libya waged a campaign to take over the independent country of Chad on its southern border, and by December 1980, most opposition had ceased. From Chad, and backed by Soviet power, Colonel Qaddafi is likely to attempt to expand his reach of influence over Chad's neighboring countries. Other French allies in the region who are edgy about the prospect of further Libyan-inspired destabilization include Niger, Mali, the Central African Republic, Cameroon, Senegal, and Gabon. Why Qaddafi is making moves which Black African states find outrageous is uncertain.

In addition, Libya continues to harbor and train terrorists for radical movements in all parts of the world. President Reagan, in a July, 1985 speech to the American Bar Association, stated:

> Colonel Qaddafi, who has a formal alliance with North Korea, echoed Kim Il Sung's words, when he laid out the agenda for the terrorist network: "We must force America to fight on 100 fronts all over the earth. We must force it to fight in Lebanon, to fight in Chad, to fight in Sudan and to fight in El Salvador."[20]

Libya remains committed to the Palestinian Liberation movement and advocates the abolition of the State of Israel as a necessary step in creating a unified Arab Nation. Libya, also supported the Polisario guerrillas in their attempt to wrest control of the Western Sahara from Morocco.

Despite Qaddafi's absence from the 18th annual meeting of the Organization of African Unity (OAU) in Nairobi, Kenya on June 24 through June 28, 1981, Libya is credited with having successfully waged a major diplomatic coup at the summit. Using his Foreign Secretary, al-Turayka, as a conduit, Qaddafi saw to it that:

● The conference did not demand the withdrawal of Libyan troops from Chad.

● Tensions arising from the Western Sahara crisis were eased.

● The next OAU summit would be held in Tripoli and that he (Qaddafi), in turn, would preside as chairman in 1982.

Sudan's then president Nemery intimated that Qaddafi bought his way through the summit. If he made full use of the chairman's potential, Qaddafi "will have an opportunity to swing this vast continent (Africa) into line behind his own ideas on international relations."[21]

Qaddafi's impetuousness reached a new peak when he authorized Libyan jets to engage U.S. carrier F-14 jets in a dog-fight over the Gulf of Sidra in mid-August 1981. In shooting down the Libyan jets, the U.S. deflected Qaddafi's claim to be the champion of the "Arab Nation" to whose leadership he aspires. This brief test took place while Qaddafi was in Aden signing a friendship pact with two Soviet allies, the People's Democratic Republic of Yemen and Ethiopia.

Libya and the so-called progressive states of the OAU suffered a setback when the OAU failed to get a quorum for the 19th annual summit scheduled for Tripoli in early August 1982. According to OAU tradition, because the meeting was to be in Tripoli, Qaddafi would have become chairman. The immediate cause of the failure was the decision by radical states to admit the Polisario guerrilla movement into the organization as the 51st member. Morocco, which was fighting the Polisario in the Western Sahara, promoted a boycott of the OAU conference. This boycott was blamed on the United States.

In 1983, the Libyan-supported insurgency in Chad developed into a serious threat to the government. Led by former President Goukouni Oueddi, the rebels quickly seized several northern outposts from government posts. As of early 1984 Colonel Qaddafi was conducting a full-scale campaign to "Libyanize" the occupied northern portion of Chad.

Colonel Qaddafi played the leading role in bringing Ft. Lt. John Rawlings into power in Ghana 1981. Libya provided arms, ammunition and oil worth some $18 million dollars to bolster Rawling's accession to power. In 1982 Qaddafi distributed his *Green Book* primer on revolution in Ghana's capitol, Accra, rather than in his own capitol of Tripoli.

In July 1985 Libya and the new government of Sudan, which came to power after the overthrow of the pro-Western government of Nemery in April, signed a military pact. The U.S. expressed "grave concern" over this development.

> In an unusually sharp warning to the Sudanese leadership, the White House and the State Department said that if the Sudan established a military relationship with Libya, this "could only impact adversely on United States-Sudanese ties."
>
> In Khartoum, the Sudanese capital, the pact was widely viewed as a sign that the Sudan's ties with Libya were warming at the expense of links to Egypt and the United States."[20]

With pro-Soviet, pro-Libyan regimes in Ethiopia, Sudan, and Northern Chad, Egypt will be encircled by hostile countries and Qaddafi's ability to threaten Western interests in the Horn of Africa will grow. With immense Soviet backing Libya has become a major factor in the struggle over the Middle East and Africa. In 1986 Sudan shifted away from Libya.

There are an estimated 1,800 to 5,000 Soviet bloc military advisers serving with the Libyan army.[21] The total number of Soviet bloc personnel in Libya was reported by a Libyan publication in January 1983 to be over 70,000, including 18,859 Romanians, 18,259 North Koreans, 10,592 Poles, 9,003 Bulgarians, 6,526 Soviets, 5,652 East Germans, 5,407 Czechs, and 1,692 Hungarians. In addition there are hundreds of Cuban, Palestinian, and Yugoslavian advisers and technicians. Libyan-North Korean relations have warmed to the point that the North Koreans may obtain access to the huge Libyan arms cache in return for their extensive technical assistance programs.

With the help of Syria and Iran Qaddafi put together the Pan Arab Command which met in Tripoli in March 1985. At the opening meeting Qaddafi declared: Under the banner of Pan-Arabism . . . "We shall prove, just as the Iranian Revolution demonstrated . . . that Islam is the religion of revolution and martyrdom."

On March 31, the Pan-Arab Command issued its first communique which specified, among others, the following aims and missions:

To fight to liberate all occupied Arab territories, particularly the liberation of Palestine and the liquidation of the usurping and alien Zionist entity because the Arab-Zionist conflict is a conflict for survival, not a conflict for borders; to combat all the imperialist-Zionist liquidation schemes and all capitulatory reactionary and annexing schemes, including the Camp David agreements, the Fex summit resolutions, the Reagan plan, the treacherous Hussein-Arafat Amman agreement, the project by the traitor Hosni Mubarak, and the Arafat-Mubarak-Hussein-Saddam axis; . . .

To confront imperialism, especially U.S. imperialism, and work toward liquidating its military bases and foil its schemes and strike at its positions and interests wherever they might exist;

To consolidate the alliance with the revolutionary forces and the peoples struggling for liberation, and consolidate the ties of friendship with the bloc of socialist countries headed by the friendly Soviet Union.[22]

The magnitude of the threat posed by the growing Soviet-Libyan connection, combined with the 1985 formation of the Pan-Arab Command for the Revolutionary Forces in the Arab Homelands was finally recognized in Washington but was only dimly perceived by the countries in Western Europe. In the past the Soviets found Qaddafi's quixotic tactics generally helpful to their program of promoting and exploiting chaos as a means of furthering their Leninist strategy but found some of his antics perplexing. They have turned down his requests for establishing consulates in their central Asian republics populated by Moslems. The Soviets were not amused when he told them that they should withdraw from Afghanistan. While predictions concerning developments in the Middle East-Mediterranean are hazardous, as long as the Soviet penchant for destabilizing actions remains, the Soviet Union will benefit from Qaddafi's ploys and interventions.

In recent years the ideological and policy differences between Qaddafi and Moscow have been muted and their political aims have become increasingly compatible. Both seek to undermine U.S. and western influence throughout the Mediterranean region and the Middle East, both will try to block any American-sponsored settlement of the Arab-Israel conflict, and both will seek to subvert pro-Western regimes in the region. Not only has Moscow made massive arms sales to Libya but has also invested billions of rubles into the buildup of military installations in Libya.

It should be obvious that the Soviet-Libyan-Pan Arab connection has grown more difficult, dangerous and irksome for the United States. The enhanced role of Libya in the political and economic affairs of the small but strategically located island of Malta could potentially damage the U.S. naval freedom of action in the Mediterranean. Libya itself has become an excellent platform for the projection of Soviet naval and air power through out all the Mediterranean area. The fundamental hostility of Qaddafi toward the United States was dramatized by the Libyan supported terrorists assaults on the Rome and Vienna airports at the close of 1985. In breaking off all economic relations between the U.S. and Libya President Reagan asserted: "The Rome and Vienna murders are only the latest in a series of brutal terrorist acts committed with Qaddafi's backing." In April 1986 President Reagan ordered air strikes against Libya in retaliation for Libyan-sponsored terrorist attacks against Americans in Western Europe. There was a noticeable decline in Libyan terrorism following these air strikes. The Soviet Union gave Qaddafi only verbal support at that time. The prospects for any *modus vivendi* between Moscow's *enfant-terrible,* Libya, and the United States are most remote. The implications of this state of affairs for future U.S.-Soviet relations are ominous.

Algeria

Whereas Egypt, Syria, and Libya have provided Moscow with naval and air bases and "facilities" in the Eastern Mediterranean, Algeria has provided the Soviet Union with support facilities for operations in the Western Mediterranean. Moscow was handicapped in early dealings with the Algerian provisional government, formed in 1958, by the Soviet relationship with France. The Soviets were also hamstrung in their relations with the National Liberation Front (FLN) by emphasizing the dominant role of the Parti Communiste Algerien (PCA) in the struggle with France. When Algeria achieved independence in 1962 under Ben Bella and the FLN, all political parties except the FLN were banned. The new government in Algeria moved steadily towards the left and began the process of nationalizing formerly French property. In November 1962, as a result of "radical reforms" initiated in March, Algeria was declared by Soviet scholars to be in the process of transition "from national liberation to socialism."

The Soviet Union opened diplomatic relations with Algeria in March 1962. The first trade agreement between the two countries was signed in November 1963 and mutual trade increased. Throughout the 1960s, Moscow's extension of aid to Algeria ran in the $100 million per annum range. Soviet-Algerian military ties were a crucial aspect of the total relationship because of Algeria's overall dependence on the Soviet Union. By 1969, Algeria's army of 55,000 was entirely Soviet-equipped, including armored infantry brigades and tank battalions. There were also an estimated 2,000 Soviet military advisors in Algeria by 1968, and another 2,000 naval advisors soon followed after Mers-el Kabir was evacuated by France.

The Algerian-Soviet relationship survived the overthrow of Ben Bella by his Defense Minister Colonel Houari Boumedienne in June 1965. Moscow recognized the new regime promptly, and for the next few years relations remained steady. During the 1967 Arab-Israeli War, Algeria's foreign policy seemed to be geared towards the Soviet Union as Algeria severed diplomatic relations with the U.S., banned (Algerian) oil exports to the U.S. and

Britain (Algeria severed relations with the UK during the Rhodesian crisis) and accused the U.S. of "acts of aggression" against Arab countries.

Soviet naval combatants began calling at Algerian ports in 1966. Throughout the 1970s Algeria's relations with the Soviet socialist camp grew stronger.

The Algerians began to rely on the Soviets for military aid in 1964. As one scholar sympathetic to Algeria's brand of socialism put it:

> It is well known in Algeria that the Soviets have provided extensive military aid to the Algerian armed forces. Thousands of Algerian officers have trained in the Soviet Union. The decisions of Boumedienne and the Revolutionary Council to accept this offer of military aid and training must be taken as expressing a judgment about the long-term direction of Algeria's revolutionary development, since the armed forces continue to be the final censor of the political leadership.[23]

In 1976 Algeria adapted the Algerian National Charter which states the orientation of Algeria's foreign policy:

> One of the principal characteristics of our time is the fundamental contradiction between, on the one hand, aggressive forces of imperialism and, on the other, the movement for liberation of the peoples of the Third World. Solidarity of Algeria with countries of the Third World . . . forms an essential element of our foreign policy and takes its place as an extension of our option for non-alignment. The United Nations Organization is for the non-aligned countries an adequate framework in which they cooperate for the reenforcement of security in the world and establishment of a just balance in the system of international relations.[24]

Upon the death of Boumedienne in 1978, Benjalid Chadl was elected president and vowed "to reinforce the irreversible socialist option and preserve Algerian independence in the broadest sense." This statement by no means reflects any ambivalence in Algerian-Soviet ties. Algeria supports the spread of socialism, but also wishes to develop beneficial economic ties with the West. Trade between Algeria and the six major industrialized nations of the U.S., France, Britain, West Germany, Japan, and Italy totals more than several billion dollars, with the U.S. being Algeria's largest trading partner. Perhaps for this reason Algeria volunteered to act as the intermediator in settling the hostage crisis between the U.S. and Iran. And, in this crisis, Algeria was helpful to both the U.S. and Iran. But serious differences remain between Algeria and the U.S., particularly concerning U.S. support of Israel and Algerian support of anti-Moroccan guerillas in Western Sahara.

At the same time, in Algeria,

> A positive attitude toward the Soviet Union is being cultivated in the armed forces. In the long run that could be significant for Algeria's future . . . if circumstances compel Algeria to give up the convenience of non-alignment and choose a camp, there is little doubt as to where it will plant its flag. The real alignment within non-alignment also indicates that the internal revolution is more radical and more determined than it appears.[25]

The 1985 visit of Algeria's President to Washington to meet with President Reagan is another indication of Algerian pragmatism.

The Polisario

A major arena of Soviet-supported conflict in Northwestern Africa has been the "off and on" war waged by the Saharan Republic (under the Polisario) against Morocco for control of what was formerly Spanish Sahara. Spain withdrew from the territory on February 26, 1976, ceding the land to Morocco and Mauritania. But the Polisario Front declared the 103,000 square mile region to be independent the very next day. Morocco annexed two thirds of the territory, and Mauritania the rest. In 1979 Mauritania turned over its part to the Polisario front. Morocco has offered to negotiate a deal with the Polisario but, so far, its offers have been rejected. At stake are rich phosphate deposits in the northern part of the country. The Soviet Union, Cuba, Libya and Algeria back the Polisario with both arms and advisors. The United States has, on the other hand, provided considerable military aid to Morocco.

Far ranging Libyan ambitions in the Sahara region may drive a wedge between Algeria and the Polisario front, if Algeria comes to view the front as a danger to its own territorial integrity. In early 1981, however, Algeria reaffirmed its support for the guerilla struggle to set up an independent Western Sahara. Most of the guerillas have based in Algeria, and most of their weapons are of Soviet origin.[26] The war has been going on for ten years with some 5,000 guerillas fighting ten times that number of Morrocan soldiers deployed behind an extensive system of walls.

> "Morroco's focus has been to halt aid to the Polisarios from Algeria, without whose support the movement likely would collapse. Algeria is not only naturally sympathetic to liberation groups—it won independence from France in 1962 after a bitter war—but it reportedly wants to keep Morocco's expansionist aims in check. And so far, it has shown no signs of wavering."[27]

The unexpected agreement reached in 1984 between Libya's Qaddafi and King Hussein of Morocco led to diminished support for the Polisarios. Continuation of the messy Polisario conflict can only harm Morocco, the one pro-Western regime in Northwest Africa. On the other hand, Libya's treaty of unity with Morocco raised doubts on the future reliability of what has long been considered as the United States' closest ally in North Africa. Hussein appears subsequently to have become more skeptical about Qaddafi's intent.

Conclusion

Since the 1950's, the Soviets have increased their political, military, and diplomatic presence in the Mediterranean and its surrounding shores. While often aided by poorly conceived Western policies, the Soviets have also benefited from patience which has allowed the USSR to overcome real, but ultimately temporary obstacles.

The balance in the Mediterranean has been definitely shifted in a direction in favor of the Soviet Union. Both Greece and Turkey have eased their dedication to NATO. The ties between Libya and Malta have become worrisome. The pro-Western regime of Libya has been replaced by Colonel Qaddafi. The transition of Egypt to an American orientation was an important change, even though Egypt is likely to renew its ties with the Soviet Union. The Soviet guiding hand in the disintegration of Lebanon through direct support of Syria guarantees that the Soviets will continue to seek to damage Western influence in the area. The shift of the Sudan away from its American connection was a temporary Soviet ploy.

Militarily, the Soviet navy continues to expand and gain new flexibility through increased seaborne resupply experience. The loss of Soviet access to Port Said and Alexandria were severe blows, but continued use of the Syrian ports of Tartus and Latakia partially compensates for them. The stationing of SAM-5 missiles and advisors in the Bekaa Valley possibly presage an increased Soviet threat ranging from Turkey and NATO in the north to Israel in the south. It is still too early to judge what will be the long-term impact of the disastrous failure of U.S. policy in Lebanon on overall superpower relations in the Mediterranean region.

The geographic advantage the West had when it was dominant on the entire southern shore of the Mediterranean has been lost. Whether the past decline of Western influence in the region can be halted or will continue to erode will be revealed in the unfolding developments of the 1980s.

Soviet access to land-based facilities in the Mediterranean, along with the tremendous growth of the Soviet navy, has allowed Moscow to maintain a powerful naval presence in the Mediterranean. The U.S. Sixth Fleet is no longer the dominant force in this strategic area. Despite some setbacks, the Soviet Union's established status in the Mediterranean has become an accepted fact in international life. The Mediterranean has become the Soviet Union's southern doorway to the world.

The Atlantic Flank

The western periphery of the Soviet Union includes the West European NATO alliance, neutral Sweden, Finland, Austria and Switzerland and the Atlantic Ocean. This Western, or Atlantic, flank can be divided into three sectors: (1) The Northern which includes Western Europe and stretches across the Atlantic Ocean to North America, (2) the Central Atlantic sector including the Caribbean Basin and (3) the South Atlantic including the Western Coast of Africa from Morocco to South Africa.

The Northern Sector

In the northern sector of the Atlantic flank, the Soviet Union has pursued a number of often overlapping strategies. In Soviet parlance, this area comprises their northwestern TVD (theater of military operations), and includes Norway, Iceland, Sweden, Finland, and Denmark with Poland, the two Germanies, the United Kingdom, and Greenland on the periphery.

Of immediate interest to Moscow is the decoupling of the United States from its NATO allies, followed by its "Finlandization," perhaps as a precursor to the neutralization of Western Europe. While Hungary, Czechoslovakia, and Poland remain secure behind occupied East Germany, Soviet interests in Western Europe have changed from direct occupation to promotion of passivity, structural fragmentation, and accommodation with Soviet power.

Soviet goals toward the European northern sector of the Atlantic flank have been remarkably consistent. The Soviets are opposed to both the continued U.S. presence in Europe under the aegis of NATO and the Gaulist dream of a united, strong, and independent Europe. What they really want is one day to bring all of Europe within their sphere of potential control. Rarely do the Soviets state this goal explicitly. Yet Vadim Zagladin, the first deputy of the CPSU's Central Committee Department on International Relations, once stated this goal plainly to two West German journalists who asked him whether the West Europeans should seek neutrality (i.e. opt themselves out of NATO): "That would be unrealistic in the short run, although we have always stood for a dissolution of the blocs and still have that in mind as a long term goal."[28] The attainment of such a goal would create a situation in which the foreign and security policies of the West European governments would necessarily be made in the shadow of Soviet influence. The West European countries would have to agree with the Soviet Union in all issues regarded as vital by Moscow.

The Scandinavian region of the northern sector may appear as an appendix to the NATO central front and Soviet strategy in the north may seem a part of its strategy against western Europe. That may be so. But there is also a separate Soviet threat against the Scandinavian countries which follows a distinct strategy with its own intrinsic logic. This implies that the northern countries, particularly Norway, are faced with special problems in addition to the common problems within NATO. While many developments have affected the strategic significance of the Nordic region (including the 1982 Law of the Seas extension of national economic zones and the expansion of northern resource development and industrialization), the most significant change has been the rapid development of the Soviet northern fleet with its home base at Murmansk close to the Norwegian border.

Moscow has used the massive military and industrial expansion along the Kola Peninsula as a pyschological tool for intimidation of Denmark, Norway, Finland, and Sweden. Powerful Soviet forces deployed along the flank countries have fostered an atmosphere of accommodation with Moscow.

The pressure issuing from Soviet power has been applied politically and psychologically against many different northern countries. Soviet policy has been able to exercise considerable influence in Finland by manipulating a number of levers, particularly the ever-present shadow of overwhelmingly proximate military strength. Finland is tied to the Soviet Union through the 1948 Soviet-Finnish Treaty of Friendship, Cooperation, and Mutual Assistance. The USSR seeks to maintain the economic dependence of Finland, particularly in the field of energy. By October of 1973, Finland was receiving over two thirds of its energy requirements from the USSR. Finland has been the chief advocate of a Soviet-inspired plan for a nuclear-free zone in Northern Europe. Such an arrangement would freeze the regional military balance in favor of the Soviet Union.

Denmark and Norway, both NATO members, and neutral Sweden, have also been affected by the fear of Soviet proximate power. Norway is the object of the greatest Soviet military and psychological pressure. The build-up of Soviet military forces is most evident in the Kola area. Within this area, the Soviet Union deploys approximately 70,000 troops (including two divisions), close to 300 fighter planes and long-range bombers, as well as helicopters, medium range transport planes and maritime reconnaissance aircraft. Several hundred naval aircraft operate with the Northern Fleet, including aircraft fitted for anti-ship and anti-submarine roles. Thirty Soviet Backfire Bombers, with more than a 2,500 nautical mile radius, are assigned to the Northern Fleet.[29] The naval capabilities available to the Soviet Union from the Northern Fleet (the Soviet's most powerful) and the Baltic Fleet (now connected by the Baltic White Sea waterway) indicate that in terms of total offensive capabilities, the Soviet Union could seal off Finland, Sweden, and Norway from the NATO countries to the South.

Both Norway and Denmark have pursued what has been called a "bases and ban" policy, that is, neither country will allow foreign (NATO) bases on its soil, nor will they allow the positioning of nuclear weapons on their territories. The Norwegian government's decision to stockpile (pre-position) American arms, ammunition, and other supplies in Norway for a USMC brigade sparked heated internal debate. In an apparent attempt to minimize left wing opposition and prevent the agreement from appearing provocative to the Soviet Union, the location of the stockpile has been shifted hundreds of miles south from the Soviet border.[30]

Sweden's long border with Finland, as well as its Baltic territories, places it on the immediate periphery of the Soviet sphere of influence. Under Prime Minister Palme Sweden's government appeared to seek "friendship and cooperation" with the Soviet Union. Since his assassination Sweden may be less inclined to do so. In 1975, a ten-year Soviet-Swedish accord on industrial, economic, technical, scientific, and cultural cooperation was signed. Contracts have been drawn for the enrichment of Swedish uranium in the USSR. In 1977, the two countries concluded a fishing agreement and in 1978 Sweden's state-owned shipyard signed a contract to build the world's largest floating drydock, which will be situated in Murmansk.[31] The Swedish government, nonetheless, more than held its own diplomatically against the Soviet Union in November 1981 when a Soviet submarine ran aground on an approach to a Swedish naval base.

Exactly one year later another series of submarine sightings were reported at Harsfjarden in the southern Stockholm archipelago. The Swedes were unable to sink or capture any of the subs despite repeated depth charging. Refuting Soviet denials, an official Swedish report issued on April 26, 1983 categorically states that "intrusion of Harsfjarden was part of a larger submarine opeation. . . . probably encompassing six foreign submarines."[32] The report also stated that of these six submarines, possibly three were of an experimental ground crawling type that enabled them to avoid detection. Video cameras lowered to the ocean floor shows the track marks left by the submarines on the floor.

The report also stated that despite Swedish protests, "foreign submarine violations of Swedish territory have continued and increased in scope."[33] The number of violations reported since the November 1981 "Whiskey" incident have numbered more than 40, with the report confirming that the intrusions were by "the Warsaw Pact . . . which is tantamount to the Soviet Union. No observation has been obtained indicating intrusions in Swedish waters of NATO submarines."[34]

The prime object of the Soviet pressure against Scandinavia is to insure control of the Norwegian Sea in time of war, as part of their Atlantic naval strategy. In this connection, Iceland is also extremely important to Soviet planners. Iceland's communist-dominated People's Alliance (PA) polled 22.9 percent of the popular vote in 1978. The PA's brand of nationalism appears to favor the USSR, e.g., the PA wants Iceland to withdraw from NATO. Such a move would be troublesome to the United States, which has operated a key installation at Iceland's Keflavik Airport for tracking Soviet submarines and aircraft in the North Atlantic. Iceland's International Airport and the USAF base in Iceland are located on the same airfield at Keflavik, some twenty-five miles from Reykjavik. A worry for NATO planners is the constant Soviet civilian air traffic on the runway which with imminent conflict could change into a Trojan horse operation.

Moscow is urging Iceland to pursue a neutralist foreign policy and to distance itself from the Atlantic Alliance. Iceland certainly feels the pressure of proximate Soviet military power as it is projected from the Kola Peninsula across the Greenland-Iceland-Faeroe-U.K. (G.I.F.U.K.) gap. The Soviet embassy is one third larger than any other diplomatic mission in

Reykjavik.[35] Icelandic leaders are well aware that the Soviet Union wants to become the dominant power in theArctic region of the North Atlantic Ocean.

The Soviets have been pressuring Norway to grant the USSR equal status with Norway on Spitzbergen. Given the overwhelming power differential between the two countries, such an agreement would be tantamount to Soviet control over Spitzbergen and the strategically vital waters surrounding it.

The status of Spitzbergen, also called Svalbard, was defined by a 1920 treaty signed in Paris by Norway and forty other nations. The treaty awarded sovereignty over the archipelago to Norway, but guaranteed all the signatories equal access to Spitzbergen's resources, guided by Norwegian law and regulations. In addition, the treaty forbade bases or permanent naval installations on Spitzbergen and declared that the archipelago "may never be used for warlike purposes."[36]

In 1975, a Soviet military colony was established in Spitzbergen, complete with electric field fencing, a road network, and around-the-clock security guards. A landing strip for helicopters was added, and Norwegian newspapers have featured reports of Soviet construction of a landing strip on Spitzbergen for planes other than helicopters. Soviet efforts to undermine Norweigian sovereignty over the Spitzbergen archipelago have been accompanied by similar efforts to detach the Faeroe Islands from Denmark. The USSR has played upon emergent Faeroese nationalism by hosting the island's prime minister. A communist party was established on the Faeroes in 1975.

Greenland, the western cornerstone of the G.I.F.U.K. gap, may also be politically unstable and has been subject to Soviet attention. Though the United States and Denmark share responsibility for the defense of this Danish possession, little attention has been paid to its importance for the defense of the Atlantic Alliance, even though it houses important early warning installations and air surveillance systems.[37] The Soviet Union has unsuccessfully sought Danish permission to establish meterological stations on Greenland. Moscow's end could be achieved through manipulation of a nascent Greenlandic nationalism. Scattered protests have occurred on the island against NATO installations located there. It is questionable whether the home rule granted by Denmark will satisfy Greenland over the long run, thus presenting Moscow with the potential opportunity to crack a crucial base in the Northern sector's defense system.

The Soviets could have their eyes on the two U.S. military bases maintained on Greenland at Sondrestromfjord and Thule—both critical for North American radar defense purposes and any future space-based missile defense system.

During the summer of 1986 a delegation of Siberian Eskimos visited Greenland to "expand links of culture and friendship," between the local Eskimo population and the Soviet Union. Using ethnic similarities between the Siberians and their Greenland cousins—also known as Inuits—the Soviets hope to gain propaganda points among the population of this strategic Arctic island.

The Inuits of Alaska, Canada, Greenland and Siberia are ethnically similar. Residing throughout the northern circumpolar regions, the worldwide Inuit population numbers some 100,000, of which 40,000 reside in Greenland and a further 25,000 in the Canadian north.

Seven Siberian Inuits led by Alexander Komarov visited Greenland from July 10–18. The trip was organized and prepared by Arqaluk Lynge, leader of Greenland's Inuit Ataqatigiit Party, a radical leftist group founded in 1978 to oppose Danish rule and Greenland's membership in the European Community (Common Market). Earlier in 1986, Lynge, 39, visited Moscow to discuss the Siberian Inuit visit, which was tied to the International Year of Peace.

Some analysts see the Soviet tour as a wedge to radicalize part of the local Inuit community, which comprises 80 percent of Greenland's total population of 53,000 people. Despite having achieved home rule in 1979, Greenland remains an integral part of Denmark.

Similarly, due to Denmark's NATO obligations and a Danish-U.S. defense agreement, Washington maintains the two vital military bases on the island.

The USAF base in Thule dates to the early 1950s, when the United States and Denmark signed a defense treaty which is in force to this day. But Thule's role is increasingly important, it being part of the Air Force's Space Command, a network which plays a key role in missile warning, space surveillance, intelligence, communications and weather survey.

Hosting the Ballistic Missile Early Warning System (BMEWS), Thule's radar net would warn the United States of any incoming missiles. Similar to sites in Alaska and England, the stations were built in 1961. Information gathered at Thule is sent to Colorado's North American Aerospace Defense Command.

BMEWS is undergoing a systems modernization to meet the growing challenge from Moscow's multiple warhead missiles. A new phased array radar expects to be operational in late 1986 thus allowing Thule to simultaneously track 80 to 100 targets. According to Col. James Knapp, the base commander, "The BMEWS upgrade is necessary since our current system works with 1961 technology—today we face multiple warhead missiles, something the 25-year-old system can't cope with."

Besides BMEWS, Thule operates a space surveillance station, a satellite tracking center which can play a role in the Strategic Defense Initiative.

The ultimate Soviet effort to dislodge U.S. strategic interests in Greenland is characteristic of their long-range penetration programs elsewhere.

Moreover, while the USSR appears to be attempting to politically anesthetize the Northern flank, efforts are also being made to push the Soviet

Northern Fleet's area of potentially safe operations out past the G.I.F.U.K. gap, thus converting the Norwegian Sea into a Soviet lake.

Soviet access to the Baltic, once restricted to the Gulf of Finland, was greatly enhanced by the annexation of Latvia, Lithuania and Estonia at the end of World War II. With the neutralization of Finland, uninhibited Soviet naval access to the Baltic is assured. In addition, the fleet is no longer bottled up at the eastern end of the Gulf of Finland, and can now deploy warships from Tallinn and Liepaja. The large Soviet naval maneuvers during the summer of 1981, concurrent with the continuing Polish food crisis, clearly demonstrated Soviet supremacy in the Baltic.

The trends of communist naval activity in the Northern and Baltic theaters, connected by the White Sea-Baltic waterway—display remarkable similarities. Just as units of the Northern Fleet have extended their maneuvers westward from the Barents Sea to project power to the NATO monitored G.I.F.U.K. gap, so the Baltic Fleet components have shifted their operations (notably amphibious landing exercises) westward towards Denmark and the Baltic exits. The main fleet exercise areas for the Warsaw Pact navies that were formerly concentrated off the USSR's Baltic republics or the Polish border are now deployed farther westward to Rugen (East Germany), 55 miles off of Denmark. Still other exercises have taken place in the Kattegat, and Soviet surveillance from both sea and air of the Kattegat and the Skagerrak have intensified. Naval activities that previously warned of impending hostilities have now become commonplace, making the distinction between an exercise and a real assault difficult to predict.

The Soviet Union conducted its biggest and most ambitious naval maneuver deep into the sea lanes of the North Atlantic in July 1985. The exercise, involving the 43,000 ton aircraft carrier *Kiev* and at least 100 combat and auxiliary vessels lasted 12 days. The Soviet show of force underlined the importance and difficulty for NATO of securing control of the North Norwegian sea before the outbreak of any hostilities.

Soviet military strategists, as well as political planners who operate in the wider geopolitical context, have a clear concept of what they want (and what they do not want) to happen along their long Arctic flank, and its Western Scandinavian approaches. Soviet intimidation is closely coordinated with political action. Today, it is evident to any observer that a new era is opening in the Nordic region and that change will be the order of the day.

Most important is the fact that this is the area where the main Soviet Navy has its chief access to international waters, and where strategic interests and national security are most directly exposed to the combined changes which follow from the new law of the sea, from offshore resource development, and from the international interest in northern area development. These changes are happening at the very time when the Soviet Union is emerging as a true maritime superpower and is beginning to learn to use its growing navy as an instrument for promoting Soviet state interest at a global scale.

The European Central Land Front

Soviet naval pressure from its powerful Northern and Baltic fleets affects not only NATO's vulnerable Scandinavian flank, but also reinforces the tendencies toward accommodation generated by the significant Warsaw Pact (Soviet) advantage on NATO's central land front. The public desire for detente, at almost any price, is sometimes shared by many of the NATO governments of Western Europe.

Economically, the West has become dependent on the East in ways not envisioned by the Nixon-Kissinger detente theory. Two recent examples of this interdependence and its effects on Western defense and cohesion are illuminating. The period of detente allowed a blossoming of financial loans to Eastern European governments. As the 1970s closed, it became increasingly obvious that the Western banks had severely overextended themselves in providing credit to governments incapable of paying off their debts. The Western refusal to declare the Polish government in default of over $20 billion dollars to avoid damaging the Western financial fabric is a sobering reminder that in international affairs the debtor nations often call the tune, to the detriment of the lender states. The 1986 U.S. decision to subsidize the sale of wheat to the Soviet Union provided a case of economic forces overcoming sound strategic judgment.

Another disturbing example of undesirable interaction was the issue of the Urengoi-Yamal natural gas pipeline from Siberia to Western Europe. Planned by the Western Europeans to ultimately supply as much as 50 percent of West Germany's domestic natural gas requirements by the end of this decade, the pipeline was opposed by the Reagan Administration as early as the 1981 Ottawa summit. European insistence on the project resulted in President Reagan's June 18, 1982 decision to forbid American companies from participating in the project. Western European reaction was negative, with French-American relations souring. The European decision to provide 85% of the pipelines costs at below market interest rates was puzzling to many Western analysts, in particular, to those in Washington arguing for a tougher stance against Soviet access to Western technologies. By the fall of 1982 French, German, and British resolve to pursue the project led to the easing of the American technological embargo. The European decision to contract for the natural gas at a fixed price is, in hindsight, a mistake, for the fall in world prices and the availability of natural gas from Dutch fields means the Europeans will be paying substantially higher prices throughout the decade than they would otherwise.

These particular cases are not alarming in and of themselves, but the overall trend these developments highlight is increased interdependence between West Europe and the East. While this is precisely what detente was to accomplish, the open structure of the Western societies as contrasted with the closed, repressive Soviet system in the East will leave the West more vunerable to exploitation. In combination with this economic interdependence, the military imbalance in Europe is generating passivity and a sense of futility among Western nations; particularly among the young who did not witness the enormous sacrifices of the immediate post-war world. Such relationships between military force, East-West relations, arms negotiations, and growing accommodationist trends in Europe have not been clearly perceived nor well understood.

General Bernard Rogers summarized the situation facing NATO as follows:

> A sound strategy for our defensive Alliance must take account of two types of threat. NATO must be able to deter overt Warsaw Pact aggression in Europe as well as to counter a subtler, more ominous threat. Through the constant amassing of military might, the Soviets continue to widen the gap between Warsaw Pact and NATO force capabilities. In my opinion, the major menace we face is that the Soviets will continue to widen, manipulate and exploit this gap until the military situation, even for a defensive alliance, gets beyond restoration. The Soviets will then be able to achieve their major objective in Western Europe: intimidation, coercion and blackmail without having to fire a shot. *NATO must have a strategy to deter both overt attack and intimidation and coercion.*[38]

As the credibility of the American deterrent is diminishing the ability of the Soviet Union to challenge Western Europe has grown. By 1981, the Soviets deployed about two hundred and fifty mobile SS-20s, each of which can deliver three nuclear warheads with high accuracy, giving the USSR the capability to destroy all major targets in Western Europe in a first strike. Together with the Backfire bomber, an aircraft capable of penetrating European air defenses, the SS-20 has tipped the Euro-strategic balance in favor of the Soviet Union.

To redress this imbalance, the NATO Council decided, in December 1979, to deploy 108 Pershing II launchers and 464 ground-launched cruise missiles (GLCMs)—beginning in 1983. These missiles eventually became the first nuclear weapons in Europe capable of striking targets in the Soviet Union. The Soviet Union launched a massive propaganda campaign against the deployment of the new U.S. missiles in NATO countries. Paradoxically, the large-scale nuclear protest demonstrations held through out Western Europe in 1981–83 were primarily directed against the United States. In addition, the split between the U.S. and its European allies over the Polish crisis undercut the NATO alliance.

The Soviet attempt to characterize the U.S. as de-stabilizing and dangerous to European security and peace found a ready audience among certain sections of the European left, particularly the youth. Realizing this, the Soviet KGB placed a high priority on infiltration of the Euro-peace movement. Soviet involvement in the peace movement is consistent with their comprehensive strategy of political, military, and ideological welfare. Each component is seen as reinforcing the effectiveness and capabilities of the others. The result of such efforts, while hard to quantify, is an appreciable pro-Soviet—or compensating anti-American bias in the Western peace community. This was apparent when over 1,000 youths assaulted Vice-President Bush's motorcade in West Germany on June 25, 1983. The state visit of Chancellor Kohl to Moscow in July 1983 confirmed the West German commitment to the NATO Alliance despite domestic violence.

In December, 1983 the U.S. began deploying its Pershing II missiles in the FDR. The Soviets walked out of the INF talks in Geneva and declared they would not resume arms negotiations unless the U.S. first removed its missiles from Europe. When they realized that this ploy was not working and that they might lose their peace image, the Soviets agreed to resume the Geneva discussions in March 1985.

The Soviet leadership was convinced that by preventing the missiles from being stationed in the Federal Republic, their deployment anywhere in Europe might be prevented. Further, the Soviets realize that this goal cannot be attained solely through the peace movement in the FRG. The struggle for this goal is not regarded by the Soviets as finished, nor will it be abandoned. According to 1987 public opinion polls Gorbachev's clever arms control strategy convinced many people in Western Europe that the Soviet Union was more serious about promoting peace than the United States. The Soviets hope to again promote virulent "peace" movements to end the deployments.

The Soviets hope for a renewed radicalization of the relations between European governments and opposition parties, and on increasing differentiation among member states within NATO, brought about by intense Soviet propaganda campaigns. Propaganda and political pressure will be focused on the Federal German Republic and increased over a long period of time. A distorted picture of the Federal Republic will be drawn for the international public, a picture showing the Federal Republic "preparing for war" in violation of the Moscow Treaty. By internationally picturing the FRG as "revanchist" and aggressive, the Soviet Union hopes to promote a return to conditions existing prior to the 1979 NATO decision, or to at least achieve some modifications in the NATO missile program.

Central to the Soviet strategy is the general concept of "consistant change in the international power relationship." From the Soviet point of view, the struggle for power among individual nation states and any associated interpretation of "balance of power" has, since 1917, been replaced by a situation of global conflict between two fundamentally different social systems. Any change in the global balance of power in favor of Soviet communism is the central focus of Soviet foreign policy and world events are consistently and exclusively interpreted from this point of view.

The key to Soviet policy with respect to Western Europe within NATO is that the Soviets want military superiority which will give them a war-waging capability that will assure the enemy's defeat in the event of war. Such a capability could then lead to a military detente were Western governments to perceive their defense preparations as inadequate and futile. The difficulty the NATO alliance experienced in adhering to its decision to deploy theater missiles underscores the vulnerability of the West to Soviet strategies of intimidation and subversion. If political influence is seen as the shadow cast ahead of military power, then the tremendous military advantages the Soviets are developing in the European sector of the NATO Atlantic flank will continue to promote accommodation with the Soviet Union at both popular and leadership levels of the countries of Western Europe.

During the course of 1986 some of the fissures that have always characterized the resilient NATO alliance have grown wider. The common market agricultural policy practically excludes U.S. farm products from Europe; in fact French wheat now competes with America in world markets. The huge U.S. balance of trade deficit coupled with the fact that the U.S. pays the larger share of NATO's security bill makes U.S.-European economic relations a source of continuing strain within the alliance.

The April, 1986 U.S. air strikes against Libya created a major imbroglio within the alliance ranks. John B. Oakes said that these strikes "endangered the North Atlantic Alliance, cornerstone of American foreign policy in the western hemisphere. . . . Mr. Reagan put the Alliance under perhaps the most severe strain in its history." For a while the U.S. seemed to be standing alone lambasted by friend and foe alike.

Allied anxiety also increased over United States arms control policy, particularly over the U.S. threat to dispose of the unratified Salt II treaty. Joseph Lelyveld concluded an article "On Arms Control, Europe Would Prefer to Speak for Itself" with a statement by Willy Brandt, the former German chancellor, who is chairman of the opposition Social Democrats in West Germany. "Consensus between the present American administration and Europe is becoming an illusion," he said. "The alliance is being drained." Gorbachev's projection that the U.S. presents a threat to world peace and stability with which all European countries, including the Soviet Union, must deal with jointly exploits the prospects of arms control as the surest hope for peace.

The hastily arranged October summit meetings in Reykjavik did little to bolster the confidence of America's allies in U.S. leadership. In Iceland Gorbachev almost pursuaded President Reagan to progressively withdraw U.S. missiles from Europe without any consultation with its allies. It almost seemed that the indispensable alliance was to be exchanged for some super power accord. Both Reykjavik and the Iranian arms deal have damaged European faith in American leadership and have aided the Soviet goal of decoupling the U.S. from Europe.

On this side of the Atlantic Canada's growing neutralism as a NATO defense partner is a matter of concern. A 1986 editorial in "Conservative

Insight," bimonthly publication of the Canadian Conservative Center, titled "Canada: Dangers of Growing Neutrality," underlined concern about the direction of the country's foreign policy. The editorial began with this statement: ". . . Canada's defense contribution to the security of the Free World ranks only above that of the little nation of Luxembourg. This is a sad commentary, in view of our significant and heroic role in joining with the Allied forces to defeat the Nazis in World War II." The editorial quoted approvingly a statement by Professor Edward Luttwak of the Georgetown Center for Strategic and International Studies that "Canada is a country that has decided to take a free ride." Mr. Luttwak described Canadian officialdom as "being essentially irresponsible children in the (NATO) alliance."

Two developments brighten this otherwise gloomy picture. First was the referendum decision by Spain to remain within NATO; second was the May re-election of the Netherlands Prime Minister, Ruud Lubbers which assured that the Dutch decision to deploy 48 American ground-launched cruise missiles in 1988 would not be reconsidered.

Henry Kissinger presented his own assessment of the NATO alliance and a possible cure in May 1986. "One early problem remains almost unchanged, although the two sides of the Atlantic have exchanged their roles. Now it is Europe that insists that the treaty's obligations do not extend to the developing world. And it is Europe that feels free to dissociate itself from U.S. actions where indigenous upheavals and Soviet efforts to outflank the Alliance produce contemporary crises. Sources of the problem can be seen in two facts: First, it is unnatural for a continent with a population larger than that of the Soviet Union and a gross national product one and a half times greater than it to rely for so much of its defense on a distant ally. Second, the prevalent strategic doctrine of nuclear retaliation is inconsistent with the realities of nuclear parity."

"A larger European role in the defense of Europe is long overdue. This will require not only a more substantial material effort—where in fact progress is being made—but also an explicit European identity within NATO. If the Atlantic relationship can encourage a European Economic Community where competition with the United States is inevitable, it should welcome a European Defense Community, in which all incentives— in case of a Soviet attack or pressure on Europe—would be for cooperation rather than dissociation. (Henry A. Kissinger. Alliance Cure; Redeployment, Washington Post, May 13, 1986, A-19)

Kissinger then proposed that the major NATO nations should set up a high level group under Lord Carrington, Secretary General of NATO to examine the devisive problems confronting the alliance and to recommend what should be done about them. In conclusion, Kissinger stated: "Such a major reassessment of the Atlantic Alliance should not be undertaken as a reaction to a transitory mutual recrimination. It should be done carefully and constructively with the goal of increasing the overall effectiveness of the defense of free peoples and of bringing the demands on political leaders into line with that which a democratic framework will sustain."

The U.S. was having trouble with allies in the Pacific as well as in Europe. Australia was outraged by the United States sale of subsidized wheat to the Soviet Union and subsidized sugar to China—actions harmful to Australia's faltering economy. There is no doubt that the U.S. is in tough economic competition with many of its allies. These trade problems will probably worsen before they improve. Yet security need not be jeopardized while we search for equitable solutions to these problems.

Unless the crisis within our alliance system is resolved the totalitarian Soviet system may be able to overcome the free societies of the west. We should heed the advice contained in Abraham Lincoln's message to Congress on December 1, 1862, "The dogmas of the quiet past are inadequate for the stormy present. The occasion is piled high with difficulty and we must rise with the occasion. As our case is new, so we think anew and act anew. We must disenthrall ourselves and then we shall save our country."

The Central Atlantic Sector: the Caribbean Basin

Cuba, under Castro, has been turned by the Soviet Union into a prominent political and military base, strategically located near its chief adversary, the United States. The relevant issues of Castro's gradual conversion to Marxism-Leninism, and the extent and timing of Soviet support at various phases of his Cuban revolution, are a matter of much intellectual controversy. Fidel Castro's transformation from a 1950 doctorate of law at the University of Havana to the leader of the successful 1959 revolution against Batista ended with his eventual open embrace of Marxism-Leninism.[39] After a brief fling at a Parliamentarian career, Castro organized an ill-fated attack on the Moncade military barracks in Oriente province on July 26, 1955. Imprisoned after the failure of the July 26 barracks raid, Castro was released from jail and travelled to the United States to seek funds for his "26 July movement," but failed. In 1956 he moved to Mexico and organized a group of some 80 revolutionaries to launch an attack in Cuba's Oriente province. Castro's group landed in Cuba in December 1956 and were almost liquidated by Batista's forces. Some dozen survivors established a base in the Sierra Maestra Mountains where Castro began a guerrilla warfare campaign against Batista's regime and earned the reputation of a Cuban Robin Hood.[40] Castro gained prestige and followers in his mountain stronghold and linked up with the urban underground, which became the main force in the anti-Batista struggle. Batista fled Cuba on January 1, 1959, and Castro seized power.

Castro's subsequent public acceptance of Marxism-Leninism and his alliance with the Soviet Union came about quickly, because of his hostility to the United States and his predilection for anti-democratic political philosophies. Castro quickly merged his "26th July movement" with leftist elements to form the new Cuban Communist Party. Moscow followed Cuban developments carefully. As hostility between Cuba and the U.S. grew, the U.S. began to prepare an intervention force recruited from anti-Castro Cuban exiles. This preparation culminated in the Bay of Pigs fiasco on April 17, 1961. This American disaster convinced the Soviet leaders that there was little risk in becoming Cuba's protector.[41]

The manner in which the Soviet Union monitors and incrementally nurtures an incipient revolutionary situation potentially advantageous to its overall strategy varies. The Soviets' ability to perceive, cultivate, and assist revolutionaries useful to their purposes was evident in the case of Cuba.

The Caribbean in the Ideological Context

A central problem involved in coping with Soviet intrusions in many parts of the world lies in differentiations between indigenous conflicts and the Soviet exploitation of such conflicts. Revolutionary activities may represent a spontaneous choice of radical methods for the solution of problems, or they may be externally prompted, or even imposed. The Communists have, in the past, specifically rejected spontaneous political developments. On one occasion Lenin declared:

> "Our task is to combat spontaneity, to divert the working class movement from this spontaneous trade-union striving to come under the wings of the bourgeoise and to bring it under the wing of revolutionary social democracy."

Nicaragua

There are many parallels between the 1959 situation in Cuba and the one that exploded 20 years later in Nicaragua. Both Cuba and Nicaragua were ideal targets for communist political warfare. Both countries were ruled by unpopular dictators, which made it easy to mask the ultimate goal of the guerrilla leaders operating against the government forces. The Cuban-sponsored campaign which finally toppled the Somoza regime in July 1979 was a long time in the making. The instrument created for this campaign was the Frente Sandinista de Liberation Nicaragua (FSLN). Many of its leaders were given specialized training in both the Soviet Union and Cuba in agit-prop, guerrilla warfare, and terrorism.

Although the Cubans have attempted to mask their support for the FSLN, the Sandinista organization clearly derives from the Cuban model. In March 1979, Castro met with the FSLN leaders and urged them to downplay the Marxist-Leninist nature of their goals and strategy and to stress their willingness to bring in other groups to forge a broad-based anti-Somoza movement. Castro had used the same tactics himself while waging guerrilla warfare against Batista. Castro, in August 1986, told the world that he had been a communist all along: This was done in France's Le

Figaro magazine in a big cover article enblazoned: *"Castro avoue"* ("Castro confesses").*

> What exactly did Mr. Castro say to the Figaro interviewer? Taxed in 1959 with having made in the United States a statement judged "totally anti-communist," Mr. Castro replied:
> "In actual fact, I was a communist. But it would have been premature, at that period, to proclaim the Marxist-Leninist character of our revolution."
> Mr. Castro added that anyone who attentively read his book *"La Historia Me Absolvera"* ("History Will Absolve Me") or his statement concerning the attack on the Moncado Barracks, both written by the early 1950s, should have realized that the author was guided by "very advanced" socialist thought. "Anyone who took the trouble could understand it."

It is ironic that the same intellectual gullibility exists today concerning the Sandinistas.

The key to the Sandinista victory in Nicaragua was the massive shipment of arms into that country in 1978 and 1979. Such aid was given to the Sandinistas by Cuba, through Panama and Costa Rica, on a large scale in order to match the well-equipped, well-trained National Guard in Nicaragua. After Somoza was ousted in July 1979, the Sandinistas quickly defeated the demoralized National Guard. Subsequently, the new regime in Managua has attempted to conceal its commitment to become a Cuban style Soviet satellite.

The Sandinista regime has tried to win over business leaders from the political opposition in the hopes that they will help improve Nicaragua's faltering economy. An umbrella association, known by its Spanish acronym COSEP, continues to side with the opposition, including business leaders, the independent newspaper *La Prensa,* and the church. The group's demands are essentially political and economic. When the U.S. government cut off aid in April 1981 because of continued arms shipments from Nicaragua to El Salvador, the Soviet Union induced Libya to provide Nicaragua with four times as much economic aid as the U.S. was giving. The worsening economic situation has helped consolidate the FSLN's power. The internal crackdown on political opposition led to the defection of many Sandinistas, the most prominent being Eden Pastora, the legendary Commander Zero of the 1979 Anti-Somoza uprising. A Sandinista Deputy Defense Minister, Pastora left Nicaragua in July 1981 and in April 1983 declared his opposition to the Sandinistas as ". . . my duty, as a revolutionary citizen, to do everything I can within my power to prevent the revolution from being aborted by Marxist obstinacy or by spurious counter-revolutionary forces."[42]

Relations between the United States and Managua continued to deteriorate throughout 1982, 1983 and 1984 as the volume of equipment, training and supplies from Managua for the El Salvadoran insurgency continued to

---

*Garier, Richard. *Castro's Confession Teaches a Lesson,* The Washington Times, Aug. 25, 1986, p. 31.

expand. The Sandinistas increasingly adopted stridently anti-American rhetoric, including the proposal to amend the Nicaraguan national anthem with the slogan "We shall fight against the Yankee, the enemy of Humanity."

The spring of 1983 saw internal discontent with the Sandinista regime erupt into open insurrection by two disaffected Nicaraguan groups, the Frente Democratico Nacional (FDN) and the Alianza Revolucionaria Democratica (ARDE). Led by the Sandinista heroes Eden Pastora, Fernando "Negro" Chamorro, and former junta member Alfonso Robelo, ARDE operated from southern bases in Nicaragua, while the FDN conducted operations in the North, staged from Honduras.

The Roman Catholic Church also began to oppose the Sandinistas, particularly after the treatment accorded to the Pope on his March 1983 visit to Managua. While addressing a crowd in Managua, the Pope was repeatedly interrupted by junta led Sandinista war chants that continued despite the Pontiff's pleas for "silencio."

The continued repression of promised pluralism led other prominent Sandinistas to leave Nicaragua and support opponents to the junta. Arturo J. Cruz, Nicaraguan Ambassador to the United States from April 1981 to November 1981, stated after his resignation "It was not secret that the hard core of the Sandinistas are Marxist, (but) nearly everyone felt that the Marxist vanguard would promote a social democracy." Disillusioned with the severity of FSLN domestic suppression, Cruz resigned and openly sided with Eden Pastora's ARDE insurgency.

The Sandinistas held elections toward the close of 1984 which were boycotted by the opposition, as opposition parties had no access to public communications. The people of Nicaragua remain under the junta's grip.

During the early months of 1985 the position of the Reagan Administration against the Sandinistas hardened. As a senior State Department official put it:

> Cuba and the Soviet Union are exploiting historical poverty and repression to advance their own strategic interests in the hemisphere. Those interests are inexorably hostile to the United States. And experience over 6 long years of crisis has amply demonstrated that the goals of the Cubans, the Soviets, and, to date, the Sandinistas are also contrary to the national interests of the region's democratic nations.[43]

The Administration attempted to obtain $14 million to support the Contras, a force of some 15,000 men fighting the Sandinistas. The Democratic majority in the House of Representatives rejected aid to the Contras in April 1985 claiming that it was wrong for the United States to attempt to overthrow another government. Yet we supported the overthrow of the Nicaraguan government when we joined other members of the Organization of American States in calling for President Anastasio Somoza to step down. Now, once again, Nicaraguan people are rising up against dictatorship. Only this time it is a dictatorship that vows in its national anthem to "fight against the Yankee, the enemy of Humanity."

Immediately after the House voted against support of the contras, Daniel Ortega, who became President of Nicaragua in the rigged 1984 elections, flew to Moscow to obtain assistance beyond the hundreds of millions of dollars the Soviet Union had already given his government.[44] This brazen trip eventually led the Democratic Congress to approve a larger amount of "humanitarian" aid to the Contras than the Reagan Administration had originally requested.

Subsequently, President Reagan announced an economic embargo against Nicaragua, which was more significant symbolically than economically. It was intended to let the House Democrats and the Sandinistas know that Mr. Reagan was looking for ways to prevent the Sandinista government from making Nicaragua "another Cuba."

At the May 1985 summit meeting in Bonn several foreign ministers took issue with the embargo imposed against Nicaragua by Mr. Reagan. Sir Geoffrey Howe, the British Foreign Secretary, and Roland Dumas, the French Foreign Minister, were reported by a British spokesman to have asserted that they did not want Nicaragua driven to greater dependence on the Soviet Union and Cuba.

The inability of Western statesmen to recognize political reality is perhaps the greatest advantage the Soviet Union has in its global assault on freedom. At a meeting in Washington, which the author attended, Pedro Jouquin Chamorro, former editor of *La Prensa,* now in exile, said that Daniel Ortega announced, on the day the Sandinistas seized power in 1979, that the war against "the imperialists" had just begun.[45] "The Cuban-Soviet alliance with Nicaragua will continue as long as the Sandinistas are in power. The requests for full democracy and power sharing will not be granted. The Sandinistas are loyal to an old Latin American tradition—that real legitimacy resides in the weapons that enable you to take power, and that once you have power, there is no reason to share it."

There are those who believe that the Sandinista regime can be led to abandon its Marxist-Leninist ambitions via negotiations, particularly those conducted by the Contadora group of Mexico, Colombia, Panama, and Venezuela. A peace treaty may be viewed by the American public and the U.S. Congress as a definitive solution to the problems in Central America, signalling that further U.S. attention to the region is unnecessary. Because treaties are not self-enforcing, such a lapse of attention could prove as dangerous as in the case of Cuba.

An acceptable Central American peace treaty must contain clear and unambiguous commitments that protect U.S. regional interests and the interests of friendly nations in the region. The requirements include:
- an end to Nicaraguan support for guerrilla insurgents and its destablization activities in neighboring countries;
- restoration of a military balance in the region;
- severence of Nicaraguan military and security ties to Cuba and the Soviet bloc; and

- the establishment of pluralistic democracy.

Since these requirements will not be accepted by the present Sandinista regime, other solutions will have to be found. Otherwise, if the Sandinistas, backed by the Soviet Union and Cuba, remain in power, Marxist-Leninist regimes will be installed in Nicaragua's neighboring countries.

The bipartisan Kissinger Commission concluded that the crisis in Central America "makes a particularly urgent claim on the United States for several reasons."[46] First, as Central America is our near neighbor, our own security interests are critically involved. Second, the crisis calls out to us because we *can* make a difference. Because the nations are small, because they are near, efforts that would be minor by the standards of other crises can have a large impact on this one. Third, whatever the short-term costs of acting now, they are far less than the long-term costs of not acting now. And, fourth, a great power can choose which challenges to respond to, but it cannot choose where those challenges come from—or when. Nor can it avoid the necessity of deliberate choice. Once challenged, a decision not to respond is fully as consequential as a decision to respond. We are challenged now in Central America. No agony of indecision will make that challenge go away. No wishing it were easier will make it easier.

Perhaps the United States should have paid more attention to Central America sooner. Perhaps, over the years, we should have intervened less, or intervened more, or intervened differently. But all these are questions of what might have been. What confronts us now is a question of what might become. Whatever its roots in the past, the crisis in Central America exists urgently in the present, and its successful resolution is vital to the future.

The battle for Central America, as was the case in Vietnam, will be decided by the battle for public opinion in the United States. The international press is courted, exploited, and carefully monitored while in Nicaragua. Religious groups are also utilized to promote the Sandinista regime.

The manner in which the Sandinistas have utilized some traces of democracy and pluralism to cover their real goals has been carefully documented by Douglas W. Payne in "The Democratic Mask—The Consolidation of the Sandinista Revolution." On the verge of the final offensive against Somoza in 1979 Humberto Ortega was able to say

> Without slogans of Marxist orthodoxy, without ultra-leftist phrases such as 'power only for the workers,' 'toward the dictatorship of the proletariat,' etc. we have been able—without losing at any time our revolutionary Marxist-Leninist Sandinista identity—to rally all our people around the FSLN.[47]

From that time on Payne charts the ingenious two-track course the Sandinista have pursued. In this fully documented history the Sandinista "strategy of power" for the "achievement of Marxist-Leninist goals emerges from beneath the carefully manufactured democratic cover, and the electoral process which is an inextricable part of it.

On November 6, 1985 President Reagan sent a "90-day Report on Nicaragua" to the Congress as required by law. The report covered recent developments in Nicaragua, and related U.S. policy. On October 15, the Sandinistas suspended civil liberties by declaring a State of Emergency. Repression of all types—arrests, harassment, press censorship—has continued and increased. At the same time, the Nicaraguan government has obstructed the Contadora process and persisted in its refusal to engage in a dialogue with the democratic opposition to their regime. The Report also contained detailed evidence of systematic Sandinista violations of human rights on a massive scale, including summary executions of hundreds of Nicaraguans considered "enemies of the revolution."

President Reagan, citing the need for military aid to counter Soviet-backed military efforts in Central America, told GOP congressional leaders that the Kremlin is watching Congress' every move on aid to Nicaragua's anti-Sandinista forces.

In an hour-long White House meeting, Mr. Reagan warned that Nicaragua's Sandinista government "could destroy everything" the United States has accomplished in El Salvador and other parts of the region.[48]

After a House set-back in April 1986 President Reagan made support of the Contras a personal issue. 1986 witnessed deepening hostility between the United States and the increasingly repressive Sandinista regime in Nicaragua. Even the New York Times in a July 10, 1986 editorial asserted that Nicaragua "is well down the totalitarian road." After much bitter debate in mid-1986 Congress finally approved a $100 million aid program for the Contra freedom fighters.

David Horowitz, a leading radical of the sixties wrote an impassioned article in the June 1986 issue of Commentary in which he concluded: "The Sandinista anthem which proclaims Yankee to be the 'enemy of mankind' expresses precisely the revolutionaries' sentiment and goal. That goal is hardly to create a more just society—the sordid record would dissuade any reformer from choosing the Communist path—but to destroy the societies still outside the totalitarian perimeter, and their chief protector, the United States.

"Support for the Contras is a first line of defense. For Nicaraguans, a Contra victory would mean the restoration of the democratic leadership from whom the Sandinistas stole the revolution in the first place, the government that Nicaragua would have had if Cuba had not intervened. For the countries of the Americas, it would mean a halt in the Communist march that threatens their freedoms and their peace." ("Nicaragua: A Speech to my Former Comrades on the Left".)

On July 29, 1986 Violeta Barrios de Chamorro, an owner of La Prensa, Nicaragua's only opposition newspaper, which the Government closed June 26, wrote an open letter to President Ortega Saavedra, who said recently that Mrs. Chamorro should be imprisoned. Her husband was assassinated in 1978. Excerpts from the letter follow.

As chairman of the board of directors of La Prensa, I was not greatly astonished to hear your recent statement that I deserve to be sentenced to 30 years in jail after being tried by the people's anti-Somocista tribunals.

You will never convince anyone that I am a traitor to my country, nor that I received money from the Central Intelligence Agency, nor that I am part of the Reagan Administration's terrorist plan. These falsehoods have been repeated so often that now nobody believes them. Commander Ortega, the same thing is happening here in Nicaragua as in other countries under Communist dictatorship: because there are so many lies every day, no one will believe you on the day when you say something true.

This is already under way, Commander Ortega, by means of repression and the banning of all contradictory opinion. Your Sandinista party has already created a great concentration camp in Nicaragua. But the Nicaraguan people are not losing their liberating spirit and will never lose it even in the worst of the gulags your mind is able to conceive." (New York Times, A-23, July 29, 1986)

There are still many Americans bewitched and befuddled by Ortega's propaganda campaign in the United States. Yet in the long run, his regime, backed by the Soviet Union, Cuba, Libya, the PLO and many communist countries will become isolated and eventually pull in its horns.

On August 19, 1986 President Reagan made his bluntist public statement about what is at stake in Nicaragua. As he put it, unless the Nicaraguan Government sought democracy, the "only alternative" for the rebels there would be, "to have their way and take over." (New York Times, August 20, 1986, .-1)

For this to happen the Contra freedom fighters must focus as much on their political image as on their military effort. They must be able to project themselves as a legitimate democratic alternative to Ortega's repressive regime. An unfortunate by-product of the November 1986 disclosure that monies paid by Iran for U.S. arms shipped by Israel had been sent to the Contras may weaken U.S. resolve to help them in their struggle against the Sandinistas.

Grenada

From the Soviet-Cuban point of view, Maurice Bishop's March 1979 ascension to power in Grenada was a case of serendipity rather than the product of a calculated plan. Two years after Bishop's coup, the People's Revolutionary government of Grenada was attempting to cope with the difficult task of fulfilling its revolutionary promises. While the results were mixed, Bishop's commitment to a Cuban-type regime was evident. Bishop pledged solidarity with Cuba, Nicaragua, the guerrillas in El Salvador, Vietnam and North Korea, but not to the Afghan resisters to the Soviet invasion. "The Cubans armed and trained a Grenadian army of 2,000, out of a population of 120,000. Both the Soviet Union and Cuban recognized Grenada's strategic location."[49]

After the Reagan Administration asserted that the Grenadan airport was expanding beyond the needs of civilian aircraft, Bishop denied the implied charge that the airport would be a base for Soviet aircraft. In June 1983 Bishop visited the United States and received the keys to the City of Washington, D.C. While in the United States, Bishop downplayed the role of the Cubans and Soviets in Grenada. However, he apparently chafed under the increasingly taut control of his Cuban-Soviet masters. In October 1983 Bishop was disposed of by a hardliner more in tune with Cuban-Soviet control. Bishop, along with members of his cabinet, was shot in cold blood. Subsequently, President Reagan, at the request of Antigua, St. Lucia, Dominica, St. Vincent, Barbados and Jamaica ordered U.S. forces to take over Grenada as essential to the security of the United States and the countries located in the Eastern Caribbean.

The Grenada scenario suggests that the Soviet-Cuban combination had taken over and occupied the Island of Grenada just as if they had conquered it by armed force. Grenada was not an independent, sovereign country, but a military outpost of Soviet-Cuban imperialism strategically located in the Eastern Caribbean. The numerous documents found in Grenada indicated that the Soviet Union and Castro were not about to create an idyllic democracy on that island.* The presence of North Koreans (masters of terrorism) and East Germans (masters of espionage) on the island plus large caches of assorted arms reflected Soviet-Cuban plans to make the island into an impregnable offensive base located on the channel through which tankers pass carrying Middle East oil to U.S. refineries. The highest-ranking Soviet general in the Western hemisphere was among the 30 so-called Soviet advisors captured by U.S. forces, indicating the importance of Grenada to Soviet Caribbean policy.

El Salvador

The successful insurrection against Somoza by the FSLN in 1979 gave renewed momentum to guerrillas fighting in El Salvador. The struggle in El Salvador could be traced to the Havana Conference of 1966. From the training camps established by the conference, the Tupamaros, Montoneros, Sandinistas, Chilean MIR (Movement of the Revolutionary Left), Colombian, and El Salvadoran guerrilla movements emerged.

The effort in El Salvador did not begin to coalesce until the early 1970s when the People's Revolutionary Bloc (BPR) and the Front for United Peoples Action (FAPU) emerged. The insurgent effort was further fractured by the emergence in 1975 of the Popular Forces of Liberation (FPL) and their front organization, the Popular Revolutionary Bloc (BPR). While the BPR became the largest Marxist-Leninist faction of the movement with 80,000 members, the more radical communist wing split away and formed the People's Revolutionary Army (ERP).

The North American Congress of Latin American Affairs (NACLA) stated that these groups formed because "they viewed armed struggle as the

---

*See "The Grenada Papers," Paul Seabury and A. McDougall, ICS Pres, San Fransasco, CA., 1984.

necessary answer to the intransigence of the bourgeoisie."[50] The fractured guerrilla movement was only moderately successful during the 1970s in promoting the social dislocation necessary for an insurgency. Although the success of the Sandinista movement encouraged the use of similar methods in El Salvador, the guerrillas were pre-empted by a coup in October 1979 that replaced General Carlos Romero by a five-man junta which promised sweeping land reform.

After the return of Duarte to San Salvador and the assassination of Archbishop Romero, the Democratic Revolutionary Front (FDR) was formed "to disseminate propaganda abroad" for the purpose of gaining credibility for the guerrilla cause. President Duarte accused the leftist guerrillas of assassinating Romero to attract international support against the right.

With the triumph of the Sandinistas in July 1979, Castro believed that El Salvador was ripe for a revolutionary takeover. In May 1980, Castro, as a precondition for greater Cuban aid and assistance in procuring weapons, demanded that the leadership of the FPL, the ERP, the FARN and the PCES set aside all their past ideological differences and form the United Revolutionary Directorate (DRU), in order to coordinate all logistics, command decisions, and propaganda in conjunction with the FDR. The DRU formed the revolutionary high command that conducted the fighting through 1981. The acknowledged leader of the Salvadoran revolutionaries was Cayetano Carpio, who headed the Unified Revolutionary Directorate (DRU), the executive body of the guerrilla factions. Carpio committed suicide in 1984 under mysterious circumstances. Carpio was Secretary General of the Salvadoran Communist Party in the 1960s and later helped form the Farabundo Marti Forces of Popular Liberation (FPL). The Soviet Union acting with Cuba, appears to be supporting a classically conceived and conducted communist campaign to gain political power in El Salvador.

The Soviet prescription for Communist revolution for Caribbean countries was published under the title *The Peculiarities of the Nicaraguan Revolution and Its Lessons Gained From the Point of View of Theory and Practice of the Liberation Movement*. This article appeared in *Latinskaya Amerika* No. 3 for March 1980 and concluded with S. Mikoyan's recommendations that Latin American revolutionary groups proceed according to general revolutionary experience and precepts. These recommendations included:

- the achievement of military superiority in order to expand influence without the use of force;
- organizational and explanatory work through radio, the press, and direct contacts with the people;
- the use of military and political fronts such as the "26 July Movement" in Cuba and the "Sandinista National Liberation Front" in Nicaragua as a substitute for proletariat political parties;

- the unification of leftist groups to avoid division on tactics, forms, and methods;
- the establishment of a social foundation in the revolutionary program which should be understood by the broad masses of the population;
- the arrangement of, in the international sphere, support and aid from all kinds of friends and allies and the isolation of adversaries in order to prevent their intervention (e.g., weakening of the Organization of American States, the "punitive instrument of U.S. imperialism");
- the establishment of revolutionary organs of power at all levels as has been done in Nicaragua;
- the replacement of armed forces by new formations with enlistment of the best and patriotic elements;
- the establishment of sober economic policies, tolerance of foreign investments and support of the pluralistic system.

This Soviet blueprint for action in the countries of the Caribbean should leave little doubt about the intentions of the Soviet Union in this part of the world. Nevertheless, the U.S. is having difficulty in obtaining the support of its NATO allies, including France and Canada, for the policy it is pursuing toward El Salvador. Mexico has warned against deeper United States military involvement in El Salvador, encouraging efforts toward a negotiated solution to the simmering civil war. The Reagan administration has been warned to stay out of the El Salvador imbroglio. The code phrase being used is the "avoidance of internationalization" of the conflict in El Salvador, even though this had already taken place on the communist side. Mikoyan's recommendations, it should be noted, have been broadly followed.

By the close of August 1981, the insurgents had gained official diplomatic support for their cause by both Mexico and France. The reasons for Mexico's alignment with the communists will be examined later. The French decision was more personal. The principal advisor on Caribbean and African affairs for the Socialist President of France, Francois Mitterand, is Regis Debray, the enthusiastic biographer of Castro's expert on guerrilla warfare, Ché Gueverra.

While the guerrillas do not now have the popular support to defeat the government in El Salvador, outside assistance is needed to prevent their victory. Only if the leftist bid for power via insurrection can be thwarted will the foundation be laid for accommodation between the opposing factions.

The U.S. government's efforts to forestall a Marxist-Leninist takeover in El Salvador was hampered by a massive, well-orchestrated propaganda campaign designed to isolate the U.S. diplomatically and to erode domestic American support for Washington's policy. Congressional concern over human rights crystallized in the December 1981 legislation known as the Boland Amendment. Continued aid for El Salvador was contingent upon a certification of improved human rights required every six months.

Realizing the conflict in Central America was being waged on several plateaus of conflict, the Reagan administration unveiled an economic package in February 1982 known as the Caribbean Basin Development Plan. This announcement preceded the March 1982 elections in El Salvador, which were held despite repeated threats from the DRU and FMLN to execute participants. Alvaro Magana was elected President and received the support of the moderate civilian groups. However, like his predecessor, Magana was unable to exert full control over the military.

Thus, inefficiency in the army and a weak political infrastructure enabled the guerrillas to grow in strength. During 1983, the insurgents won several major victories. Facing major difficulties in Central America, President Reagan created the bi-partisan Kissinger Commission to draft a long-term policy and program for the region. In February 1984 the Administration asked Congress to increase this year's military aid to El Salvador from $64.8 million to $243.5 million as part of an $8.9 billion Central American aid package recommended by the Kissinger Commission. President Reagan promised he would work with Congress "to make certain that our assistance is used fairly and effectively."

Congress reluctantly cooperated with the Reagan administration. After testifying before a key House subcommittee Secretary of State Shultz exploded:

> Here we have an area, right next to us, which a cross section of Americans on a bipartisan commission have studied carefully, really worked at it, have concluded is in the vital interests of the United States, referring to the panel headed by former Secretary of State Henry A. Kissinger.
>
> There are problems there, he said. We all know that. What you're telling me is that because there are problems, let's walk away.[51]

Because the March 1984 chaotic presidential elections in El Salvador did not produce a winner, runoff elections were held in May and were won by Jose Napoleon Duarte, the Christian Democratic Party candidate. As of 1985, three groups were competing for the destiny of El Salvador: a small violent right, which sought to nullify the land reform program and overturn the current government; externally supported guerrillas, estimated at about 7,000, who seek a Marxist-Leninist regime and refuse to participate in elections; and a broad coalition of political parties from democratic left to conservative, democratic unions, and most of the military, religious, and civic institutions.

The coalition has opposed both the violent right and the communist left. It won the March 31, 1985 elections which assured Duarte's Christian Democratic Party a majority in the National Assembly. The example of El Salvador has shown that with adequate aid and tenacity the victory of democracy in Central America is possible. The battle for El Salvador, however, is not over as urban guerrillas resumed terrorist operations in San Salvador since the spring of 1985, but the overall situation as of 1987 favors

Duarte even though a damaging earthquake in San Salvador added to his problems.[52]

Mexico

According to Stanford's Richard R. Fagan, adverse consequences would follow if the United States attempted to "internationalize" the conflict in El Salvador.[53] U.S. military assistance given to prevent the extreme Left from gaining power in El Salvador would do particular damage to U.S.-Mexican relations. Mexican policies are rooted in an historically skewed understanding of the social forces at work in Central America. Mexican President Jose Lopez Portillo went out of his way to stress Mexico's close ties with Cuba just three days after a United States delegation arrived in Mexico with what it called "proof of Havana's support for Salvadoran guerrillas." Mexico's foreign policy is always to the left of that of the U.S. Although Mexico appears stable in contrast to many other countries in Latin America, this appearance may be deceptive. Mexico faces vast internal problems for which she has yet to find answers.

In Mexico, the most widely read newspapers in the universities, cultural circles, and the labor movement are owned and controlled by well known pro-Soviet and former Cuban figures.[54] The intellectual role of thousands of Spanish loyalists living in Mexico is a key factor in Mexico's leftist orientation. The Mexican penchant to show independence in its foreign policy and strong nationalism has brought it close to Cuba at times, even though Cuba provides a dismal model to follow. Like its patron, the Soviet Union, Cuba has become a militarized, totalitarian state.

Mexico chooses to ignore the role of both Cuba and the Soviet Union in the turmoil in Central America. While in Moscow, Manuel Bartlett Diaz, Mexican Minister of Government, stated the Mexican position bluntly on March 14, 1985: "Mexico and the Soviet Union coincide in their policy towards Central America."

Many people in Europe and the United States believe that the negotiations undertaken by the so-called Contadora Group, composed of Mexico, Colombia, Venezuela and Panama represent the best opportunity for solving the Nicaraguan problems. The United States supports the spirit of this peace process, yet is at odds over verification provisions for such matters as the withdrawal of foreign military personnel.

The Machiavellian role played by Mexico in the formation of the Contadora group has been described by Gonzalo J. Facio, Foreign Minister of Costa Rica from 1970 to 1978. The Mexican government actively promoted the formation of the mediator group which adopted the name of the Panamanian island where it initially met. What did Mexico have in mind? Mexico's political objectives in Central America can be found in the French-Mexican Declaration of 1980 and the so-called Peace Plan proposed by President Lopez Portillo in 1981. Facio asserts that:

The French-Mexican Declaration professed to recognize the Farabundo Marti guerrillas as the most genuine representation of the Salvadoran people. Lopez Portillo's Peace Plan began with the premise that the Sandinista regime is the true expression of the self-determination of the Nicaraguan people. For this reason, the plan concluded, all of Latin America should cooperate to consolidate the Nicaraguan revolution, faced with threats from Yankee imperialism.

These past events underscore how the Mexican PRI government promoted the Contadora Group to achieve two goals: 1. the establishment of a "shared government" in El Salvador which would allow the Marxist guerrillas to share power that they have not been able to gain either by vote or by force; 2. to promote international aid to maintain a regime in Nicaragua that, by merely declaring itself anti-imperialist and by hurling insults at the U.S. government, attempts to justify the imposition of a military dictatorship totally submissive to Fidel Castro's influence.[55]

According to Facio,

Independent analysts think that the Mexican government by proclaiming itself the defender of Leninist revolution in the Caribbean, is seeking in return that the Soviets do not encourage a Leninist revolution in Mexico, since it is known that the objective conditions for revolution, as defined by Marx, are more present in Mexico than in any other Latin American country.[56]

Facio concluded,

With the pretext of stopping an inter-Central American war, the efforts of Contadora have been directed at consolidating the Sandinista regime while trying to keep the Nicaraguan rebels from receiving the economic and military aid that the rebellion needs to triumph.

Although to declare this is to commit the sin of heresy, the truth is that the Contadora Group's efforts have not fathered peace nor, much less, the progress of democracy in Central America.[57]

Facio's analysis does not bode well for the United States. An August 14, 1983 meeting between President Reagan and Mexican President Miguel de la Madrid in La Paz, Mexico failed to reconcile U.S. and Mexican policies towards conflicts in Central America. In fact, de la Madrid used this occasion to chide President Reagan for ordering deployment of U.S. naval forces off the coasts of Nicaragua. The two Presidents met again in the summer of 1986. At this meeting de la Madrid finally conceded difficulties to bring peace to Central America via the Contadora approach. The next few years of U.S.-Mexican relations are not going to be easy as long as Mexico ignores the fact that the Soviet Union and Cuba have a long-term program of supporting revolutionary groups in order to create, in furtherance of their strategic aims, conditions for revolutionary takeover. In short, "the Soviet threat in Latin America represents one part of the Soviet global strategy.[58] Mexico aids and abets that threat. The Mexican economy is in chaos and unemployment and widespread corruption is rampant. The fact that Mexico has become in the past three years the principal pusher of drugs into the U.S. further complicates U.S.-Mexico relations.

In addition Mexico provides a "safe haven" for massive spying operations against the United States. U.S. officials in Mexico City assert that the

Soviet Embassy is being used to mount espionage operations against the United States and that it has become a major conduit for the illegal transit of advanced technology to the Soviet Union.

Mexico has fewer than 50 people stationed at its embassy in Moscow. But the Soviet Embassy here, with more than 300 people, is one of the largest Soviet diplomatic missions in the world, even though Moscow has few official dealings with Mexico. Less than 1 percent of Mexican exports are sold to the Soviet Union.

The problem, U.S. officals say, is the Mexican acquiescence in the Soviet spying.

A senior Mexican government official acknowledged that there were espionage operations in Mexico City. But he defended Mexico's policy of permitting one of the largest overseas contingents of the Soviet intelligence and internal security agency, the KGB, to operate with virtual impunity.

Mexico, he said, is "an open country," and any country is allowed to have as many diplomats stationed in Mexico City as it chooses.[59]

While Mexicans may fear the consequences of "internationalizing" the conflict in Central America, the governments of Costa Rica, Honduras, and Guatemala have already noticed the spread of regional instability because of Cuban-Nicaraguan support for insurgencies.

Honduras

In Honduras, the first election in nine years elected Roberto Suazo Cordova president in January 1982. Despite this edging towards democracy, Honduras has been harrassed by El Salvadoran and Nicaraguan insurgents that use Honduras as a pipeline for arms transfers to the El Salvadoran insurgency. According to Sandinista defectors, the transfer of Nicaraguan arms to El Salvador through Honduras began almost immediately after the revolution deposed Somoza in July, 1979. These infiltrations used an estimated 15 to 20 overland routes through the Honduran Pacific coastline. In addition, Nicaraguan smugglers would leave the Pacific Nicaraguan port of Potosi and hug the coastline until reaching the El Salvadoran coastline where the weapons would be off-loaded.

U.S. and Honduran attempts to interdict the transfer of arms have been only partially successful. Managua reacted to this effort by stepping up Honduran-Nicaraguan border incidents and the encouragement of instability in Honduras. Tension between Nicaragua and Honduras is likely to continue as long as the Sandinistas continue to funnel arms and aid to the insurgency in El Salvador.

A domestic political crisis began to develop in Honduras in the spring of 1985.

After more than three years in office, Mr. Suazo appears to have reached a low in popularity. The armed forces, until now apparently neutral in the conflict, have quietly backed the unionists opposed to Mr. Suazo, according to army officers and Western officials.

The dispute centers on who will have the power to nominate candidates in the presidential election scheduled for November. The labor officials and a majority of legislators are demanding primary elections to select candidates.[60]

A major political upheaval in Honduras could hamper U.S. efforts to maintain pressure on the Sandinistas in Nicaragua. For the remainder of 1985 President Suazo prevented the delivery of supplies to the U.S. supported Freedom Fighters (Contras). The administration of President Jose Azcona which assumed office on January 27, 1986 lifted the ban on shipment of aid to the Nicaraguans fighting the Sandinistas.

Guatemala

Political violence in neighboring Guatemala is contingent upon the outcome of the struggle in El Salvador. A recent issue of *Latinskaya Amerika,* published by the Soviet Academy of Sciences, and edited by Sergei Mikoyan (son of former Soviet President Anistas Mikoyan), specified that, after Nicaragua and El Salvador, the next country to erupt will be Guatemala. For well over a quarter of a century leftist guerrillas have been waging a conflict against the military government of Guatemala. In recent years, the traditionally passive Indians have been joining the ranks of the rebellious insurgents for the first time. In the aftermath of the Sandinista triumph in Nicaragua, the tide of communist-supported revolutionary activity swept north into both El Salvador and Guatemala.

After the March 1982 elections, moderate Alejandro Aguirre was replaced by a military coup led by young officers intent on political reform. Though advocating political reform, the regime of General Efrain Rios Montt came under increasing pressure from the Roman Catholic Church, private enterprise and even the army to continue with a long-promised "political opening."

On August 8, 1983 the army overthrew the Montt regime, and replaced Montt with the Defense Minister Oscar Victores. The emergence of a pluralistic democracy is possible in Guatemala but the internal disintegration could be exploited by Cuban or Nicaraguan backed agents to create a totalitarian Marxist regime in the confusion.

After an involved election process, Guatemala has a new democratically elected leader, Vinicio Cerezo. The 43 year old Christian Democrat was inaugurated on Jan 14, 1986 after winning 68 per cent of the vote in December run-off elections. Cerezo got off to a good start with working relations with the Army that has run the country for the past thirty years. He runs a country faced with tremendous poverty, several insurgencies and a history of violence. The U.S. will try to help the new regime.

Costa Rica

A small country of two million inhabitants, Costa Rica is placed between Nicaragua and Panama. Despite its small size (it is slightly smaller than West Virginia), Costa Rica's location makes it of prime importance to both the Sandinistas and their opponents.

Long a prosperous nation, Costa Rica abolished its army in 1949, but possesses a small police force. This state of unarmed prosperity has traditionally enabled guerrilla movements to use Costa Rica as a base of operations without hindrance. Because of its border with Nicaragua, Costa Rica served as a base for the Sandinistas and later the Pastora and Robello led ARDE. However, the lack of armed forces and an economic slowdown has resulted in increased subversion and terrorist activity in the capital, San Jose and surrounding country.

> To a remarkable degree, Costa Ricans are united by the belief that they face a threat from neighboring Nicaragua. They perceive the small but growing American military presence here as necessary to guard against that threat.[61]

The success or failure of U.S. efforts to curtail the Soviet backed Cuban and Nicaraguan creation of regional instability will determine the fate of Honduras, Costa Rica, and Guatemala.

Surinam

In a bloody army coup led by Desi Bouterse in December 1982, Surinam came under the control of an avowed Marxist-Leninist government which turned to the Soviet Union and Cuba for support. This was the first time a self-proclaimed communist government was established on the mainland of South America. On the day the U.S. invaded Grenada, however, Bouterse expelled Cuban advisors and began ruling in coalition with labor unions and businessmen. Subsequently, Surinam began to re-open its ties with Castro's Cuba.

A Caribbean Survey

Although Nicaragua was the center of U.S. security concerns south of the border in mid-1986, the entire Caribbean region stretching from the northern countries of South America through Central America to Mexico and the many island nations in the sea all face significant domestic problems which could present the Soviet-Cuban combination with opportunities to make trouble for the United States. The prospects of renewed guerrilla warfare in Colombia confronts its new president, Virgilio Barco Vargas. In November, 1985 many members of Colombia's supreme court were killed in their offices in the Palace of Justice. Nearby Surinam and Guyana are both ruled by leftist leaders who generally collaborate with Cuba. In adjacent Panama evidence has circulated that "the army commander of Panama, a country vital to the United States, is extensively involved in illicit money laundering and drug activities and has provided a Latin American guerrilla group with arms. According to evidence collected by American intelligence agencies, Senior State Department, White

House, Pentagon and intelligence officials evidence also showed that the Commander, Gen. Manual Antonio Noriega, who is in effect the leader of the country, had been tied to the killing of a political opponent. They also said that for the last 15 years, he had been providing intelligence information simultaneously to Cuba and the United States." (The N.Y. Times, July 12, 1986, p. 1)

Further to the north, Mexico is facing a gigantic economic crisis, political corruption and criminal activities associated with its role as the major drug trafficker to the United States. In 1985 the staff of the Senate Foreign Relations Committee prepared a report for the chairman, Sen. Richard G. Lugar with forecasts that Mexico loomed as the most significant foreign policy problem of 1986. Senator Lugar said, "The problems are extraordinarily serious but the Mexicans have been attempting a good number of reforms and have announced others." He called the warnings from the C.I.A. and elsewhere "a legitimate fear, but all these people who talk of collapse give the impression that there are no pillars in place in that society, and there are." Serious instability, he said, "is conceivable but not inevitable." (N.Y. Times, May 25, 1986, p. 10)

Meanwhile Cuba appears to be becoming more totalitarian than its Soviet model. In the Soviet Union so-called private plots produce over 30 percent of the food grown by Soviet farmers. On May 19, 1986 Fidel Castro said Cuba halted a six-year old experiment with free peasant markets, calling it "a source of enrichment for neo-capitalists and neo-bourgeois." The Cuban radio said Mr. Castro announced the end of the free markets aimed at giving farmers an incentive to increase production by allowing them to sell produce themselves after satisfying government quotas. "The peasant free market will pass without glory, leaving behind a great lesson, much damage and many millionaires," Mr. Castro was quoted as having said.

The free peasant markets were among several measures taken in recent years to relax government control over the economy. In 1982, about two years after the free markets began, the Government announced new restrictions, including a 20 percent tax on farmers' profits.

In August 1986 the Soviet Union imposed stiff terms on Cuba for a 1986–1990 trade pact. Cuban sugar will be sold to the Soviet Union at a fixed price of $1,275 a ton instead of the former price of $1,425. The price of Soviet oil sold to Cuba will remain $39 per ton despite the steep drop in world oil prices since November 1985. Moscow can be quite capitalistic in dealing with its communist clients.

Turning to the Caribbean Islands, Haiti is in a virtual state of anarchy and it would not be surprising to one day learn that Cuban agents had finally restored order and discipline—Castro style—to the unhappy people who live there. As a New York Times editorial put it: "The discouraging news from Haiti—unrest in the cities and a slide toward anarchy in the countryside—casts doubt on the hopes excited by the fall of the house of

Duvalier. But the country's sizable problems still would be manageable if there were someone managing. Sadly, there isn't." (N.Y. Times, July 27, 1986, p. A-34)

On July 29 the opposition People's National Party (PNP) of pro-Soviet former Prime Minister Michael Manley appeared headed for a big win in municipal elections. The state-owned Jamaica Broadcasting Corp. and the independent Radio Jamaica put the PNP ahead of the ruling Jamaica Labor Party (JLP) in 12 of the 13 local districts. The elections were seen as a major test of Prime Minister Edward Seaga's pro-Washington economic and foreign policies.

The Meaning of the Soviet Caribbean Penetration

The Caribbean area is of special importance in the defense of the United States. Preventing the positioning of military forces or offensive weapon systems so as to threaten the security of the Panama Canal is of vital interest to the U.S. The military linkage which the USSR has established from its European bases across the North Atlantic to its Western anchor in Cuba is a daring strategic masterpiece. The Soviet SLOCs (sea line of communication) to Cuba cut across the U.S. SLOC from North America to NATO Europe and the North-South SLOC from Western Europe to the Persian Gulf via the southern tip of Africa. The powerful and sophisticated Soviet military facilities in Cuba greatly enhance the capabilities and staying power of the Soviet naval forces, including submarines criss-crossing the Atlantic Ocean.

Soviet exploitation of Castro's triumph in Cuba has been of enormous strategic value to Moscow. The Soviets have made Cuba into one of the most useful military and intelligence bases in the world. They have deployed a Soviet Army Brigade there to train Cuban expeditionary forces for deployment in Africa, the Middle East, and Central America.

A 1985 joint State Department Defense Department analysis summed up the situation succinctly:

> The Soviet Union sees in the region an excellent and low-cost opportunity to preoccupy the United States—the "main adversary" of Soviet strategy—thus gaining greater global freedom of action for the USSR. While the Soviets are not likely to mount a direct military challenge to the United States in the Caribbean Basin, they are attempting to foment as much unrest as possible in an area that is the strategic crossroads of the Western Hemisphere. Working through its key proxy in the region, Cuba, the Soviet Union hopes to force the United States to divert attention and military resources to an area that has not been a serious security concern to the United States in the past.[62]

The fundamental goal of the Soviet Union in this area is to promote the destabilitation of the United States. The possible breakdowm of the Mexican political, economic and social structure might well be exploited by the Soviets via Central America. If Mexico explodes into chaos the U.S. might face an unmanageable problem on its southern border. The Soviet-Cuban intrusion into the Caribbean Basin is an intrinsic part of Soviet global strategy. Cuba has frequently been the cutting edge of this unfolding strategy. With the Soviet penetration into the Caribbean, an operational link has been placed between the Northern (European) and Southern (African) sectors of the Soviet Atlantic Flank.

The Southern Sector

Soviet naval expansion along the coast of West Africa aims toward the achievement of a position by which the Soviet Union could exert control, if necessary, over the southern Cape sea route to the Indian Ocean. Southern Africa, the major free world source of strategic minerals indispensable to the functioning of a modern industrial society, may be the ultimate target area which links Soviet strategies for the Persian Gulf and Western Europe. Control of both the communication routes around the Cape and of strategic mineral supplies may well be at stake. The spread of Soviet influence coupled with the diplomatic isolation of South Africa could severely handicap U.S. naval deployments from Norfolk, its principal Atlantic base, into the Indian Ocean.

The Soviets have equipped many clients around the periphery of Africa with modern MIG jets, to an extent possibly obviating the need for Soviet deployment of aircraft carriers around the littoral of Western Africa. The Soviet Union is strengthening relationships with several governments along the west coast of Africa and is developing a naval off-shore capability from which friends might be protected or hostile governments toppled.

Africa was not an important sector in Soviet global strategy until the 1967 Arab-Israeli War demonstrated how easily the Suez Canal could be closed. Soviet planners then decided to establish an alternate SLOC from European Russia to Vladivostok around the southern tip of Africa. Although the newly independent states in Western Africa were vulnerable to Soviet penetration, it took many years for the Soviets to operate successfully in the African milieu. An initial Soviet thrust into the Belgian Congo (soon to be Zaire) followed the 1960 rebellion against Belgian rule. This intrusion was short-lived and remembered mainly because of the establishment of the Patrice Lumumba University in Moscow for the training of black Soviet agents in Africa.

In the mid-1970s three factors changed the pace and level of Soviet efforts in Africa: an across-the-board build-up of Soviet military power; the collapse of the Portuguese Empire; and the ending of the American involvement in the Vietnam War. The Soviet Union has achieved entry into many ports in Western Africa at a time when the United States and Western Europe have reduced access. Thus, an imbalance of naval presence has developed in a region where the SLOCs are more important to the West than to the Soviet Union. In its operations on the Coast of Africa, the Soviet

Union appears to have effected a division of labor with the Cubans and East European allies; the Soviet Union deploys naval forces and fishing fleets in the region, while military and intelligence operations are left primarily to its Cuban and East German surrogates. "East Germany's African policy is an extension of Soviet foreign policy."[63] Along the west coast of Africa, the Soviet Union, frequently assisted by its Cuban front-line forces, has attempted to gain access to naval or air facilities. In West Africa Soviet presence has been evident in the Cape Verde Islands, and intermittent in Ghana, Guinea, Equatorial Guinea, Guinea Bissau and, most significantly, in Angola.

Ghana was clearly in the Soviet camp as long as Nkrumah was in power. After his 1966 ouster, Ghana began to move toward the West. On December 31, 1981, First Lt. Jerry Rawlings took power in a coup. Libya's Qaddafi immediately began to support the almost illiterate Ghanaian leader. Rawlings is disliked and the country is economically in ruins, but there is no well organized opposition to Rawling's erratic and oppressive rule. Qaddafi will, it seems, maintain influence in Ghana, and help pave the way for a Soviet return.

Meanwhile other Soviet ties with Ghana are being developed. Hundreds of Ghanaians have been sent to Libya to work in the oil and petroleum industry. Ghanaian students have been sent to Libyan colleges to study Arabic. Likewise, with the Soviet return, scholarships have been awarded to over 150 Ghanaian students to study in the Soviet Union. The Soviets have promised economic assistance and continue to run a propaganda campaign from their embassy. Some two hundred and fifty Cuban soldiers provide training, intelligence and Rawling's personal security guards.[64] Paradoxically, despite Ghana's pro-Soviet orientation, what little economic progress has been made in a country that was once the jewel of the West African coast has been made possible by Western (IMF) credits.[65]

In 1976 Guinea Bissau agreed to a union with the Cape Verde Islands, 400 miles off the African coast. The Soviet Union has displayed a keen interest in the Cape Verde Islands, which have an important port and naval base on Mindelo and an international airport on Sal capable of handling large jets.[66] The importance of the Cape Verde Islands for the protection of the trade routes around the Cape to Europe has long been recognized. In the former Portuguese colony of Guinea-Bissau, the ruling Africa Party for the Independence of Guinea and the Cape Verde Island (PAIFF) is under Soviet influence.

President Sékou Touré maintained a Marxist regime in Guinea since 1958 until his death in 1984. His regime has been referred to as "black Stalinism." Soviet arms transfers to Guinea in 1969–70 made possible the establishment of base rights, both for Soviet air and sea operations in the Atlantic Ocean. In 1975 Soviet air patrols began flying regularly over the Gulf of Guinea and the Southeast Atlantic. Guinea accumulated a sizable inventory of Soviet weaponry in the process, including tanks, armored personnel carriers, aircraft and patrol boats. Following Touré's death a military junta seized power and vowed to promote free enterprise and respect human rights.

A coup against Touré's successor, Brig. Gen. Conté, was attempted by Col. Diara Traoré in early July 1985 but failed. Traoré and his fellow conspirators were shot.

> In the Touré years Colonel Traoré, who is now 50 years old, spent nearly a decade in the Soviet Union as a trainee officer and then as Guinean military attaché. He was General Conté's associate in a military coup in April 1984, a week after Mr. Touré died in the United States following surgery.[67]

Since 1974 Soviet influence also developed in Benin (formerly Dahomey), and the state apparatus there has been structured along Soviet lines.

Equatorial Guinea had been largely under Soviet influence when President Nguema Biyoto Masie was in power. Soviet vessels fished the rich waters in the Gulf of Guinea; Soviet naval combatants have made port calls since 1970, and Russian personnel were quartered at the port city of Luba (used for fishing, the rotation of personnel to Angola, and as a spying and communication facility for Soviet operations in West Africa). In addition, the Soviets still have access to the port of Fernando. In 1975, President Masie allowed Soviet transport planes to stop over during the airlift to Angola, but since the August 1979 coup against Masie, the ruling Obiang junta annulled the fishing agreement with Moscow and Equatorial Guinea appears to be moving closer to the West.

During the 1966–69 Nigerian Civil War, the Soviet Union ignored the principles of "wars of national liberation" and supported the federal position against the Biafran seccessionists. Maladroit Soviet diplomacy reduced the political gain this military assistance should have rendered, and while there have been economic technicians in Nigeria from East European nations, there have been no military advisors. Despite the December 1983 military coup against an elected leader, Nigeria leans toward the West.

The Nigerian economy has been faltering over the past several years due to the decline in world oil prices. On April 15, 1985, the Nigerian government ordered 700,000 aliens to leave the country within two weeks. Two years ago Nigeria drove out about two million people in a chaotic exodus. Most of the aliens are from Ghana, Niger, Chad, and Cameroon. They came to Nigeria to escape the drought and to find work.

The Nigerian military regime which seized power in Africa's most populous country at the end of 1983 has sought to end widespread corruption.

> Nigeria closed the borders with its four neighbors—Benin, Niger, Chad and Cameroon—in April 1984 when a new currency was introduced as part of the campaign against corruption.
> A primary objective was to render worthless the large sums of the old currency believed to have been smuggled out to escape taxes. . . .

Military tribunals have convicted former government officials of corruption and
sentenced several to prison terms of more than 20 years.[68]

As of 1986, because of maldroit diplomacy, the Soviets have not been
able to exploit Nigeria's domestic difficulties.

Southern Africa: The Conflict Zone

The deep political, ideological differences between South Africa and the
neighboring black states make these countries a natural target for Soviet
penetration and support. The root of the antagonism lies in South Africa's
domestic policies which are detested by the black states as well as by the
international community as a whole.

South Africa has become a target of its neighbors with pro-Marxist
forces in the forefront. South Africa's fear is that a belt of Soviet-backed
Marxist states stretching from the Atlantic to the Indian Ocean could be
formed thus presenting a grave threat to the survival of the country.

The Namibian conflict is another major issue and, for neighboring Angola, it is of more immediate concern than the South African apartheid. The
black states are committed to end South Africa's control of Namibia and to
support the South West African People's Organization (SWAPO), as they
have dedicated themselves to the "struggle against apartheid" through
support of the South African liberation movement, The African National
Congress.

Because the sea lanes around South Africa constitute the West's main oil
artery and because southern Africa as a whole is the major storehouse of
strategic minerals in the non-communist world, the destruction of the
existing balance between South Africa and its neighbors could have a
disastrous impact on the global strategic equation. Let us now turn to the
key countries in southern Africa.

Angola

The major Soviet gain along the Western littoral of Africa came when
they decided to move into Angola in 1975. Soviet intervention (with massive arms shipments) in the civil war in Angola gained Moscow a series of
naval/air strong points along the west coast of Africa. The Soviet stronghold in Angola is even more advantageous than prior Soviet military access
to Nigeria—including Soviet use of Lagos for the ships of its South Atlantic
squadron. The Angolan crisis of 1975 gave the Soviet Union a windfall
which they exploited decisively. By utilizing a Cuban expeditionary force,
the Soviet Union imposed a Marxist-Leninist regime on Angola. Thus,
they obtained a base for operations into Zaire, Rhodesia (Zimbabwe),
Namibia, and, ultimately, against South Africa.

The Soviet Union assisted Agustino Neto's MPLA victory over UNITA in Angola, and by 1978 there were Soviet advisors in Angola along with some 19,000 Cuban military personnel.[69] The MPLA government has received Soviet military aid, including T-34 and T-54 tanks, large numbers of PT-76 amphibious light tanks and armored personnel carriers, MIG-15 and MIG-21 fighter bombers, and various other weapons. The ports of Luanda and Libito are both available to the USSR. Moscow signed a 20-year Treaty of Friendship and Cooperation with Angola in October 1976.

Angola also serves as a staging area for the Southwest African People's Organization (SWAPO) raids into Namibia. Since South Africa deployed troops in Northern Namibia in the mid-1970s, the SWAPO guerrillas have received increasing support from the Soviet Union, much of it channeled through Angola. In early September 1981, South Africa conducted a large-scale raid against MPLA, Cuban and SWAPO forces in Southern Angola. They killed several Soviet officers, captured one and seized thousands of tons of newly delivered Soviet military equipment estimated to be worth 200 million dollars. In Angola, the Soviets and Cubans provide support for combat operations against the rival liberation movement UNITA (National Union for the Total Independence of Angola). The East Germans also provide advisors.

Subsequent developments since 1975 have not been altogether favorable to the Soviet Union. By 1980, the Soviet-supported MPLA was badly split since its leader, Neto, died in Moscow. He was succeeded by Eduardo dos Santos, who has visited the GDR and Czechoslavakia and is firmly tied to Moscow. The disastrous state of Angolan economy has been reported by David Lamb of the Los Angeles Times who visited Luanda in 1981.

Angola is a fragile and wounded country in a state of utter deterioration . . . A 2,600 mile trip through four provinces produced little evidence of anything save decay and stagnation, incompetence and inefficiency.[70]

The Cuban mercenaries in Angola are losing control of considerable parts of the countryside to UNITA. As of 1986, the Angolan resistance under the direction of UNITA and the leadership of Dr. Jonas Savimbi continued to gain in the struggle for independence from the Cuban invaders. UNITA governs a territory containing three million people—more than half of Angola's population. According to Dr. Savimbi, there are 35,000 Cuban soldiers, 3,500 East German soldiers, and 3,000 Soviet "advisors" in Angola. Despite their military power, UNITA is in control of the southern and eastern portions of the country, and its power is growing.

In regard to Namibia, Dr. Savimbi favors independence for Namibia from South Africa, but he stresses that a stable and democratic structure will be impossible in Namibia so long as Cuban, Soviet and East German forces are in Angola on the northern border of Namibia. They will foster revolution and violence through SWAPO (South West Africa People's Organization), a Marxist organization which uses Angolan territory as a base for terrorist attacks in Namibia.[71]

Although the U.S. backs the contras fighting the Sandinistas in Nicaragua and the Afghan freedom fighters fighting the Soviet forces in Afghanistan, it refused for years to back Savimbi in Angola or even to contact him. In December, 1985, however, the U.S. government endorsed covert military aid to support Savimbi's forces.[72]

While the U.S. is exploring ways of improving our relationship with Angola and seeking to bring about circumstances that will make possible agreement on Namibian independence, the stumbling block is the continued presence of Cuban troops in Angola.

> The Cuban troop issue is not an issue we made up; it is an objective reality at the core of the question of regional security. The South Africans, whose concurrence and cooperation must be secured for any agreement leading to Namibian independence, have repeatedly made clear that they regard the Cuban troop issue as fundamental to their security concerns. Quite apart from that, the United States, as Vice President Bush said in Nairobi on November 19, 1982, "is not ashamed to state the U.S. interest in seeing an end to the presence of Cuban forces in Angola," just as we seek internationally recognized independence for Namibia. Such an outcome would contribute to both regional security and a global climate of restraint.[73]

Unfortunately, this policy has no chance of success. The Cubans are the praetorian guards of the Angola government. If they departed, President dos Santos and his mullato colleagues would soon be dead. Nowhere is there a better opportunity for rolling back the advance of communism than in Angola. Savimbi has the will and the manpower to win, only U.S. recognition and aircraft are needed. Such open aid may come eventually.

Zimbabwe

In 1980, after years of civil war in Rhodesia, Robert Mugabe was elected as the second Prime Minister of a key country in Southern Africa now known as Zimbabwe. In applying sanctions in the 1960s, the West did not, at first, inhibit Rhodesia's economy. It did, however, make the country into a kind of international outcast, and its policies encouraged Rhodesian black radicals to launch a terrorist war against Ian Smith's government, after the fall of Angola and Mozambique, to Communist domination.

The so-called Front Line States (FLS)—Angola, Botswana, Mozambique, Tanzania, and Zambia—also played a role in promoting the eventual triumph of Mugabe in Zimbabwe. Only Botswana, Mozambique, and Zambia were actually "front-line" on Zimbabwe. The FLS, former white-ruled colonies (now ruled by black Africans), have all played and continue to play an important role in the struggle against the remaining white-rule in Africa. With the partial exception of Tanzania, all are one-party states where Western ideas and institutions of political and personal liberties quickly disappeared after independence. All of them have special relations with the Soviet Union, Cuba and East Germany. Their economies have progressively deteriorated since independence.

During the long insurgency campaign against Ian Smith, and subsequently against Muzorewa, Mugabe's Zimbabwe African National Union (ZANU) operated from Mozambique. Joshua Nkomo's Zimbabwe's People's Revolutionary Army (ZIPRA) operated from Zambia. Mugabe is a member of the Mashona tribe which comprises over 80% of Zimbabwe's population. Nkomo is a member of the Matabele tribe, whose members number less than 15% of the population. During the struggle for independence, differences of opinion in the Patriotic Front sometimes led to fighting between the Nkomo and Mugabe factions. In February 1981, Prime Minister Mugabe ordered his former foes, the white-led regular army and air force, to smash guerrillas loyal to Nkomo, his former coalition partner.

On February 21, 1981, the government of Mugabe finally agreed to establish diplomatic relations with the Soviet Union. The price the Soviets paid was to cut all ties with the minority Patriotic Front Party of Nkomo, the organization that Moscow heavily supported during the seven-year guerrilla war for black-majority rule.

As a clever, pragmatic politician, Mugabe is avoiding abrupt moves to break Zimbabwe's cumbersome economic dependence on South Africa. His policies of nationalization are driving many of the whites out of Zimbabwe. Despite his pragmatism, Mugabe's long-term intentions may indeed be the creation of a Marxist-Leninist state.

In the area of international relations, Mugabe envisages an "alliance between the fighting peoples of Zimbabwe and the socialist countries." The six bilateral trade agreements that have been signed by Zimbabwe since independence have all been with Soviet bloc, Communist, or Socialist regimes: Bulgaria, the GDR, North Korea, Mozambique, and Ethiopia. In public statements, Mugabe has also firmly aligned himself with the pro-Soviet Polisario movement, the PLO, SWAPO, and the officially banned African National Congress. He did not condemn the Soviet Union for shooting down the KAL airliner, although he attacked the U.S. for invading Grenada. Mugabe has also brought some 200 North Koreans into the country to train his army. After Sékou Touré died, Mugabe described him as a "loss to the entire African continent."

The prospects for political stability and economic progress in Southern Africa will be profoundly influenced by Mugabe's efforts to achieve a harmonious multi-racial society in Zimbabwe. Few people familiar with Southern Africa believe that such a goal is Mugabe's real aim. If most of the whites depart, Zimbabwe is likely to decline economically, but because its infrastructure is in good shape, it may not reach the disaster level of, say, Angola, or, even worse, Mozambique.

The Mugabe government faces dissension, unrest, and violence particularly in Matabeleland, stronghold of Joshua Nkomo. Nkomo, Mugabe's former ally in the Patriotic Front, was sacked from the cabinet by the Prime Minister. This has caused considerable dissatisfaction among Nkomo's followers, who also bear a grudge against Mugabe for persecuting Nkomo's supporters.

The upshot has been a spate of violence reminiscent of the days of the Rhodesian bush war against Ian Smith. Violent incidents occur regularly, the main perpetrators being former Zipra fighters loyal to Nkomo. Zimbabwe's infant national army has also been plagued by these divisions, as reflected in a high number of politically-inspired desertions. Nkomo's Zapu, it should be added, is still a legal political party, but Mugabe has made plain his intention of introducing a one-party system in the foreseeable future. Unless Mugabe and Nkomo reach some reconciliation, the prospects for stability in Zimbabwe are uncertain.

On July 6, 1985, following his party's landslide victory in Zimbabwe's first general election since independence, Prime Minister Robert Mugabe moved quickly toward a socialist, one party state. He served notice to whites that those opposed to his policies would have to leave the country and suggested a further crackdown on the African People's Union led by his long-standing rival, Joshua Nkomo. He may further fan hostilities between his government and Nkomo, leading to more violence.[74]

There is a danger for Zambia if armed conflict develops in Zimbabwe. Zambia's rail line, e.g., runs through Zimbabwe to the East African coast. Increasing upheaval in Zambia could only enhance the Soviets' opportunities to exploit chaos to strategic advantage in Southern Africa. In December 1985 on a visit to Moscow, Zimbabwean Prime Minister Robert Mugabe signed his country's first economic and technological cooperation agreement with the Soviets. While the two countries stopped short of outright military aid, following the meeting Mugabe said they had "looked at our own military capability and how we can strengthen ourselves against the threat from South Africa."[75]

Namibia

Toward the end of the 19th century a colony was established by Imperial Germany on the southwest coast of Africa. After World War I, administration of this area was transferred to neighboring South Africa under a League of Nations mandate. In 1966, this mandate was revoked by the United Nations with U.S. support, although no specific determination of the UN as the successor of the League of Nations exists. South Africa has refused to accept this decision. The conflict over independence for the people of Namibia, and the transition to majority rule, has become more intense in recent years, with increasing clashes between South African forces and SWAPO guerrillas.

SWAPO originated in the Owamboland People's Congress in the late 1950s. Sam Nujoma joined this group in 1959 and by 1960 had formed the SouthWest African People's Organization, or SWAPO. The name SWAPO was selected to attract a broad base of support. Most of SWAPO's adherents come from Owamboland. Owamboland, enjoying adequate rain-fall, is separated from the rest of Namibia by several hundred miles of desert. A substantial rift in SWAPO developed in the early 1970s between many members of the organization and Nujoma. Many of those fighting in South-West Africa charged Nujoma and his leadership group residing in Lusaka, Zambia, with corruption, nepotism, and incompetence.

In spring of 1977, the five Western members of the UN Security Council, the United States, Britain, West Germany, France, and Canada (the so-called "contact group") launched an unprecedented joint effort to resolve the Namibia problem peacefully. Discussions began between representatives of the "contact group," South Africa, and SWAPO. Throughout the discussions, the Western Five kept all Namibian political groups informed of significant developments in the talks. The neighboring African states of Zambia, Mozambique, Angola, Tanzania, and Botswana as well as others in Africa, were deeply involved by the Western "contact group" in each stage of the negotiating process.

South Africa cooperated in this process and by mid-1978 the negotiations produced an agreement between South Africa and SWAPO to cease hostilities and to proceed with a prompt transition to independence and majority rule through UN supervised elections. Subsequently, the UN Security Council endorsed this agreement and launched the process for establishing international peacekeeping and supervision during the critical transition period to Namibian independence.

In early January 1981, a conference was convened in Geneva that brought the contending factions in Southwest Africa together for the first time. The agreement they were to approve called for a cease-fire, to be followed by the phasing out of most South African forces and the phasing in of a United Nations peacekeeping force that would be stationed mainly in a demilitarized zone on both sides of the territory's northern border with Angola, an area of guerrilla struggle. Then, under international supervision, there would be an election for a constituent assembly.

At the Geneva Conference, there were representatives of the political parties that had combined to form the Democratic Turnhalle Alliance—a multiracial grouping opposed to SWAPO. Sam Nujoma headed the SWAPO delegation. The Geneva Conference failed to achieve accord on the agreement. The Western and African participants at the Conference had promised the Turnhalle group that the United Nations would stop providing funds for various nonmilitary programs for the insurgents and that the equal status of the parties in the territory would be confirmed in a General Assembly resolution that would have the effect of annulling the Assembly's seven-year old endorsement of SWAPO as the "sole and authentic" people of Namibia. This never happened. The Reagan Administration proposed in June 1981, that a comprehensive settlement over Namibia would require the withdrawal of Cuban troops from Angola. Initially cited as a precondition for U.S. recognition of Luanda, the presence of Cuban troops subsequently became a U.S. and South African item of negotiation over Namibia. South Africa has frequently reaffirmed its backing for a negotiated settlement along the lines of the 1978 United Nations plan, augmented by a set of constitutional principles that all parties would be asked to endorse in advance of elections for a constituent assembly.

The constitutional principles were meant to serve as "confidence-building measures" for the South Africans, who want to make sure that the rights of the 100,000 whites in the Namibian population of one million will be protected, and that a dictatorship by the South West African People's organization is ruled out.

American, South African, and Angolan negotiators continued to meet and by early June 1983 announced that an accord over Namibia might be forthcoming. The Angolan refusal to negotiate the Cuban presence apparently subsided.

Towards the end of August 1983, UN Secretary General Javier Perez de Cuellar visited southern Africa in an attempt to end the stalemate over Namibian independence. His visit included Capetown, Windhoek, and Luanda. He sought to visit Windhoek to prove that the UN is not blindly committed to SWAPO. Mr. Perez conceded that his five-day mission "had not been a success."

In February 1984, South Africa concluded security pacts with both Angola and Mozambique, which were sharply condemned by the Organization of African Unity (OAU).

Presumably, the Security Pact with Angola will lead to the disengagement of South African forces from Southeast Angola. Coincidentally, South Africa authorities have announced a major infiltration of SWAPO insurgents into Namibia. It is possible that SWAPO is seeking to strengthen its position in Namibia in case a truce in Southern Angola leads to a settlement in Southwest Africa.

In Southwest Africa, the avowed United States plan is to seek a settlement in tandem with a withdrawal of Cuban troops from Angola. According to Western diplomats, the intention is to use the withdrawal of South African troops from southern Angola—which they have been occupying for over two years—to press Angola's Marxist leadership for a statement that a Cuban presence is no longer justified.

This would bring closer United States recognition of the Angolan Government—withheld because of the Cuban presence—and would facilitate United Nations plans for elections and the creation of an independent Namibia.[76] In the spring of 1985, South Africa again set up a local government in Windhoek, but one lacking power in foreign policy and in security matters.

On June 30, 1985 South African forces again battled SWAPO rebels in Angola.

General Meiring, commander of the South-West Africa Territory Force, said Angola and the South-West Africa People's Organization had been warned repeatedly that

South Africa would resume raids across the border if the guerrilla group "continues to
sow death and destruction among the civilians of South-West Africa."[77]

The prospects of a peaceful settlement in Southwest Africa (Namibia)
are slim as long as the United Nations holds SWAPO to be the "sole
representative of the people of Southwest Africa." This position is the core
of the problem. The West tends to overlook the strong Soviet support of
SWAPO, and the fact that Cuban troops in Angola enable SWAPO to have
bases in that country. There were some indications following the 1984
South African moves toward Angola that Cuba was considering the withdrawal of its troops from that country. Yet the conditions that Castro has
imposed for such a withdrawal will most likely be unacceptable to South
Africa so that peace in Southwest Africa remains, at best, a distant prospect.

Mozambique

Although Mozambique fronts on the Indian Ocean rather than on the
Atlantic, it is included within the southern Africa conflict zone since it is
the last link in the encirclement belt of South Africa which the Soviet Union
is seeking to create.

The independence of Mozambique in 1975, the Soviet-Cuban imposition
of a Marxist-oriented regime in Angola in 1975 and the French expulsion
from Diego Suarez in Madagascar by 1975 brought the Soviet Union access
to key port facilities along both the West and East African approaches to
the Cape of Good Hope.

In March 1977, the Soviets signed a Friendship Treaty with Mozambique. Maputo, the capitol, is now available to Soviet warships, as is
Nacala, the best deep water port in East Africa. Nacala is believed to be
defended by Soviet-supplied anti-aircraft guns and surface-to-air missiles.

In Mozambique, the Portuguese handed the reins of power to Frelimo, a
communist party, without any test of political opinion. Since then, the
government of President Samora Machel had been trying to transform
Mozambican society into the Marxist-Socialist mold.

This has led to major dislocations due to the exodus of several thousand
skilled Portuguese. Given the repressive nature of the Frelimo regime,
opposition was bound to find extra-constitutional expression, the main
vehicle being the Mozambique National Resistance guerrilla movement.
Over the last few years, the MNR has been waging a guerilla war against
Frelimo in many parts of Mozambique.

The Mozambique National Resistance, which has been pro-American
and anti-Soviet has been increasingly successful. Yet, the State Department decided to give $40 million U.S. tax dollars to prop up the failing
Marxist-Leninist dictatorship of the Soviet puppet Samora Machel in Mozambique, and to aid his Communist troops. The Christian Science
Monitor reported on January 14, 1985:

In what one official calls a major change in policy, "The Reagan Administration will soon seek Congressional approval for military aid to Mozambique . . . We won't replace the Soviets," notes Robert Gelbard of the State Department's Office of Southern African Affairs. "But we hope to encourage a policy of real nonalignment."

It is expected that the aid will help Mozambique, a Marxist state, fight a rebel movement known as the Mozambique National Resistance (MNR) . . .

In 1984, the MNR—which has about 12,000 fighters, according to intelligence estimates—was in every province and contributed to disruption to the nation's fragile economy . . .

What justified this aid to a Marxist regime with a worsening human rights record? It would seem that the timing correlates closely to the signing of the Nkomati agreement vigorously promoted by the State Department. This agreement establishes a qualified detente between South Africa and Mozambique. Conditions are that Mozambique will no longer permit ANC bases and that South Africa will discontinue support of the MNR. The State Department has also claimed that Machel is also moving away from the Soviet Union.

There is incredible naivete in the present U.S. policy toward Mozambique. In testimony before Congress, Mr. Crocker made the following statement:

This administration took office just as the United States' relations with Mozambique reached a low-water mark. Communication with the Mozambican government was practically non-existent, that country's policies seemed unalterably aligned with those of the Soviet Union and its satrapies, its perceptions warped by hostile disinformation. But the utter incapacity of Marxist economics to cope with the problems of a developing country, and the conspicuous inability of the Soviet Union to assist Mozambique with security and political problems stemming from its isolation, led to indications that the Mozambican government wished to reestablish communications with the United States. We responded by making clear that we were interested in a positive relationship . . . We believe that a solid basis now exists for a meaningful improvement in relations between us.[78]

Unless such illusions in current U.S. policy toward Zimbabwe and Mozambique are corrected, U.S. policy will continue to make southern Africa safe for Marxism. A fundamental shift in policy toward Mozambique is key to this situation. U.S. political and diplomatic support for the MNR would not only promote a quick end to the Marxist dictatorship in Mozambique, it could also establish a government in Maputo that would prevent Mugabe in Zimbabwe from moving to a total Marxist dictatorship. The anti-Soviet MNR has spread the war through all of Mozambique's 10 provinces.

On February 11, 1985, President Reagan, at the urgings of the State Department, signed an agreement to provide a further $40 million to Mozambique in aid and, in addition, to provide its soldiers with U.S. military equipment and training.

Toward the close of 1985, Joaquim Chissano, foreign minister of Mozambique, met with Soviet leader Mikhail Gorbachev to discuss "further development" based on a treaty of friendship and cooperation between Moscow and Maputo. Samora Machel's government is mired in a guerrilla war with the Mozambique National Resistance. Without a coherent ideological program and unable to penetrate the country's major towns, the guerrillas have contented themselves with blowing up power lines and blocking roads. In August, Machel's North Korean-trained troops succeeded in overrunning a major resistance base in the foothills of Gorongosa Mountain in central Sofala Province. Despite this, the conflict remains a "no-win situation," according to one regional military expert, with neither side likely to gain the upper hand without substantial outside support.[79]

Ironically, in Mozambique the U.S. and the Soviet Union appear to be backing the same side.

On October 19, 1986 President Samora Machel of Mozambique died in a plane crash inside the border of South Africa en route from Zimbabwe to Mozambique. According to documents found in the wreckage of the plane he, along with Muggabe and Soviet and Cuban officials had been plotting a coup against Malawi's President Banda, whom Machel called a criminal for harboring rebels of the Mozambican National Resistance. Machel's successor, former foreign minister Joaquim Chissano dos Santos, was hand picked by Marcelin. dos Santos, Moscow's hard-line man in Maputo. While posing as a moderate to obtain more U.S. dollars he will pursue policies hostile toward the West and helpful to Soviet goals in Southern Africa.

The Deepening Crisis in South Africa

During the first half of 1986 the complex racial crisis in the Republic of South Africa grew progressively worse. Black resistance to the oppressive apartheid regime became increasingly more violent. In order to quell the violence the South African government issued a set of tough emergency decrees. Under the surface of a strained calm there is an intense struggle of blacks against whites, whites against whites, blacks against blacks and with coloreds and East Indians also caught up in a melee of racial antagonism. The split in the white community (some 15% of the population) widens the gap between the hard-line Afrikaners and the more liberal people of English descent; The Zulus, the largest black tribe, are often at odds with other black tribes whom they once dominated. The two million Coloreds and the one million East Indians have recently been given a chance to participate in a Rube-Goldberg kind of a parliament. The blacks are excluded from any form of participation in the South African political process. Time is running out for a negotiated settlement which will open a door toward some form of black political participation.

Many liberal observers of the South African scene believe that only "a one man—one vote" solution will prevent an impending disaster. These proponents of a "quick and dirty" solution overlook the historical fact that it took all Western democracies, including the United States, many years to move from a limited to a full political franchise. Full voting rights now for all qualified blacks is a better answer. Unless some such process is reached for political participation for educated blacks, the bitter struggle in South Africa could end in bloody chaos. According to John B. Oakes, former Senior Editor of the New York Times, "The Reagan-Thatcher temporizing on sanctions paves the way for the ultimate collapse of white control in a tragically unnecessary debacle of blood bitterness and chaos." (N.Y. Times, op-ed July 18, 1986) Oakes continued: "This government will not yield control until it is beaten to its knees", says a prominent white churchman, "The crisis may not come soon but when it comes a catastrophe will take place. Our country will be totally ruined but we whites need this as a catharsis to change our minds from thinking in terms of race and color. Instead of white Europeans, we have to become white Africans, working along side the blacks—not over them—to create a new country from the ruins." More than likely a black totalitarian, pro-Soviet regime will be established upon the ruins. After all the Soviet Union is entrenched in Angola, retains a strong hand on Mozambique, is backing SWAPO to the hilt in Namibia, is closely aligned with Mugabe's tight one-party rule in Zimbabwe and fully backs the African National Congress. If disaster in South Africa results in an enhanced Soviet role in all of Southern Africa the global balance of power could shift in favor of Moscow.

On July 10, 1986 the Heritage Foundation commented on a May 1986 secret document of the South African Communist Party Politburo, first captured by South African authorities.

> The document not only reveals the close links between the ANC and the communists and the way in which the communists exploit the ANC to manipulate Western opinion, but it also echoes the success that Communist Parties have had in the past in Czechoslovakia, Poland, Vietnam, Nicaragua, and elsewhere in fooling the West by hiding behind the respectable front of "genuine" reformist national liberation movements.

> The document points out that no longer is the Communist Party-ANC alliance viewed merely as an "agitational opposition"; instead, it is seen increasingly as "the immediate alternative power." Because of this change—and specifically, the increased visibility of the ANC—the Party has felt it necessary to reassure its membership that it still controls what it calls the revolution in South Africa.

> While the ANC's own literature claims as its ultimate goal a "national democratic revolution," the secret communist document rejects this thesis. Instead, the national democratic revolution is described as "a stage towards the struggle for social emancipation in the epoch of the world transition from capitalism to socialism and within the context of the struggle against imperialsim."

> The document discusses the breakdown of consensus among the white ruling elite, noting that "there appears to be a proliferation of new groupings which consider themselves to be a part of the forces for change." The Communist Party is willing to use these groups for what they can offer, and then cast them aside. This, of course, is what communist parties have done in a dozen other countries since 1945.

> The Politburo study states candidly its view of these liberal South African reformers: "Let us be clear. The 'liberal' bourgeoisie seek transformations of the South African society which go beyond the reform limits of the present regime but which aim to

preempt the objectives of the revolutionary forces. . . . They seek transformation through negotiation and not the kind of conflict which would culminate in a revolutionary seizure of power."

Though it is essential for the liberation front to be seen by the international community as sincere in its desire for peaceful change, this must not divert attention from the main goal: "Nor must a genuine desire to project a public image of 'reasonableness' tempt us to paddle softly on the true nature of the liberation alliance and its revolutionary socioeconomic objectives. . . . The main thrust of our present strategy remains a revolutionary seizure of power." The talks which so far have taken place between the ANC and reformist elements in South Africa therefore are only tactics in a much broader strategy.

On July 22, 1986 President Reagan delivered a long-awaited speech on "Policy toward South Africa." In this speech the President condemned apartheid four separate times , condemned the emergency laws promulgated by Botha, asked for a timetable for the elimination of apartheid laws, called for the release of political prisoners, for the release of Nelson Mandela, and for "unbanning" black political movements.

The President, however, rejected the immediate use of sanctions. Liberals in the Congress were outraged. Senator Kennedy said that "Mr. Reagan doesn't speak for the American people." Bishop Desmond Tutu, winner of the Nobel Peace Prize, stated, "President Reagan is the pits as far as blacks are concerned. . . . He sits there like the great, big white chief of old. . . . I am so angry . . . I found it quite nauseating. I think the West, for my part, can go to hell."

The fact that sanctions have been ineffectual everywhere they have been tried as an instrument of foreign policy is overlooked by those who advocate this approach to coping with South Africa's complex problems.

Some people living within South Africa take a more balanced view; One such person is Roley Arenstein an avowed white communist, recently released from detention. He said that the outlawed African National Congress was wrong to seek change through guerrilla warfare and through the demand for the immediate socialization of the economy. Rather, Arenstein said it is only a matter of time before apartheid disappears contending that the prophecy would be hastened by organization of labor and political opposition rather than by guerrilla warfare. (New York Times April 14, 1986, A-2)

The powerful Zulu tribe also seeks a middle grouping in the present struggle. The Zulu Chief, Mangosuthu Gatsha Buthelezi says he is ready to contemplate some sort of political federation that will take into account whites' concern about their survival under black rule; the African National Congress seeks a unitary state ruled by the majority. Chief Buthelezi has criticized congress leaders, once his allies, for purportedly sending young blacks to die as cannon fodder. (New York Times July 13, 1986, p-12)

Helen Suzman, a long-time fighter against apartheid and a member for many years of the opposition in South Africa's Parliament, wrote a persuasive article in the August 1st, 1986 New York Times Magazine making a powerful case against sanctions, "Sanctions against Pretoria Would Hurt Blacks Most of All." The clamor for sanctions in Congress, by the Catholic bishops and liberal activists has nothing to do with rationality but alot to do with politics. Everyone wants to be on the "right" side of this emotional and vote-catching issue. The absence of objectivity with respect to the sanctions issue demonstrates how difficult it is for the American democracy to conduct a rational foreign policy in a chaotic and complex global environment.

Despite misgivings over the efficacy of economic sanctions Congress passed a Sanctions Bill over a Presidential veto. Whether this will aggravate or ameliorate the internal situation in South Africa remains to be seen.

The future of all Southern Africa is linked to what happens in the Republic of South Africa. There is no easy, immediate solution for this strife torn country. The solution must be found among the contending groups within the land itself. Let up hope that naive, simplistic Western impatience will not prevent a continued Western presence in a region so vital to the security of all free democratic nations.

In this context Max Singer writes, "The last thing the United States should be doing is to encourage or endorse the African National Congress. Those of us who are most eager to help the blacks in South Africa should be at the head of the pack fighting any attempt to persuade the Reagan Administration to flirt with such a policy. Giving aid and comfort to the ANC might not be racism, but it certainly is a sad crime against the blacks of South Africa." (N.Y. Times, July 23, 1986, op-ed, A-37)

The early November 1986, Oliver Tambo, leader of South Africa's South African Congress met with Soviet General Secretary in Moscow and obtained more arms and supplies from the Soviet Union. He informed reporters that the ANC would soon set up a mission in Moscow and expressed immense satisfaction that the Soviet Union would do everything possible to assist the ANC (Washington Times Nov. 7, 1986 p.7-A).

Despite such clear evidence of the ANC's close and warm links with Moscow, Secretary of State George Shultz invited Oliver Tambo to meet with him in his office on January 28, 1987. What diplomatic purpose was served by this meeting is beyond comprehension. It certainly was not a triumph for sagacity.

Conclusion

Many Western observers have come to believe that Soviet influence in Africa has reached its peak. They overlook the significance of Soviet geopolitical objectives and the patience with which the Soviets pursue their goals.

Despite its abortive support of revolutionary forces in the Belgian Congo (later Zaire) and in Ghana, Soviet intrusions into Western and Southern Africa did not become significant until the mid-seventies. The success of Soviet strategy in the southern sector of its Atlantic Flank has been made possible by systematic exploitation of post-colonial attitudes against the West and the complex racial conflicts rampant in Southern Africa, abetted by the guilt-ridden, hypocritical policies of many Western countries.

Moscow's strategy has been to appear as the chief supporter of the "anti-imperialist" and "anti-racist" countries in the region. The growth of the Soviet capacity to project its own forces into the area, as well as major military assistance programs, has bestowed an image of power upon Soviet representatives. The Africans respect authority, and so when the Soviets present a "show of force," as in Angola and Ethiopia, they gain respect. Accordingly, Soviets have deployed naval and air forces along the west coast of Africa to back up their policy. A Soviet West-Africa patrol has operated in the South Atlantic since 1970. This naval force could move to the waters off Southern Africa on short notice. The Soviet air and sealift capabilities permit the Kremlin to dispatch its own troops and/or those of its allies in strength into the area.

Soviet capacity to deal with Africa militarily is quite impressive. As the world's major arms producer, the Soviet Union has the capacity to supply enough arms and military advisers to Southern Africa to sustain prolonged guerrilla struggles throughout the area. Soviet military deliveries to Africa (excluding Egypt) jumped nearly fortyfold from 1972 ($55 million) to 1977 (more than $2 billion). Moscow now supplies some three-quarters of all weapons imported into Africa. In addition to these huge amounts of material supplies, numerous personnel—some 4,000 Soviet and East German "advisers"—supplement another 40,000-plus Cuban combatants scattered in various spots across the continent. The increasing flow of Soviet arms to Africa indicates its growing importance. Whereas in 1972 Africa (excluding Egypt) received a mere 5 percent of Soviet arms deliveries to non-communist developing states, by 1977 this level had increased to about 60 percent. The Soviets also employ various forms of military aid and "political assistance," they prefer to obtain influence and access covertly and by "peaceful means," rather than by overt intervention. Thus, if Soviet-backed local forces are met with armed hostility, as in the case of Angola, supporting troops will be provided indirectly from another source.

Moscow would clearly like to broaden its political bases in Africa. Soviet leader Chernenko used the occasion of a three-day March 1984 state visit to Moscow of the Ethiopian chief, Mengistu Haile Mariam to counter Western allegations that the Soviet intrusion campaign into Africa was suffering setbacks. He proclaimed continued support for Angola, Mozambique, and other "frontline" states fighting for the liberation of Southern Africa. The Soviets also denounced any proposed linkage of South-West African settlement with the withdrawal of Cuban forces from Angola.[80]

The increasingly unstable political and military situation in South Africa—the ultimate Soviet target—is, and will continue to be, crucially sensitive to the wisdom, or lack of wisdom, of the policies pursued there and to the steadfastness and patience with which they are carried out.

The Indian Ocean: Center Stage

The strategic importance of the Indian Ocean issues from the continents on its littoral and the strategic maritime choke points along its periphery. Surrounded by the Eurasian land mass, Africa, Indonesia, Australia, New Zealand, and Antarctica, the Indian Ocean serves as a staging area for powers competing for regional influence. The ocean can be sealed by the choke points along the Cape of Good Hope, the Strait of Hormuz, the Strait of Malacca, and the various passages in the Indonesian archipelago between Australia, New Zealand and Antarctica which increases the competition for control of the littoral, particularly adjacent to the above choke points.

As advancing communications have bound the countries of the world closer together, the waters between Africa, Australia and Southern Asia have become the pivotal area in the one global ocean. Many years ago Admiral Mahan wrote that, "During the 21st century, the fate of the world will be decided on the Indian Ocean." He added, "He who controls the Indian Ocean dominates Asia." These geopolitical factors underlie Soviet policies in the region.

For the USSR, the Indian Ocean and its littoral is a vital sea line of communication (SLOC), and is a major area of Sino-Soviet competition. The region contains many newly independent states which are courted by both Beijing and Moscow.

The first major display of Soviet naval force in the Indian Ocean basin occurred in March 1968, when a relatively small squadron from the Pacific Fleet entered the ocean via the Strait of Malacca.[81]. Subsequently, there emerged a noticeable pattern in the naval activity of the Soviet Union in the Indian Ocean. A "major force"—usually a cruiser and one or two destroyers, plus support vessels, and/or submarines—leaves Vladivostok before the onset of winter, and arrives in the Indian Ocean in December or January. A "minor force"—consisting of nothing larger than a destroyer—arrives shortly before the major force departs by July.[82]

Since the Soviet expulsion from Egypt, Moscow is no longer certain of unrestricted naval transit through the Suez Canal. Consequently, the Soviet Union has increasingly focused on sea routes around Africa into the Indian Ocean.

The Southwest Sector

In addition to Mozambique which has already been discussed, this sector includes Malagasy (Madagascar), Mauritius, Tanzania and the Seychelles Island Republic.

In the Malagasy Republic, (formerly Madagascar) President Ratsiraka's leftist vanguard of the Malagasy Revolution Party (AREMA) remains in control. Ratsiraka defeated Monja Jaona, leader of the National Movement for the Independence of Madagascar (MONIMA) in bitterly contested 1982 elections. Jaona was placed under house arrest, but was subsequently released. It is difficult to ascertain the full degree of Soviet penetration into this former French colony, although the Soviets have been granted access to certain base facilities, particularly the naval base at Diego Surzoz in northern Madagascar.

Moscow signed a fishing agreement with Mauritius in July 1970. Since 1969, Soviet warships made regular visits to this island nation. On July 17, 1982, a Tripartite Alliance was announced in Port Louis, Mauritius, which had turned pro-Soviet. The alliance comprised Mauritius, Malagasy and the Seychelles and represented a Soviet attempt to gain control of the southern part of the Indian Ocean. Malagasy has since ratified two economic agreements with Libya.[83] In August 1983 elections were held in Mauritius in which Paul Berenger's pro-Soviet militant movement was defeated by a multi-party alliance led by Prime Minister Aneerood. Under the new Prime Minister this island nation has begun to move back toward the West.

In the Seychelles, Moscow initiated diplomatic relations only two days after independence was declared in June 1976. However the fiery revolutionary president, Albert Rene, has moved from a radical leftist stance to a moderate middle position in the East-West conflict. The Seychelle group, on which 70,000 Seychellois live, comprises 92 islands and controls 500,000 square miles of seabed resources. The islands are located astride the oil routes from the Persian Gulf to the Cape of Good Hope. Mauritius has claimed title to the British-owned, U.S.-leased island of Diego Garcia, which is the location of the only U.S. Indian Ocean naval base. This claim is supported by the Seychelle regime and Madagascar.

There was a bungled coup attempt in the Seychelles in 1981 led by a South African mercenary, Michael "Mad Mike" Hoare. Some of Rene's ministers claim that the CIA was involved in this abortive attempt. While claiming to pursue a policy of non-alignment, Rene's government has provided strategically important facilities to the Soviet Union. Thus, while the Seychelles has shifted away from its previous alignment with the Soviet eastern bloc, this should not be interpreted as portending any definitive disassociation.

Soviet access to the Seychelles plays an important part in the improvement of Soviet naval and air power along the Indian Ocean flank of Africa. If the gradual drift toward Soviet military predominance in this area continues, Moscow might gain ultimate control of the Cape route oil flow so important to Western Europe and the United States.

Tanzania, while not bordering on South Africa, has been a prime member of the so-called "Front-Line" states opposing Pretoria and particularly its reluctance to cooperate with the UN plan to move Namibia toward independence. Julius Nyerere, President of Tanzania for 23 years, voluntarily stepped down at the close of 1985. In October a Tanzanian delegation of military commissars visited Moscow and was given a pledge of "unswerving solidarity."

Kenya, to the north of Tanzania, has for many years followed a pro-Western policy and has provided facilities for the United States, not for the Soviet Union.

The Northwest Sector

This sector includes the two Yemens located on the eastern approach to the Red Sea from the Indian Ocean and the countries on the western approach, known as the Horn of Africa. These include Somalia, Ethiopia, Djbouti, and Sudan.

Yemen and the PDRY

The Soviet Union has had long-standing contacts and interests in Yemen. Following British withdrawal and the establishment in November 1967 of the People's Democratic Republic of Yemen (PDRY), also referred to as South Yemen, Soviet activities in southern Arabia focused upon the Marxist-oriented National Liberation Front (NLF) government in Aden. Such involvement formed part of a major Soviet effort to acquire naval facilities in the PDRY, particulary in the port of Aden. In return for Soviet aid, the USSR was granted use of port facilities at Aden and of nearby facilities at the former RAF airfield in Khormaksar. The Soviets also maintain forces and facilities near the Island of Socotra (part of the PDRY), which has a key Indian Ocean airfield.

The vacillations in relations between the PDRY and YAR (Yemen Arab Republic, or North Yemen), have reflected a complex web of internal, regional, extra-regional, and global rivalries. The assumption of power by the NLF in South Yemen toward the end of British rule, led to years of abortive efforts by the Saudis to undermine the NLF. The emergence in 1969 of the extreme leftist faction of the NLF as the dominant power put an end to any early hopes for reconcilation.

Saudi Arabia continued to court Aden, and Moscow became quite apprehensive over Saudi policies. V. Kudryavtsev, senior political commentator of *Izvestiya,* expressed indignation at what he suggested were attempts by Saudi Arabia to promote arrangements in the Red Sea area detrimental to non-Arab and non-Red Sea states.[84]

Egyptian President Sadat's visit to Jerusalem on November 19, 1977, and the ensuing (direct) peace negotiations between Jerusalem and Cairo ended the PDRY's brief pro-Western swing and secured Soviet presence and influence in southern Arabia. The subsequent split of the Arab world into "rejectionists" and "supporters" of Sadat's initiative offered the PDRY the opportunity to break its isolation without having to compromise itself ideologically or politically. Aden was thus among the first and the most vocal member of the "rejection front." Not only was this group supported by the USSR but the fact that among its members were two Arab oil-producing states, Libya and Iraq, offered alternative (and less politically objectionable) sources of financial aid to the PDRY.

On December 19, 1977, Aden announced its claim to territorial waters extending 12 miles from shore (rather than 3 miles formerly claimed), a move which challenged Saudi security plans for the straits, and which further discouraged attempts for unification. In early February 1978, following weeks of mounting tension along their common border, Saudi Arabia and PDRY entered into open, if limited, armor and air hostilities in the Wadia Oasis of the Rub al-Khali desert.[85] In Aden, there were increasing manifestations of an intensified power struggle between Rubayyi and his political (and personal) rival, Ismail. The struggle was "resolved" in late May, when, at the order of Ismail, 150 officers among Rubayyi's supporters, all allegedly opposed to Ismail's proposed establishment of a new Marxist party, were arrested. During the weeks just prior to the bloody power struggle, Soviet, East European and Cuban officals dealt exclusively with individuals on Ismail's side of the dispute.[86]

The outcome of the struggle was certainly to Moscow's satisfaction. The pro-Moscow faction was in firm control of domestic, defense and foreign policies.[87] A few days later, details were reported of a secret military-cooperation agreement concluded during Soviet Admiral Gorshkov's visit to Aden on May 18, 1978. The fifteen-year agreement stipulated that the USSR would aid the PDRY in the event of foreign aggression, that Soviet warships would be stationed at Perim Island, and that Soviet command over PDRY military foces on the island would be established. The agreement also called for the construction of a Soviet airbase.

Soviet naval vessels have made more port calls to the PDRY than to any other Indian Ocean littoral nation. That the PDRY was to be of special significance to Soviet maritime strategy was demonstrated in May 1979, when the new aircraft carrier *Minsk*, the amphibious landing ship *Ivan Rogov*, and a *Kara* class cruiser docked at Aden for a "good will" visit on their way to Vladivostok.[88] The Soviets now have the use of the most important naval base in the Indian Ocean.

By the fall of 1983, the USSR looked to consolidate its interests in the southern portion of the Arabian peninsula. Re-unification of the two

Yemens seemed more feasible since the YAR then had several hundred Soviet advisors there, and since the YAR's Salih had rejected U.S. arms offers in favor of Soviet weapons. Such re-unification would be a major coup for Soviet Middle East strategy, allowing them yet more bases and ports in the strategic Red Sea region. In addition Saudi Arabia would face a greater threat. Arafat's PLO forces, long supported by Moscow, were deployed to North Yemen, after being expelled from Lebanon for the second time in December 1983. Arafat moved his headquarters into Jordan in the summer of 1985. In early 1986, civil war broke out in the PRY, South Yemen, to the surprise of everyone, including the Soviet Union. Rebel forces seeking to oust President Ali Nasser Mohammed al-Hassani were led by Abdul Fattah Ismail—the hardline former President who after five years in exile was later accepted by the Soviets. By permitting and apparently encouraging his return, the Soviets set the stage for the bloody conflict which broke out on January 13, 1986, Ali Nasser Mohammed was ousted and he and several thousand of his followers found refuge in North Yemen. As late as November 1986 Nasser Mohammed promised an early return to Aden. Most observers believe that the struggle in Aden was an embarassment for Gorbachev.[89] The civil war in the PDRY threatened the Kremlin's efforts to gain the confidence of moderate countries in the Arabian Penninsula that were showing success with the establishment of relations with Oman and the United Arab Emirates. Both factions in the PDRY struggle profess friendship with the Soviet Union. The PDRY is the only Arab country ruled by a self-professed Marxist Party. No matter which rebel faction comes out on top, the Soviets will still retain, considerable influence in that pivotal country.

The Horn of Africa

The expansion of Soviet influence into the Horn of Africa was the outgrowth of a policy aimed at creating a strong position in the Gulf of Aden and the Indian Ocean. Soviet overtures in the Horn of Africa were initially directed towards Ethiopia. Full diplomatic relations and the exchange of embassies were completed in 1956. But the Soviet focus in the Horn of Africa shifted to Somalia in 1960s. An initial Soviet arms agreement with Somalia, concluded in 1963, provided for the training of Somali military cadets in the USSR and the establishment of a Soviet military mission in Mogadishu, the capital. The initial extension of credits were based on the hope of having the port of Berbera become available to the Soviet Navy.

The 1969 coup in Mogadishu, which replaced the government of the Western-educated and oriented Egal with the regime of General Mohammad Siad Barre, was welcomed by the Soviet Union.[90] Increased Soviet involvement in Somalia was undertaken when Moscow's difficulties with the Sudan and Egypt underlined the importance of a "progressive" regime in Somalia. Consequently, the Soviets supported the Somali struggle for

"Scientific Socialism," and its efforts to regain the Somali populated, but Ethiopian controlled, Ogaden province. Podgorny's July 1974 visit to Mogadishu led to the signing of the Treaty of Friendship and Cooperation, the first such treaty the Soviets concluded with a black African state.

Close Soviet-Somali relations made the ports of Kismayu and Berbera available to the Soviet Union. The investment in Berbera had its beginnings when the Soviets enjoyed access to port facilities in both North and South Yemen, and prior to their eviction from their Egyptian bases on the Red Sea. This was a manifestation of the Soviet policy of cultivating alternative relationships as a precautionary measure against sudden shifts in political orientation by unpredictable regimes. While the Soviets were solidifying their position in Somalia, developments elsewhere in the region were to affect their relations with Mogadishu.

Soviet influence in the near-by Sudan had blossomed since 1968. Sudan purchased large quantities of arms from the Soviets and closely coordinated its policy with that of Egypt. With the Nemery revolution of May 1969, Soviet influence was further enhanced. the Soviets utilized the small, yet tightly organized and disciplined, communist party to improve relations and to encourage Nemery's pursuit of socialist policies. This pro-Soviet trend ended abruptly in July 1976 as the result of an attempted overthrow of Nemery's regime. Clear evidence of a Libyan role in planning the coup and in financing and equipping the rebels, and allegations of Soviet involvement in the coup attempt (through the Soviet embassy in Khartoum), led to a major shift in Sudan's foreign policy. Nemery soon became the Soviet Union's most outspoken adversary on the African stage, Nemery, in turn, was disposed of in an April 1985 coup. Sudan has since made a military pact with Libya and began a shift away from the West.[91]

In Ethiopia, the Provisional Military Administrative Council, known as the Dergue and headed by Colonel Mengistu Haile Mariam, deposed the Imperial Ethiopian regime in March 1975. In February 1977, Ethiopia, a new "Democratic People's Republic," was launched on a radical course of "socialization."

An article in Pravda, March 10, 1976, expressed surprise concerning the revolution.

Almost no one could have foreseen that disturbances in the army would result in such serious political consequences. But the fact is that these events only revealed the social crisis that had come to a head in society. What had been hidden from outside observers suddenly erupted on the surface and resulted in an explosion whose significance is already apparent. Ethiopia is on the threshold of major changes.[92]

Not only were the Soviets surprised by the events in Ethiopia, they even referred to their position in the revolution as that of an outsider, awaiting the outcome for a change. The issue of Eritrean independence and the war over the Ogaden added to the chaotic situation in which the Dergue came to power. Ethiopia was becoming threatened by the independence movements in Eritrea and by the Somali war, and badly needed weaponry. An opportunity for the Soviet Union to establish a close relationship with Ethiopia arose in the context of this perceived vulnerability.

The Soviet Union initially attempted to maintain friendly relations with both Somalia and Ethiopia. However, the decision to support Ethiopia in 1977, inevitably dragged it into the internal conflict of the Horn. While the United States continued its military support of the Addis Ababa regime, the Soviet Union, in much the same way as in other regions, concluded the initial arms deal with Ethiopia through East European allies.

During the first week of February 1977, following an internal power struggle, Mengistu emerged as the new leader of the Provisional Military Administrative Council. The Soviets quickly supported his leadership.[93] The Carter Administration, however, looked upon the new regime as a flagrant violator of human rights. Not anticipating any serious damage to American interests, the United States suspended military aid to Ethiopia,[94] and Ethiopia turned completely to socialist countries for its arms. The arms were needed to quell an Eritrean independence movement in Northern Ethiopia.

The Soviet Union then began the delicate maneuvers to reposition between a potentially valuable, former U.S. ally, Ethiopia, and the long-established alliance with Somalia. Following a ten-day visit to Libya, Fidel Castro paid visits to both Mogadishu and Addis Ababa. During his visit to Ethiopia, Castro departed to an "unknown destination" on the 16th of March 1977. As was later learned, Castro met secretly with Mengistu and Barre in Aden where he presented a Soviet proposal for a regional confederation comprising Ethiopia, Somalia, Djibouti, and, possibly, PDRY. Moreover, Eritrean political aspirations were to be resolved within the framework of the confederation which would provide for Eritrea's autonomy. Somalia's Siad Barre rejected the proposal and, in the face of rapidly improving Soviet-Ethiopian relations, sent a signal to Moscow that his political allegiance should not be taken for granted.[95]

By the end of April, the shifting alliances on the Horn of Africa became apparent. In its search for arms, Ethiopia appealed to the USSR, and Moscow, failing to successfully mediate between Somalia and Ethiopia, sided with the latter. Cooperation between the two countries found its immediate expression in major Soviet arms sales to Ethiopia and in Ethiopia's demands for an American evacuation of the Kagnew communications facility near Asmara in Eritrea.

Mengistu quickly paid a state visit to the USSR. On May 6 Podgorny and Mengistu signed a declaration "on the basis of relations of friendship and cooperation between the USSR and Ethiopia."[96] Soviet military assistance was extended to the Mengistu regime. In order not to arouse Somalia, the Soviets presumably shipped arms from South Yemen and Libya. Incidentally, Soviet arms and ammunitions stored in Libya, in quantities far exceeding Libyan needs, had been intended for precisely such uses: to supply third parties without direct Soviet involvement at the moment of crisis.

By July, Somali leaders realized that the Soviets had made their choice. Consequently, Somali shifted to an active search for cooperation with the region's anticommunist regimes and for alternative sources of arms. The Somalis apparently concluded that without prompt action their military superiority would be reversed due both to declining Soviet military aid and to the rapid build-up of Soviet armaments and advisers and Cuban troops in Ethiopia. Consequently, Barre made preparations for a military campaign to win claims to both the Ogaden and adjacent Djibouti. Initially, it appeared as though Barre's decision—to turn from the Soviet Union—was about to pay off on the all-important military front. Within a few weeks his forces were in control of much of the Ogaden. Equally important, on July 26, the Carter Administration announced that it would provide military assistance to Somalia. This apparent American "green light" for Somalia to pursue its military initiative[97] was quickly followed by similar announcements from Paris and Britain concerning the sale of military equipment to Somalia.

The Americans stated, however, that American arms could not be used offensively, but solely on Somali territory. By late July, Somalia found it increasingly difficult to drive the Ethiopians out of the remaining Ogaden areas.

Upon returning home from an unsuccessful visit to Moscow, the Somali President learned that the United States, having belatedly realized the consequences of its initial offer of arms, made the offer contingent upon the withdrawal of Somali troops from the Ogaden. Similar conditions were set by France and Britain. Ironically, this turnabout of the major Western powers coincided with a stepping up of Soviet supplies to Addis Ababa. Moscow was determined to prevent Ethiopia's defeat. This commitment found its expression in a $220-million Soviet arms deal with Ethiopia.[98]

The lack of support and shortages of arms, ammunition and spare parts, coupled with urgings by friends and foes alike, produced a qualified Somali willingness to compromise, conditional upon Ethiopian recognition of the right of the Somali residents of the Ogaden to self-determination.[99]

Ethiopian requests for massive injections of Cuban troops were met by Cuban and Angolan objections, yet it took only two weeks for these forces to be transported from Angola. To encourage an increase in direct Soviet (and Cuban) involvement in the conflict, the Ethiopian regime launched a campaign geared to project a "progressive" socialist image. Addis Ababa announced plans for the rapid transformation of the country and its readiness to establish a Marxist-Leninist party.[100]

On November 13, Mogadishu ordered all Soviet advisors to leave Somalia within one week; ended Soviet use of strategic naval and air facilities on the Indian Ocean; abrogated the 1974 Treaty of Friendship and Cooperation; and broke diplomatic relations with Cuba. While the U.S.

was surprised by the Somali moves, Moscow was not. Several pro-Soviet Somali officials had apparently informed the Russians ahead of time. Advance notice, however, could not mitigate the damage. In addition to the collapse of design for a socialist federation along the strategic waterway, and the political consequences of the abrogation of a Friendship Treaty by a second Third World country in eighteen months (Egypt was the first), the Soviets lost the important base at Berbera, other naval facilities in Kismayu and interior airfields, such as Uanle Uen from which long-range TU-95 aircraft patrolled the northwest portions of the Indian Ocean.[101]

The Soviets, having concluded that the Barre regime was unlikely to reverse its decisions on relations with Moscow and Havana, took steps to guarantee that its Ethiopian client would win the war decisively. Taking both regional and Western intelligence by surprise, on November 26, 1977, the Soviets launched a massive airlift surpassing any previous demonstration of its capacity to intervene decisively in distant places within a short period of time. MIG fighter-bombers, T-34 tanks, medium-field and anti-tank guns, heavy mortars, SAM-7 anti-aircraft missiles, medical supplies and food and petroleum were air-shipped to Ethiopia. Some 250 Soviet transport planes—about 15 percent of the Soviet air fleet—were utilized. The planes were dispatched continuously and simultaneously from different bases, violating the airspace of many of the region's anti-Soviet countries en route to Ethiopia. The most dramatic phase of the airlift took place during the first week of December when the Soviets drew on their stockpiles in Tashkent and Alma Ata; closed rail lines to regular traffic so that war supplies could be transported to seaports and airports; and launched Cosmos-964, a military reconnaissance satellite, apparently to assist in coordinating this campaign.

Currently, there was a significant increase in the number of external Communist-bloc personnel in Ethiopia. In mid-January, Cuban Defense Minister Raul Castro, his deputy and ten other senior officers were joined in Addis Ababa by General Koliyakov, cmmander of Soviet forces in Libya, along with five other senior Soviet officers, several East German officers and the PDRY's Chief of Staff.

The implications of the Soviet massive support of Addis Ababa reached far beyond the immediate Somali-Ethiopian context. When contrasted with what appeared to be American impotence, the message to other Third World countries was clear: when faced with a perceived military challenge to vital interests, only one superpower could be relied upon to act—the USSR. The airlift had an additional purpose. It was tactically designed to test Soviet ability to move massive quantities of supplies and troops to distant places, in this instance Northeast Africa and the Middle East.[102] The Soviet airlift to Ethiopia revealed that: (1) the USSR was capable of surprising Western intelligence with massive airlifts; (2) within the first ten hours of such an airlift, the Soviets could move more than three divisions to arms depots in Iraq, Libya and Aden; and (3) the presence of ground and command crews and storages of fuel in PDRY compensated considerably for the loss of the Somali bases.

In addition to the military operation, the Soviet Union also strengthened its position politically in Ethiopia. This involved a series of purges of anti-Soviet individuals within Mengistu's close circle and their replacement by more sympathetic ones. By mid-January, 1978, Ethiopian pressure—orchestrated and, to a large extent, executed by the Soviets—already led to a Somali retreat from Ogaden. By early February, Western sources confirmed that Soviet ships were steaming toward Ethiopia carrying thousands of Cuban troops for a final thrust against Somali forces.[103] More than 3,000 Cubans and 1,500 Soviet advisers were allegedly already in Ethiopia. Cubans were also reported to be flying combat missions on behalf of Ethiopia. The Soviets, themselves, expanded their role of coordinating (with South Yemeni troops) the fighting in Eritrea,[104] building up a force of some twenty naval vessels in the southern Red Sea and assisting in the air defense of Cuba by flying MIG-21s over Cuban skies, so as to free Cuban pilots for combat in the Ethiopia-Somali conflict.[105]

The formerly French colony of Djibouti, located on the Red Sea, is frequently involved in the continuing conflict between Somalia and Ethiopia over the Ogaden. Many Ethiopians have fled to Djibouti where they find life in refugee camps more attractive than the barren, hard existence in their own country.

After the announcement of Somalia's decision to withdraw its forces from the Ogaden, Moscow publicly established the pretext for its continued military presence in Ethiopia, a presence it defined as a matter of internal Ethiopian affairs. Eritrean guerrillas, according to *Pravda*, were "international enemies of socialism" trying to "weaken Ethiopia . . . (and) to liquidate the possibilities of its access to the sea."[106] The importance to Soviet interests of access to the Red Sea had been confirmed a few weeks earlier. An East German delegation discussed the possibility of modifying and expanding the Eritrean port of Assab; on February 10, 1978, an Ethiopian-GDR agreement allowing East Germany to carry out these plans was signed.[107]

After losing facilities in Somalia the Soviets moved personnel and equipment from Berbera to Aden. With continued access to Aden and to anchorages off Socotra, the loss of Berbera should not significantly hamper Soviet naval operations around the Horn. The Soviets enlarged the existing Ethiopian naval base at Massawa, which, along with Assab, had become available to Soviet naval units operating in the Red Sea. The Soviet Union also has the use of naval facilities on the Dahlak Islands in the Red Sea. A solid foothold in Ethiopia, however, has provided Moscow with an invaluable base for operations in Central Africa, as well as for naval and air operations in the Red Sea and Indian Ocean, which could conceivably be used to apply pressure against Saudi Arabia.

A number of converging events in the winter and spring of 1985 affected the unstable situation in the countries of the Horn and their relations with external powers. Ethiopia was increasingly plagued by a devastating combination of famine and fighting. The Tigre People's Liberation Front (TPLF) and the Eritrean People's Liberation Front are both putting up stout resistance to the Ethiopian Army's efforts to subdue them. In addition, Ethiopia was the country hardest hit by the continuing drought sweeping across Africa.

Ethiopia is one of the poorest countries in the world and the continued drought and the government policy of forcing rebellious people to move into barren areas has produced a staggering number of deaths. In 1983,

The Reagan administration increased its humanitarian aid to the drought-stricken area after critics charged that such aid was being withheld because of the Ethiopian regime's Marxist stance and its close ties to the Soviet Union. Relief efforts have been hampered by bad roads, lack of trucks, and the fact that antigovernment guerrillas control many of the affected areas.[108]

In 1985:

Relief officials and diplomats said that as many as 60,000 refugees, including children, pregnant women, and the ill were driven out of a relief area by soldiers over a three-day period at the end of April. M. Peter McPherson, the American aid administrator, termed the banishment "a death sentence" for up to half of the people who had occupied the camp.

The United States is the largest donor of emergency aid to Ethiopia, which is a Soviet ally. Mr. Janson quoted Colonel Mengistu as having said that local officials had been responsible for the evacuation and that the national authorities had not been informed.[109]

The U.S. in May 1985 announced a plan to provide development assistance to Ethiopia because of a change in U.S. law.

The change in United States law comes at a time when many aid officials are saying that the emergency relief effort here is accomplishing about as much as can be expected but that the prospects for Ethiopia becoming economically self-sufficient remain dim. Ethiopia with a population estimated at 43 million is now considered the poorest country in the world, with about eight million people on the brink of starvation.

Those experts added, however, that projects connected with many programs—for example, the organizing of Soviet-style collective farms and a Government plan to resettle more than a million famine victims from the north in parts of the west and south—will not receive American support.[110]

Addis Ababa owes the Soviet Union over $2 billion for arms; it must also pay for the upkeep of Cuban forces as well as its own large standing army. The anomaly of the U.S. enabling the Soviet Union to maintain its strategic position in Ethiopia while the U.S. attempts to feed its starving population should be obvious. Meanwhile, hundreds of thousands of Ethiopians have fled into neighboring Sudan creating a massive problem for that poor country.

The United States was the chief supporter of Sudan's President Gaafar Nemery who was overthrown in April 1985 while in Egypt on his way back to Sudan from a visit to Washington.

Sudan's new military rulers have sought help from its former enemies, Libya and Ethiopia. The Sudanese announced that they were restoring relations with Libya and that its leader, Col. Muammar el-Qaddafi, had promised to help end the rebellion in southern Sudan.

The northern Moslems who try to govern the drought-ridden and destitute Sudan are seeking a negotiated peace with the southerners, largely Christian or animist, who have received weapons from Libya and sanctuary in Ethiopia.

The United States, which is at odds with both Libya and Ethiopia hopes for an end to Sudan's north-south conflict and thus has reason to encourage negotiations. The fighting has compounded Sudan's inability to pay the $1 billion in annual interest on its foreign debt and has halted oil exploration and economic development.[111]

Heavy fighting continued between Sudanese Government troops and the Sudanese People's Liberation army after the military pact had been made between Sudan and Libya.[112] Fighting continued in 1987.

Likewise rebellion against the central government in Ethiopia appeared to grow in the summer of 1985. The Eritrean People's Liberation Front, which seeks secession from Ethiopia, claimed to have captured Barentu, a city about a third of the way from the Sudanese border and the Red Sea. The rebels claim they control "more than 85%" of the Eritrean countryside.

"The Ethiopian Government is also fighting insurgencies in the region of Tigre, just south of Eritrea. The main rebel group in that area, the Tigrean People's Liberation Front, is seeking not only independence but also the downfall of the Government in Addis Ababa."[113]

Fighting, suppression and starvation plagued Ethiopia in 1986. Combined, these chaotic developments have tended to improve the Soviet position in the Horn of Africa. The payoff for the Soviet Union is as much psychological as strategic. The military advantages the Soviet Union has gained in Ethiopia are important, but no less important is the Soviet Union's growing image as an effective power willing to help revolutions. While few in the Third World find the Soviet Union an attractive model to imitate, yet "Soviet action in Africa has done much to reestablish the credibility of the Soviet Union as an effective leader of the world communist movement."[114]

The Persian Gulf

The Persian Gulf extends Northwest between the Arabian Peninsula and Iran. On its western shore are located Iraq, Kuwait, and the Arab Emirates, Saudi Arabia and Oman. The richest oil deposits in the world are located in these countries.

The Soviet Union's interest in the Persian Gulf region is a longstanding one. In November 1939, during the period of the Nazi-Soviet Pact, Soviet

Foreign Minister V. M. Molotov told Hitler's ambassador in Moscow that the Soviet government was prepared: ". . . to accept the text of an agreement . . . provided that the area south of Batnum and Baku in the general direction of the Persian Gulf is recognized as the center of the aspirations of the Soviet Union."

The turmoil in the region created by the Iranian revolution, and the Iraqi-Iranian War, and the Soviet invasions of Afghanistan will lead to far reaching changes in the political alignments of the region.

Throughout history, developments in the Persian Gulf region and the Indian sub-continent have frequently been intertwined. Despite the political turbulence in India, Bangladesh, and Pakistan in the closing years of the seventies, the subcontinent was a model of stability compared to the explosive Persian Gulf region. The fact that India was both the dominant and most stable country on the subcontinent may account for the difference. South Asia, however, was not immune to the storms arising in Southwest Asia. This was particularly true of heterogeneous Pakistan, with its lack of a solid and durable political system and struggling economy. In recent years, turbulence in the Persian Gulf area has been centered in Iran and Afghanistan. Their internal conflicts have had catalytic effects on each other and have also spilled over into their immediate neighbors, Iraq and Pakistan, respectively.

The presence of hundreds of thousands of Palestinians in the Persian Gulf states links the Arab-Israeli conflict in the Middle East with Persian Gulf developments. The Palestinian presence in the Gulf states is a favorable factor for the Soviet Union, which actively backs the PLO in its struggle against Israel.

In this respect the Soviet-Kuwaiti communique, issued in conjunction with the official visit of the Kuwaiti Foreign Minister to Moscow April 23–25, 1981, is most revealing. The Kuwaiti foreign minister, Sheik Sabah, representing the Gulf Cooperation Council (which includes Saudi Arabia) reached a consensus of views with the Soviet leaders. Sabah declared that the Gulf area is threatened not by the Soviet Union, but by the United States, and that the Gulf states will act to prevent deployment of American forces into the area. As the communique states: ". . . both sides expressed their continued support for the just struggle of the Palestinian people for securing their legitimate rights under the leadership of the PLO, their sole legitimate representative." In this context, the Kuwaiti side expressed its high appreciation of Soviet support for the just Arab cause.

Saudi Arabia

Saudi Arabia is the prime organizer of the Gulf Cooperation Council, a military arm of which was established in 1984.[115] The Council has created a Rapid Deployment Force, united under Saudi command, for the purpose of "deterring aggression." This force might be used in response to attempted coups by internal groups. The first example of successful self-defense by any of the Council's members was the Saudi's destruction of 1 or 2 Iranian F-4s that intruded into Saudi airspace in June 1984.[116]

The importance of Saudi Arabia in international affairs cannot be overestimated. Located strategically in the Middle East and Persian Gulf region, controlling the world's largest reserves of easily exploitable oil, and possessed of significant economic influence, Saudi Arabia occupies a key position on the international political stage. The future of the United States, Western Europe, and Japan is inextricably connected with future Saudi policies. The U.S. and its allies need a steady flow of Saudi oil, and the Saudis need the Western markets for sales and investments, and a security guarantee from the U.S.

Parallel assessments of Soviet goals in the Middle East and Persian Gulf region have led to cooperation between the U.S. and Saudi Arabia. The Saudis clearly recognize the Soviet threat to themselves and to the West. A member of the Saudi royal family has charged that the Soviets threaten eventual denial of Western access to Persian Gulf oil and that:

> The Soviet military presence in Cuba is not nearly so serious a threat to Western security as the military presence of the Russians in the Gulf and in the Horn of Africa.[117]

Some time later, while reporting on future world oil demands and production levels, the Saudi Arabian Oil Minister, Sheik Ahmed Zaki Yamani, gave further evidence in support of the view that the Soviet invasion of Afghanistan was a move toward the Middle East oil fields.[118] Minister Yamani asserted that he expected all of Eastern Europe to be facing oil shortages in the late 1980's, thus threatening the USSR's military and economic hegemony in that region. Such a development would put great pressure on the Soviets to offer alternative sources of supply (e.g., Middle East oil) to their clients. Responding to questions concerning Soviet goals in the Middle East, the head of Saudi Arabian Intelligence, Prince Turki al-Faisl, candidly stated:

> The answer is simple: our oil . . . At this moment we do not expect an invasion, but we do expect the Soviets to use their power to maneuver themselves into a position to make arrangements for a guaranteed oil supply.[119]

The Soviet threat to Saudia Arabia and the Middle East, and indirectly, to the United States and its allies is clearly recognized by the U.S. Yet despite pledges to assist Middle East states against Soviet aggression, and significant amounts of advanced weapons and U.S. military training offered to Saudi Arabia, the Saudis have occasionally threatened to "play the Soviet card" against the United States. The Saudis occasionally talk of opening direct diplomatic relations with Moscow, of possibly bringing the Soviets into broader Middle East peace negotiations, and of potential arms deals with the USSR (a la Kuwait).[120] Rumors circulated when Soviet

Ambassador Anatoly Dobrynin was invited to dine at the Saudi Embassy in Washington.

Saudi hints about improving ties with the USSR are intended to put pressure on the U.S. For the USSR, the development of open relations with Saudi Arabia would be a significant diplomatic breakthrough, setting the stage for a much wider Soviet role in the Middle East and Persian Gulf. Rumors of a Saudi-Soviet rapprochement have appeared particularly during U.S. Congressional debates on major weapons sales to Saudi Arabia. Such stories circulated during the debates of the Carter Administration's sale of F-15s, the 1981 AWACs sale hearings,[121] and during the debates over the unsuccessful sale of Stinger missiles to Saudi Arabia. Significant differences, however, exist between the Soviets and the Saudis which inhibit any major policy change toward the USSR. The Saudis have made the improvement of relations with Soviets contingent upon a withdrawal from Afghanistan, a reduction of their military presence in Ethiopia and South Yemen, an end to Soviet propaganda attacks against the Saudi government, and greater religious freedom for Soviet Muslims.

The Soviets appear to be positioning themselves for pressuring Saudi Arabia from every direction—from the north via either Syria or Iraq, from the east from Afghanistan, from the south from the PDRY (Aden), from the west from Ethiopia via the Red Sea, and from offshore via Soviet naval power. The Soviets count on a combination of external pressure and internal upheavals to one day place Saudi Arabia under their control.

Iraq

The Soviets broke diplomatic relations with Iraq, established in 1944, when in February 1955 the conservative, Western-oriented regime of Nuri as-Sa'id committed Iraq to the Baghdad Pact. Meanwhile, Soviet interests in the Middle East focused on Egypt, Syria and Yemen. The July 1958 revolution (which the USSR supported) in Iraq and the subsequent withdrawal of Iraq from the Baghdad Pact led to an immediate thaw in the Soviet-Iraqi relationship. Moscow's attitude towards Iraq improved dramatically with the overthrow of the Ba'athists in November 1963 by a military junta led by General Abd as-Salam Arif. Under Arif and his brother, Abd ar-Rahman Arif, who succeeded him in April 1966, the closeness of Soviet-Iraqi relations improved, especially following the June 1967 War with Israel. Soviet relations with the Iraqi government continued to expand, culminating in the 1972 Soviet-Iraqi Treaty of Friendship and Cooperation.

Until the mid-1970s, Iraq's military power was tied down by Iranian-supported Kurdish separatists in the northeast. In 1975, the Shah of Iran reached an agreement with the Iraqi government whereby Iran would cease to provide support for the Kurdish rebels in return for one half of the strategically located Shatt al-Arab waterway. The Shatt al-Arab waterway is important to both countries; both rely on the waterway for the shipment of oil—from Khorramshahr and Abadan in Iran and Basra in Iraq—into the Gulf, and then on to the West and Japan. Prior to the 1975 agreement, Iraq had allowed Iran to navigate and transit the waterway, although Iraqi sovereignty extended all the way to the Iranian bank. Of primary importance to both Iraq and the Soviet Union is the fact that the oil ports of Basra and Umm Qasr are located along the Shatt. Both naval "facilities" had been made available to the Soviet fleet. Although Iraq has, to a large extent, been militarily dependent on the Soviet Union since the 1958 coup, the Iraqis have since 1975 sought the aid of other nations. The French, for example, have provided Iraq with fighter bombers, as well as tanks, antitank weapons, and naval vessels for the Gulf.

Soviet-Iraqi relations have cooled considerably in the past couple of years. Whereas in 1972 (following the Soviet-Iraqi Friendship Treaty) the Iraqis obtained 95 percent of their arms from Moscow, Iraq has subsequently obtained less than 60 percent of its military supplies from the Soviets. The Iraqis appeared, even before the 1980 war with Iran, to be slowly drifting away from the Soviet orbit. By 1986 most of Iraq's military equipment came from Western countries and the PRC.

Iran

Soviet-Iranian relations were bitter following Soviet attempts in the aftermath of World War II to penetrate the northern Iranian province of Azerbaijan. In post-Mossadegh Iran, Moscow had to deal with the avowedly anti-communist regime of Shah Mohammed Reza Pahlavi. The Shah entered, to Moscow's chagrin, into the Baghdad Pact in 1955, and signed a bilateral military agreement with the United States in 1959.

But Moscow's relationship with Tehran took a turn for the better in the early 1960s. In 1962, Iran assured the Soviets that it would not allow any foreign state (U.S.) to have rocket bases on Persian soil. A Soviet-Iranian arms agreement was signed in January 1967, whereby the Soviet Union provided Iran with anti-aircraft guns, trucks, and armoured vehicles. During the 1970s, the Soviet Union and Iran expanded their mutual trade relations. Relations between the USSR and Iran, however, grew markedly cooler in the mid-1970s. An Iranian effort to refurbish its military arsenal was viewed with alarm in Moscow; more worrisome was the fact that the Soviets saw Iran as moving closer to the West.

Afghanistan

Soviet-Afghan diplomatic relations were established in 1919, with a friendship treaty following in 1921 and a non-aggression and neutrality pact in 1930. Khrushchev and Bulganin included Afghanistan on their December 1955 "barnstorm" tour of South Asia, which came, by no coincidence, three months after the May 1955 Pushtunistan crisis. Full support was extended to Afghanistan in this dispute with Pakistan, and the 1930 Treaty of Neutrality and Non-Aggression was extended for another ten years. Moscow concluded its first arms agreement in Southwest Asia with Afghanistan in August 1956.[122] Arms transfers and sales included fighter planes (MIG-21s were among the planes delivered), tanks, artillery, and large quantities of small arms.

The geopolitical relationship between Iran, Afghanistan and Pakistan (as well as India) played a crucial role in the Soviet drive toward the Indian Ocean. Moscow's longstanding goal of a warm water port on the Arabian Sea had long been frustrated by anti-communist Iran and Pakistan. Two related intraregional disputes—between Afghanistan and Pakistan on the one hand, and Afghanistan, Pakistan and Iran on the other—have provided Moscow with opportunities to penetrate the "land link" between the Middle East and South Asia by exploiting either the Baluchistan or Pushtunistan issues.

Baluchishtan

For roughly 100 years, prior to the advent of the British Raj, an independent Baluchi confederacy flourished along the Makran coast as a semi-autonomous tributary to the Pushtun-dominated Afghan empire. The Goldsmid line, which divides Iran from Pakistan, places one million Baluchis in Iranian Baluchistan, 1.5 million in Pakistani Baluchistan, and a small portion (300,000) in southern Afghanistan.

The declaration of independence of India and Pakistan in 1947 did not settle the Baluchistan question. The Khan of Kalat still refused to join either new nation (as had the Maharaja of Kashmir and the Maharaja of Hyderabad), opting instead for an independent Baluchistan. A short-lived Baluchi insurrection was suppressed by Pakistan in 1948, and Baluchistan was incorporated into West Pakistan.

The continuing Baluchi independence movement in Pakistan has sparked hopes in Moscow of a potential client state on the Indian Ocean. Should a future Baluchi insurrection succeed, as did the 1971 Bangladesh rebellion in what was formerly East Pakistan, Moscow could open direct transit lines between Soviet Central Asia, via the client state of Afghanistan, to Gwadar in Pakistani Baluchistan (reportedly modernized with Soviet aid) or Chad Bahar in Iranian Baluchistan.

Pushtunistan

The Pushtunishtan dispute centers on Afghani irredentist claims to Pushtun-populated territories in Pakistan east of the Durand Line and west of the Indus. Most estimates place roughly half the total Pushtun population east of the Durand Line (in Pakistan's Northwest Frontier Province (N.W.F.P.) and Baluchistan).

From the Soviet perspective, the further disintegration of Pakistan, a U.S. ally, and the incorporation of the N.W.F.P. and Baluchistan into Afghanistan or the creation of an independent Pushtunistan or Baluchistan would be a tremendous coup. Overland access from Soviet Central Asia to the Indian Ocean could become a reality. A Soviet base or access rights to facilities along the Makran coast could provide a launching ground for closing the Strait of Hormuz, or, at least, a staging post for Soviet naval operations in the Indian Ocean and a link-up for Moscow's strategic assets in the Middle East/Horn of Africa.

Afghanistan and Iran in the 1970s

Moscow's relations with Afghanistan illustrated the marriage of strategic considerations and ideology in Soviet policy. Nothing in Afghanistan's semi-feudal social structure, and outlook, would seem to justify this nation becoming one of the Soviet Union's principal aid beneficiaries in the Third World. Under Daoud (1953–1963), Zahir Shah (1963–1973) and then again under Daoud (1973–1978), Afghanistan remained in the hands of the old Afghan monarchy, the Mohammadzai clan. Following Daoud's return to power, in a July 1973 coup engineered by a group of Soviet-trained military officers, Afghanistan continued to move into the Soviet orbit. In May of 1974, Daoud gave qualified support to the Soviet Asian collective security scheme, so long as there was not conflict with internal concerns. Following Daoud's June 1974 Moscow visit, his support became more explicit.[123]

There has been much speculation about the Soviet role in the 1973 coup in Afghanistan, particularly through the two pro-Moscow communist parties, Khalq and Parcham. The party which was to be known as Khalq (since 1966) emerged in 1965, following the fall of the first Daoud government and the relaxation of government pressure on opposition groups. It was called the Democratic Party of the Masses, with Nur Mohammad Taraki as General Secretary. Khalq drew its support from the Pushtuns and from among the rural population.

Sources monitoring events in Kabul have asserted that Parcham, the new splinter party of the Khalq, was the military backbone of the 1973 coup. The Soviet connection in Afghanistan has largely been through the Afghan army. Specifically, two hundred Afghan officers were being instructed in the USSR yearly through training which had both a military and an ideological component. Following the 1973 coup, Daoud, as he had in the 1950s and 1960s, emphasized his commitment to Baluchistan and Pushtunistan, issues popular among the Pushtun majority army. However, in an apparent maneuver to consolidate his power, he turned on his Parcham supporters, especially within the army, replacing leftist Parcham officers and civil servants with those loyal to him personally.

The Shah's Promotion of Stability

Soviet aspirations in the Persian Gulf area in the early 1970s were checked by the mid-1970s, largely due to the efforts of the Shah of Iran. The Shah sought to diminish Soviet influence and presence in South and Southwest Asia by offering the regional states alternative sources of trade, aid, and transit and by attempting, through the manipulations of commercial, economic, and diplomatic levers, to stabilize the intra-regional tensions so often exploited by Moscow.

In May 1974, Indian Prime Minister Indira Gandhi made a state visit to Tehran, which was returned by the Shah in October. Credits amounting to $1 billion were offered to New Delhi.[124] Prime Minister Bhutto followed Mrs. Gandhi's footsteps to Tehran, returning to Pakistan with a $500 million credit.[125] Further, the Shah stated that he would intervene militarily to protect Pakistan in the event of a threat to its integrity.

The Shah continued to defuse intra-regional conflict in the mid-1970s by signing a treaty with Iraq in 1975 which settled their border dispute and ended Iranian support for the Kurdish rebellion against Baghdad. In return, Iran terminated its propaganda campaign and military support for a "Greater Baluchistan."[126]

Having eased tensions on his western flank, the Shah turned eastward to Afghanistan and Pakistan. In April 1975, President Daoud followed Prime Minister Indira Gandhi and President Bhutto to Tehran, where he received $2 billion in Iranian economic commitments, much of it for the construction of the Kabul-Kandahar railway.

As Iranian-Afghani and Iranian-Pakistani relations improved, Daoud's policies towards Pakistan began to change. In June 1976, Daoud invited Bhutto to Kabul. As a result of their cordial talks, the two governments agreed to suspend hostile propaganda attacks against each other and to reestablish relations according to the "spirit of Bandung."[127] The Shah's efforts to promote stability in Southwest and South Asia were, of course, not in the interests of the Soviet Union; Moscow's ambition to gain a foothold in this strategic area depended upon the existence of intra-regional hostilities. If Afghanistan and Pakistan ceased to be adversaries, Afghanistan's reliance on the Soviet Union for arms, trade, aid and transit rights would diminish, and Moscow's hope for a Greater Baluchistan or Pushtunistan would fade. And, if India no longer needed Soviet support against China and Pakistan, her need for continuing the "special relationship" with Moscow would become less vital.

The Two Revolutions 1978–1979: Afghanistan and Iran

The hopes of the Southwest Asian states for a new era of stable intra-regional relations were shattered by the 1978 anti-Daoud coup in Afghanistan, and the civil strife in Iran, which led to the departure of the Shah in January 1979. A related development was the replacement of Bhutto by Zia ul-Haq in Pakistan.

On April 27, 1978, a group of the more radical officers of the People's Democratic Party (PDP) Army and Air Force (most of whom had been trained in the USSR) engineered a bloody coup which elevated Taraki Khalai to the offices of President and Prime Minister of Afghanistan.[128] Daoud was executed during the coup and a 35-member Revolutionary Council, under Taraki, assumed power. The new government was recognized in quick succession by the USSR, Bulgaria, Cuba, and India. Hafizullah Amin, also a Khalqi, was named Deputy Prime Minister and Foreign Minister. From Parcham, Babrak Karmal was named Vice-President and Abdul Khadir was appointed as Minister of Defense. Although Taraki was known to be both a nationalist and a moderate, both Babrak Karmal and Hafizullah Amin were rigid ideologists and hardline communists.[129]

Whether by coincidence or not, the internal stability of Iran deteriorated rapidly after the fall of Daoud in Afghanistan in April 1978. As a result of a skillfully waged psychological warfare campaign conducted from Paris by Ayatollah Khomeini, the Shah's political support in Iran rapidly eroded in the closing months of 1978.

In the face of widespread protest against his rule, Mohammed Reza Pahlavi departed Iran in January 1979. In the wake of the Shah's expulsion, Iran was thrown into political and economic chaos. The succeeding regimes of Shahpur Bakhtiar and Mehdi Bazargan, were unable to restore order or to prevent the various successionist or autonomy minded ethnic groups in Iran (Kurds, Baluchis, Azerbaijani), from arming themselves and reviving their struggle for autonomy.

Subsequently, power in Iran fell into the hands of the mullahs, under the control of the Ayatollah Khomeini. Two short-lived care-taker governments rose and fell—before supreme power was assumed by the Ayatollah Khomeini. Since then, national referendums have declared Khomeini the unquestionable leader of an Iranian Islamic Republic for life.

Khomeini would not move Iran closer to the Soviet Union, but he quickly severed Iran's formerly close ties to the United States. Although the February 1980 elections in Iran vaulted Abolhassan Bani-Sadr to the office of the Presidency, his government never functioned independently of Khomeini and the mullahs. In fact, Bani-Sadr fled into exile in 1981 and was condemned to death, in absentia, by the Iranian Parliament.

The Shah sought refuge in Egypt, Morocco, the Bahamas and Mexico, before entering the United States for medical treatment. Resentful of what they believed to be the U.S. protection of a national criminal, a group of student demonstrators—with the tacit approval of the Ayatollah—stormed the U.S. Embassy in Tehran in early November, taking 90 U.S. personnel hostage. President Carter, for his part, attempted to make a show of force in the Persian Gulf area by dispatching a three-carrier task force centered on the U.S. carriers *Midway, Coral Sea* and *Kitty Hawk*. A subsequent U.S. rescue mission failed disastrously. Eventually, a complicated deal involving release of frozen Iranian assets led to the release of the U.S. hostages on January 20, 1981.

In neighboring Afghanistan the Soviet presence in Kabul rapidly increased following the spring 1978 coup. The armed forces had been trained and equipped by the Soviets for some time. A new factor was a growing Soviet role in the economy and planning. Cooperation between Afghanistan and the Soviet Union expanded with the signing of a Treaty of Friendship and Cooperation in December 1978.[130] Although Taraki vowed to remain officially non-aligned, it seems clear that Afghanistan was already in the Soviet camp. Since the coup, Soviet advisors in Afghanistan increased at least fourfold, to 5,000.

In March of 1978, Deputy Prime Minister and Foreign Minister Amin replaced Taraki as Prime Minister and was considered to be the strongman behind the government. In mid-September of 1979, Amin staged a bloody coup; Taraki was fatally wounded. Brezhnev and Kozygin lost no time in congratulating Amin on his "election" to the posts of General Secretary of the PDP, President of the Revolutionary Council and Prime Minister of the Democratic Republic of Afghanistan. On December 27, 1979, Amin was ousted from power and executed in a coup supported by Soviet troops.

On December 27, the Afghan radio announced that Babrak Karmal, a former Vice-President who had been living in exile in Eastern Europe, was the new President and Secretary General of the ruling PDP.[131] Karmal was brought into power by Soviet troops flown into Kabul.

The implications of this ruthless Soviet move into Afghanistan are frightening. The Soviets again demonstrated their capacity to airlift sizeable forces beyond their borders in relatively short order. The Soviets will be using existing (and building additional) air bases in Afghanistan. Soviet airfields in Afghanistan would have a critical effect on American and Western interests in the region. Operating in conjunction with Soviet fighters based in Southern Yemen, Soviet planes in Afghanistan could more than balance fighters and attack bombers on American aircraft carriers in the Indian Ocean. In addition, the Soviet presence threatens the cohesion of Iran, and will affect the post-Khomeini succession struggle in that country.

Perhaps the most important knowledge that the West can learn from the Soviet invasion of Afghanistan is the utter ruthlessness with which they conducted the operation. An article, "Report from Afghanistan," by Claude Malhuret, a French doctor who spent several years in Afghanistan providing medical service to the Afghan guerrillas stated that "Soviet antiguerrilla tactics are fundamentally different than those employed by Western governments and armies." According to him, the Soviets operate on the principle that an anti-guerrilla war can only be won by the "side that succeeded in making terror reign." He continued "This does not involve a warm bath/cold shower tactic, but the exclusive use of boiling water—again and again and again, until both the guerrilla fighters and the population ask for mercy." Malhuret concluded: "The Soviet strategy involves: the use of mass terror . . . The Afghan resistance might not be beaten . . . if in the coming years there is a profound change in the international balance of power and in the reaction of Westerners to Soviet totalitarianism."[132]

The Soviet campaign to swallow Afghanistan has lasted over seven years. While now and then talking the possibility of peaceful settlement, the Soviets are instituting a long term program for absorbing this country into their orbit. They are conducting a cruel war of attrition against the Afghan freedom fighters. In the spring of 1986 the Soviets put the head of their Afghan Secret Police, Najib, into the top spot of their puppet government. In December Najib visited Moscow amid Soviet hints to end the war. He told Western correspondents that Afghan freedom fighers were no longer able to mount major attacts against government troops. The Afghan resistance receives some aid from the United States and the PRC but not enough to expell the Soviet forces. Speaking in Vladivostok on July 28, 1986, Mikhail Gorbachev told the world that he would order a 6 percent Soviet troup pull out in return for a cut in western aid to the Afghan guerrillas. (N.Y. Times, July 29, 1986, p. 1) The brutal Soviet assault on Afghanistan would scarcely be affected by such a minor pull-back. The brazen duplicity of this Soviet bid reveals the mendacity of the Soviet leader.

The Gulf War

Middle East tensions soared to new heights when, in September of 1980, Iraq launched an attack on Iran. The first assault saw the capture of the territory spanning from Qasr-i-Shirin to Ilam, near the tentative boundaries of Kurdistan. But the Iraqis had grossly underestimated two things: first, the military tenacity of Iran, which, although not as formidable as Iraq's, did inflict a considerable degree of damage to Iraqi facilities; and second, the resolve of the Iranian people to rally around Iran's efforts to stave off the Iraqis—the government did not topple, as the Iraqis had expected.

There are many reasons which explain Iraqi aggression. First, there has been a long history of both land and sea border disputes between the two countries, particularly with regard to the Shatt al-Arab waterway. Second, Hussein was extremely irritated by Khomeini's attempts to incite Iraq's Shiites to rebel against the minority Sunni Muslims who wielded the power of Iraq.

The Soviet role in the Gulf War is not vividly clear. Moscow, initially denied Iraq military re-supplies and assistance, but in 1983 began to supply both sides. After Iraq launched the war against Iran, the Soviet Union concluded a Treaty of Peace and Friendship with Syria, Iraq's neighbor and bitter opponent. Libya, Syria, and North Korea—all linked to the Soviet Union—sent arms to Iran. Jordan and Saudi Arabia backed Iraq in this conflict. In 1981, as a possible response to the Iraq-Iranian War and the

Soviet invasion of Afghanistan, Saudi Arabia again attempted to coordinate some forms of a Gulf Security System that would include Oman, the UAE, Bahrain, Qatar, and Kuwait. The war has dragged on without resolution in sight. The Iranians have succeeded in driving the Iraqis back into Iraqi territory with suicidal "human wave" attacks of the Iranians using children as cannon fodder. If anything, the war intensified in 1985—1987. Iran has used thousands of young, ill-armed boys in the fray in attempting to win by a war of attrition. On August 24, 1986—

> Ayatollah Ruhollah Khomeini said Iran must reject any arbitration in the Persian Gulf War, fight until victory and "finish off" Iraqi President Saddam Hussein.
>   "We should continue the war until victory—and it is near. If our nation wants to bring this victory closer, it must prepare in the true sense of the word to . . . finish off this man [Mr. Hussein]," the ayatollah said in a broadcast speech.

Iraq has increasingly used airstrikes against Iranian refineries, ports and ships. In response Khomeini has threatened to close the Strait of Hormuz. The United States has vowed to keep the Hormuz Strait open at any cost— as closure would cut off gulf oil moving toward the West and Japan.

Speaking for the Soviet government, the Soviet Press Agency, *Tass*, in March, *1984*, claimed that U.S. acts in the Persian Gulf imperilled peace.

> "The U.S. Government should understand," the *Tass* statement said, "that it will bear full responsibility for the possible dangerous consequences of its policy and for its attempts to interfere in what is taking place in the Persian Gulf area."

The USSR, with contacts in both camps, may seek the role of peace-maker to enhance its claim to be the final arbiter of the Persian Gulf area. The fates of the countries of the so-called Northern Tier—Turkey, Iran, Iraq, and Pakistan—are all interconnected, along with the future of Afghanistan. The USSR would reap immense strategic benefits were it to gain a dominant position in this region. Iran plays a key role in these strategic maneuvers—Soviet invasion of Afghanistan may prove ultimately to be directed towards Iran. Despite the dissolution of the Tudeh Party, Moscow may still be capable of influencing events in Iran. Several thousand technical and economic advisers remain in the nation as do Soviet bloc diplomats. In mid 1986 Iran resumed shipment of natural gas to the Soviet Union.

Gaidar Aliev, a 1982 addition to the Soviet Politburo, has told of his personal hope that Iranian Azerbaijan would someday be united with its Soviet counterpart. Iran shares a porous 1250-kilometer border with the Soviet Union and another 400-kilometer border with Soviet occupied Afghanistan. In the chaotic post-Khomeini situation that will develop in Iran, Moscow will play every card in its hand, including possible intervention under the 1921 Soviet-Iranian Friendship Treaty, and/or support for volunteers from dissident Kurds, Azerbaijani, and Turkomen ethnic groups.

As this book goes to press it is difficult to judge what the long term impact of the Reagan Administration's abortive arms for hostages deal will be. There is no doubt that the Soviet Union sees a net gain from the confused Washington revelations. On December 8, 1986 Deputy Foreign Minister Alexander Bessmertnykh told a Moscow press conference that the clandestine U.S. arms sales to Tehran proved Soviet claims that the Reagan administration has acted in duplicitous ways and even lied in its negotiations with Moscow. As he put it:

> "It is simply that the situation of supplying arms to Iran proved that we are right when we say that there are cases where the U.S. administration has lied, and from this point of view this episode is interesting to us."[133]

Iran's future orientation will have a tremendous impact on the future of the region and of the world. As of 1987, there appeared to be little chance that the Iraq-Iranian war would end soon. Khomeini will not stop a war with an enemy he has vowed to destroy. Opportunities to end this costly conflict may arise only after his death.

The North Central Sector

In this sector of the Indian Ocean littoral, Soviet policy after Stalin was largely focused on India, with some attention to Afghanistan, Sri Lanka, and Burma. U.S. sponsored multilateral security systems such as CENTO and SEATO enclosed India and Afghanistan between Iran, Thailand and the two wings of Pakistan. In addition, the U.K. signed a mutual defense agreement with Sri Lanka in 1947 whereby an RAF base was maintained at Katunayake and a naval base was permitted at Trincolmalee. The treaty was renewed in 1960 with permission for use of an airfield at Gan and permitted British access until 1986. As a result of the confinement of British defense activity to NATO areas, the base at Gan is no longer used by the RAF.

The choice of India as the focus for Soviet attention was a logical one. India was the largest and strongest regional power and, as Nehru was emerging as the preeminent leader of the "non-aligned movement," solid ties with New Delhi could only add to Moscow's prestige and influence in South Asia, as well as in the Third World in general. Moreover, India's archfoe, Pakistan, had joined the West-oriented mutual security systems of SEATO and CENTO (in September 1954 and September 1955, respectively), possibly promoting Soviet fears of encirclement or hostilities close to home. Several Indo-Soviet trade and aid agreements had been consummated since the mid-1950s and the Soviets generally extended economic credits for India's five-year plans. The first Indo-Soviet military agreement was reportedly concluded in October 1960. A second arms agreement was concluded in September 1964, for the purchase of bombers and fighter planes, tanks, artillery, and small arms.

Following Nehru's death in 1964 and the India-Pakistan War of 1965, Moscow pursued a more balanced policy towards India and Pakistan (as well as between Pakistan and Afghanistan). Soviet neutrality in the intra-regional disputes of the South Asian nations was prompted by a number of considerations. First, Pakistan's bilateral foreign policy in the early 1960s had led to a growing closeness with the PRC and a loosening of ties with the U.S., despite Pakistan's continuing membership of CENTO and SEATO. Second, the Soviets were fearful of the enhanced role the PRC might aim at playing in the sub-continent. During the 1965 war, China was threatening to cause trouble for India on her Northern border during the fighting. Finally, Soviet fears of a right-wing resurgence in India, following the death of Prime Minister Shastri at Tashkent in 1966, were intensified by the nomination of Morarji Desai, a conservative, for the leadership of the Congress, and Indira Gandhi for Prime Minister. These signals led the USSR to widen its options in South Asia by opening the door to Pakistan, via a Soviet-Pakistani arms deal.[134] Indians demonstrated in front of the Soviet embassy in New Delhi and there was general discontent within the government. Yet, the Soviet arms agreement was largely a symbolic act designed to offset a growing Chinese influence in Pakistan and to widen Moscow's options on the sub-continent. The Soviet move to warm up to Pakistan, however, proved to be short-lived.

When, in March 1971, President Yahya Khan of Pakistan made the fateful decision to repress the separatist movement in Pakistan's Eastern Wing by military force, among the results was a huge outflow (numbering many millions) of Hindu refugees from East Pakistan into Indian territory. By degrees, the Indian government became convinced that the only way in which they could rid themselves of this refugee burden was to help the Bengalis in their fight for independence, even if this entailed—as it did—war between India and Pakistan. India knew this was a risky course of action. The 1971 Indo-Soviet Treaty of Friendship and Cooperation was therefore entered into as a form of insurance. And it has led, over the years, to a steady strengthening of India's sense of affinity with the Soviet Union.

In the aftermath of India's decisive 1971 victory over Pakistan, Soviet policy considerations towards South Asia were pervaded by the objective of maintaining the intra-regional military and political status quo. At the local level, Mrs. Gandhi and the Congress (R) party were at the peak of their national popularity in India. She, as Prime Minister, had gained tremendous grass roots support for her election promise to "abolish poverty." The defeat and dismemberment of Pakistan, a nation supported by both the U.S. and the PRC, further demonstrated to the world that India was, indeed, the paramount power on the sub-continent, with aspirations of becoming a major influence in global affairs.

As India's only major supporter, the Soviet Union benefitted from the hostilities which resulted in the formation of Bangladesh. The Soviet Navy has enjoyed access to facilities at the Indian submarine base at Vizagapatnam (which Moscow helped to develop) and at Bombay and Cochin. But the Indian government categorically denies that Moscow enjoys any base rights in India other than the normal port-of-call privileges granted to all nations.

In the wake of the Indian victory, Sheikh Mujib Rahman became President of Bangladesh. In early 1972, Mujib immediately established linkages with the USSR. And, in the same year, a 25-year Indo-Bangladesh Treaty of Friendship and Cooperation was signed.

After the Bangladesh War, Indo-Soviet policy objectives coincided (but for different reasons), fostering an atmosphere for mutual accommodation. Between 1972 and 1974, the USSR and India concluded as many as 40 agreements or protocols for economic, technological, scientific, and cultural cooperation. In November 1973, a 15-year economic cooperation agreement was signed with India and since that time, the USSR has been India's largest regional trading partner. Brezhnev again visited India in 1980.

From Pakistan, Bhutto visited the Soviet Union in early 1972. He was told that Moscow did not regret its 1971 intervention in the Bangladesh liberation and that if another "Bangladesh" occurred—implying a situation of similiar circumstances with respect to the Pakistani provinces of Baluchistan and the N.W.F.P.—the USSR would take a similar stand. With respect to Bangladesh, the USSR openly encouraged the fledgling nation's close ties with India and Mujib's warm feelings towards the USSR. In January 1972, the USSR became the first major power to recognize Bangladesh.

A shared Indo-Soviet concern over the containment of a tacit U.S.-PRC alliance in South Asia was translated into positive Indian reactions to Moscow's Asian Collective Security concept. In February 1972, in an interview with *Tass,* Indian Foreign Minister Swaran Singh described the Soviet collective security scheme as "an initiative aimed at promoting peace and security and reducing international tensions."[135]

By 1973 initial Soviet objectives in South Asia had been achieved, with India's help through the 1971 Indo-Soviet treaty, the substance of various Indo-Soviet communiques, the strength of their economic, political and military ties, as well as the coincidence of Indo-Soviet views on certain foreign policy positions (i.e., hostility toward China, the United States, and Pakistan). Finally, India made various supportive diplomatic gestures toward the USSR—the elevation to ambassadorial level of her representation to North Vietnam (January 1972), the recognition of the GDR (October 1972) and North Korea (December 1973), a pro-Arab stance on the Middle East controversies and support for the Communist victory in Vietnam (1975), and support for Vietnam's invasion of Kampuchea (1979). All of these actions affected Moscow's international position favorably.

Between 1974 and 1976, a confluence of domestic, regional and global factors precipitated a loosening of Indo-Soviet ties. In India, the euphoria of the Bangladesh struggle had, by 1974, begun to fade, as did the popularity of the Gandhi government. On June 26, 1975, Fakhruddin Ali Ahmed, President of India, at Gandhi's urging proclaimed under Article 352 of the Constitution that a grave emergency existed, whereby the security of India was threatened by internal disturbances.

Meanwhile, in Bangladesh, the charisma of Mujib had rapidly faded in the wake of political corruption, economic disaster, and public disillusionment. On August 15, 1975, a group of disaffected young army officers (majors and colonels) staged a coup which resulted in the death of the Sheikh and his immediate family. After an Indian-supported counter-coup failed, Major-General Ziaur Rahman took over the new government in Bangladesh and almost immediately embarked upon improving relations with the Indo-Soviet arch foe, the PRC.

By 1974, Mrs. Gandhi felt that India's post-Bangladesh position was secure enough to resume the process of normalization of relations with China. Sino-Indian rapprochement was slowed down by China's apprehension over India's explosion of a nuclear device (May 1974) and the incorporation of the Himalayan protectorate of Sikkim into the Indian Union. On April 15, the Government of India annouced the appointment of the first Indian ambassador to the PRC since the 1962 war.

Soviet apprehensions over the Indian and Bangladeshi drift towards the PRC were compounded by improvements in Indo-Pakistan and Pakistan-Bangladesh relations, as well as by Indian overtures to the United States. Thus, by 1976, the Soviet posture in South Asia had received some setbacks. Yet Indo-Soviet relations were to remain close despite Moscow's reservations about trends in India's regional and global relations with other countries. In April of 1976, the two countries signed a new five-year trade agreement; and in June, Mrs. Gandhi's visit to the USSR reassured the Soviets that India's decision to improve her relationship with China did not represent a threat to the long-standing relationship between Moscow and New Delhi.

The period between 1977 and 1979 witnessed increasing internal instability among the nations of the sub-continent and its periphery. At the local level in India, public displeasure with Mrs. Gandhi's emergency rule increased. Despite large scale public discontent, she called for an end to the emergency, with national elections to be held in March 1977. The results of the 1977 Indian national elections were devastating for her. She and her son were defeated in their bids for a seat in Parliament. The Janata front and its allies captured 328 of the 542 seats.[136] The key posts of the new government were filled by the winning coalition and its supporters, with Desai as Prime Minister. The Desai government publicly expressed the desire for a "more balanced" foreign policy.[137]

Overtures to the United States and PRC (begun during the Gandhi years), however, did not mean a shift away from the Soviet Union; rather, India continued her "special relationship" with the USSR. Three new Indo-

Soviet agreements followed a 1977 visit by Soviet Foreign Minister Gromyko. The first provided for a Soviet loan of 250 million rubles for the import of equipment for Indian steel, coal, and other industries. The second called for an increase in total Indo-Soviet trade. The third provided for the improvement of telecommunications services between the two countries.[138]

Desai's ruling coalition began to split during the summer of 1979. By the middle of July, 80 Janata members of Parliament had defected, along with a number of cabinet ministers. On July 15, Desai resigned as Prime Minister, facing an impending vote of "no confidence" in the Lok Sabha.

Meanwhile, in Pakistan, national elections were held in March 1977. Bhutto and the Pakistan People's Party (PPP) were returned to power by a 75 percent majority; yet, the opposition (a heterogeneous grouping of political parties) demanded the resignation of Bhutto and refused the compromises offered by the Bhutto government. Bhutto was ousted on July 5, 1977 (and executed in 1979), and Army Chief of Staff Zia ul'Haq proclaimed himself Martial Law Administrator. Under Zia, US-Pakistani ties have remained intact, although they were shaky following a wave of anti-Americanism in late 1979. The sale of F-16 fighter aircraft to Zia was a major factor in maintaining the level of US-Pakistani relations, as was the 1983 visit by Secretary of State George Shultz.

General Zia is Pakistan's third military ruler. It is doubtful whether some form of civilian, or quasi-civilian government can be brought about without unleashing a further outburst of popular unrest. There is also a continuing threat, if not of outright Soviet military attack, of substantial attempts at subversion in Pakistan by the Soviets, particularly directed at fomenting Baluchi and Pushtun separatism. The Soviets are also seeking to destabilize Pakistan because of its support of the Afghan resistance. The return of former President Bhutto's daughter to Pakistan in mid 1986 led to increased domestic violence.

In Bangladesh, Major-General Ziaur Rahman unilaterally assumed the title of President in April 1977. In February 1979, the Bangladesh Nationalist Party of the President won a two-thirds majority in Parliamentary Elections. Few pro-Moscow or pro-Beijing leftists gained seats in the election.

The January 1980 Parliamentary elections in India resulted in the return of Mrs. Gandhi to power and her breakaway political party, Congress (I).

The Aftermath: The Soviet Invasion of Afghanistan and the Iraq-Iranian War

The Soviet invasion of Afghanistan set shock waves throughout the entire littoral of the Indian Ocean. Following a January 1980 meeting with British Foreign Secretary Lord Carrington, Mrs. Gandhi reportedly stated that there was no justification for the Soviet intervention. Clearly, New Delhi has been wary of the Soviet move into Afghanistan.

The dilemma facing New Delhi is whether a strong Pakistan, capable of withstanding Soviet encroachment is worse than the eventual Soviet take over in Afhanistan. U.S. efforts to bolster the Zia regime, such as the 1981 sale of F-16 fighter aircraft, alarmed India as has the expansion of Pakistani-PRC relations.

Close relations with the Soviet Union remain the cornerstone of Indian foreign policy. The six-day visit of Soviet Defense minister, Dmitri Ustinov, in March, 1984 led to the Soviet agreement to furnish India with a variety of up-to-date military equipment. Signs of close relations between New Delhi and Moscow remain abundant in cultural and academic areas. India is vital to the Soviet Union because it is the dominant country in South Asia, on the Soviet Union's southern border, and because China is next door.

For Pakistan, the coincidence of the Soviet invasion of Afghanistan to the north, coupled with Pakistan's own internal situation of instability—posed unique dilemmas for this strategically located South Asian nation. Zia feared that, on the one hand, separatist tendencies in Iraninan Baluchistan could spill across the border reviving the fervor of the 1973–1977 Pakistani-Baluch insurrection or that on the other hand, that Soviet Afghani-orchestrated uprising could be fomented over the Pushtunistan or Baluchistan issues. As of 1983, there were some 1,000–5,000 Baluchis in exile in Afghanistan and they were reported to be receiving training in insurgency warfare from Soviet and Afghan advisors.

Pakistan would like to receive economic and military aid from the United States and the PRC, yet it is sensitive to possible hostile responses in Iran and in India. Pakistani-American perceptions of the threat to Pakistan posed by Soviet intervention in Afghanistan are convergent. The bilateral relations of these two countries suffer from American apprehensions that Pakistan is developing nuclear technology for military purposes and from Pakistani dissatisfaction with the low-level U.S. support accorded during her 1965 and 1971 wars with India. The 1981 Pakistani acceptance of the large-scale American aid package was a diplomatic turnabout for the United States.

The 1984 assassination of India's Prime Minister Indira Gandhi and the subsequent election of her son Rajiv may create greater flexibility in Indian foreign policy. On May 1 1985 in an effort to establish a U.S. arms relationship with India in the face of virtual Soviet monopoly, Fred C. Ikle, undersecretary of defense for policy, began three days of talks with senior Indian officials in New Delhi. Ikle's visit was intended to counter Indian anxiety over Washington's sale of sophisticated weapons systems to India's traditional enemy, Pakistan. It was also designed to take advantage of a "window of opportunity" for better U.S.-Indian relations, presented by the election of Prime Minister Rajiv Gandhi. A major policy objective of the U.S. administration is to encourage diversification of Indian arms purchases beyond the Soviet Union, which has been India's major foreign arms supplier for years.

On November 25, 1986 Secretary General Mikhail S. Gorbachev began a four day visit to New Delhi: He was welcomed by Indian Prime Minister Rajiv Gandhi as a "crusader for peace."

> Mr. Gorbachev hailed "the life of new India" under Mr. Gandhi and said he expected that Soviet-Indian relations would make "constant headway on the solid foundation of mutual respect, mutual benefit and common aspirations for peace."
>
> (New York Times, November 26, 1986, p - A - 3

The visit led to increased Soviet military and economic assistance to India.

The situation in the North Central sector of the Indian Ocean following the end of the Iraq-Iranian war will present grave dangers for Western security, as well as unique opportunities for the Soviet Union. The Soviet Union may in fact, eventually play the role of peacemaker, as it did at Tashkent. The Soviets would, of course, like to be the most influential power in both Baghdad and Tehran. If, however, they were forced to choose, they would prefer to gain power in Iran. They faced a similar choice between Ethiopia and Somalia and, finally, chose Addis Ababa over Mogadishu.

Taking into account these developments in the three countries that comprise the core area of the sub-continent, Soviet strategy toward Asia during the remaining years of the eighties will be to continue to focus on the "special relationship" with India, while attempting to counteract the PRC's relationship with Pakistan and Bangladesh.

Sri Lanka

Sri Lanka is of strategic significance to both superpowers because it rests astride the major SLOCs across the Indian Ocean. With excellent port facilities and airports, Sri Lanka could serve as a replenishment depot, or as a staging post for naval and air units operating in the Arabian Sea and Bay of Bengal. Two parties have alternated in the exercise of political power since Sri Lanka became independent in 1948. The first is the Sri Lanka Freedom Party (SLFP) under the leadership of Mrs. Bandaranaike, the second is the United National Party (UNP). Mrs. Bandaranaike's nationalization of major assets of American and British-owned petroleum companies in Sri Lanka, and reluctance to pay adequate compensation, led to the suspension of U.S. aid.

In the general elections of March 1965, the UNP was again returned to power, with Dudley Senanayaka as Premier. During his five-year rule, Sri Lanka's domestic and foreign policies shifted back to a Western orientation. The 1970 victory of the SLFP-dominated United Front was a clear gain for the Soviet Union. The pro-Moscow communist party was included in the front and a communist was appointed to the cabinet. The new government soon recognized East Germany, North Korea, and North Vietnam, while it severed ties with Israel. In the wake of a rebellion against the regime in 1971, led by ultra-leftist students, Moscow delivered six MIG-17 fighters to the Colombo government to combat the insurgents; the MIG-17s were practically useless. On the other hand, Sri Lanka did receive more appropriate military assistance from many other countries including the Peoples' Republic of China, Yugoslavia, Great Britain, Australia, and the United States.

In the latter part of 1971, when the war between Pakistan and India broke out, Sri Lanka sided with Pakistan because of her fear that if Pakistan were completely eliminated, Sri Lanka would enjoy very little independence against India. Mrs. Bandaranaike permitted airplanes from West Pakistan to bring supplies to Dacca in the eastern wing of Pakistan to refuel at Colombo.

The political tables again turned in July 1977, with the UNP, under J.R. Jayawardene, winning 135 seats of 168 in the Sri Lanka Parliament. Jayawardene stated that he would follow a more non-aligned course in foreign policy than the previous Bandaranaike government, with less hostility towards the United States and the West.

Jayawardene's government began to face growing unrest by the Tamil minority, a Dravidian people brought from Southern India by the British. On May 12, 1983 the government was forced to proclaim martial law and used government troops to suppress the growing militancy of the Tamils. Amid growing speculation that the Tamils were receiving support from the pro-Moscow communists, the government announced the suspension of press freedoms and imposed mandatory curfews and censorship.

Radio Moscow condemned this move, claiming, "The government is an agent of reactionary imperialism. The Communist Party of Sri Lanka has issued calls pleading for the unification of the island."[139] In July 1985 talks between the Tamil rebels and the Government of Sri Lanka began as a result of pressure put on the Tamils by Prime Minister Rajiv Gandhi of India. Little progress was made in those talks. During 1986, the domestic situation in Sri Lanka continued to deteriorate. The Soviets will try to exploit instability in Sri Lanka to further Soviet designs for naval facilities in the Indian Ocean.

The most significant 1986 development in South Asia was the growing intensity of the civil war in Sri Lanka whose 16 million people are divided into hostile camps. The Tamils who originally came from India's state of Tamil Nadu make up 18 percent of the population. "Experts on all sides agree that the guerrillas were able to become strong by using southern India as a sanctuary and supply base." (N.Y. Times, March 31, 1986). Further, "U.S. intelligence experts indicate that the Tamil terrorist factions are being supported by three countries with close ties to the Soviet Union— North Korea, Libya and India—and say there are indications that the

Soviets are encouraging Tamil efforts to overthrow Sri Lanka's government in order to obtain control of the strategic Trincomalee deepwater harbor." (Insight, May 19, 1986)

The Tamils are a classic case of a minority that believes it has been wronged by the ruling majority. The Sinhalese, too, have the outlook of a minority. Time and again the argument is heard: "We are but 12 million people alone in the world. No one else speaks our language, shares our culture. Who else is the guardian of our Buddhism? And here we are on a small island staring north at 50 million Tamils." (International Herald Tribune, July 3, 1986, p. 4)

Developments in Pakistan and Sri Lanka are India's most pressing concerns. Both countries have turned to the west for security assistance. American warships now make routine recreational stops at Sri Lankan and Pakistani ports, and Pakistan has stepped up aid to Sri Lanka—prompting Indian officials to warn of a "nexus" of influence that could undermine attempts to maintain what New Delhi calls a "neutral zone of peace" in the Indian Ocean. The situation is "disconcerting" said Mr. Venkateswaran, India's foreign Minister, although "not a threat to security." (N.Y. Times, May 11, 1986, p. E-7)

Sri Lanka faces an ever deepening civil war. The Soviets are keeping a watchful eye over developments and will seize whatever opportunity that may arise to establish their presence there.

Burma

The geographical position of the Socialist Republic of the Union of Burma, the largest country in Southeast Asia, offers easy access to the Indian Ocean, Indochina, and even the strategically important Malacca Strait. Burma, located between India and China, has always maintained closer relations with Beijing than with Moscow. Burma's withdrawal from the Havana Summit of non-aligned nations and its withdrawal from the non-aligned movement in late 1979—due to the fact that Burma saw the non-aligned movement as becoming increasingly pro-Soviet (under Cuba's manipulation)—has no doubt exacerbated tension with the Soviet Union. At best, Soviet-Burmese relations can be characterized as "cool."

Burma, however, may become a prize in the struggle between the pro-Moscow and pro-Beijing forces in Asia and could lose its buffer status between China and India. Further, the Socialist Republic of Vietnam (SRV), the Soviet surrogate in Southeast Asia, is aiding the Burmese White Flag Communists, one of the country's several insurgent groups, adding yet another to Burma's mounting problems. The death of Ne Win will undoubt-edly set off a struggle over the future orientation of Burma between the PRC, on the one hand, and the Soviet Union, India, and Vietnam, on the other.

As the Soviet-Vietnamese alliance grows tighter, Hanoi's involvement in the Burmese insurgency problems might bring the BCP under direct Soviet influence. Although Burma has so far escaped Soviet expansionism, the country's future within the context of the ongoing international power struggle is, of course, uncertain. That Ne Win has no institutionalized system of political succession will allow the Indians, in addition to the Chinese, to attempt to place their own candidates in power following his demise. Whoever succeeds Ne Win is likely to face an escalation in Soviet and Vietnamese efforts to bring Burma into the Soviet camp. Burma is truly non-aligned and, therefore, diplomatically isolated. Whether Rangoon can survive Indian, Vietnamese, and Chinese designs is uncertain. Should India gain the upper hand Burma could play a role in Soviet efforts to encircle China.

Conclusion

The Indian Ocean is a region of potentially decisive strategic importance to outside powers. The Western absence created by Britain's withdrawal from the region has been partially filled by the periodic presence of a U.S. naval task force in the Indian Ocean and by French naval forces based on France's residual possessions in East Africa, by India, and, most importantly, by Soviet naval power. Interplay among these powers, along with regional disturbances, has transformed the Indian Ocean into an arena of chaotic rivalry and confusion.

Soviet planners grasped the strategic significance of the Indian Ocean long before their American counterparts. The initial Soviet move toward Indonesia in the early 1960s foreshadowed their subsequent strategy. Soviet strategy is most effective in an environment of chaos and anarchy, conditions prevalent in many areas on the Indian Ocean. The Soviets have shown little interest in mitigating these regional conflicts.

Passage through the Indian Ocean is essential to the unification of the western and eastern sectors of the Soviet empire, and Soviet gains in the Indian Ocean arena would influence situations throughout the globe. Soviet dominance of this crucial ocean would strongly aid Soviet strategic planners in their efforts to cope with the PRC. Current high levels of Soviet naval activity and base acquisition efforts from the Cape of Good Hope to the Strait of Malacca are informed and guided by such considerations.

The Pacific Flank

China, potentially either a friend or foe, remains the focus of the Soviet Union's Asian policy. Before assessing Sino-Soviet conflicts of interest in Southeast Asia, Taiwan, Japan, and the Korean peninsula, a brief review of recent confrontation between the two powers is in order.

The Soviet-Chinese Confrontation

In the aftermath of Hanoi's victory in Indochina, the struggle between China and the Soviet Union has intensified. The Soviet Union has attempted the establishment of a *cordon sanitaire* around China and has also sought to weaken it internally and pressure a change in its anti-Soviet policy.

Mao's death in September, 1976, created an opportunity for a new phase in Sino-Soviet relations. The Central Committee of the Communist Party of the Soviet Union (CPSU) sent a message to its Chinese counterpart expressing "deep condolences" on his death. Soviet gestures toward reconciliation were, however, rejected by China and Beijing was determined to continue rapprochement with the United States.

By early 1977, Moscow expressed obvious irritation with Beijing. An *Izvestiya* political observer, Aleksandr Bovin, accused Beijing of "carrying on the old anti-Soviet line." A flurry of diplomatic exchanges in the winter of 1977–1978 ended in a continued impasse. *The People's Daily* declared that Moscow repeatedly broke promises, and that the Chinese would not negotiate until "the Soviet side comes forward with concrete deeds."[140] Following diplomatic overtures, Brezhnev undertook a 13-day, 5,000 mile train tour across Siberia to Vladivostok. The objective of the trip seems to have been to emphasize the Soviet rejection of Chinese demands to withdraw from the border and Mongolia. Meanwhile, a serious disturbance was brewing in China's southern flank. In December, 1978, the Vietnamese launched an attack against the regime of Pol Pot in Cambodia. This opened a new Soviet *point d'appui* for applying naval and air pressure on China.

Southeast Asia

Southeast Asia is the active area of confrontation between the Soviet Union and China. Southeast Asia, historically and geographically, offers the best opportunity for China to expand its influence.

The presence of millions of ethnic Chinese throughout Southeast Asia ensures considerable political influence for the PRC. These "overseas Chinese," although only six percent of the population, have extraordinary economic influence in every Southeast Asian state. These states are concerned that the ethnic Chinese could form a fifth column for China.

There are two central issues of Sino-Soviet conflict in Southeast Asia. One involves the Soviet-backed Vietnamese campaign to consolidate control over Indochina. The other involves the campaign to gain influence in the ASEAN (Association of Southeast Asian Nations) noncommunist countries of Southeast Asia. The leaders of Thailand, Malaysia, Singapore, Indonesia, and the Philippines express the hope that a balance of influence by all the major powers will develop in Southeast Asia. ASEAN, established in 1967, is the only functioning political and economic regional

organization. ASEAN has become a political power in Asia, and its importance is recognized by the United States, Japan, the Soviet Union, and the
PRC.

There are potentials for the expansion of Soviet power in Southeast Asia.
Indonesia and Thailand are most susceptible to Soviet intrusion. Thailand
may become more affected by Vietnamese and Soviet policy if Vietnam
consolidates control over Cambodia, and if the Vietnamese decide, with
Soviet support, to destabilize Thailand. Indonesia, with immense natural
resources, faces serious economic and social problems that make it vulnerable to Soviet influence.

Indonesia

Indonesia was one of the first states in the Third World to receive Soviet
attention and assistance, and its strategic location explains their interest.
One of Moscow's goals has been to ensure the freedom of navigation
through the Malacca, Lombok, Sunda, Ombai (Timor) and Makassar
Straits, the five principal passages through the Indonesian archipelago.

Relations with the Soviet Union expanded when the Indonesian regime
was faced with a separatist insurrection in 1958. The Soviet Union was
quick to come to President Sukarno's aid. Within days, Soviet vessels were
docking in Indonesian harbors, followed by the arrival of Soviet planes.

In the wake of Khrushchev's February, 1960 visit to Indonesia,
Moscow's interest in that country grew conspicuously. Over a short period
(1958–1961), Indonesia received more than $1.5 billion from Soviet-bloc
states, most of which was in the form of military assistance. The Soviets,
nevertheless, failed to influence the main anti-communist force in the
country—the army. For years, President Sukarno managed a precarious
balance between the Indonesian Army and the Partai Kommunist Indonesia (PKI), playing one against the other. But eventually, the PKI, which
had considerable influence in the air force, gained ground and, with Sukarno, allied more closely with Beijing. On September 30, 1965, the PKI
apparently* attempted a coup d'etat which relied on air force personnel.
The coup was quickly crushed by General Suharto and the army.

While the PRC suffered the most from Sukarno's 1965 ouster, Soviet
relations with Indonesia were also affected. The Soviet Union then turned
to Vietnam as its focus in Southeast Asia. The Soviets, however, have not
abandoned their efforts to regain influence in Indonesia. Soviet "agitprop"
stresses the threat to Indonesia posed by the indigenous Chinese.[141] Indonesia maintained relations with both the Soviet Union and North Vietnam
during the Vietnam War, and subsequently Indonesian official relations
with both Hanoi and Moscow have been characterized as "cool but cor-

---

*There is still confusion as to who was primarily responsible for this coup—Sukarno or the
PKI.

rect." The Soviet Union's largest Southeast Asian embassy is in Djakarta, which underscores the importance of Indonesia. Djakarta is reputedly the center for Soviet intelligence operations in Southeast Asia.

Indonesian authorities face the problems of a low standard of living (approximately $300 per capita annual income), an ossified social and political structure, and increasing turbulence among students and Moslem groups. Given these circumstances, the Soviet Union appears content to wait for changes in Indonesia's internal political situation hoping to regain its former advantageous position in that country.[142]

In a July, 1985, dedication of the new Jakarta airport, named after the independence leader Sukarno, President Suharto made peace with Indonesia's troubled past, but also opened a door to the PRC. Beijing sent its foreign minister, Wu Xugian, to the ceremony, just after signing an agreement to reestablish direct commerce between the two countries after a lapse of 18 years. The Soviets will now face greater competition for influence in this key Southeast Asian country.

The PKI has become the only pro-Soviet communist party in any ASEAN state. In the event of domestic political instability, the PKI represents a way for Moscow to re-establish a strong diplomatic position in Indonesia. When the present generals retire, the question is not only who will replace them, but also how this will affect Indonesian foreign policy. The two nationalist newspapers, *Merdika* and the *Indonesian Observer* are pro-Soviet and pro-Vietnamese in their editorials, arguing that it is logical for Vietnam to control all of Indochina.

If there is another revolutionary upheaval, Moscow will again try to reap the benefits. If the Soviet Union reestablishes itself in Indonesia, Moscow will enjoy a dominant position at both ends of Southeast Asia: on the border of China in the Socialist Republic of Vietnam and in the strategic straits connecting the Pacific and Indian Oceans.

Thailand

Thailand's importance lies in its strategic location, its large population, and its key position in ASEAN. It is the only ASEAN state where all superpowers (U.S., USSR, and PRC) vie for influence. If Thailand can survive as a non-communist state, it will stand up in sharp and favorable contrast to Vietnam, Laos, and Cambodia.

Thailand does not exercise effective control over most of its border areas. Although the indigenous insurgency movement—approximately 4,000–5,000 armed guerrillas as of 1986 does not pose an immediate threat to the government, it could, with external support, become disruptive in border areas.[143]

Thailand and the Philippines are more pro-U.S. than the other ASEAN countries. Thailand sent 20,000 troops to assist American forces in South Vietnam. The Thais also provided 15,000 volunteers to fight in Laos against the Pathet Lao, and they allowed 40,000 U.S. airmen to be stationed in the country during the Vietnam War. Until 1977, SEATO (South East Asia Treaty Organization) headquarters were located in Bangkok. After the communist victory in South Vietnam in 1975, Thailand obtained much military equipment (especially planes and ships) from the South Vietnamese fleeing to Thailand. Moreover, Thailand has given refuge to some of Pol Pot's beleaguered forces, and has allowed them to return to Cambodia to continue the battle against the Vietnamese and the government forces. Lastly, the Thais have allowed the Chinese to transport supplies across their territory to the Khmer Rouge forces.

Vietnam holds several grievances against Thailand, and Thailand would be a target if the Vietnamese decide to expand their interest in Southeast Asia. Moscow's policy has been to work against a Thai-Chinese rapprochement, to encourage Thai-Vietnamese accommodation, and to improve all facets of Soviet-Thai relations. Despite considerable efforts the Soviets have still not been able to achieve success.

Soviet support for a Vietnamese policy hostile to Thailand could destabilize this pro-U.S. state, and could also directly affect the viability of ASEAN itself. Huge numbers of refugees, and long borders with two pro-Vietnamese states, Laos and Kampuchea, have made the Thais justifiably sensitive about national security. Soon after the Vietnam invasion of Kampuchea (Cambodia), President Carter sent a diplomatic message to Moscow and Hanoi that the United States would defend Thailand in the event of attack. The Thais, regarding Vietnam as their chief threat look to both the PRC and the U.S. for support.[144]

On March 31, 1981, the Thai government of Prime Minister General Prem Tinsulanonda was the target of a coup staged by General Sant Chipatima. Prime Minister Prem was able to quickly re-establish control and reaffirm Thai commitments to ASEAN and the U.S. Thailand is economically healthy and their pro-U.S. stance will likely continue. Vietnam's incursions into Thai territory, close to the Cambodian frontier present a serious security problem to Thailand.

In 1983, Soviet Deputy Foreign Minister Mikhail Kapitsa threatened that the Vietnamese would support insurgents in countries opposed to the Vietnamese regime in Kampuchea. Following this, Vietnam, with Soviet-bloc help, set up training camps in Laos for their guerrillas.

In July, 1985, Secretary of State George Shultz, at a meeting of ASEAN foreign ministers, pledged U.S. support to these allies and reaffirmed U.S. security pledges to Thailand. He also visited Kampuchean refugee camps on the border, but avoided a commitment to greater U.S. support for their struggle against the Vietnamese. Another coup attempt against Prem's government in September 1985 was quickly crushed. Thailand is prosperous and resilient and will stay on even keel.

Malaysia

Soviet strategic interest in Malaysia centers on its location on the north of the Malacca Strait, the major route between the Indian and Pacific Oceans. Malaysia regards the strait as part of its territorial waters, but the Soviets feel this threatens their Black Sea-Vladivostok passage.

The Soviets have no ties with the guerrilla movements of Malaysia, which are either pro-Chinese or nationalist. Insurgency in Malaysia might offer a vehicle for Vietnamese, and thereby Soviet, influence. The Soviets have emphasized to Malaysian leaders that it is the Chinese, not they, who support Malaysian rebel groups.

Singapore

The geographic hub of Southeast Asia and the fourth busiest world port, Singapore is a vital link between Northeast and South Asia. Port facilities in Singapore would provide a strategic location for the Soviet fleet at an important point on the European-Pacific route. Since the Chinese invasion of Vietnam in 1979, however, Singapore has often refused service to Soviet naval vessels.

The expansion of the Soviet navy into the Indian Ocean explains much of the Soviet interest in Singapore. Singapore was very receptive to the idea of adding a security role to ASEAN. Indeed, in October, 1977, *Pravda* sharply rebuked Singapore's Prime Minister, Lee Kuan Yew, for advocating a greater U.S. role in Southeast Asia.[145] Lee insisted that in the event of a withdrawal from South Korea, U.S. troops should be stationed "somewhere else in the western Pacific." The prime minister has also urged the U.S., "to match the Soviet build-up in the Pacific step by step."[146]

The Philippines

After three years of negotiations, the terms of the 99-year base agreement between the United States and the Philippines were revised in 1979 and gave the Philippines explicit sovereignty over the bases.

The Soviets vigorously supported Philippine demands for greater control over U.S. bases, which Moscow deemed a security threat. Moscow was resigned to support whatever policy Manila pursued but hoped for a blow to the United States. Subic Bay, the largest U.S. naval complex in Southeast Asia, services the U.S. 7th Fleet. From here, the United States patrols sea and air lanes in the Western Pacific and the Indian Ocean.

The Soviets now have a close relationship with the Philippine communists.[147] Their Libyan associate, Colonel Qaddafi, has supported the Muslim rebellion against the Philippine government. The Soviet attempt to capitalize on Philippine apprehension about an increase of Japan's military has turned into a waiting game. The August, 1983, assassination of Benigno

Aquino, long a political opponent of President Marcos, has plunged that country into political turmoil. Opposition leaders have accused the government of complicity in Aquino's death. Massive anti-government demonstrations erupted in the country since the assassination. Continued unrest could damage U.S.-Philippine relations, as could any congressional cutback of U.S. bases.

During 1985 the political and economic situation in the Philippines deteriorated drastically. The New People's Army (NPA) is the military arm of the "new" Communist Party of the Philippines which is a Maoist, pro-Chinese party. Large-scale rebellions are taking place in many parts of the country and thousands of people have been killed.[148] Strong opposition to President Marcos and considerable U.S. pressure led to a decision to hold Presidential elections in early 1986.

Marcos claimed to have won the election. The subsequent ouster of Ferdinand Marcos from the Philippines and the accession to power of Corazon Aquino in early 1986 appeared to herald a new and favorable phase in U.S. involvement in that strategically vital nation. But events since then have raised some doubts as to whether the Philippine return to democracy will be untroubled. For one thing the communist threat to reviving democracy in that country remains very real. The communist party is active in all the nation's provinces and controls some 20 percent of the population through "Shadow Governments." The chief of the Philippine Armed Forces, General Fidel V. Ramos has openly asserted that communist rebels had taken advantage of the "liberal atmosphere" of the new government of President Aquino to resume their local influence.

At the same time, he said the military is struggling to dig itself out of a "big black hole" of inefficiency and corruption as it begins to effect long-waited changes that would help it combat the insurgents. (Seth Mydons, New York Times, June 5, 1986, p. A-3)

The illegal communist party of the Philippines and its armed wing, the New People's Army, whose strength Ramos put at 16,500 regular fighters, have increased their local influence around the country in the first five months of the year. General Ramos said that the number of villages influenced or infiltrated by the communists had increased by 9 percent since 1985 to 7,631, or 18 percent of the country's 41,615 villages. These are spread through 62 of the 74 provinces. "The situation remains well under control but may deteriorate seriously if political and economic instabilities persist."

He stressed, as he has in the past, that "for counterinsurgency to succeed, military efforts are not enough." He urged greater coordination among the military, the civilian government and the private sector.

There is also a considerable and long-simmering Moslem insurgency in Mindanao. Again according to General Ramos, after initial peace feelers toward the new government, the largely dormant Muslim insurgency on the southern island of Mindanao "has lately stepped up armed activities."

Forty-six Muslim rebels were among the 421 insurgents he listed as killed during a three months period.

Marcos left the Philippines with much loot and left the country in economic disarray. Aquino needs a far greater package of fast economic aid than she has thus far received. In mid August, 1986, Richard C. Lugar, Chairman of the Senate Foreign Relations Committee, said that her September 1986 visit to Washington would be helpful in persuading Congress to approve increased economic support. Japan has also pledged economic aid.

Another of Aquino's problems is her tendency to be conciliatory to her die-hard opponents and enemies. Nothing was done to block obvious preparations for the coup attempt by Marcos supporters. When the coup failed nothing was done to discipline people who acted treasonably against her government. The notorious inefficiency and corruption of the Philippine army has already been noted. These problems, taken together assure Aquino a troubled future. Only if she demonstrates greater strength and resolution can she succeed.

Acquino did just that in late November 1986 when she fired her defense minister, Juan Ponce Enrile, and most of her cabinet. Enrile had been her most outspoken public critic. Subsequently she deftly awarded Enrile the Philippine Legion of Honor.

The Sino-Soviet Struggle in Indochina

Sino-Soviet conflict in Southeast Asia was defused during the Vietnam War, for Hanoi refrained from conflict with either power. The end of the war and the emergence of a Soviet-Vietnamese alliance introduced a third major power into the region.

The Soviet-Vietnamese alliance has grave implications for peace and stability in Southeast Asia. The Lao Dong Party, headquartered in Hanoi, seeks to rule over all of Indochina. By the end of the war it was firmly in control of Laos and seeking control over Kampuchea.

In Laos, the Communist Pathet Lao soon eliminated all moderates from power and replaced them with pro-Vietnameses. The Pathet Lao power grows from the barrel of a Vietnamese gun, and they have governed Laos as a satellite of the Indochinese Communist Party. Since 1976, when the 600-year-old monarchy was replaced by the Lao Democratic Republic (LPDR), the North Vietnamese have had 40–60,000 soldiers in Laos. Bases accessible to the Soviets have been established on the Laotian-China border.

The reintegration of North and South Vietnam, is a top priority in Hanoi.[149] The Vietnamese-Soviet relationship is based in large part on Soviet willingness to help the Vietnamese achieve their foreign and domestic goals.

Marking the second anniversary victory in Vietnam, Premier Phan Van Dong visited the USSR in April, 1977, and requested membership in the

Council of Mutual Economic Assistance (CMEA); and by June of 1978 the SRV was admitted, to the surprise of other members.[150] While this event was a political coup for Moscow in its competition with Beijing, there were also compelling incentives for Hanoi to join CMEA. Membership should make it easier for Vietnam to obtain needed technology, machinery, and aid from CMEA, largely east European countries. Soviet aid should increase since Vietnam has concluded a treaty of friendship with Moscow and joined Comecon.

There are other factors in the Vietnamese alliance with the Soviet Union. There is an historical and cultural enmity between China and Vietnam. In addition, Hanoi's regional policies bring conflict with Beijing. Finally, Hanoi's alliance with Moscow reinforced its hostility toward Beijing.

In 1978, Vietnam attacked Kampuchea, and quickly captured all the major cities and controlled communications in Cambodia. In supporting Vietnam, the Soviets gained strategic naval position in the Indian Ocean and South China Sea. In particular, the Soviets sought Cam Ranh Bay, a major anchorage supported by shore installations that were built by the United States during the war.

With access to Cam Ranh Bay, Moscow could control approaches to the Strait of Malacca, as well as outflank the PRC South Sea fleet from Whampoa, Chankiang, and Yulin and counter U.S. forces at Subic Bay and Clark Air Force Base. But it is not known whether use of Cam Ranh Bay was conceded to the Soviets in the November 1978 Soviet-Vietnamese Friendship Treaty. Vietnamese permission to use these facilities was a quid pro quo for demonstrated Soviet support and Soviet restraints imposed on Beijing in negotiations with Hanoi.

By the end of 1980, the Soviets had permanently established a South China Sea Eskadra (squadron) and elevated the operations of their newly acquired naval facilities in the SRV to equal their principal Pacific fleet base at Vladivostok.

Soviet maritime expansion has continued. Construction of base facilities at Kompong Som, Kampuchea, 100 miles from the Thai border, was begun in 1984. When finished, this port will provide the USSR Navy with a deep bay, major submarine base and an excellent anchorage.[151]

The Soviet Union and China in the Kampuchean-Vietnamese Conflict

Beijing and Moscow have both used the Kampuchean Vietnamese conflict as leverage against the other. Anti-Vietnamese Cambodian guerrillas have claimed that the Vietnam-Khmer Rouge conflict is a result of the Vietnamese goal of dominating Indochina. In the 1930s, Moscow (through the Comintern) supported the Viet Minh's claim to leading the revolution in Indochina. There is little evidence that a strong pro-Vietnamese faction existed in the Khmer Rouge after Shihanouk's deposal in 1970.

The Cambodians may have perceived Soviet collusion and support in the Vietnamese plans to dominate Kampuchea. In 1977, they began large-scale attacks upon Vietnam. In August 1977, following major Cambodian-Vietnamese battles, the Soviet Union demonstrated support by sending a military delegation to Vietnam.

The Soviets wanted to avoid a pretext for China to involve itself in the Kampuchean-Vietnamese conflict, and they urged a resolution of the Kampuchean-Vietnamese border dispute. The Soviets pointed to Vietnam's relations with Laos as an example for Cambodia, and having "significance for Southeast Asia as a whole."[152] The Laotian model gave little incentive for Phnom Penh to begin negotiating with Hanoi.

Beijing was reported to have offered in July, 1977, to mediate the Kampuchean-Vietnamese dispute. Until early 1978, Beijing was circumspect in its policy regarding Kampuchean-Vietnamese conflict. China wished to avoid pressure on Hanoi and avert a situation in which Vietnam might become more obliging toward Soviet requests for a naval base at Cam Ranh Bay.

Hanoi decided to attack Kampuchea in 1977. The realization that it was not prepared to overtake the Pol Pot regime led Hanoi to withdraw in late January, 1978 and to offer new proposals for a settlement. Subsequently, China embarked on a policy of brinksmanship to check Vietnam which involved threats against Kampuchea for its shift toward the Soviets, for its claims over islands in the South China Sea, and for its mistreatment of the indigenous Chinese. By summer, 1978, about 180,000 ethnic Chinese had fled from Vietnam to China, and in September, 1978, China-Vietnam talks on refugees were suspended.

As a logical outgrowth of these actions, Vietnam and the Soviet Union entered into the Treaty of Friendship and Cooperation on November 3, 1978. One prominent Soviet spokesman explained that the treaty was necessitated because, "The political climate in Southeast Asia is being poisoned by the Chinese leadership.[153] The Soviets intimated that the treaty would contribute toward the policy of encircling China.

The Soviet-Vietnamese treaty has forged one more link in the system of treaties of alliance between the fraternal socialist countries.[154]

An immediate result of the treaty was the visit to Kampuchea of a delegation led by Wang Dongxing, deputy chairman of the CCP, who stressed Chinese backing of the Pol Pot regime. Both Beijing and Phnom Penh seemed to believe that the Soviet-Vietnamese treaty presaged new developments. As Beijing built up its forces on the Vietnamese border, Moscow moved to strengthen Vietnam, and in December, 1978, delivered two Petya II-class frigates to the Vietnamese navy.[155]

The Kampuchean Invasion

Hanoi undertook to topple the Pol Pot regime in December, 1978, because Vietnam could not begin rebuilding the South as long as the problems remained in Kampuchea. On December 3, 1978, Hanoi announced the formation of the Kampuchean United Front for National Salvation (UFNS) in the eastern section of Cambodia. The UFNS consisted of dissident Cambodian elements receptive to Vietnamese influence. Though the UFNS had few armed troops, their forces were helped by the estimated 100,000 men Hanoi supplied for action against Kampuchea.

Beijing, meanwhile, became more belligerent, calling Vietnam "the Cuba of Southeast Asia." China warned of a "limit to China's forebearance and restraint toward Vietnam.[156] By mid-December, 1978, Hanoi had consolidated its gains in eastern Cambodia and was ready to strike at Phnom Penh. Vietnam's success in securing eastern Kampuchea was attributed to supplies from the USSR.[157]

The Vietnamese assault began before Christmas, 1978. Phnom Penh fell on January 7, 1979, just as the Pol Pot government was requesting UN support to resist Vietnam. The Soviets promptly recognized the new Cambodian government led by Heng Samrin. Moscow reportedly counseled Hanoi to proceed cautiously in consolidating control of Cambodia, for the Soviets did not wish to provoke a Sino-Vietnamese conflict.

The weeks following the fall of Phnom Penh saw intensified fighting in Cambodia. The new government's reliance on the Vietnamese made it difficult for Hanoi to have sufficient troops to counter the Chinese buildup on their border. The Vietnamese had to bolster their original Kampuchean invasion force for invasion was easier than occupation. After the conquest of most of Cambodia, China began supplying Pol Pot's guerrilla forces via Thai ports.[158] The Chinese buildup along the Vietnamese border had by January, 1979, reached one-half million troops.

The Soviet navy was deployed off the Vietnamese coast during the offensive against Kampuchea, and these forces were divided into two groups. One consisting of intelligence-gathering vessels and gunboats, was positioned between the Chinese island of Hainan and the northern Vietnamese coast. Its purpose was to spy on Chinese military communications on the Vietnamese border and ascertain Chinese military intentions for Hanoi. The other was dispersed in the South China Sea and consisted of two heavy *Kresta*-class cruisers and other ships. Their mission was to block a Chinese move against the Vietnamese-held Spratly Islands,[159] or, at least, to warn Beijing that an attack on the Spratlys would involve the Soviet Union. Chinese control over the Spratlys could mean domination of vital sea lanes.

China's invasion of Vietnam on February 17, 1979, was preceded by a considerable buildup of forces on both sides of the border. China sought to demonstrate to Vietnam that its alliance with the USSR would not harm

Chinese interests in Southeast Asia, and also to "punish" Vietnam for antagonizing China by invading Kampuchea. The Chinese also wanted to reduce Vietnamese military pressure on the Khmer Rouge guerrillas in Cambodia.

Initial Soviet reaction to the Chinese invasion of Vietnam was guarded. Soviet intervention would risk war with China. Soviet forces on the Chinese border would require considerable reinforcement for a large-scale offensive against China, and extreme Siberian weather makes winter troop movement almost impossible. Preserving U.S.-Soviet detente also mitigated against Soviet intervention in the invasion. In fact, Soviet officials vigorously asserted that a principal goal of the Chinese invasion (and Deng's trip to the United States just before it) was to drive a wedge between the United States and the USSR, scuttle detente, and wreck the possibility of a SALT II agreement. The dominant view in Moscow seemed to be that the United States was guilty of complicity.[160]

In response to the Chinese invasion, Moscow chose to supply Vietnam with military assistance and diplomatic support. Following the invasion, a Soviet military delegation went to assess and report on the military situation. Moscow also airlifted minor supplies to Vietnam, indicating that the SRV forces were not short on supplies.

The Soviets deployed more ships to the South China Sea including the Soviet Pacific Fleet Flagship, which was capable of directing air and naval operations. These Soviet naval deployments in 1979 were the first show of force by the USSR in the region.[161]

As the Vietnamese position deteriorated with the fall of several provincial capitals, Moscow's admonishments to Beijing became sharper. There were indications that the Soviets favored action against China.[162] When a battle between Chinese and Vietnamese forces for the city of Lang Son seemed likely, the Soviet Union warned of the dangers and declared their readiness to honor obligations of the Soviet-Vietnamese Treaty.

Soviet assistance also provided aircraft to transport Vietnamese troops from the southern front (Kampuchea) to the northern front (China).[163] Moscow's predicament—maintaining political credibility in Hanoi and the rest of the Third World, without war with Beijing—was resolved by China's withdrawal from Vietnam in mid-March. By capturing the provincial capital of Lang Son, and forcing Vietnam to redeploy troops from Laos and Cambodia to northern Vietnam, and by demonstrating its superior capability (vis-a-vis the USSR) for intervening in Indochina, the Beijing leadership could convincingly argue that it had achieved its "limited objectives."

Anchoring of three Soviet naval vessels in Cam Ranh Bay in late March, 1979, (a guided missile cruiser, a frigate, and a mine sweeper) was the culmination of increased naval involvement in the region. Ironically, China's invasion was a significant factor in Hanoi's decision to allow Moscow use of one of the world's best naval bases. Soviet facilities at Da

Nang and Cam Ranh Bay are reportedly under Soviet administrative control and entirely independent of the Vietnamese military command.[164]

The implications of a Soviet base at Cam Ranh Bay were realized in mid-April when the Japanese Defense Agency reported that Soviet electronic spy planes were also being based there.[165] These reconnaissance aircraft take off from Vladivostok and fly along the Chinese coast monitoring Chinese movements, landing at Cam Ranh to refuel and return. They also monitor U.S. vessels in the region. The Soviet base at Cam Ranh Bay will improve their global military position by linking their Indian and Pacific Ocean naval forces.

The Soviet Union appears to have won the latest round in the struggle for Indochina. Generally the Chinese invasion of Vietnam was poorly executed and Moscow did not need to extensively support Hanoi. At the start of 1987, however, Cambodian resistance to the 20 or so Vietnamese divisions in that country continued.

There is evidence that Moscow is dominating Hanoi's policy toward both Cambodia and China. Hoang Van Hoan, a former Vice Chairman of the Vietnamese National Assembly who defected to China in 1979, stated publicly that Vietnam was no longer an independent country but totally subservient to the Soviet Union.

Vietnam provides the USSR with a formidable ally in a region where it has long sought influence. Soviet support for Vietnam has enhanced their prestige and contributed to perceptions of growing Soviet power. Finally, Soviet naval and air presence in Vietnam provides greater potential for interdicting U.S. naval movements from the Pacific to the Indian Ocean and countering U.S. military presence in the Philippines.

During the 1985 dry season, Vietnam launched its longest and most violent campaign against the three resistance groups in Kampuchea. Resistance continued, however, and the U.S. Congress is considering giving two of these groups financial support.

1985 marked the tenth anniversary of the fall of Saigon. Life in Vietnam is barren and harsh; the country stays afloat with Soviet arms and inadequate Soviet aid. Some 10,000 Vietnamese remain in reeducation camps. Many thousands of Vietnamese opponents of Hanoi have been executed. Amnesty International has called these "forced labor camps, whose prisoners subsist on meager rations and sometimes only one cup of water a day."[166]

In mid-1985 there were indications that Hanoi would like to end the diplomatic isolation imposed by the 1979 invasion of Kampuchea. Vietnamese Foreign minister Nguyen Co Thach proposed negotiations about Kampuchea that included:

"A withdrawal from Kampuchea by Hanoi's troops in return for a simultaneous cutoff of Chinese aid to the Khmer Rouge and a denial of sanctuary for the guerrillas. Thach also suggested that Heng Samrin, the Vietnamese-backed President of Kampuchea, and former Head of State Prince Norodom Sihanouk should negotiate a sharing of power as part of a transitional process."[167]

In 1986 the economy of Vietnam was in shambles, that of Kampuchea far worse. Yet the SRV is going ahead with plans to consolidate its control over that unfortunate country. One device it is using is to settle thousands of Vietnamese who are trained to speak Khmer and to adopt Khmer names.

Pressures from grass-roots party organizations prompted sweeping changes in the Vietnamese Community Party leadership in December, 1986. Economic hardships, including wide-spread malnutrition, combined with bitterness over Soviet influence in Hanoi led to a major Politboro shake-up.

We can only speculate what the future holds for Moscow in Southeast Asia. The area that was Moscow's "weak link" can no longer be so described. The Soviet Union as a strong new force in Southeast Asia has created unease in the ASEAN states, which was greatly reinforced by the Soviet invasion of Afghanistan in 1979. The emergence of Soviet-Vietnamese power presents a challenge to American foreign policy in Southeast Asia.

The Northeast Asian Closure

Sino-Soviet conflict in Northeast Asia has been less violent than in Southwest and Southeast Asia. Yet, in the long run, this struggle may be of greater strategic significance, because Japan is the pivotal point in the battle for Asia. Japan, perceiving a growing Soviet military threat, has been moving closer to the PRC. Japan's security is greatly affected by the status of Taiwan and the Republic of Korea. If the Soviet Union or the PRC should dominate either country, the security of Japan would be jeopardized.

Taiwan's location in the Soviet sea lane between Cam Ranh Bay and Vladivostok makes it an important factor in the development of Soviet strategy in Asia.

Taiwan, or the Republic of China (ROC), had been the link between U.S. security in Northeast and Southeast Asia, and part of the defensive perimeter of Japan and South Korea. U.S. military access to Taiwan has supported all deployments in the western Pacific. Taiwan's several harbors can accommodate the entire U.S. Seventh Fleet, and its air bases can service any aircraft in the world. The island also offers intelligence facilities to monitor Soviet naval activities in the Far East.

The U.S. decision to terminate the U.S.-ROC Defense Pact has created a number of uncertainties. If this results in Sino-Taiwanese negotiations that incorporate Taiwan into the PRC, the Soviet Union, Japan, South Korea, and many nations of Southeast Asia would feel gravely threatened. Once an integral part of China, Taiwan would assure Beijing control of the Taiwan Strait and ability to challenge both the Soviet navy and Japanese shipping. After PRC-U.S. normalization, Deng Xiaping made it clear that two situations require military force against Taiwan: refusal to negotiate reunification or appeals to the Soviets for help.

There is deep concern in Japan regarding U.S. security commitments to Taiwan because the country will remain part of the Japanese security perimeter regardless of changes in its diplomatic status.

Normalization of China-U.S. relations introduced delicate nuances into U.S.-Japanese security relations. The Soviets regard Japan as a major threat in the Pacific. Japan, as a partner in the U.S.-Japan Security Treaty and as a potential economic and political ally of China, is a Soviet nightmare. In time, Japan may be able to block the Soviet naval fleet through the Straits of Soya, Tsugaru and Tsushima on their way from Vladivostok to the Pacific Ocean.

Soviet objectives have been to sever the U.S.-Japanese connection, to prevent Japan from closer alliance with Beijing, and, if possible, to obtain Japanese help for economic development of Siberia. Yet, because of unresolved issues and incredible Sovet heavyhandedness, Soviet-Japanese relations can hardly be described as normal. Key issues involve a peace treaty, the dispute over the northern territories, Siberian development, fishing controversies, and security questions.

To further complicate Soviet-Japanese relations, China clouds Soviet-Japanese relations. The development of mutual defenses between Japan and China would pose a serious threat to the Soviet Union. The development of an anti-Soviet coalition between the United States, Japan, and China would pose the gravest possible threat to Moscow. Both developments are possible, though unlikely, in the immediate future.

Japan as a global economic power, has wanted a stable four-power equilibrium in the Pacific. Tokyo carefully sought an equidistance policy with Moscow, Beijing, and even the United States. But, in 1979, Japan abandoned this effort and has assumed that cooperation with the PRC and stronger ties with the U.S. are vital. Japanese public opinion has shown a definite warming toward China, while Japanese distrust of the Soviet Union is increasingly evident. Moscow's unilateral abrogation of the Neutrality Pact of World War II and Soviet occupation of the northern territories provoke intense resentment.

Japan does pursue a policy of equidistance in economic trade. Japan can not afford to alienate either China or the Soviet Union because of the need for raw materials and markets and growing trade difficulties with the United States and Western Europe. Politics have not interfered with Soviet-Japanese trade as it has with Soviet-American trade. The Soviet Union is apparently acquiescing to the Japanese penchant for separating economics from politics.

Tokyo has discovered that Beijing and Moscow have different assets and liabilities and that maintaining balance between the two is extremely difficult. Japan's overwhelming reliance on economic power and the lack of political and military leverage has prevented development of an effective foreign policy. China presents Japan with advantages of cultural affinity, geographic proximity, large consumer markets, a significant political lobby, and, most of all, no perceivable threat. In contrast, the Soviet Union, although it may offer greater economic opportunities, arouses greater apprehensions. The advantages offered by China appear to outweigh those offered by the Soviet Union by a considerable degree.

Soviet-Japanese relations are much more restrained than Sino-Japanese relations. Understandably, improved Sino-Japanese relations are a serious Soviet concern. The territorial issue is significant to the Japanese. Successive Japanese governments have refused to conclude a peace treaty with the Soviet Union until the Kunashiri, Etorofu, Shikotan, and Hamobai Islands are returned; but Moscow contends that Japan has no title to them. The Soviet Union rejected the last Japanese demand in January, 1978, during a visit to Moscow by Japanese Foreign Minister Sunao Sonoda. In September, 1981, Japanese Foreign Minister Suzuki visited northern Hokkaido to dramatize the Japanese demand for the return of these islands. The outcome of this territorial dispute is a matter of endurance. It will take much more than the unlikely return of the northern territories to alter Japanese animosity toward the Soviet Union.

Growing Soviet deployments in Asia have generated fear and anti-Soviet feeling in Japan and an increase in defense. Noting the imbalance between Japanese and Soviet forces, the Japanese defense chief lamented a defense system of "bamboo spears against Soviet machine guns."

Soviet air and naval bases and sustained deployment of forces in East Asia and the Western Pacific enhances Soviet ability to pressure the PRC and Japan. It also complicates U.S. support of its Manila Pact partners, the Philippines and Thailand, and naval movements between the Pacific and Indian Oceans. The Soviets have continued to upgrade their Pacific fleet. A Kiev-class carrier joined the Soviet Pacific Fleet in mid-1979, and Soviet military presence throughout the Far East has risen dramatically in the 1970s.[168] The Soviets now deploy 650,000 ground troops in the Far East, with 46–50 divisions along the Sino-Soviet border reinforced by approximately 12,000 tanks and 1,600 war planes. Air capabilities have also risen with one-fourth of the Soviet SS-20 missile force targeted against Asia.[169]

Between 1970 and 1980, as the United States reduced its Pacific fleet, the Soviet Pacific fleet increased submarines by 50%, guided missile cruisers by 100%, destroyers by 20%, and guided missile frigates by 1000%. It also acquired a Kiev-Class carrier equipped with VTOL aircraft.[170] The Soviet Pacific fleet has 89 principal surface combatants, 112 other combatant ships, 245 combatant craft, 235 auxiliaries, 102 attack submarines, and 440 naval aviation planes. In 1984, the Pacific fleet acquired a second Kirov-Class nuclear powered guided missile cruiser and two attack submarines, two major surface combatants, 13 fighter-bombers, 12 ASW helicopters, and a third Kiev-Class carrier. A carrier with a full-length flight deck is under construction but will not become operational until the end of the decade.[171]

Two other developments between 1978–1979 showed deviation from the Japanese equidistance policy. The first was the Sino-Japanese Treaty of Friendship of August, 1978, and the second was the Japanese Defense Agency's Fifth White Paper of July, 1979, which focused on the Soviet threat to Japan's survival. Prime Minister Yasuhiro Nakasone, first elected in 1982 and former chief of the Japanese Defense Agency has sought to involve Japan more closely with the Western defense community. He has even described U.S.-Japanese ties as an "alliance," a term the Japanese are generally reluctant to use.

Nakasone's open embrace of the Western community is welcome in Washington and Europe but has brought him condemnation at home and in Moscow. The Soviets are displeased by his support for the deployment of intermediate range missiles in Europe, and they have reminded Japan that its densely populated country is vulnerable to nuclear attack.

The Soviets would like to generate policies of accommodation within Japan's leadership. Some Japanese believe that the U.S. no longer dominates the Pacific and that their country should adjust its policies to the new leading power, the Soviet Union.

The lack of a balance of power in the Pacific creates an unsettling and a dangerous state of affairs.

The Koreas

The interests of four major powers intersect in the Korean peninsula, where tension remains high 30 years after the Korean War. The government of South Korea sought a rapprochement with North Korea shortly after the United States normalized relations with the PRC at the end of 1978. Ideological and economic differences, not to mention mutual hatred, cloud the outcome of such overtures.

The North Korean government may still be searching for an opportunity to attack and defeat the South.* General John A. Wickham, Jr., Commander of United States Forces in Korea, testified before the U.S. House Armed Services Committee on February 20, 1981. He described the military situation on the Korean peninsula as most threatening, with the military forces of North Korea far outnumbering those of South Korea. The North Korean forces are ready to attack without warning and can move independently of both Moscow and Beijing.

A Sino-American alliance could prompt North Korea to obtain additional Soviet support for increased military pressure on South Korea or for an

---

*The bizarre assassination of South Korean President Park Chung Hee on October 26, 1979, may have been one such opportunity. Park had ruled South Korea since he seized power by a coup in May 1961 and his passing introduced a new phase into that country's turbulent political history. The United States warned North Korea of moving against the South.

offensive. A tighter alliance between North Korea and the Soviet Union could precipitate more Sino-Soviet differences.

The intensity of Sino-Soviet competition over the Korean peninsula is readily understandable given its strategic location and their heavy investment in North Korea. North Korea takes full advantage of the Sino-Soviet conflict to assert its independence and to play one against the other. Both Moscow and Beijing are North Korea's treaty allies and military suppliers. Both, in part because of their political rivalry, publicly support North Korea's call for American troop withdrawal from the South.

Moscow has a clear security interest in preventing any country from having a predominant position in North Korea. Current Soviet policy toward Korea is affected by policies toward other big powers, as well as by its bilateral relations with North Korea. To keep pace with Beijing, Moscow has from time to time supported the reunification of Korea. Moscow would like reunification of the Korean peninsula with a minimum of direct Soviet involvement.

In the event of a North-South conflict, Moscow would not hesitate to militarily assist North Korea and try to preempt a similar effort by Beijing. Moscow originally sponsored the establishment of the Democratic People's Republic of Korea and helped the government seated in Pyongyang plan the initial invasion of South Korea in 1950. Chinese intervention proved necessary to rescue North Korea from total collapse following the unexpected and successful U.N.-sponsored American involvement. Sino-North Korea relations have been termed a "militant friendship sealed in blood" as a result of their shared struggle.

During the Korean War and until the early 1970's Beijing and Pyongyang shared the perception that Washington and Tokyo were their main enemies. Beijing now regards the USSR as its main adversary, and this must trouble North Korean leadership. North Korea must have felt abandoned and betrayed when Beijing normalized relations with Washington, disregarding the 1953 Panmunjom Armistice Agreement between the two countries. During 1984 Beijing even opened some contacts with Seoul.

North Korea promised both the PRC and the Soviet Union that neither could establish a base in its territory. Since 1979, North Korea has allowed Soviet merchant ships and tankers to use the year-round port of Najin and transport petroleum and other supplies from there to Vladivostok by rail when that harbor is closed by ice.

There is little chance for reconciliation between the two Koreas in the forseeable future. The attempted assassination of ROK President Hwan in 1983 in Burma will not soon be forgotten in Seoul. Nor did the Soviet downing of a KAL aircraft reduce South Korea's resentment against Pyongyang's powerful ally.

President Hwan's second visit to Washington in April, 1985, bolstered the strong relations between the U.S. and the ROK.

Moscow controls two of the three Asian countries that share borders with both the Soviet Union and China, Afghanistan and outer Mongolia. Only the Korean peninsula is still contested between the two Asian giants.

The Soviets have been observing with concern the strengthening of U.S. security ties with Japan, South Korea and the PRC. At the same time, Soviet commentators deny that Soviet actions, statements, and deployments are responsible for these moves.

The up and down course of the Sino-Soviet split and its consequences for U.S. and PRC relations remain in the fog of the future. Even former president Nixon who was a zestful collaborator in the rapprochement with Peking, when asked whether his China initiative is likely to survive the 2000th year, was obliged to confess that he did not know the answer. Nixon made the right answer since prophecy is a hazardous undertaking.

The precarious and unstable situation in Northeast Asia is likely to continue. If Moscow perceives this as threatening, its likely response would be to strengthen its military presence in the region. This ominous prospect needs careful monitoring.

The struggle in Indochina, the dramatic events in Korea, troubles in Iran, turmoil in the Philippines, and the Soviet invasion of Afghanistan have made Asia a primary concern of Soviet foreign policy. With the war between Iran and Iraq that began in September, 1980, three armed conflicts were being waged simultaneously on the southern flank of Asia. Soviet suppression of resistance in Afghanistan, and Soviet-backed Vietnamese efforts to control Kampuchea were other cases of active fighting.

The Chinese are opposed to the Soviet involvement in Kampuchea and to the invasion of Afghanistan. Chinese policy in Asia currently favors stability and peace, while Soviet policy favors instability. This condition makes U.S. ties with the PRC very important.

The growth of Soviet naval power in the Pacific was marked by a 1985 Soviet fishing agreement with the island state of Kiribati, some 600 miles from the U.S. ballistic missile testing station on the Kwajalein Atoll. Kiribati's neighbor state, Tuvalu, was reported to be considering its own agreement with Moscow.

Soviet interest in fishing in the South Pacific is evidence of Moscow's interest in areas once the preserve of the U.S. and West European powers.

In meetings between Secretary of State Shultz and Australian Foreign Minister Bill Hayden in Canberra, July 15th, 1985, much attention was given to New Zealand's absence from the ANZUS talks. They focused on Soviet efforts to sign fishing agreements with newly independent island states, such as Kiribati, and the risk of similar Soviet overtures to other islands. More than fishing rights are involved, however. U.S. officials fear that Soviet fishing trawlers in the area would be used to conduct covert intelligence activity. The United States is "working on fishing agreements with some of the nations involved" to prevent further Soviet gains, Shultz said.[173]

Soviet fishing fleets also serve the Soviet navy with surveillance, espionage, and communications.

Soviet policy in the Pacific and Asia reflects Soviet fears and confidence. The Soviet Union is concerned about an alliance between the United States, China, and Japan that would curtail Soviet actions in Asia. This concern, however, is counterbalanced by confidence in Soviet military power. The strategic balance in Central Asia increasingly favors the Soviet Union.

The growth of Soviet power on its Pacific flank threatens the stability of all East Asia. Developments in one part may set off actions elsewhere. For example, it may be argued that the PRC-Japan friendship treaty of August, 1978, triggered the November 1978 Soviet-Vietnamese friendship treaty. In turn, the USSR-SRV treaty might have accelerated Sino-U.S. normalization. Sino-U.S. normalization might have affected Vietnam's invasion of Kampuchea, and Soviet support of the invasion.

Expanding Soviet power is a conspicious factor in Asia's becoming the world's largest area of conflict. In collaboration with Vietnam, the Soviet Union controls Laos and Cambodia and has extended its control of Afghanistan. The Chinese assert that the invasion of Afghanistan and Kampuchea bespeaks Soviet double strategy aimed at control of the Persian Gulf and the Strait of Malacca.[174]

Soviet Inroads Into the Pacific

There were a number of 1986 developments in the far flung Pacific region which reflect a growing Soviet challenge to U.S. interests in this immense area. The evidence of a continuing overall build up in the region was unmistakable. A book published in 1986 by Auburn House, straightforwardly assesses the character of the Soviet military buildup in the Far East to determine effective U.S. and allied responses. This timely work examines the challenge the United States faces in maintaining a strong nuclear capability in the Asian-Pacific region without giving rise to political tensions among its allies. ("The Soviet Far East Military Buildup: Nuclear Dilemmas and Asian Security", Edited by Richard O. Solomon and Masataka Kosaka, Auburn House Publishing Co., Dover, MA, 1986)

Closely related was the decision by New Zealand's Prime Minister David Lange, to ban U.S. nuclear powered and nuclear-armed ships from its territory. This came at a time when the Soviet Union was increasing its military presence in the Asia-Pacific region dramatically and was seeking to exploit a growing "peace movement" in the South Pacific.

The New Zealand Labor government ostensibly seeks to promote a foreign policy "less aligned" with such traditional allies as the U.S. and Britain. Lange wants an alliance that does not require New Zealand to be defended by nuclear weapons. He further wants to promote his policies as an example for the rest of the Pacific to follow.

The Soviet Union is expanding its military capability in Asia and apparently intends to gain a foothold among the vulnerable South Pacific microstates. Western officials were troubled by the sounds coming out of Vanuatu. In July, 1986 the tiny South Pacific republic announced that it would establish diplomatic relations with the Soviet Union, less than a month after entering negotiations with Moscow over fishing and aircraft-landing rights. In 1985 Kiribati became the first South Pacific country to sign a fishing-rights treaty with Moscow. Fiji has expressed a similar interest. While U.S. officials warned against "Soviet subversion" in the region, New Zealand Prime Minister Lange was undisturbed. "The tiny South Pacific countries are loyal to the West," he said, wryly adding, "Their structures of government do not leave themselves to being hijacked by people with thick accents or big wallets." (Time, July 14, 1986, p. 28)

The huge naval and air base on Vietnam's coast that for many years was the key supply hub to the U.S. war effort in that country has gradually been transformed into what the U.S. Pacific Command now calls "the largest Soviet naval base" for forward deployment of warships outside the Soviet Union.

Admiral Ronald Hayes, commander in chief of the U.S. Pacific Command, said the Soviet buildup at Cam Ranh Bay is "the most significant development in this theater [of operations] in recent years. When you look at it from a strategic sense" he said, "Cam Ranh Bay gives them the warm water port that they have been seeking since Catherine the Great." (Branigan, William, "Soviet Military Operations Seen Increasing in the Pacific", The Washington Post, Aug 1, 1986 p. A12)

The 1986 Japanese Government White Paper, entitled "Japan's Paper," released over the weekend of August 9–10, emphasized that "the Soviet Far East buildup has been most significant in strategic intermediate-range nuclear missiles, which are within striking distance of Japan."

The annual report by the Japan Defense Agency points out that the military circumstances faced by the nation have become increasingly "severe" as a result of the Soviet buildup.

The report says the number of Soviet SS-20 intermediate-range nuclear missiles has increased by 27 from last year to more than 162 in the region and that the number of TU-22 strategic Backfire supersonic medium-range bombers in the same region has now reached 85. It says that Japan is within range of the SS-20s deployed in central Siberia and east of Lake Baikal.

The paper notes that Japan's defense posture has worsened due to expansion of Soviet military power in the area since Japan's national defense program was outlined a decade ago by the Cabinet of then-Prime Minister Takeo Miki.

The paper stated that Soviet military capabilities are now on a par with those of the United States in nuclear as well as conventional weapons, and added, "If some country thinks that it can commit an act of aggression against Japan with conventional weapons, the nuclear deterrence provided by the United States will not be adequate to prevent such an act. The Japanese self-defense forces would play a crucial role in the country's defense should this ever occur." (Branigan, Op.cit., A-24)

Admiral Hays summed up the implications of the Soviet military surge in the Pacific in an interview at his headquarters. Hays said the Soviets are able "to interdict essential sea lines of communication, to strike lucrative targets that are shockingly undefended at this time, like the Aleutians, Guam and the Philippines. And we actually see them conducting simulated strike missions against these areas."

Expanding Soviet Empire

This review of Soviet activities has shown that the scope, diversity, and intensity of Soviet global activity reveals a coordinated and massive effort of influence and control. These are consistent with the strategic concepts and designs set forth in the first three chapters.

The ominous and massive character of the Soviet threat to democratic societies is finally being recognized. Until the Soviet invasion of Afghanistan, the prevailing view was that Soviet motives were primarily defensive. Soviet buildup on its European and Chinese frontiers seemed only natural for a country threatened on two flanks. In truth, the buildup including space and nuclear weapons has been consuming some 14 percent of the Soviet GNP. The Soviet government increasingly seems to be presiding over an insecure system of imperial power. As the challenges to the system build, the Soviet Union's military power extends the system's frontiers, and, in the process, saves it from internal disintegration.

What conclusions can be drawn from the record of Soviet performance over the past thirty years? Has the Soviet Union become a purely imperialistic power?

Soviet policy and expansionism is informed by an underlying strategy, but the Soviets do not seem to be pursuing a detailed plan for world domination. Nevertheless, the growth of Soviet power into distant regions does indicate a desire for an empire with frontier provinces in every continent. If the world's political map of 1945 were compared to the map of 1987, one would conclude that the Soviets had many victories and that the United States and its allies had suffered many disastrous defeats. Above all, the Soviets have demonstrated a willingness to spend their military currency at every opportunity.

The world is witnessing the steady global expansion of the world's only remaining empire.

The expansion may rely directly on the Soviet military, as in Eastern Europe or Afghanistan, or on an indigenous but Soviet-supported military as in Cuba, Nicaragua and Vietnam.

This chapter has traced the Soviet record of expansion in the Mediterranean—Middle East region, the growth of Soviet influence in Western Europe and Scandinavia via a combination of intimidation tactics and peace overtures. Their movement, with Cuba, into Central America, Soviet-Cuban efforts to de-stabilize Chile by shipping arms to Communist factions in that beleagured country is matched by their growing beach-head in anti-American Peru.

There has also been an enhanced Soviet presence across the Northern borders of the Republic of South Africa, the deep Soviet penetration into Ethiopia, its military presence in Aden, its on-going invasion of Afghanistan, its military presence in Vietnam, as well as Soviet assistance to Hanoi's campaign to supress resistance to its rule in Kampuchea, add recent Soviet moves into the small nation states of the South Pacific and finally the Soviet Union has tightened its alliance with North Korea. All in all it has been an impressive Soviet performance.

The incremental manner in which existing social structures are changed makes the process of Sovietization of its satrapies in many regions of the globe difficult to recognize. For example, Nicaragua has not yet become a completely Marxist-Leninist state and many Western leaders are not able to discern the true goals of the Sandinista government.

After the U.S. Congress in April 1985 rejected aid to the Contras, President Ortega flew to Moscow. There he met with the new Soviet leader, Mikhail Gorbachev, who promised continued economic aid for "friendly Nicaragua."

The amount of aid wasn't specified—although some Western estimates put it at $200 million a year—and there was no mention at all of military assistance. That subject probably was discussed by the two sides, but the Kremlin was careful to make no publc commitment; neither delegation to the talks included the customary complement of military men. The Soviets seem to regard Nicaragua as a low-cost, low-risk investment. They are happy to score propaganda points, and they will do what they can, short of major military and economic aid, to maintain the Sandinistas as an irritant to the United States.[175]

On his way back from Moscow Ortega also visited several Western European countries to seek political support and economic help. He sat with Prime Minister Felipe Gonzales of Spain, with whom President Reagan had recently met. At a news conference Gonzales said:

I think the Nicaraguan revolution is extraordinarily attractive, though I disagree with a number of things.

Mr. Gonzalez was blunt in saying that Nicaragua still lacked some political liberties such as freedom of the press and limited political participation.

'I would like to see limits in Nicaragua disappear,' he said, although he also said, 'I believe Nicaraguan leaders would like to see this, too.'[176]

According to Elliot Abrams, Assistant Secretary of State for Interamerican affairs:

There is, by now, no question that the Sandinista regime is repressive and undemocratic, and that it is subverting neighboring democratic Governments. The evidence has been mounting for years.

Abrams concluded, the only sensible U.S. policy is to continue and increase the pressure on the Sandinistas to accede to the wishes of the Nicaraguan people—for democracy, for freedom and for peace.[177]

The longer the Sandinistas remain in power, the more restricted the political liberties in Nicaragua. The way that a Marxist-Leninist, such as Ortega, gradually suppresses freedom should be obvious to most intelligent observers. The fact that it is not, and the fact that few democratic political leaders understand the full range of the sophisticated and devious Soviet strategy accounts for much of the success of the Soviet empire builders. Lord Pitt, who launched Great Britain on its imperialist path in the mid 18th century would acclaim the achievements of his twentieth century emulators.

The implications of Soviet global strategy for the future are set forth in the concluding chapters.

NOTES

1. The Soviet Government stressed the unique position of the Black Sea and the Turkish Straits as vital to their security, just as was the Panama Canal to the security of the United States. Thus, it regarded the "Black Sea" as "closed sea." See the *New York Times,* October 11, 1946.
2. *Radio Moscow* (in Turkish), March 17, 1978.
3. *New York Times,* April 30, 1985, p. A8.
4. MENA, January 15, 1955.
5. *New York Times,* January 20, 1956.
6. Dragnich, George, "The Soviet Union's Quest for Access to Naval Facilities in Egypt Prior to the June War of 1967," in McGwire, Booth & McDonnell, *Soviet Naval Policy* (Praeger, NY. 1975), p. 269.
7. "The Soviet Intervention into Egypt," *Born in Battle Magazine* (Israel), March 1980, p. 43.
8. *Egyptian Gazette,* July 19, 1972;
9. McLane, Charles, *Soviet Third World Relations,* Vol. 1 (Central Asian Research Centre, London, 1973), p. 120.

10. Walid Khalidi, *Conflict and Violence in Lebanon: Confrontation in the Middle East,* 1979, Published by the Center for International Affairs, Harvard University, p. 83.
11. *New York Times,* May 16, 1983, p. A-1.
12. *New York Times,* March 11, 1984, A-10.
13. *New York Times,* March 15, 1984, p. 1.
14. *New York Times,* July 11, 1985, p. A-7.
15. *Times,* London, June 29, 1956.
16. *Welt,* Hamburg, July 23, 1970.
17. *Deadline Data on World Affairs,* DMS Inc., Greenwhich 1976 "Libya", p. 50.
18. Cooley, John K., "The Libyan Menace," *Foreign Policy* (No. 42, Spring 1981), p. 86.
19. *Ibid.*
20. *New York Times,* President Reagan's address to American Bar Association, July 9, 1985, p. A-12.
21. *The Economist,* July 4, 1981, p. 37.
22. Focus on Libya. The Qaddafi Doctrine Pencon Ltd. 905 16th St. Washington, D.C. Sept. 1985.
23. Morray, J.P., *Socialism in Islam: A Study of Algeria,* The Institute of Theoretical History, Monmouth, Oregon, 1980, p. 88.
24. *Ibid.,* p. 161.
25. *Ibid.,* p. 89.
26. Tworney, "The Long Battle For a Lifeless Desert," Philadelphia Inquirer, July 8, 1985, A-1.
27. *Ibid.*
28. "Speigel" interview with Vadim Zagladin, in Der Spiegel, June 8, 1981, p. 119.
29. Leighton, Marian, *The Soviet Threat to NATO's Northern Flank,* Agenda Paper 10, National Strategy Information Center, New York, 1979, pp. 10–11.
30. *Washington Post,* December 8, 1980.
31. Leighton, op. cit., p. 72.
32. Report from Swedish Embassy, Washington, DC, published April 26, 1983. This report compliments a more exhaustive 86-page treatment of the role of the Swedish Navy in handling the crisis.
33. *Ibid.*
34. *Ibid.*
35. Leighton, *op cit.,* p. 67.
36. *Ibid.,* p. 14.
37. *The Military Balance 1980–1981,* International Institute for Strategic Studies, London, 1980, p. 6.
38. Rogers, General Bernard, Supreme Allied Commander Europe, "Nato Strategy: Time to Change?" The Alliance Papers, No. 9 October 1985.
39. Suchlicki, Jaime, *Cuba, From Columbus to Castro,* Charles Scribners Sons, New York, 1974. This is one of the best surveys of Castro's political evolution available.
40. The favorable press in the United States is best examplified in the articles by Herbert L. Matthews in the *New York Times,* in 1957. The series was influential in gaining support for Castro.
41. Suchlicki, *op. cit.,* p. 181.
42. *New York Times,* April 15, 1983.
43. Statement by Langhorne A. Motley, Assistant Secretary for Inter-American Affairs, before the Subcommittee on Western Hemisphere Affairs of the House Committee on Foreign Affairs, Washington, D.C., April 17, 1985. Current policy no. 687, Department of State, Washington, D.C. April 17, 1985.
44. *New York Times,* May 4, 1985, p. 1.
45. Conference on Totalitarianism vs. Democracy, sponsored by the National Republican Committee, International Affairs Institute, May 2–3, 1985.

46. Report of the National Bipartisan Commission on Central America, To the President of the United States, Jan. 11, 1984.
47. Payne, Douglas W. The Democratic Mask, The Consolidation of the Sandinista Revolution, A Freedom House Publication, 48 E. 21st St. NY, NY 10010, 1985, p. 17.
48. *The Washington Times,* Jan. 22, 1986, p. 1.
49. Leiken, Robert S., "Eastern Winds in Latin America," *Foreign Policy,* No. 42, Spring 1981, p. 101.
50. Armstrong, Robert, *El Salvador—Why Revolution?* NaCla, Report on the Americas, Vol. VIII, No. 2, March-April 1980, p. 27.
51. *New York Times,* March 7, 1984, p. 1.
52. "Wandering if War Will Creep Back to the City," by Marguerite Del Giudice, *Philadelphia Inquirer,* May 6, 1985, p. 2.
53. Op Ed, *New York Times,* January 4, 1981.
54. Leiken, Robert S., *Op. Cit.,* p. 105.
55. A statement by Gonzalo J. Facio, former foreign minister of Costa Rica from 1970–1978, on his view of the origins and motives of the Contadora Group seeking to negotiate a peaceful solution to the conflict in Central America. Published by Council for Democracy in the Americas, Washington, D.C. The Group, made up of Mexico, Panama, Colombia, and Venezuela, has arrived at 21 principles of "democratization" of the isthmus. So far, no final agreement has been reached.
56. *Ibid.*
57. *Ibid.*
58. Leiken, *Op Cit.,* p. 105.
59. International Herald Tribune, June 24, 1985, p. 3
60. *New York Times,* May 5, 1985, p. 5.
61. *New York Times,* July 11, 1985, p. 2.
62. The Soviet-Cuban connection in Central America and the Caribbean, released by the Department of State and the Department of Defense, March 1985, Washington, D.C.
63. Starrels, John M., "Beyond the Wall in Berlin," *New York Times,* August 13, 1981.
64. S. Agyeman-Mensah, *New York City Tribune,* June 5, 1885, p1B
65. *Financial Times,* London, June 20, 1985.
66. Cottrell, Alvin J. and Hahn, Walter F., "Naval Race or Arms Control in the Indian Ocean?" (New York, National Strategy Information Center, 1978, Agenda Paper, No. 8) p. 33.
67. *New York Times,* July 7, 1985, A-8.
68. *New York Times,* May 4, 1985, p. 5.
69. Rottenberg, Morris, "The USSR and Africa: New Dimensions of Soviet Global Power," Advanced International Studies Institute, 1980, p. 82.
70. Harwood, Richard, "Angola: A Distant War," *Washington Post,* June 22–29, 1981. See David Lamb, *Los Angeles Times.*
71. *Washington Report,* ASC, Boston, Virginia, Jan. 1982.
72. *The New York Times,* Dec. 15, 1985, Section 4, 2E
73. *The Search For Regional Security in Southern Africa,* U.S. Department of State, Current Policy No. 453, February 15, 1983.
74. *New York Times,* Zimbabwe After Vote, July 8, 1985, p. 3
75. Insight, Dec. 30, 1985, p. 36
76. *New York Times,* March 17, 1984, p. A6.
77. *New York Times,* July 1, 1985, p. A-3.
78. *New York Times,* July 7, 1985, p. A-3.
79. Insight, Dec. 30, 1985, *op. cit.,* p. 31.
80. *New York Times,* March 29, 1984, p. A-3.
81. McGwire, Michael, "Foreign Port Visits by Soviet Naval Units," in McGwire, Booth and McDonnell, *op. cit.,* pp. 412–413.

82. Jukes, Geoffrey, "The Indian Ocean in Soviet Naval Policy" *Adelphi Paper No. 87*, International Institute for Strategic Studies, London, 1972, p. 1.

83. *Africa Economic Digest*, July 9, 1982.

84. *Izvestiya*, April 16, 1977.

85. *MIS*, February 1–15, 1978: AFP Agence France Presse, February 26, 1978.

86. Some reports in the Arab world attributed responsibility to the Soviet Union, Cuba and East Germany for events which took place during May and June in both North and South Yemen, *Washington Star*, June 28, 1978, quoting *al-Liwa* (Beirut); Cairo Domestic Service, July 2, 1978.

87. For sources on the various developments of the last week of June, see, for example, *TASS* (in English), June 25–28, 30, 1978; *New York Times, Washington Star,* June 28, 1978.

88. *New York Times*, May 31, 1979.

89. *The Washington Post*, Jan. 22, 1986, p. 1.

90. *Pravda*, October 24, 1969.

91. *New York Times*, July 10, 1985, p. A-9.

92. Vladimir Ozerov, "Winds of Change over Ethiopia," *Pravda*, March 10, 1976, p. 5. In the *Current Digest of the Soviet Press*. Volume 26, 1976.

93. Radio Moscow, February 1977. (in Amharic)

94. Secretary of State Vance explained the Administration's policy in the following words: "In each case we must balance a political concern for human rights against economic or security goals." Testimony before the Subcommittee on Foreign Operations of the Appropriations Committee, U.S. Senate, February 24, 1977.

95. Barre News Conference as reported by *Washington Post*, May 17, 1977.

96. Radio Moscow (in English), May 1977.

97. In the context of events taking place in the Ogaden, Barre must have interpreted it as such. See his interview in *Newsweek*, February 13, 1978.

98. *The Daily Telegraph*, September 3, 1977.

99. This condition expressed on behalf of the Western Somalia Liberation Front, was made by the Somali envoy to Rome on September 20, 1977.

100. *Pravda*, October 12, 1977; Moscow Domestic Service, October 18, 1977.

101. Interesting, was Barre's admission of having provided the Soviets with facilities. See his speech of November 20, 1977.

102. *New York Times*, January 7, 1978.

103. *New York Times*, February 7, 1978.

104. The Guardian (London), February 2, 1978.

105. *New York Times*, February 14, 1978.

106. *Pravda*, March 15, 1978.

107. Addis Ababa Domestic Service, February 10, 1974.

108. Africa Report, December 1983, p. 48.

109. *New York Times*, A3, May 7, 1985.

110. *New York Times*, "U.S. Will Give Development Aid to Ethiopia", May 9, 1985, A8.

111. *New York Times*, April 28, 1985 E2.

112. *New York Times*, July 15, 1985, A. 3

113. *Ibid.*

114. Kenneth Maxwell, "A New Scramble for Africa?" In *The Conduct of Soviet Foreign Policy*, eds. Erik P. Hoffman and Frederic J. Fleron, Jr. New York, Aldine Publishing Co., 1980. p. 516.

115. "Six Nations to Join Gulf Force," *New York Times*, November 30, 1984, pA9.

116. "Saudi Arabian Downing of Iranian Fighter," *New York Times*, June 7, 1984, pA30.

117. "Saudis, Stressing Regional Stability, See Soviet Threat," *New York Times*, February 8, 1980, Sec. Ap. 6.

118. "Saudi Charges Soviets Acted in Afghanistan from Fears about Oil," *New York Times*, October 4, 1979 Sec. A. p. 6.

119. "Saudis awaken to their Vulnerability," *Fortune Magazine,* March 3, 1980, p. 56.
120. "Saudis Deny Rumors that They Plan to Establish Ties With USSR," *Christian Science Monitor,* May 9, 1984, p. 14.
121. Proposed Sale of Airborne Warning and Control Systems (AWACs) and F-15 Enhancements to Saudi Arabia. Congressional Report of Hearings before Committee on Foreign Affairs, House of Representatives, held September 28, October 1,6,7, 1981.
122. McLane, Charles B., *Soviet-Third World Relations,* Vol. 2, (Central Asian Research Center, London, 1973), p. 14.
123. *FBIS,* June 10, 1974, p. J4.
124. Tahir-Kheli, Shirin, "The Foreign Policy of a New Pakistan," *ORBIS,* Vol. 20, No. 3, 1976, p. 756.
125. *Christian Science Monitor,* July 29, 1974.
126. Tahir-Kheli, "New Pakistan," *op. cit.,* p. 484.
127. Syed, "Pakistan in 1976: Business as Usual," *Asian Survey,* Vol. 17, No. 2, 1977, p. 189.
128. *New York Times,* May 7, 1978.
129. *New York Times,* June 12, 1978.
130. *New York Times,* December 6, 1978.
131. FBIS-MEA-79-251, December 28, 1979, Vol. V. (Supplement).
132. Malhuret, Claude, Report from Afghanistan, *Foreign Affairs,* Winter 1983/84, pp. 426 and following.
132. *New York Times,* March 8, 1984, p. A-4.
133. The Washington Post, December 9, 1986, P-A-16
134. McLane, Charles, *op. cit.,* Vol. 2, p. 68.
135. Chatterjea, Basant, *Indo-Soviet Friendship* (S. Chand & Co., New Delhi, 1973), pp. 234–235.
136. Weiner, Myron, "The 1977 Parliamentary Elections in India," *Asian Survey,* Vol. XVII, No. 7, July 1977, p. 623.
137. *New York Times,* March 28, 1977.
138. *Times of India,* March 31, 1977.
139. *New York Times,* March 15, 1984, p. A-16.
140. *People's Daily,* September 29, 1976.
141. *TASS,* November 19, 1977.
142. Leifer, Michael, "Conflict and Regional order in Southeast Asia" *Adelphi Papers,* No. 162, The International institute for Strategic Studies, London, 1980, p.8.
143. For an analysis of Thai Communism see R. F. Zimmerman, "Insurgency in Thailand," *Problems of Communism* (May/June 1976) Vol. XXV, No. 3.
144. See Milton Asborn, "Kampuchea and Vietnam: A Historical Perspective," *Pacific Community,* (April 1978), p. 251.
145. *Pravda,* October 16, 1977.
146. *Far East Economic Review,* October 26, 1979, p. 18.
147. Tillman, Dundin, "Phillippine Communism," *Problems of Communism* (May/June, 1976), pp. 40–48.
148. Whitehall, John, Options in the Philippines, Freedom at Issue, March-April 1985.
149. Douglas Pike, "Vietnam's Foreign Relations," Report prepared for the Subcommittees on Asian and Pacific Affairs, Committee on Foreign Affairs, U.S. House of Representatives, June 1979, p. 11.
150. *Christian Science Monitor,* July 3, 1978, reported that even some of the East European countries appeared to be caught off guard by Vietnam's admission.
151. Bradley Hahn, "Threat Perceptions in ASEAN, Japan, and PRC," (FPRI). See also *Intelligence Digest Weekly Review* (Cheltenham, England), September 17, 1980, pp. 3–4.
152. *Pravda,* July 29, 1977, p. 5.
153. *New Times,* November 1978, No. 46, p. 5.
154. Text of Soviet-Vietnam Friendship and Cooperation Treaty, *New Times,* (November 1978), p. 6.

155. *Christian Science Monitor,* December 14, 1978, p. 2.
156. Fox Butterfield, "Foe Nears Cambodian Road," *New York Times,* December 15, 1978.
157. David K. Willis, "Kremlin Exults at Viet Gains," *Christian Science Monitor,* January 9, p. 1.
158. *New York Times,* February 8, 1979.
159. The Spratly's are claimed by the PRC, Taiwan, the Philippines, Malaysia and Vietnam. The latter occupies six islands, the Philippines seven.
160. The U.S. deployment of six naval vessels in the South China Sea, including the carrier Constellation, reinforced such a Soviet view since its only purpose could be to discourage Soviet intervention, which in effect benefitted China.
161. This observation is based on a review of Soviet naval diplomacy in James McConnel and Bradford Dismukes, "Soviet Diplomacy of Force in the Third World," *Problems of Communism* (January/February, 1979).
162. Harrison Salisbury has observed that, "There exists in the Soviet general staff, and has existed for ten if not twenty years, a body of opinion that holds that war with China is inevitable and that, being inevitable, the sooner it is fought and won the better. These generals do not see time on the Soviet side; particularly if Deng Xiaoping's technological and military goals can be achieved as a result of closer and closer Sino-American collaboration," *New York Times,* February 27, 1979.
163. Joseph C. Harsch, "The Far East Arena: Who Will Dominate," *Christian Science Monitor,* March 23, 1979.
164. Frederick Mortiz, "Vietnam: A Sign of Backing Off," *Christian Science Monitor,* March 27, 1979.
165. *Christian Science Monitor,* November 28, 1979.
166. *Newsweek,* May 13, 1985, p. 49.
167. *Time,* July 8, 1985, p. 22
168. For an excellent and comprehensive survey of the existing distribution of military power in the Asian-Pacific region see *Asian Security, 1979 through 1985.*
169. *The Washington Times,* April 22, 1985, p. 1.
170. Luttwak, *The Grand Strategy of the Soviet Union,* p. 221.
171. *Soviet Military Power,* 1985. Department of Defense, p. 64.
172. *The Wall Street Journal,* December 26, 1985, p. 1.
173. *The Philadelphia Inquirer,* July 16, 1985, p. 12a.
174. The author was so informed during an exchange in Beijing in September 1980 with members of a Chinese Strategy Institute.
175. *Newsweek,* May 13, 1985, pp. 45, 46.
176. *New York Times,* May 12, 1985, p. 3.
177. *Op. ed., New York Times,* Jan. 13, 1986, A-15.

CHAPTER V

Soviet Global Strategy In Retrospect

The Soviet Record In The Round

This volume has focused on Soviet strategy and its manifestations around the globe. The Soviet effort to extend its power is enormous in size and scope. What can we learn by analyzing Soviet expansionism?

Soviet strategy though fundamentally political, relies on military power to force accommodations to its designs. The Soviets apply outward pressure to the west, south and east from the Soviet heartland astride Eurasia. All along its vast periphery, the Soviet Union has used military power against its neighbors. Many of these countries are also subjected to the more subtle pressures generated by increasingly widespread Soviet naval deployments from ports in European Russia and Siberia.

Chapter IV summarized the Soviet operational record in the Mediterranean and other theaters that form a chain around the coastal region of the Afro-Eurasian land mass. These theaters are: Western Europe (mostly NATO members); Africa, particularly southern Africa, which oversees the important sea lane around the Cape, and which also contains the greatest strategic mineral resources of the non-communist world; the arc stretching from the Horn of Africa through the Eastern Mediterranean and across the Arabian Peninsula into the Persian Gulf region and on into Afghanistan, (this area contains the bulk of the world's proven oil reserves); the South Asian subcontinent, which is dominated by India, an important associate of the Soviet Union; the Southeast Asian peninsula and its adjacent Archipel-agos, which lie along the sea routes linking the Indian and Pacific Oceans; Northeast Asia, where the Soviet Union continues to build forces to intimidate Japan and to strengthen its links with North Korea. From the Persian Gulf to Vladivostok, Soviet naval power pressures the PRC while strong Soviet land forces oppose China on crucial portions of the long Sino-Soviet frontier.

Finally, in the Western Hemisphere, Soviet encroachment into Central America and the Caribbean Basin, aided by Cuba, poses a serious threat to American strategic interests. If the United States becomes embroiled in the Caribbean, it could be diverted from opposing further Soviet encroach-ments into areas on the periphery of the Afro-Eurasian land mass.

Each major link in the Afro-Eurasian and Caribbean operational chain presents the Soviet Union with unique problems and opportunities.

Analyzing Soviet global endeavors reveals the scope and regional varia-tions of Soviet expansionism. Those preoccupied with upheavals in their own regions might better understand the Soviet role locally if they exam-ined Soviet global strategy. For example, Mexican political and intellectual leaders, who equate Soviet-Cuban strategy in the Caribbean with revolu-tionary traditions indigenous to Latin America, might think differently if they examined parallel Soviet operations in the Horn of Africa, the Persian Gulf, or Southeast Asia.

The Search for Sea Lanes

A concern of Soviet expansionist strategy is to gain control of specific sea lines of communications (SLOCs). The sea lanes between the Soviet Union's European and Asiatic provinces are important for Moscow's com-mercial and industrial needs, and are vital to ensure communication and coordination between the four fleets of the Soviet Navy.

The development of secure sea communications between the Soviet Union's European ports and its remote Siberian maritime provinces is necessary regardless of strategic goals. The Soviet internal transportation system linking east and west is inadequate compared to the dense highway and rail networks of Western Europe and the United States. In real eco-nomic terms, transportation costs from Vladivostok to European Russia via the Trans-Siberian Railroad are greater than shipping via water, because official rates on the railroad are kept artificially low. Furthermore, keeping the railroad open during the long Siberian winter is both difficult and expensive.

Western analysts do not have accurate data comparing the volume of overland freight between European Russia and eastern Siberia with the volume that goes by sea. The sea shipments represent over half of the total—The Soviet's claim that the long sea route via the Indian Ocean is vital to the survival of the Soviet Union is essentially correct. The underlying purpose of such a claim is to legitimize their economic and military presence in the many countries along the way. As one Soviet author stated:

> In view of its geographic position, the USSR needs a large fleet in order to maintain the necessary internal contacts with remote parts of the country. Vitally important communication routes linking the European with Asiatic and Far Eastern ports of the USSR pass through the Mediterranean and across the Indian Ocean. It is quite clear that the existing land routes cannot be any substitute for these more economic and convenient sea routes.[2]

To strengthen the connection between its western and eastern extremities, the USSR reinforces its internal rail and air transportation networks with a large and growing fleet of naval and merchant vessels. Soviet vessels are capable of navigating between Murmansk and Vadivostok, via the Arctic, for only a few months each summer. The southern sea lanes, via the Indian Ocean, can be used throughout the year, and Soviet expansionism has focused on the latter route.

A distinction must be made between peacetime and wartime problems facing the Soviet Union when analyzing the effectiveness of the total Soviet transportation system. In peacetime, the Soviets can ship supplies to military bases at points along the Europe-Asia-Pacific sea lanes. Under conditions of war, Soviet sea lanes would be vulnerable to Westen interference, particulary at the critical areas that their ships must pass through en route from Europe to Siberia.

As the record shows, the Soviet Union is attempting to develop—around the Cape, across the Indian Ocean, and through the Strait of Malacca—an assured maritime route to the Siberian Pacific coast. To reach Vladivostok, the main base for the Far Eastern fleet, Soviet ships must transit the Sea of Japan and the Korean Strait. Soviet vessels sailing from Vladivostok to Odessa must cross such strategic waterways as the Taiwan Strait, the Strait of Malacca, or other passages through the Indonesian archipelago, before reaching the Indian Ocean. Finally, these ships must cross the Indian Ocean before going through the Strait of Bab al Mandab, and through the Suez Canal to reach Odessa, or sail around the Cape of Good Hope and past Gibraltar and the Dardanelles.

Justifying the crucial importance of the Indian Ocean to the Soviet Union, Georgii Arbatov, Moscow's leading U.S. specialist, once said, that "for us the Indian Ocean plays the same role, as, say, the Panama Canal does for the United States, being a seaway connecting the West and East of our countries."[3] This reasoning attempts to justify Soviet claims to naval positions as well as access to one half of the global ocean.

Wartime and peacetime arms and troop transport are served also by the Trans-Siberian Railroad. Troops stationed along the long Sino-Soviet frontier are an indispensable element of any Soviet deployment against China, and the Trans-Siberian Railroad is a prerequisite for any such deployment. To secure this land link against possible Chinese interdictions, the Soviet

Union has spent billions of rubles to develop an alternate route from Lake Baikal to Vladivostok, hundreds of miles from China's northern border.

In addition to this highly expensive strategic precaution, the USSR seeks complementary land and sea links to protect its Pacific maritime provinces. This has been accomplished by developing close political ties with countries located along the lengthy Baltic-Black Sea-Vladivostok sea lanes.

In these countries, the Soviets have obtained facilities both for Soviet merchant ships and naval vessels, as well as for air transport and reconnaissance aircraft. When these facilities are linked by the Soviet navy, Moscow can use the facilities of potentially pro-Soviet states to secure their strategic goals.

Soviet positions in the sea routes of the Indian Ocean can facilitate Soviet moves in Southeast Asia and a containment policy toward China, while at the same time easing communications between Soviet Black Sea and Far Eastern ports. The Soviet Union, by establishing positions in the Indian Ocean and its littoral, may check Chinese expansion southward in much the same fashion as Britain checked Czarist Russian expansion in the nineteenth century.

Some Western scholars perceive a Soviet drive to dominate the Indian Ocean, among them, Dr. Alvin Cottrell.

> The presence of Russian ships in the Indian Ocean has ensured for Moscow a seat at the conference table on a whole series of issues where previously the Soviet voice was not heard. Soviet vessels are now endeavoring to enchance Moscow's image at the expense of the West—and of China—on all shores of the Indian Ocean.[4]

The main base of the Soviet Pacific fleet is at Vladivostok, located in the Sea of Japan. The exits through the Strait of Tsushima or the Sea of Okhotsk are vulnerable. The Arctic-Northern Sea route can be used for only about three months each year. Hence the Pacific fleet must be completely self-contained.

The Pacific fleet has become the largest in the Soviet navy. It has about twenty ballistic missile submarines, some sixty attack submarines, a number of cruisers equipped with guided missiles, guided missile destroyers, and destroyer escorts. Altogether there are over fifty major Soviet combat ships in the Soviet Pacific fleet. As of 1981, the aircraft carrier Minsk was deployed to the Soviet Pacific Fleet at Vladivostok.

Soviet naval excursions throughout the Pacific region grow each year. Soviet naval forces travelled far beyond the Sea of Japan as early as 1959, when a Svedlov-class cruiser and two destroyers visited Djakarta. Subsequent political and naval discussions between the Soviet Union and Indonesia led to the transfer of a number of warships and auxilliaries to Indonesia.

In September, 1971, a Soviet task force of 10 ships sailed into Hawaiian waters. The flotilla steamed past Pearl Harbor and the U.S. CINCPAC (Commander-in-Chief-Pacific) headquarters. Soviet naval activity in the Pacific continues to grow in the Philippines and Australia and through the

Strait of Malacca into the Indian Ocean. The Soviets have also obtained from some of the small island countries of the mid-Pacific refueling and other privileges.

The advantage the Soviets have gained by use of Cam Ranh Bay have already been discussed. Soviet buoys have been anchored east of the Philippines to resupply Soviet ships in the Pacific. Soviet acquisition of "strategic islands" in Southeast Asia would obviously solidify the Soviet naval chain from the Black Sea to Vladivostok.

The Soviet intrusion into the Caribbean-Central American region has also been described in considerable detail. The Soviet access to Cuba cuts across U.S. SLOC's to Western Europe and Western European allies SLOC's around the Cape of Good Hope to Persian Gulf oil. They also gain positions to threaten one of the world's vital points–the Panama Canal.

The Choke Point Focus

Geography establishes critical naval choke points–those which might contain the Soviet Navy within coastal seas and those which are essential to Western commerce.

These critical points determine the division of the Soviet navy into four main fleets, which are based at Murmansk, in the Baltic and Black Seas, and at Vladivostok. The Soviet Union has attemped to neutralize countries adjacent to the seas which each fleet passes on its way to the oceans beyond. In the Northern and Baltic Fleet areas, Sweden, Norway, Denmark and Iceland have been targets for Soviet pressure. The presence of massive Soviet military power deployed in the Kola Peninsula is an intimidating factor. Iceland has been a target of Soviet attempts to disassociate it from the NATO alliance.

The Soviets must have assured passage from the Black Sea to the Aegean and then to the Mediterranean, and so Moscow has encouraged internal subversion within Turkey, and has sought to capitalize on the antagonism between Greece and Turkey over Cyprus. The Soviets have also pressed Turkey not to close the Dardanelles to their warships.

If there is a general war in the Middle East, it is likely that the Suez Canal would again be closed, leaving Gibralter as the only Soviet exit from the Mediterranean. The European side of the Strait of Gibralter is relatively stable, but on the African side the Soviets have supported the struggle of Polisario guerillas, backed by Algeria and Libya, against Morocco. The United States has sought to counter with military aid to Morocco to keep both sides of the Strait in pro-Western hands. The 1985 meeting between President Reagan and President Chadli Benjedid, presages a weakening of the Polisario Movement.

The two principal bases of the Soviet Pacific Fleet are Vladivostok and Petropavlovsk. Vladivostock is the home port for three-fourths of this fleet, while one-quarter is based in Petropavlovsk. The Sea of Japan has three usable exits–the Korea Strait between Korea and Japan, the Tsugaru Strait between Hokkaido and Japan's main island of Honshu, and the Soya Strait north of Hokkaido. The Soviets have concentrated on the Soya Strait for a sure exit, although they control only the northern side of it. To diminish anti-Soviet attitudes, the Soviet Union has conducted sophisticated and subtle psychological warfare against the Japanese fishing population on Hokkaido. The Soviets are aware of Japanese potential in controlling the exits from the Sea of Japan in the event of war, and it is likely that Soviet war plans provide for overtaking at least the northern tip of Hokkaido. Japan's self-defense forces are well aware of this possibility, and Japan's best airplanes, ground equipment, and troops are deployed in Hokkaido.

The Soviet government has attemped to break out of its encircled positions not only by pressures on countries adjacent to its four fleet bases, but also by "leaping over" the containment line. Thus, the Soviet Union has established three primary strategic positions far from its continental shores, in countries once aligned with the West. The Soviets acquired advance bases in Cuba in 1962, in the People's Republic of Yemen (Aden, Socotra) in the early '70's, and in the Socialist Republic of Vietnam in the mid-70's. These bases have become points of entry for Soviet operations against Central America, Saudi Arabia, the Persian Gulf States, the PRC, and states in Southeast Asia.

The superpowers have conflicting objectives regarding choke points and, for the most part, different approaches to these objectives. As long as conditions of "peace" have continued the United States has sought to prevent deterioration of political situations and to preserve its alliances with nations near Soviet exit positions, to block Soviet operations in the event of a general war. On the other hand, the Soviet Union uses subversion to attempt political dominance in the countries located on or near choke points. Only a few of the more than 100 straits or choke points that are 24 miles wide or less are vital to international commerce. These include the passages into the Caribbean and the Panama Canal, the Straits of Magellan, Gibralter, Suez and Aden, the Cape of Good Hope, Hormuz Strait, and the five principal passages through the Indonesian archipelago, which extends some 3,000 miles between Malaysia and Australia.

Resource Denial

It is worth noting that two critical choke points are also major sources of energy and strategic minerals, vital to democratic industrial societies.

The Soviets seek to deny the West of such vital resources as Middle Eastern oil and the minerals of southern Africa. Soviet efforts to gain control over such resources have been aptly dubbed a "strangulation strategy," with respect to Western Europe, Japan and, to a lesser extent, the United States.

The significance of this element of Soviet strategy was clarified by a conference conducted by the World Affairs Council of Pittsburgh in 1980. It was concluded that:

> Insofar as access to strategic minerals (including oil) is concerned, the Soviet Union must be regarded as a hostile state, whose leaders may be attempting to injure the U.S. and its allies by impeding their access to strategic minerals.

According to the panel of this conference the Soviet mineral trading pattern has changed in a way that endangers Free World access to many strategic minerals: "Soviet exports of certain raw minerals to the West are declining sharply." At the same time the Soviet Union has begun to import certain strategic minerals for itself and its allies from countries whose output had previously gone to the U.S. and its allies. The Pittsburgh panelists believed that the new pattern may well signal an historic shift.

> This new pattern clearly spells trouble for the West . . .
> The new Soviet international minerals behavior could become an effective strategy for crippling Western industrial production by cutting off access to strategic minerals.

The pattern will worsen with respect to energy also. By the end of this century, the United States will import 60% of its oil needs, Western Europe, 70%, and Japan almost 100%.

The influence of the Soviets in Syria, the Soviet occupation of Afghanistan, and its military presence in Libya, Ethiopia and South Yemen have increased the Kremlin's ability to interrupt the flow of Middle East oil as well as exert influence on conservative Arab states and Iraq, Iran, and Pakistan.

Unless there are significant discoveries outside of the Middle East, the major industrial states will be dependent upon oil exported from the Persian Gulf and North Africa. By 2000 the Gulf states are estimated to account for 80–90% of the world's export potential, with Saudi Arabia's share being 40–45% of the total. Soviet proximity to the volatile Persian Gulf region demands an overall U.S. strategy that combines political, economic, and military objectives, as well as support from allies, to counter Soviet aggression in the area and assist friendly regimes. Unfortunately, the Soviets may possess the better cards in the contest over the Persian Gulf.

Geopolitical Goals

Contained within the goals of choke-point control and resource denial are certain geopolitical aims. The most rewarding—and difficult—Soviet objective would be separation of the United States from its allies in Europe, East Asia, and the Middle East. If U.S. power and influence are confined to the Western Hemisphere, no force in Eurasia could withstand Soviet demands. The Soviet intrusion into the Caribbean through Cuba may divert the U.S. from combatting Soviet acquisition-denial strategy along the coastal areas of Afro-Eurasia.

Other goals may be more readily attainable. First is to guarantee the protection of aligned Marxist-Leninist regimes, such as Cuba, Nicaragua, Angola, Afghanistan, Vietnam, the People's Democratic Republic of Yemen, and Ethiopia. Closely related is the goal of marshalling support for the "positive correlation of regional forces," which favors countries such as India, who have tolerable relations with the Soviet Union.

Finally, the Soviet Union seeks neutralization of the People's Republic of China. The reasons for Sino-Soviet enmity have been discussed in depth by many experts. Robert Scalapino observes that "at every level of Soviet society, an unconscious if not outright fear persists that whatever the gain of the moment, the problem of coexistence with China will represent the gravest single problem to be faced in the next century."[5] More than ideological and territorial disputes, the source of Chinese hostility toward the Soviets is their belief that Moscow, even during the heyday of the alliance, wanted to keep China in a position of subordination and inferiority. As the rift between China and the Soviet Union widened, the Soviets deployed large numbers of troops along the border. Soviet strategists perceive that the "China Problem" can be alleviated by securing a dominant position on the strategic sea routes linking the European and Far Eastern ports, thus completing a land-sea encirclement of the PRC. The Chinese experimentation with free market economics may also present an ideological challenge to the rigid and centralized Soviet economic model.

The record of Soviet actions over the last quarter of a century indicates that the Soviets have pursued their global strategy through separate but interlocking policies in three geographic theaters surrounding their perimeter. In the West, the Soviet Union confronts NATO—its most formidable military opponent. The southern sector beckons to Soviet leaders with both adventure and opportunity. Control of the oil resources of the Middle East could be a key to the future of the balance of power. On the east, the Soviets are confronted with their most implacable foe, the People's Republic of China.

Within its overall strategy, the Soviet Union appears to be pursuing three related goals: (1) resource strangulation of Western Europe, Japan and, to a lesser extent, the United States; (2) isolation of the United States from its Western European, Middle Eastern and Asian allies; and (3) the neutralization of China. The primary Soviet strategic goal is to confine the United States within the Western Hemisphere.

The Soviet Union has a flexible timetable and a variety of methods to pursue its long-range strategic goals. Soviet aggression uses a wide range of methods—changing the fields of battle, military weapons, and the non-military instruments of subversion, propaganda, and sustained pressure.

As the December, 1979, invasion of Afghanistan indicated, the Soviet system of conflict, maintains that if political warfare is unsuccessful, military means are an accepted alternative. Lenin's view of "just" and "unjust" wars rationalize Soviet military attack on "inferior" social systems, as progressive, and not an aggressive act. Soviet political warfare is quite pragmatic. Within the political spectrum, groups are probed for both vulnerability and utility. The Soviet Union's strategy is not at all concerned with the concepts of "left" or "right" as they are defined in the West. Soviet support of Argentina during the 1982 Falkland War is a case in point. They will support groups identified as either or both if they can gain incremental victories this way.

Soviet analysts perceive that the world situation is unfolding satisfactorily according to their strategic design. According to Boris Ponomarev:

> Our epoch is one in the transition of mankind from capitalism to socialism on a *worldwide scale*. It is precisely because the socialist orientation, or the trend toward socialism, proves its vital strength that imperialism is attacking this force with particular violence. Imperialism, together with the forces of domestic reaction, is constantly trying to undermine progressive regimes. These attempts are very dangerous. It is enough to mention the examples of Egypt and Somalia. Diversions; plots and mutual confrontation of peoples against each other, even overt intervention as in the case of Afghanistan, speculation with economic difficulties, with backwardness and taking advantage of hostilities between different tribes—these are all opportunities used by imperialism.[6]

Ponomarev goes on to describe the United States and its allies in terms that accurately fit Soviet operational practices.

The Soviet Union, the world's most formidable imperialistic power, is clearly on the march. Although the Soviet Union appears to be replaying earlier imperialist roles once enacted by nineteenth-century European powers, one should not conclude that the noncommunist world is facing a traditional challenge. In the countries along the sea lanes between Europe and Asia and elsewhere, the Soveit Union seeks political, ideological, psychological, and military preeminence.

Moscow's spokesmen have written about "a radical restructuring of international relations"[7] in favor of the Soviet Union. Attempts to restructure international politics so that the Soviet Union attains world leadership are intrinsically offensive, and thus the Soviet global strategy is an offensive one, admirably suited to advance a restructuring of the international system.

The Matter of Soviet Intentions

The growth of Soviet military capabilities is now generally accepted and this volume has documented Soviet expansionism over the past quarter of a century. It is now useful to question the Soviets' ultimate intentions—is

Soviet expansionism and militarism the result of Western threats to Soviet security, or do they reflect the desire of the Soviet leadership to extend their system worldwide?

In any intelligence analysis, it is far easier to estimate an adversary's capabilities than his intentions. Consequently a prudent military planner prepares to meet his opponent's capabilities and not his intentions, which are difficult to perceive and easily changed. Unfortunately, conflicting perceptions of Soviet intentions in the West frequently distort or override carefully calculated estimates of Soviet capabilities. In America, the wide range of opinions concerning Soviet intentions makes a consensus concerning U.S. policy toward the Soviet Union almost impossible. Nor can every opinion concerning Soviet intentions be correct. Then how can one judge Soviet intentions?

If one matches Soviet capabilities and actions with assessments of intentions, realistic interpretations of Soviet objectives can be identified. Following are official U.S. and Soviet appraisals of the other's intentions, as well as the assessment of several Western scholars of Soviet intentions toward the West.

Official Soviet announcements since the beginning of the USSR have stressed the unremitting conflict between communism and capitalism, and the inevitable doom of the latter. Even during the height of detente, ideological warfare and supporting "wars of national liberation" were a feature of Soviet statements and propaganda. During the first Reagan Administration, the fundamental hostility of the Soviet Union toward the United States became more open.

Soviet Foreign Minister Andrei A. Gromyko in his September 22, 1981, address to the United Nations General Assembly, charged that the United States was responsible for all international tensions:

> The Soviet Union has never threatened anybody and is not threatening anybody now.
> In examining and solving international problems, we rely on the ideals of freedom and progress of nations, on the principles of respect for the independence of all states and all peoples. We aim for consolidating the foundations of life, rather than for preparing the funeral of mankind.
> There exists, however, another trend in world politics which pursues quite different goals. That is the course followed by militarist circles of imperialist states. The sum and substance of that course is to seek domination over other countries and peoples: domination that means imposing one's will upon them, their economic exploitation and the use of their territories for military strategic purposes.

In making these incredible charges, Gromyko ignored the letter which President Reagan had sent to Soviet President Brezhnev on the same date. According to the State Department, President Reagan wrote:

> There are two aspects of such Soviet actions which have been of particular concern to the United States.
> First, the USSR's unremitting and comprehensive military buildup over the past 15 years, a buildup far exceeding Soviet defensive needs and one which carries disturbing implications of a search on the part of the Soviet Union for military superiority.

Secondly, the Soviet Union's pursuit of unilateral advantage in various parts of the world—through direct and indirect use of force in regional conflicts. The role of Cuba in Africa and Latin America is particularly destabilizing.

Officially, the U.S. and the Soviet Union blame each other for the deteriorating relations between them. Historically, detente between the Soviet Union and the West occurs when the West accommodates to Soviet policies. When the West (mainly the U.S.) defends its interests, Soviet hostility become more open.

Many observers of the Soviet Union are convinced that domestic problems are so deep and insolvable that the idea of a substantial Soviet threat to non-communist nations should not be taken seriously.

Former U.S. Ambassador to the Soviet Union George Kennan pictures the Soviet Union in such dire straits that it is incapable of harboring designs against Western Europe or other areas.

Their whole motivation in external relations is basically defensive. . . . It is absurd to picture these men as embarked in some new and dark plot to achieve the subjugation of, and the domination over Western Europe.[8]

Marshal Shulman, a special advisor on Soviet affairs to former Secretary of State Cyrus Vance, stated in hearings before the House Committee on International Relations:

The Soviet Union looks upon present and future history as leading toward the triumph of communism on a worldwide basis.[9]

Shulman responded to a question concerning Soviet prospects for economic growth:

In human affairs there is always the capability of systems muddling along in ways that may not represent a clear choice of alternatives. Yet somehow things continue to function.[10]

Harrison E. Salisbury, a long-time student of Soviet affairs, described Soviet society as stagnant and almost beyond the possibility of regeneration.[11] At the same time, Salisbury acknowledged that Soviet power would soon pass from the group of aged leaders to a generation of younger men. Since Salisbury wrote that in 1981, leadership shifted from Brezhnev to Andropov to Chernenko, and finally, in 1985, to the youthful Gorbachev. In an insightful article, "Gorbachev's Great Push and the Reluctant Public" (Dec. 18, 1986), veteran New York Times correspondent Serge Schmemann told how Gorbachev's plea for a profound "restructuring" to check the economic stagnation, the political corruption and the blight of drunkness has had little impact. Unless the overall situation improves Gorbachev may decide that the best way to cope with massive internal problems is to launch new adventures outside Soviet borders.

George Feifer's article, "Russian Disorders," claimed that food shortages, alcoholism, and corruption have marked the end of the Soviet dream.[12] Feifer, who has written many articles and books about the country, wrote a devastating account of the fundamental and irreversible flaws in the Soviet system. Yet, according to Feifer, rarely has there been any active opposition to Moscow's foreign policy. Instead, Soviet domestic media distorts world news so effectively that Soviet leaders can count on the blind obedience of the masses. Although the Soviet people realize how badly they have been treated they accept their dismal fate. Feifer concludes, "even with this realization, they'll shoot whom they're told to."[13]

A revealing insight into Soviet perceptions of the world and intentions toward its adversaries appeared in an article in *Isvestia* on May 9, 1983, which was written by Marshal Nikolai Ogarkov, then Chief of the General Staff of the Armed Forces of the Soviet Union, on the 38th anniversary of victory over Nazi Germany.

In his review of World War II Marshal Ogarkov, after praising the leadership of Stalin, concluded: "There is no force in the world that could stop the victorious march of socialism (i.e., the Soviet rulers' power) on the planet—nor will there be!" Marshal Ogarkov continued: "The United States continues to escalate its undeclared war against Afghanistan. . . ."

After claiming that the United States "provoked the senseless war between Iran and Iraq," and was, "abetting the Israeli aggressors in the Middle East," the Marshal continued: "Today, as in the 1930s, the threat of a new world war is growing. World imperialism, international Zionism and reaction are trying to carve up the world in their own way." Ogarkov's articles are widely circulated among the Soviet military and as of the close of 1986 he was the leading candidate to replace the ailing Marshall Sakolov as Minister of Defense.

Soviet leaders frequently speak and act as if they were already at war with the U.S., their principal imperialist enemy. Hence, Soviet capabilities reflect intentions which rule out accommodation and which stress unrelenting conflict until one of the powers is vanquished.

Ideological Imperatives

When the Bolsheviks captured Russia, they discarded the Pan-Slavic vision which had inspired their predecessors, and replaced it with the system of Marxism. They added the conspiratorial tactics of Lenin to the Byzantine diplomacy practiced by the Czars. Lenin's work, *Imperialism: The Highest Stage of Capitalism*,[14] provided the ideological rationale for an unrelenting campaign to destroy the Western democratic, industrial system.

Many Western observers tend to downplay the role of ideology in Soviet strategy and operations, contending that the Soviet masses are either indifferent or hostile to it. Yet, while the Soviet intelligentsia is indeed cynical about Soviet ideology, it does provide a rationale for Soviet leaders to undermine and destroy the West. Mikhail Suslov, for many years chief Soviet ideologist, stressed the significance of ideology as follows:

> It should be stressed, Comrades, that in all our ideological work the slightest slackening of the struggle against reactionary bourgeois ideology is impermissible . . . it is precisely the struggle in the ideological sphere—the sphere where peaceful coexistence between capitalism and socialism does not and cannot exist—that is assuming particular urgency.[15]

The Bolsheviks, believing themselves the agents for moving mankind from "capitalism" to communism, held that they must destroy the old society by any means to establish the new. When their victims resist, the communists accuse them of aggression. As L. Brezhnev expressed it:

> The more restricted imperialism's possibilities of dominating other countries and peoples become, the more fiercely do its most aggressive and myopic representatives react to this.[16]

Ideologically antagonism between the Soviet Union and the non-communist world will continue as long as the Soviets adhere to Marxism-Leninism as a basis for policy. Milovan Djilas, a defiant and knowledgeable confidant of both Stalin and Tito, holds that, "Communism is ideologically and structurally incapable of transforming itself into a democratic, parliamentary, pluralistic polity. . . ."[17]

An insightful analysis of the role of Marxist-Leninist ideology in Soviet political behavior was made by Max M. Kampelman speaking about the years of negotiations with the Soviets over their adherence to the Helsinki Final Act.

In an address to a committee of the American Bar Association Kampelman stated:

> Now I was not a novice to Soviet matters. At one point I taught political science as well as law, and I taught a course on problems of democracy and another course on Marxism-Leninism. I wrote a book on the effort of the Communist party to capture the American labor movement. So I didn't come to the issue as a total novice.

He mentioned several things that he had not anticipated that had surprised him.

> I had not expected to find the degree of committment to Leninism that I actually did find in the heads of the Soviet delegation. I am not prepared to generalize and to say that that degree of committment went through the whole delegation. I didn't meet every member, or at least didn't have intensive conversations with every member of the Soviet delegation. Nor am I prepared to say this necessarily means that Leninism has deep roots within the Soviet society. I do not know. What I can say, however, is that I was surprised by the degree of committment to Leninism that existed in the leadership of that delegation. When you are spending 400 hours in conversations, and particularly if you feel you are a little bit familiar with the concepts of Marxism-Leninism, it isn't difficult to find yourself involved in conversations about Marxism-Leninism. I expected to find a more pragmatic view, maybe a more cynical view.

Kampelman continued:

Let me tell you about the meetings I had with two different heads of delegations of the Soviet Union. Both were deputy foreign ministers—I think there are a total of five deputy foreign ministers under Gromyko. One of them, when the meeting started, was a 75-year-old man, a very capable man who had been a "survivor." He had his ups and downs, but was at the time a member of the Central Committee of the Communist Party, a very powerful man. He had spent 11 years as head of the negotiating team with the Chinese. As the Chinese negotiations were moved to the front burner, he was moved back into those negotiations, and was succeeded at Madrid by another man who was also a deputy minister. He was a man who our government told me was of considerable importance within the system. In both of them I did find this kind of committment to the tenets of Marxism-Leninism.[18]

For tactical reasons ideology is sometimes subordinated but it still is the rationale guiding Soviet global behavior.

The Policy-Power Syndrome

When the Soviet Union was relatively weak, the necessity for cooperation with its "capitalist" adversaries was obvious. According to a resolution of the 1928 Sixth World Congress of the Communist International, "The peace policy of the proletarian state does not imply that the Soviet State has become reconciled with capitalism," . . . "it is merely a more advantageous form of fighting capitalism, a form which the USSR had consistently employed since the October revolution."[19] Peace offensives and detente continue to be important aspects of Soviet strategy.

While Soviet strategy and tactics vary as the correlation of forces between the superpowers changes, the ideological commitment to eliminate all but Marxist-Leninist political systems remains. Soviet leadership devotes vast resources to propagating this archaic ideology, which bestows the harsh Soviet system with some legitimacy. A *Pravda* editorial of June 9, 1979, stressed "the strength of ideological conviction" and "conviction of the rightness of our cause, of our Marxist-Leninist ideology."

Most Western analysts who have studied the Soviet Union see little evidence that the Kremlin shares real interest with Western democracies in the development of a peaceful and cooperative world community. Nor is there any evidence that the ultimate objective of Soviet foreign policy is to establish Soviet-American accord. The Soviets saw detente, which flowered in the aftermath of the 1972 SALT Agreement, not as a step toward joint Soviet-American dominion, but as an opportunity to gain strategic advantage over the U.S. The rapid erosion of detente began when the Soviets, following Hanoi's capture of Saigon in 1975, pursued a more activist policy. The first manifestation of this was the 1975 Soviet-Cuban intrusion into Angola. The Soviet invasion of Afghanistan in December, 1979, will not be the last Soviet foray into the world beyond their frontiers.

With the fading of detente, the Soviet global position has become much stronger than it was during the Cold War period. The Soviets operate on the fundamental principle of the irreversibility of the socialist revolution. Soviet strategy probes takes advantage of Western weaknesses and exploits socio-political conflicts in unstable countries to change the global correlation of forces in their favor. Their objective appears to be Soviet hegemony. The Soviet record over the past twenty years supports this conclusion.

This pessimistic conclusion is reinforced by the prolonged Soviet military build up that far exceeds the requirements of a prudent defensive posture. Secondly, Soviet, or Soviet-Cuban, or Soviet-Vietnamese intrusions since 1975 into Afghanistan, Angola, South Yemen, Ethiopia, Nicaragua, Kampuchea, and Syria have all been supported indirectly by Soviet arms and, directly or indirectly by Soviet soldiers. Finally, the increasing brazenness with which the Soviets and their surrogates conduct their operations reflects self-confidence and disdain for their opponents.

Operational Principles

We have explored the history of Soviet interventions into the regions bordering the long sea routes from ports in European Russia to Vladivostok. In each region, the Soviets have used a variety of tactics to establish themselves. Methods and instruments have been adapted to the unique characteristics of countries in each region. From our review of Soviet policy and activities in the global sphere as well as in Mediterranean, Atlantic, Indian, and Pacific Ocean areas, some general conclusions can be drawn:

1. The Soviet Union is willing to pay heavily for strategic gains—its big investments in North Korea, Indonesia, Cuba, Egypt, India, Vietnam, Somalia, Angola, Ethiopia, People's Democratic Republic of Yemen (PDRY), Turkey, and Afghanistan, are proof of that. It focuses on strategic target countries, and does not spread its resources randomly.

2. The Soviets have utilized internal conflicts in other countries to penetrate into Western-dominated regions, perpetuate local disputes to prolong dependence on Soviet arms, and control local conflicts to prevent all-out wars, which could escalate and necessitate Soviet military forces.

3. The Soviets promote relations with "stand-by" countries regardless of the state of existing ties, recognizing that many Third World governments are unstable and unpredictable. This tactic minimizes the impact of changes in political factions and has enabled the Soviet Union to cut its losses and shift to another near-by target country. This flexible approach operated in conflicts between Turkey and Greece following the 1974 Cyprus crisis, Syria and Egypt after the 1973 Yom Kippur War, India and China following the 1962 border war, PDRY and YAR in 1978, Ethiopia and Somalia in 1977–78, and Vietnam and Indonesia after the 1965 coup.

4. The Soviets intrude into the power structure of a strategically valuable Third World country with diplomatic and/or economic penetration, spearheaded by adroit political warfare, followed by military support. At the very least, military paraphenalia provides the Soviets with opportunities for increasing their influence.

5. The Soviets generally give full support to countries whose policies serve their own aims—Soviet support of Cuba and Vietnam vis-a-vis the United States, and Vietnam vis-a-vis Kampuchea and China, are striking examples of this principle.

6. In the past, ideological factors played a marginal role in Soviet calculations, but recently, the Soviets have preferred ideological commitment over tactical expediency in supporting national leaders. This principle is illustrated by Cuba, Vietnam, the People's Democratic Republic of Yemen, Afghanistan, and Ethiopia. Ideological commitment, however, needs interpretation. Ideology, from the Soviet viewpoint, may be a tool guaranteeing loyalty of the client rather than an end in itself. A leader who adopts the Soviet model is likely to stay in power longer, since the model is effective in maintaining political control; likely to remain dependent longer, since he needs guidance and assistance in executing the model; and, likely to share interests with the Soviet Union. Of course, if the Soviets decide to dispose of an ideologically committed leader, as they did with Amin in Afghanistan, the first point is more likely to apply to the successor!

7. The Soviets have become increasingly adept at using proxies for combat which advances their interests. The Cuban legionnaires are the most notable force employed by the Soviets, but North Koreans and, in some situations, the Vietnamese may assume this role.

8. The Soviets disdain world public opinion on issues of strategic importance.* They will defend, preserve, or expand their interests regardless of international opinion. To put it differently, they prefer to be respected and even feared rather than liked—the Soviet invasion of Czechoslovakia, their support of Neto in Angola and the Vietnamese in Kampuchea, the use of their own troops in Afghanistan, illustrate this principle. They display some sensitivity on other than strategic issues, but they ignore world opinion on vital matters.

9. Soviet strategy is essentially conservative, and it tends to avoid unnecessary risks. But when the Soviets do move, they move massively, as in Ethiopia and Afghanistan. Their strategy of incremental gains is well-suited to the nuclear age, particularly in the post-Vietnam period. They have become increasingly adept at interpreting the mood in Washington. They took full advantage of American passivity during most of the 1970's, while avoiding measures that might have aroused the United States to act.

---

*The calloused contempt the Soviets displayed toward world opinion in defending their action in shooting down an unarmed Korean Airliner was a classic example of their disdain for the rest of the world community. Likewise was their justification of the unprovoked murder of U.S. Army Major Nicholson.

In summary: patience and persistence characterize Soviet strategy. The USSR has achieved the status of a global power, and claims that developments in every area of the world affect their interests. The tide of the East-West conflict is difficult to assess, yet the Soviet Union's ubiquitous presence in the world, practically non-existent at the end of World War II, is now a powerful factor.

Do the Soviets want to return to a relationship of detente with the United States, which brought the Soviets strategic gains, and the U.S. strategic set-backs? Would the Soviets attempt cooperation at the expense of giving up active influence in areas of vital interest to industrialized democracies? This is not likely. Instead, the expanding military power of the Soviet Union will continue to support an activist Soviet policy. The Soviets, of course, will continue to portray themselves as the chief proponents of peace, disarmament, and progress.

Brent Scowcroft, former National Security Advisor to President Ford, has critically assessed the U.S. response to the Soviet challenge. After stating that the Soviets "comprehend far better than we the political value of military power," he continued:

> The other basic source of the troubles which now confront us is none other than we ourselves. The Soviets basically have a hostile and expansionist view of the non-Communist world. The Soviets' constant buildup of military might is designed to counter Western hostility and serve the USSR's expansionist world outlook. In contrast, the West in general and the United States in particular have treated the Soviet threat as being episodic rather than permanent. We have been stimulated to great efforts by specific threatening events such as Korea, "missile gaps," and Berlin crises. But we have not been able to sustain our concern over long periods of time.
>
> Indeed, on the basis of the historical evidence of our behavior, the Soviets have reason to believe that time favors them and that ultimately their policies will be successful. Thus far, each burst of American energy has been only a temporary phenomenon, following which we have lapsed again into complacency and left the USSR free to resume its careful but persistent tactics of encroachment.
>
> In a way, then, the United States, as the leader of the West, has actually encouraged the Soviet Union to behave as it has.[20]

How does this appraisal augur for the future?

NOTES

1. Since the Soviets rarely, if ever, publish reliable statistics on goods shipped between European Russia and the Soviet Far East, we must restrict ourselves to analogies with comparable logistical choices. The alternate costs of shipping heavy goods material between the East and West coasts of the United States by rail or by ship certainly favor sea shipment.
2. Kozlov, Svyatoslav, "The Truth About the Soviet Presence on World Oceans," *Soviet News* (London) 17 April 1973, p. 175.
3. *The London Observer,* November 12, 1978, p. 15.
4. P. N. Burrell and Alvin J. Cottrell, *Strategic Review,* "The Soviet Navy at the Indian Ocean," U.S. Strategic Institute, Fall 1974.

5. *Asia and the Road Ahead* (Berkeley: University of California Press, 1975). Also see Morris Rothenberg, *Wither China: The View From the Kremlin* (Miami: Center for Advanced International Studies, University of Miami, 1977).
6. Ponomarev, Boris (Article specially written for RABOTNICHESKO DELO by Boris Ponomarev, "Socialist Orientation and Social Progress"), February 1981, pp. 1–6, emphasis supplied.
7. N. Lavedev, "The USSR's Effort to Restructure International Relations," *op. cit.,* (Moscow), no. 1 January 1976.
8. Kennan, George, "Are all Russians 8 Feet Tall," *Freedom at Issue,* September–October, 1978, No. 37, p. 16.
9. "The Soviet Union: Internal Dynamics of Foreign Policy Present and Future United States Policy Toward the Soviet Union," (Wednesday, October 26, 1977), House of Representatives, Committee on International Relations, Subcommittee on Europe and the Middle East, Washington, DC, p. 2.
10. *Ibid.,* p. 323.
11. Salisbury, Harrison E., "The Russia Reagan Faces," *The New York Times Magazine,* February 1, 1981, p. 51.
12. Feifer, George, "Russian Disorders," *Harpers,* 1981, p. 55.
13. *Ibid.,* p. 57.
14. Lenin, V.I., *Imperialism: The Highest Stage of Capitalism,* in *Collected Works,* Vol. 31, April–December 1920, Lawrence & Wishart, London (Moscow: Press Publishers) 1966.
15. Moscow, *Tass International Service,* June 20, 1972.
16. Speech at meeting with voters, February 22, 1980, Novosti Press Agency Publishing House.
17. George Urban, "A Conversation with Milovan Djilas," *Encounter,* December 1979, p. 13.
18. *Law and National Security Intelligence Report,* American Bar Association, Volume 7, Number 2, February 1985.
19. *The Struggle Against Imperialist War and the Tasks of the Communist,* 2nd ed., New York: Workers Library Publishers, July 1934, p. 22.
20. "Soviet Dynamics-Political, Economic Military," A report of the World Affairs Council of Pittsburgh, 1978. Rapporteur's Summary by Lt. General Brent Scowcroft, USAF (Ret.)

CHAPTER VI

Soviet Global Strategy in Prospect: A Forecast

A New Try

The 1985 arrival of the second Reagan Administration and the promotion of Mikhail S. Gorbachev to the top Soviet leadership at the beginning of the second Reagan administration has been met with a cautious effort by the United States to put superpower relations on a more tolerant basis. President Reagan set the stage for another round of arms control talks in a speech to the United Nations on September 24, 1984:

> We are ready for constructive negotiations with the Soviet Union. We recognize that there is no safe alternative to negotiations on arms control and other issues between our two nations, which have the capacity to destroy civilization as we know it. I believe this is a view shared by every country in the world and by the Soviet Union itself.

Gorbachev's rise to power following the death of Chernenko in 1985 was widely interpreted as bringing a new style into the Kremlin which could lead to improvements in Soviet-American relations. President Reagan told a group of magazine publishers that he believed the Soviet leaders were "really going to try and, with us, negotiate a reduction in armaments."[1]

Yet Gorbachev had demonstrated his capacity for playing Leninist hardball politics within a few hours of assuming power. A flurry of coarse threats, broad hints and general muscle-flexing had laid the groundwork for a previously untried linkage between U.S. backing of rebels in Afghanistan and Soviet military build-up and actions in Central America. At a meeting following the mid-March 1985 Chernenko funeral ceremony, Gorbachev warned Pakistani President Zia ul-Haq that his country's continued support of Afghan rebels would affect Soviet-Pakistan relations "in the most negative ways."[2] Gorbachev wanted to link Soviet pressure on Pakistan, a U.S. ally, to U.S. treatment of Nicaragua, a Soviet ally. To add weight to his threat to Pakistan, Soviet troops immediately moved into border areas, raids were carried out on Pakistani villages, and air strikes were made within Pakistani territory.

The West has not yet grasped the Soviet stake in Afghanistan nor the depth of Soviet commitment. As the leader of the Soviet Union, Gorbachev will continue to pursue Soviet goals with the tenacity of his predecessors. Despite the November 1985 summit meetings in Geneva and the October 1986 meeting in Reykjavik, a meaningful East-West accomodation is unlikely in the near future.

The Old Soviet Pattern

In the remainder of this decade, as Soviet domestic problems intensify, Soviet leadership will continue to exploit global opportunities by manipulation of the differences among the Western industrialized nations. U.S. policy toward the Arab-Israeli dispute is increasingly opposed by its European allies; there is growing division between the U.S. and its allies regarding economic policies and toward the Soviet Union; Japan is reluctant to increase its defense effort to the level sought by the United States. These tensions and the economic dislocations confronting most of the industrialized democracies are seen by the Soviets as indications that the final "crisis" of capitalism is imminent.

Although the future is uncertain for both the Soviets and their opponents, the Soviets possesses several advantages. The Soviet Union is fundamentally a totalitarian regime resting on the "legitimacy" of "scientific" Marxism-Leninism and the Soviets derive operational advantages from being a closed society. They can more easily manipulate the populations of their foes while insulating their own from foreign influence.

Despite chronic domestic problems, the Soviets continue to allocate a large percentage of economic, technological and industrial resources to the acquisition of power, particularly through military development. This effort has accelerated in the last 20 years to the extent that the Soviet economy has assumed a wartime structure.

As a result, the Soviet Union has surpassed the U.S. in every aspect of military development except naval force. Furthermore, the Soviets are much better prepared to mobilize for further expansion, although lagging behind the U.S. in critical areas of advanced technology.

While the Soviets are pursuing a total strategy aimed at imposition of their social system on the global world order, the US and its allies are pursuing a loosely coordinated and largely reactive defensive strategy. Soviet grand strategy combines superiority in space, in strategic warfare, and in conventional and growing maritime capabilities with political/psychological subversive intrusions into crucial Third World countries so as to bring about a fundamental and irreversible shift in the world correlation of forces. The final "victory" over disintegrating capitalism is sought without war. The Soviet building blocks are in place for a race for world mastery. The two areas in which the contest may be decided are the scientific-technological frontier and the psychological dimension.

The Scientific-Technical-Economic Dimension

During the entire post World War II period the United States has relied on technological superiority to maintain a military advantage over the Soviet Union. The Soviet Union seeks to eliminate that advantage by an aggressive pursuit of technological equivalence, or even superiority.

Marshall Goldman of the Harvard University Russian Research Institute has published an interesting study entitled, *The U.S.S.R. in Crisis: The Failure of an Economic System.* By Western standards, the USSR has been in crisis since its inception. A farming population twice that of Western Europe and America combined has failed to feed the country adequately. According to Goldman in 1981:

> This is the first time since WW II that it [the USSR] has suffered three disastrous crop failures in a row. After hitting a production record in 1978 of 235 million metric tons of grain, the harvest fell to 79 million tons in 1979, to 189 million tons in 1980, and is expected to reach no more than 175–180 million tons this [1981] year. They probably will need 40 million metric tons—astonishingly, the equivalent of about 20% of their total grain needs.[3]

The economic and political consequences of such harvest shortfalls carry over into later years. By 1983, economic and agricultural problems had become so acute that the Politburo introduced radical economic reforms and made large purchases of U.S. grain. Ironically, the reforms allowed decentralized decision making at the plant-managerial level and established independent production incentives, proposals made by Khruschev prior to his fall for "economic heresy." From the viewpoint of the average citizen, there has been a decline in Soviet consumer goods in recent years.

The defects in the Soviet agricultural system seem to be structural. A recognized Soviet scientist, A.P. Fedoseev, has stated: "The [Soviet] system can not be perfected, if only because it is already perfect, and to adapt it to human needs and rationality means to destroy it . . .".[4] This discredited agricultural system is maintained solely because of the centralization of power that it confers upon the CPSU apparatus. Any diffusion of power to an independent sector of the population would weaken the authority of the central government. In the words of a Soviet emigre writer, " . . . if such a stratum should appear, then tomorrow they would come up against an organization of independent trade unions, and after that, before you know it, against something else even more terrifying."[5]

The Soviet economic system treats "workers as cogs in the economic mechanism" and creates problems of "lower worker productivity and motivation."[6] Marginal diffusion of authority and minor increases in incentives will be insufficient to relieve the economic malaise of low productivity combined with large military investments.

However, while the Soviet domestic economy stagnates, the military-scientific industrial complex in the Soviet Union is continuing developmental patterns established in the late 1960s. This sector has traditionally enjoyed individual incentives and decision-making perogatives; Soviet weapons, e.g., are designed in competitive systems similar to those of the West. According to Secretary of Defense Weinberger:

> For the Soviet Union, the goal of world leadership in science and technology includes a high level of resource commitment that essentially involves the integration of two approaches:
> - The establishment and expansion of a large indigenous technology and production base to support their industrial and military development programs.
> - The acquisition and assimilation of Western technologies to reduce the time, cost, and risk involved in supporting their programs. The Soviet political and military intelligence organizations, the KGB and the GRU have for years been training scientists and engineers to target and acquire advanced technology from the United States, Western Europe, Japan, and elsewhere.[7]

The KGB effort to obtain advanced technology in Western Europe and Japan has been described. Soviet efforts to acquire technology in Japan are particularly intense and Western counter-intelligence officials view KGB activities in Western Europe with equal alarm. According to a West German counterintelligence official: "We see a multiplication and intensification in the technology sector that must reflect unusual pressure to perform. It wasn't there before in the same degree. They've become very aggressive."

The Soviets have acquired billions of dollars worth of Western technology by purchase (legal or illegal), by theft, espionage, and bribery, and from scientific exchanges and U.S. open literature. Using these techniques, the Soviets are able to introduce new technologies into their weaponry without costly R&D or trial and error. Western production methods and radar and guidance technologies have been particularly useful to the Soviets. In addition, the Soviets continued to spend more than twice the U.S. in Research and Development and to educate more than twice the U.S. number of physical scientists and engineers.

The economic, scientific, and technological growth of the Soviet base has occurred within the context of a "planned economy." The theme of the

10th 5 Year Plan (1976–1980) was intensification of economic production. This intensification was to be based primarily on "the acceleration of scientific-technical progress, the rise in labor productivity, and the improvement in the quality of work by all possible means in all sectors of the national economy."

Throughout its history, the Soviet Union has stressed scientific education as a means of increasing productivity and furthering state interests. This resulted in various attempts to legitimize the Soviet system through technological-economic exploits, such as the feats of "Stalin's Falcons" in the 1930s. However, this emphasis on technology in education has produced many asymmetries between the Soviet and US educational bases. According to a May 1981 report by the Stanford Research Institute:

> The Soviet general secondary school curriculum is quite accelerated in both science and mathematics as compared with most curricula in US high schools. The entire school population is exposed to the mathematics-science oriented curriculum in Soviet secondary schools rather than only selected students as is the case in the United States. Thus, in general, the Soviet secondary school graduate has a better training in mathematics and science than does his or her US counterpart.[8]

In sum, the Soviet educational system is producing a talent pool for future scientific and technological innovation. Important conclusions can be drawn relating the Soviet educational system and the development and enhancement of Soviet power. First, this emphasis on science, and particularly mathematics, in secondary education results in an increasingly qualified manpower pool for military research. Thus, the qualitative edge in hardware design favoring the West and the United States is in danger of soon disappearing. In the military sphere the Soviet Union is on the verge of technological equality with the United States and, if present trends continue, the Soviets may surpass the U.S. by the close of the century. Thus, the U.S. will soon be unable to rely on superior technology to offset Soviet numerical superiority in men and weapons systems.

Such technological improvement in military hardware may well stimulate the lagging Soviet economy. For this to occur, however, Soviet leadership will have to resolve the chronic lack of productivity in the Soviet labor force. This problem can often be traced to alcoholism, absenteeism, and lack of motivation, factors that technologically sophisticated production techniques can not completely overcome.

Western analysts have detected acute Soviet manpower shortages and expect a possible energy crisis within the decade. Such domestic difficulties, however, may even accelerate Soviet expansionism as the leadership seeks to reduce the impact of energy or manpower shortages through foreign policy initiatives.

Despite economic strains, the Soviet Union is not facing a domestic crisis. The Soviet leadership has always placed a higher emphasis on acquiring power than on satisfying domestic consumer needs or comforts. A Soviet domestic crisis *would* occur if the USSR were to fall permanently behind in advanced technology or if the system of internal control should fail. The Soviet Union has frequently faced severe social and economic difficulties since the 1917 revolution. Control over the population, however, has not faltered, nor has the drive for industrial and military expansion waivered.

Three factors explain this situation: First, the Soviets plan industrial development as thoroughly as their foreign policy of expansionism. Second, control over the populace insures obedient, if at times, unenthusiastic support for Soviet programs. Third, the USSR systematically and single-mindedly pursues the increase of its strength, perceived power, and actual influence.

Social control of the many by the few, although the foundation of present and future Soviet capabilities, has faced the Soviet leadership since the revolution. When, for example, problems of integration have been exacerbated by a multi-lingual and ethnic population, the CPSU has sought to reverse these trends by emphasizing the uniformity of the Soviet socialist citizen and enforcing rigorous training in the Russian language. Ethnic relations remain complex, particularly in strategically important Central Asia, populated almost exclusively by Muslims. These problems are made more sensitive as a result of high birthrates among Muslims in Central Asia, the Sino-Soviet cleavage, and the revival of Muslem fundamentalism in neighboring states. In an unusual display of openness in December 1986 Soviet-TV reported anti Russian riots by Muslims in Kazakhstan.

The resources devoted to ensure domestic control are considerable. They range from indoctrination to coercive techniques and, while often unpleasant or intolerable by Western standards, the methods are remarkably effective; the Soviet leadership can rely on the loyalty of a vast majority of its people.

As the 1980s progress, the appeal of communism as a universal ideology has deteriorated, especially after the Sino-Soviet split, which weakened the legitimacy of the communist movement world-wide. The lack of uncontested ideological authority weakened the Soviet Union by removing its claim to be the sole source of Marxism-Leninism. The Moscow brand of Marxism has lost whatever attractiveness it might have once had.[9]

While the ideological appeal can be expected to decline still further, the Soviet leadership will still be guided by Marxism-Leninism. The Soviet government has other means of insuring its control, from continual reminders of the sacrifices during the Great Patriotic War to the use of the KGB. The KGB is quite effective at maintaining party control in the Soviet Union, using Draconian principles in its operations. Victor Krasin's story, "How I Was Broken By the KGB," is a devastating account of how this totalitarian instrument of oppression operates.[10] The internal enemies of the Soviet state are not only those who criticize, but those who fail to actively support the CPSU. Without the KGB, the present conditions within the USSR would likely force the Soviet leadership to radical changes. However, the political clout of the KGB grew significantly after its former Chairman, Yuri Andropov, became leader of the Soviet Union.

The Soviet government is faced by severe economic and ethnic problems, but with stringent internal control mechanisms, these will not develop into the economic and social disaster predicted by Salisbury, Feifer and others. Analysts who predict such developments overlook Soviet production of scientific-technological helots, trained to operate in the context of control and coercion. The few dissidents which exist can often serve as safety valves for the system.

At the fifth annual Sakharov Hearing held in London to honor Andrei D. Sakharov, Louise Shelley, an associate professor at the American University in Washington who specializes in Soviet law and justice, said that ordinary citizens are now being affected by the government's increased use of law as an instrument for social control. "Parents can be penalized if their child gets drunk with them," she said in an interview. "It is now a criminal offense for a husband to stay home while his wife works. This . . . is affecting the man in the street with a degree of control they haven't known in a long time."[11]

The Political and Psychological Dimension

The combination of massive Soviet misinformation, the political naivete of many Western leaders and the tendency of the Western media to focus on the inequities and flaws of their own societies (while glossing over the flaws in communist systems and movements) makes it difficult to persuade many people of the threat to democratic societies implicit in Soviet global strategy.

The increasing willingness of the Socialist International to act in parallel with the Soviet Union on such issues as disarmament and "wars of national liberation" in Southern Africa and the Caribbean is another cause for concern. The SI apparently refuses to accept that Soviet dominance has not resulted in socialism or democracy, but rather implies an erosion of freedom in Western Europe. Many Western intellectuals are also unaware of the danger posed to the West by Soviet policies and apply a double standard in their appraisal of Soviet and American behavior. The Western media is usually the vanguard of opposition to Western, and particularly American, efforts to protect the vital interests of Western democracies.

In an article in *Encounter*, Robert Elegant examined the behavior of the media regarding Vietnam and discussed the role of Western media in furthering Soviet strategy. According to the article:

> The press reacted—and could well again act—as a multiplier of the prejudices of the Western intelligentsia, whose tender conscience moves it to condemn the actions of its own side while condoning related deeds of enemies who are either "immature" or "feel themselves threatened".[12]

U.S. network television reporting of Vietnam was crucial in shifting public focus away from facts and in arousing emotions against the government. The role of media in future conflicts could be the same.

Public discussions of nuclear weapons and arms control issues are conducted quite differently in the West than in the Soviet Union. In the West, nuclear weapons and strategies are treated with opprobrium; in fact, for many Western intellectuals nuclear war has become the only evil facing mankind. Conversely, Soviet journals and media actively support Soviet nuclear development and strategy. The capacity of the Soviet Union to exploit the freedoms of the West while insulating its own society from Western reporting of its activities gives the Soviet Union a major psychological advantage in the East-West struggle.

There has been a remarkable fusion of the nuclear peace—freeze campaigns with opposition to U.S. involvement in Central America in both the United States and Western Europe. There is a growing body of evidence that the Soviet Union is deeply involved in assorted and related peace and disarmament campaigns on both sides of the Atlantic.

The Soviets have always viewed peace as a weapon of ideological subversion. Through their principal front organization, the World Peace Council, the Soviets conduct their campaign of subversion in the name of peace. The manipulation of the Western desire for real peace to serve Soviet goals was openly stated by the Central Committee in a letter which appeared in *Pravda* July 14, 1963;

> The struggle for peace and peaceful coexistence weakens the front of imperialism, isolated its more aggressive circles from the mass of the people and helps the working class in its revolutionary struggle . . . The struggle for peace and for peaceful coexistence is organically bound up with the revolutionary struggle against imperialism.

In a remarkably insightful book, Jean-Francois Revel painted a dismal picture of the psychological vulnerability of democracies:

> Democracy probably could have endured had it been the only type of political organization in the world. But it is not basically structured to defend itself against outside enemies seeking its annihilation, especially since the latest and most dangerous of these external enemies, communism—the current and complete model of totalitarianism—parades as democracy perfected when it is in fact the absolute negation of democracy. . . .
> Communism is more skillful, more persevering than democracy in defending itself. Democracy tends to ignore, even deny, threats to its existence because it loathes doing what is needed to counter them. It awakens only when the danger becomes deadly, imminent, evident. By then, either there is too little time left for it to save itself, or the price of survival has become increasingly high.[13]

The system of Soviet fronts and misinformation sources in Western Europe has worked well. In castigating U.S. policies towards Central America, even friendly newspapers do not take at face value official U.S. reports on developments in the region. Instead, they will assert that the U.S. "claims" particular occurrences, and continuing to ignore the practices of the Sandinista regime in Nicaragua. The fusion of the anti-missile deployment campaign and the anti-U.S. Central America campaigns has been extraordinarly successful in Western Europe.

It is worth noting the skill of the Soviets in infiltrating and utilizing these movements. For example, the slogan "No New Missiles in Europe" which was conceived by a Soviet front organization in West Germany in 1981 and which was widely used in the intense propaganda campaign against deployment of the U.S. systems tactitly condoned the presence of the Soviet SS-20 missiles targeted at Western Europe by demanding "No *New* Missiles in Europe."

The U.S. is clearly faltering in this psychological battle before a massive, well-organized psychological campaign to discredit its foreign policy. The White House leadership crisis resulting from the Iranian Arms deal and irregular funding of the Contras has been a Soviet phychological windfall. In addition to the expenditure of billions of rubles to psychologically disarm the West, the Soviet Union also finances equipment for jamming Western radio broadcasts to the Soviet Union.

The Western media is often used by the Soviet Union to spread misinformation. For example, Western journalists may be invited to visit a model guerrilla camp in El Salvador, where young, selfless, clean-cut guerrilla fighters are taught to fight against their oppressors and Yankee imperialism. These newsmen then carry the message back that the U.S. is backing the wrong side in the struggle for social justice. As this message is repeated in newspapers, it finally works its way into the editorial pages which condemn U.S. involvement as vigorously as Tass. On Sunday, July 27, 1983 the New York Times published a broadside editorial against President Reagan entitled "Forget the Maine." It closed as follows:

> There are many things the United States should be doing for hemisphere stability, democracy, prosperity, and to defend its genuine interests, diminish Soviet influence, and to dispell the impression that it is threatened by social justice in Latin America. What it should not be doing is overthrowing containable leftist regimes or fighting for lost reactionary causes, launching war games and invasions in the service of blind doctrine.

The U.S. media constantly glosses over or ignores leftist terrorism and focuses on rightist atrocities in countries such as El Salvador. The advance of democracy in El Salvador in the past several years under Duarte's leadership has largely been ignored.

Many Americans are intellectually aware of the danger posed by the Soviet Union yet few understand the virulence of the underlying hostility behind the effort. A typical example of malicious Soviet propaganda follows:

> Gangs of "Contras", employed by the Reagan Administration in its efforts to overthrow the Nicaraguan government, receive lavish handouts from U.S. money-bags. According to AP News Agency, the counterrevolutionary grouping, which calls itself "Nicaraguan Democratic Forces," makes use of large "donations" by the firm "Miner

and Fraeser" to arm bandits. Edgar Chamorro, former ringleader of the "Nicaraguan Democratic Forces," admitted that the "Human Development Foundation" corporation initiated the setting up of the so-called "Fund of Nicaraguan Refugees" to finance the dirty war waged by Washington against Nicaragua with the hands of "Contras." The accomplices of the Nicaraguan counterrevolution have launched a vigorous campaign to raise funds from "private sources," one of the goals of which is also an attempt to conceal from the public opinion the true proportions of the CIA financial aid to the hirelings who commit bloody crimes against the Nicaraguan people.[14]

Simultaneously, the Soviet Union creates the illusion that it is seeking constructive dialogue through press releases that are reasonable and bland. For example, the July 5, 1983 press release from the Soviet Embassy in Washington stated:

> The USSR is doing everything possible to reckon with the considerations of its partners in the talks and to reach a mutually acceptable agreement, taking into account the interests of both sides. Meanwhile, the US position boils down to the demand for unilateral disarmament of the Soviet Union with the preservation of the NATO's countries' medium range nuclear arms arsenals intact.

While the Soviets release statements reflecting general accomodation and reasonable intent, their true bargaining position is much more negative and contentious.

The record of Soviet behavior and the acknowledged Soviet endorsement of the Marxist-Leninist philosophy suggests that the Soviet Union is not a status quo power. The massive Soviet military build up required by expansionism becomes even more impressive when one realizes the enormous internal economic obstacles that were overcome to create such an establishment.

Except for some relatively minor hard core allies such as Vietnam, Cuba, Third World dependents (Angola, Ethiopia and the PDRY), and occupied Eastern Europe, the expansionist policies of the Soviet Union have created a diplomatic isolation. India is the only major power that gives general, although not complete diplomatic support for Soviet policies. In the UN General Assembly censure of the Soviet invasion of Afghanistan, only 18 countries voted with the Soviet Union by opposing the resolution calling for the removal of all foreign troops from Afghanistan. It would appear that when acting to further their policies, the Soviets would prefer to be a feared, rather than popular, member of the world community.

The Soviet Course for the Future

The global situation presents both difficulties and opportunities for the Soviet Union. The Soviets will hope to exploit tensions and disagreements within the Western alliance and with Japan in the hopes of further weakening the U.S. forward deployment strategy. Likely areas for Soviet efforts include promotion of European opposition to U.S. policies in Latin America, Asian and Japanese resistance to the re-arming of Japan. The Middle East will also be an area for possible Soviet gains, especially after the disastrous failure of U.S. policy in Lebanon.

The oppression of Solidarity in Poland and the use of Soviet troops to invade Afghanistan highlight the internal contradictions and brutality of the Soviet system. Yet, the inability of the West to defend itself adequately because of its faltering will, its addiction to the welfare state and resistance toward defense expenditures will enable the Soviets to cope with these stresses with little fear of Western intervention.

As the 1980s began, the Soviets became concerned when the West, and particularly the United States, undertook serious efforts to redress the military imbalances that had developed in the 1970s. By 1986, the consensus for such a sustained effort has waned in the U.S. Congress and the Reagan Administration defense budget requests have been reduced. Meanwhile, despite continued economic dislocation and stagnation, the Soviets have maintained the military expansion program launched in the mid 1960s, strengthening the Soviet belief that they can deal with their security needs far more readily than can Western societies. The central quesiton asked by Politburo strategists is, how to expedite the "burial" of capitalism with the least risk to themselves?

Within the above context, the strategic policy the Soviets are likely to pursue in the future will be chosen in relation to the following factors:

• The Soviet commitment to the destruction of "capitalism", as enunciated by Lenin, remains. Gorbachev reads Lenin constantly.

• This goal has always been central to the design of Soviet strategy, the form of which has varied according to the means available to the Soviet Union and its opponents.

• Until the beginning of the 1970s, the Soviets waged protracted conflict—a form of conflict which enables a determined weaker opponent to overcome an intrinsically stronger but strategically incompetent adversary. With the attainment of at least strategic equivalence, the Soviets can assert their interests directly, as they have done in Angola, Ethiopia, and Afghanistan.

• By the 1980s, the USSR must deal with incipient rebellion in some of its provinces, such as Poland. The aftermath of the 1983 Papal visit has apparently eased the pressures on Warsaw, but such pressure may return in the future, although not in present form.

• The Soviet Union must also cope with the reality of the Sino-Soviet hostility. Though Soviet strategies in Asia are butressed by a considerable technological and industrial lead over the PRC, Soviet Asian strategy must account for a 4–1 Chinese advantage in population.

• Under the Reagan Administration, a group of men came into power who understand Soviet strategic ambitions. Defense programs begun under the Reagan Administration have focused on the advantages of exotic, high technology characterized by the Strategic Defense Initiative, popularly called "Star Wars." The aim of this program is to neutralize, if possible, by the mid-1990s the advantages the Soviets now enjoy in strategic nuclear warfare.

The American acceleration of RTD&E and strategic modernization programs may eliminate the Soviet advantage within a decade. The prospect of losing their strategic advantage may induce Moscow to step up the tempo of their expansionist aims.

In 1985 the Soviet leadership group, recruited and trained during the Stalin era, began to pass power to a younger generation headed by Mikhail S. Gorbachev. Having grown and matured after the ravages of World War II, these new leaders will have known the Soviet Union only as a global superpower; there will also be no memories of the mobilized capabilities of the industrialized West. This has serious ramifications for Soviet-American relations.

Most of the successors to the Andropov-Chernenko generation came from the upper levels of the party-government bureaucracy. To have advanced that far, they will have to be experienced party bureaucrats and infighters, capable of imposing discipline and adherence to Marxist-Leninist ideology. They are acceptable to the military, to the KGB and to the increasingly influential Soviet scientific and technical community. They can also be expected to maintain a privileged status for the ruling elite.

Gorbachev and his Politburo colleagues face severe problems. Though most of these have existed since the founding of the USSR, they will become more acute during the 1980s and 1990s. Internally, the disastrous performance of Soviet agriculture must be addressed. In addition, the unsolved nationality question will continue to grow more vexing as the Russian birthrate decreases while Asiatic Muslim rates soar. The resurgence of Islamic fundamentalism south of the border in Iran and the effects of occupying Islamic Afghanistan could also pose potential problems.

Though not as vulnerable as some Western analysts predict, the Soviet economy requires overhaul. The commitment to military projects retards Soviet economic growth, but a shortage of modern equipment, high rates of alcoholism and absenteeism, and the lack of a genuine work ethic also contribute to the economic ills.

As serious as these problems are, it can be expected that they will either be corrected or endured. The Soviet Union has faced greater challenges, including fighting and winning the most devastating war in history and the subsequent development of the world's largest military machine. The impact of Soviet internal troubles on its foreign strategies is of major concern to the West.

The new Soviet leadership will have to choose from three broad policy options: (1) abandonment of expansionist strategies; (2) maintaing the present position and playing for time and opportunities; or (3) pushing forward against the U.S. alliance systems, seeking to neutralize the U.S.

by the 1990s, paving the way for the subsequent handling of the PRC. A variant on this would be to address the PRC first and to then turn on the U.S.-led alliance system. From the Soviet perspective, the merits of each of these options is summarized below:

1. *Retrench*

This policy would be based on the recognition that the Soviet Union has become over-extended and that the costs of expansion exceed gains. However, this policy cannot be chosen by the Soviet leadership group for two reasons. First, it abandons the concept of "the inevitable triumph of Communism" which bestows legitimacy on the CPSU and on other allied communist parties. Secondly, such a policy would most likely lead to increased accomodation with the West, with the subsequent loosening of Soviet control in Eastern Europe. Both developments are unacceptable to Moscow.

2. *Stand Pat*

This strategy has several attractions for Soviet leadership. An apparently conciliatory Soviet Union would be able to diffuse Western and particularly European resolve to restore the military equilibrium.

Furthermore, if the American economy continues its vigor, a conciliatory Soviet Union would strengthen those seeking to transfer funds from the defense modernization program to social services.

Since a global situation is developing favorable to Soviet interests, however, there is a question whether the Soviet leadership or its allies in Vietnam, Aden, Angola and Cuba have the patience to mark time.

3. *Push Ahead*

The third alternative is also a plausible course for Soviet activity. The ability of the U.S. or its allies to oppose a concerted Soviet drive until the late 1980s is questionable. The risks of such a policy increase with each new success. The Soviet Union can not be certain whether success will breed accomodation with the Soviet Union or antagonize adversaries causing them to form cohesive alliances. In particular, continued Soviet expansion in the Middle East would threaten Western access to vital oil supplies. In addition, it would add to Chinese fears of Soviet encirclement. Whether such moves would force Japan and Western Europe to seek accomodation with the USSR or strengthen the U.S. alliance structure is uncertain.

Soviet doctrine stresses the danger of collapsing capitalist societies, predicting a death spasm by dying capitalism against the socialist states. This option holds the promise of success but contains the possibility of strengthening the alliance system of its chief adversary.

If the Soviets should choose the first option, the West will have little to worry about in the next decade or so. And if the Soviets conduct their foreign policy along the lines set forth in the second option, the next decade for the United States will be turbulent but not fatal. The desire to exploit

Western weaknesses while Soviet strategic superiority exists would make the third option a logical choice for Soviet leadership. Whether this proves to be true depends on several factors: the post Solidarity situation in Poland, the magnitude of the Soviet agricultural disaster, and the situations in Afghanistan, Central America, the Middle East, and Europe. It is conceivable that the Soviets could implement the second option, while laying the groundwork for the third option.

Whatever mix of these options the Soviets may choose, the developing situation facing the U.S. and its allies is one of enormous danger. This assessment may at first glance somewhat contradict the assertion made in Chapter II that the Soviet strategists are under no compulsion to gain victory within a set period of time. This assertion remains valid, but is qualified by two parameters. The first is the Soviet avoidance of reckless adventurism, such as the Krushchev plan to introduce IRBMs into Cuba in 1962 which was condemned by his colleagues as a "hair brained scheme". The second qualification is the Soviet desire to perceive and grasp an historical opportunity when it presents itself. The Soviet achievement of strategic superiority is such an opportunity. Whether they will take advantage of it so that the U.S. can not restore the military balance is an open question.

The decision makers who will recommend options for the Soviet leadership are unknown in the West. The same men who decided the support for the Sandinistas in Nicaragua, the MPLA in Angola, the large scale intervention in Ethiopia, or the Soviet invasion of Afghanistan will most likely estimate the emerging "correlaton of forces" which will determine Soviet policy options vis-a-vis the United States.

Equally unpleasant is the probability that most Soviet scholars with whom Americans discuss U.S.-Soviet relations may also be ignorant of the decision-making process in the higher levels of the Soviet government. The Soviet people know little of Soviet involvement in foreign interventions. In this way, the Soviet government does not need to generate domestic support for whatever it chooses to do in any part of the globe.

The peoples living within the Soviet Union are not responsible for the strategy outlined within this book. They are, in Samantha Smith's words, ". . . people like everyone else", but their government is like no other on earth. The peoples in the Soviet Union deserve our sypmapthy and our support. Except for the accident of birth, many of us in the West might have to endure the grey existance that is the lot of most people living in the USSR.

Outcome Unknown

The ideological and geopolitical perceptions of Soviet strategists would logically induce them to advance the expansion of the Soviet Empire during the course of the 1980s. There is no guarantee, however, that the Soviet

Union will succeed in pursuing this or any other goal they might choose to adopt. History is not determined by blind, deterministic forces, but by mortal men. There are no fixed parameters that dictate the outcome of the struggle, one way or the other.

The West possesses vast resources which, if mobilized, can safeguard Western civilization and culture from the threat posed by Soviet totalitarianism. Though the Soviets have sought the ability to absorb a nuclear strike against them, the uncertainties of the outcome of such a nuclear war may constrain their expansionist policies.

The Soviet leaders are also sensitive to the imponderables of the domestic situation as well as to the intrinsic unattractiveness of their system to subject people. The societal weaknesses of the Soviet system could become a real source of vulnerability if the West were to mount a campaign to exploit them.

Churchill said in 1950: "The Soviets fear our friendship more than our arms. We must labor to create the reverse." If the Soviet Union wishes to enter into the long-term international cooperation which mankind so desperately needs, it will have to shift its policy to something far more benign than peaceful coexistence and the continuation of warfare that the term implies.

Some conflict between systems is inevitable even in a stable world, but such conflict need not result in an irreversible shift of the global balance of power in favor of the Soviet Union. In this respect, remarks made by President Kennedy at American University on June 19, 1963 are appropriate:

> World peace, like community peace, does not require that each man love his neighbor: it requires only that they live together in mutual tolerance, submitting their disputes to a just and peaceful settlement. And history teaches us that enmities between nations, as between individuals do not last forever.

The Soviet Union is not impervious to the global developments demanding a cooperative solution. Failure to solve environmental and resource problems affecting all mankind could wreak havoc on the Soviets as well as everyone else. This being so, the U.S. should try and hasten the advent of true international cooperation by inducing the Soviet Union to participate in the international community in a more mature responsible manner. There is no way for the U.S. to avoid this arduous and dangerous task, first enunciated in National Security Memorandum 68 in April 1950, if freedom is to survive. Haphazardly executed in the past, this task has recently become more complicated by the increase in relative Soviet military strength.

With two superpowers in the world, it should be in the long term interest of both to keep their competition within limited bounds. It is hoped that one day the Soviets will share this point of view. Until they do so, the struggle will continue.

The U.S.-Soviet rivalry issues both from the clash of basic political ideology and conflicting security interests in the global arena. If the creativity, comprehension, and efficacy of their strategies can be judged objectively, Soviet strategy throughout the long confrontation has been superior. As Revel put it, political democracy . . .

> is under worldwide attack as it has never before been in its brief history. And that attack, which is being waged with unexampled vigor, scope and intelligence, is catching the democracies in a state of intellectual impotence and political indolence that disposes them to defeat and makes a Communist victory probable, if not inevitable.

Marxism-Leninism, as it has evolved in the Soviet Union, is an amalgam of imperial Czarist Russia with Lenin's adaptation of Marx, to create a new Soviet state under the total control of the Communist Party. Under Lenin, and more completely under Stalin, the state became supreme over the utopian aspects of communism. By imposing totalitarian party control over the apparatus of the state and over the military, the new rulers transformed the Czarist empire into the Soviet empire. This new Soviet empire, moving in accordance with what was to be called the theory of "scientific communism," set about to fulfill its goal of triumphing over the enemy, the "imperialist" state-system led by the United States. Because no convergence of capitalism and communism is possible under this Marxist-Leninist theory of history conflict is a permanent condition. Yet, many Westerners find this kind of Soviet behavior difficult to grasp.

> Many of us still want to believe that the problems that separate us are problems that can be resolved by negotiation and mutual good will. But unfortunately we must realize that we cannot find lasting peace through negotiation because what the Soviets really want we cannot negotiate. We cannot cede to them the right to progressive imperial conquest. We cannot negotiate away our freedom. We must face the fact that the antagonism between our two civilizations is not superficial but fundamental and that we are condemned to this state of affairs for the long term. There is no easy solution, no quick fix.[15]

Soviet communist ambitions have been explicitly stated by Lenin and all of his successors in the Kremlin. As recently as April 1984, the Soviet foreign Minister Andrei Gromyko, stated the Soviet view of the world with brutal frankness:

> The Soviet policy of peaceful co-existence is a specific form of socialism's class struggle against capitalism. This struggle is ongoing and will continue in the field of economics, politics and, of course, ideology, because the world outlook and the class struggle are *irreconcilable*.[16] (emphasis supplied)

The American response to the Soviet drive for global preeminence must be met by American society as a whole. If we lose the global struggle with the Soviet Union, it will be because we permitted it to occur. A Soviet victory is not foreordained; the Soviets can be checked and prevented from manipulating events to their advantage. This requires, however, that the countries cooperating with American leadership must devise a strategic plan superior to that bequeathed to Moscow by Lenin. The development of such a strategy is the most important task confronting the United States. Equally, if not more important, is the imperative for the American and allied governments to generate the will of their respective peoples to see this struggle through until the survival of free men on this globe is assured.

Gorbachev Year One: 1985

There are almost no parallels between Soviet strategy and the strategy pursued by the United States. While American strategic thought posits a dichotomy between war and peace, the Soviets see a continuum. The United States has no peacetime strategy with which it seeks to confront Soviet expansionism with the combined arms of diplomacy, economic powers, psychological operations, and potential military might. Not surprisingly, it is difficult for Westerners to understand how seriously the Soviet leaders focus on conflict, on preparations for war, and on their continuous assault on free societies.

Will this pattern continue under Gorbachev? The question that must be asked is whether Gorbachev is a dedicated devotee of peace or a calculated, glib dissembler. If he is a convinced Marxist-Leninist, he can only be the latter. Since we are dealing with a man who rules the world's only remaining empire and who commands the greatest military machine ever created it is important that we try to find out the well-springs of his behavior.

If one examines what Gorbachev has said and written in recent years one can conclude that he believes in the eventual triumph of communism over capitalism even though he must sometimes modify his public stance and actions for the sake of tactical expediency. This has always been the practice of Soviet leaders. Except for being younger, more sauve, and more glib Gorbachev fits into the mold of his predecessors all the way back to Stalin and Lenin.

It is worth noting that Gorbachev, a protégé of Andropov, became a leader of the Komosol at the age of 17, in charge of 30,000 young Komosol students at Moscow University at the age of 21 and chose a career calculated to climb the party ladder to the very top. It is interesting to note that Gorbachev was national party secretary in charge of agriculture during three successive years of crop failures. Yet this dim performance record did not lower his standing with Andropov, who set the stage for Gorbachev's subsequent rise to power in March 1985.

Before the Central Committee, CPSU, on April 23, 1985 Mikhail S. Gorbachev revealed the intensity of his devotion to Marxism-Leninism and took major steps toward gaining personal control of the ruling Politburo. In a speech which Stalin would have been proud to deliver, Gorbachev said that "with all certainty the responsibility for the present situation rests in the first place in the United States. They are seeking to sabotage the

Geneva arms talks, dominate the Third World, undermine the international economy and attain military supremacy over the Soviet Union." The trigger for this comprehensive attack appeared to have been the Soviets' growing anger with the U.S. negotiating strategy at the then six-week-old Geneva arms talks. Gorbachev said that the Americans, in arguing the case for continued research on the "Star Wars" space defense, were violating the pre-conditions of the talks and thus were not serious about an agreement. He further remarked with respect to the Third World:

> The United States openly claims the "right" for itself to interfere everywhere, ignores and, not infrequently, directly tramples underfoot the interests of other countries and peoples, the traditions of international intercourse and existing treaties and agreements. It constantly creates seats of conflicts and war danger, heating up the situation now in one area of the world, now in another. The United States is threatening militarily today the heroic people of Nicaragua in an effort to deprive it of freedom and sovereignty, as was the case in Grenada.

In the economic sector, Gorbachev claimed:

> The economic expansion of the United States is being broadened and stepped up. Manipulation of bank rates, the predatory role of transnational corporations, political restrictions in trade, all kinds of boycotts, and sanctions create an atmosphere of tension and distrust in international economic relations, disorganize the world economy and trade and undermine its legal basis.

And in the Communist bloc, Gorbachev said:

> imperialism has stepped up its subversion in recent years and is coordinating its actions against socialist states. These activities extend to all spheres—political, economic, ideological and military.

At the close of this malicious caricature Gorbachev hinted about a possible Soviet walkout from the Geneva arms control talks:

> It is impossible to reconcile an arms race and disarmament talks. This is clear if one does not indulge in hypocrisy and does not try to mislead public opinion. The Soviet Union will not encourage such a course, and let this be known to all those who are now engaged in a political game and not serious politics. We would not like to have a recurrence of the sad experience of the previous talks.[17]

At the same April meeting of the Central Committee in which he fired broadsides against the U.S. Gorbachev solidified his personal position by placing three allies on the Politburo. Named to full membership were Yegor K. Ligachev, the national party secretary in charge of high-level appointment; Nikolai I. Ryzhkov, the economic specialist in the party's Secretariat, and Viktor M. Cherbrikov, head of the KGB security police.

All three of the above men had been promoted to their current positions under Mr. Gorbachev's own mentor, Yuri V. Andropov. Like Gorbachev, these men rose through the party apparachik.

Subsequently Gorbachev eliminated his chief rival, Grigory V. Romonov, from the Politburo and elevated Andrei A. Gromyko to the largely ceremonial position of President of the Soviet Union. As 1986 came to a close, however, there was still some question as to whether Gorbachev fully dominated the Politburo. Initially Gorbachev acted with more than normal restraint abroad which may have helped set the stage for the first Reagan-Gorbachev summit meeting in Geneva in November 1985. The immediate reaction to the Geneva Summit was one of restrained optimism by the leaders on both sides. Though they failed to agree on arms control, human rights and many other questions, President Reagan and Mikhail S. Gorbachev, the Soviet leader, were widely praised for establishing a climate of rapport that could permit hard bargaining on crucial issues.

In a ceremony marking the end of the summit conference, Gorbachev stated

> the significance of everything which we have agreed with the President can only, of course, be reflected if we carry it on into concrete measures. If we really want to succeed in something, then both sides are going to have to do an awful lot of work in the spirit of joint commission—of the joint statement which we have put out.[18]

In the follow-up to these remarks President Reagan added:

> Before coming to Geneva, I spoke often of the need to build confidence in our dealings with each other. Frank and forthright conversation at the summit are part of this process. But I'm certain General Secretary Gorbachev would agree that real confidence in each other must be built on deeds, not simply words. This is the thought that ties together all the proposals that the United States has put on the table in the past, and this is the criteria by which our meetings will be judged in the future.
>
> The real report card on Geneva will not come in for months or even years. But we know the questions that must be answered.[19]

On his return to Washington President Reagan told the cabinet that:

> his talks with Mikhail S. Gorbachev had 'cleared the air' and that the two leaders had agreed to 'keep in touch, keep in contact' even before they meet again next year.
>
> Mr. Reagan acknowledged that he had failed to soften the Soviet leader's opposition to the Administration's space-based missile defense plan, and that the United States and the Soviet Union remained divided on major issues.[20]

Mikhails S. Gorbachev was warmly received when he returned to Moscow and ". . . there was a palpable sense of optimism among many Russians over his meetings with President Reagan."[21]

According to Leslie H. Gelb,

> The summit meeting . . . was widely seen by officials on both sides as a victory for President Reagan, who wanted to emphasize process and play down substance, and a setback for Mikhail S. Gorbachev, who had staked so much personal prestige on an arms control breakthrough at the two-day encounter.
>
> Before the meeting, Mr. Gorbachev gambled that by threatening a failure in Geneva, he could elicit concessions from Mr. Reagan on space-based defenses. By all current accounts, it did not work. Now, according to Soviet officials, he will revert to a longer-term strategy of trying to turn American and allied opinion against Mr. Reagan's Strategic Defense Initiative.[22]

The burden of this book is that the Soviet Union is an expansionist power which under Gorbachev still embraces the thesis espoused by Lenin: "As long as capitalism and socialism exist, we can not live in peace. In the end, one or the other will triumph."

Lenin's appraisal is not negated by the summit's joint U.S.-Soviet statement that a "nuclear war cannot be won and must never be fought." This study contends that the Soviets will continue to seek victory over the United States without war.

The author agrees with former President Richard Nixon that:

> . . . tensions between the two nations are due not to the fact that we do *not* understand each other but to the fact that we *do* understand that we have diametrically opposed ideological and geopolitical interests. Most of our differences will never be resolved. But the United States and the Soviet Union have one major goal in common: survival. Each has the key to the other's survival. The purpose of summit meetings is to develop rules of engagement that could prevent our profound differences from bringing us into armed conflict that could destroy us both.[23]

In an interview given a few days before flying to Geneva, President Reagan commented:

> . . . I recently read a statement I'd like to quote: 'Nations do not distrust each other because they are armed; they are armed because they distrust each other." So our negotiations should be aimed *at eliminating the distrust*. This would require not just words between us but deeds—actions that we both could take that would help convince the other side that we mean no first strike and no harm.[24]

While we may mean no harm to the Soviet Union the converse may not be true. In the same interview President Reagan discussed the issue of distrust from another angle.

> . . . we're not out to destroy their system or change it, nor are we going to allow them to change ours. We recognize that it is an advantage to both of us to have continued peace and to go forward with the systems under which we presently exist—but to eliminate the distrust between us.[25]

It is quite true that the United States and the West have not tried to change the Soviet system. But the Soviets have continuously sought to undermine and change the social and political system of their opponents. A careful reading of Gorbachev's news conference held on the morning after the end of the Geneva summit meeting will reveal Soviet adherence to its goal of victory over the United States and its allies.

Gorbachev's news conference was a masterpiece of disingenuousness. As a dedicated practitioner of Leninism and married to a University lecturer on "Marxist-Leninist Philosophy" Gorbachev astutely plays the game of Active Measures involving double agents, influence peddlers, front organizations, and the skillful manipulation of public opinion among Soviet opponents. His post-Summit news conference conveyed his desire to walk with President Reagan toward common goals on the one hand while continuing to mastermind the Soviet strategy aimed at undermining the West. Our goals are not the same nor can they be as long as the Soviets believe that their mission is to extend their oppressive system over all the earth.

Mr. Gorbachev began his press session by noting "how far the militarization of the economy has proceeded".[26] Presumably he was referring to the American economy. He glossed over the fact that the Soviet Union devotes twice as much of its GNP to arms as does the United States. Over ten years ago the Peking Review stated: "The entire Soviet economy has taken a peculiar form of war economy."

The Chairman then asserted: "And we did our utmost to lay the basis for a mutual understanding before the meeting would get under way, to improve the political atmosphere." This statement was not true. In fact, the Soviet Union stepped up its domestic anti-American propaganda barrage in the weeks and days before the summit. Western diplomats suggested that the stepped-up propaganda could be designed to put extra pressure on Reagan.

After stating that "a nuclear war cannot occur" Gorbachev continued: ". . . we are for competition with the United States, for active rivalry with the United States." Noting the emergence of divergences, Gorbachev assured the press that ". . . we're certainly prepared to come up with some sort of mutually acceptable solution, provided there is no arms race in space."

Gorbachev deftly ignored the military aspects of the Soviet space program:

> I must say we did get the impression that the Americans are certainly very strong in certain areas of technology, particularly in computer sciences, in radio communication, and of course there's the desire too for us to grab onto that and gain some sort of superiority.
>
> But one could even quote President Johnson, way back, who said that whoever manages to gain power in space will rule the earth. And they're just itching to get their hands into it. They're just itching to get this world domination and look down on the world from on high. It's an old, longstanding ambition.

In response to President Reagan's focus on the role of regional conflicts Gorbachev commented as follows:

> The tension—this is what we said both to the President and the American delegation, conflicts and even whole regions and wars, the wars which take place in this or that region between this or that country, whichever part of the world it's in—these are all based upon what happened in the past, and upon the social and economic conditions in which these countries and regions are existing today.

While present regional conflicts can often be traced to the past, Soviet intrusion has been instrumental in a number of countries including Nicaragua, Angola, Ethiopia and Afghanistan. Gorbachev claimed "We have nothing against discussing regional problems here or there. . . . But at the same time, we continue to stress, and I want to say now, we want to do it without any interference in the internal affairs of any country."

This standard Soviet line has worn extremely thin. Gorbachev, however, saved his strongest rhetoric to underscore his position that the "star wars" program will not only lead to a further arms race, but it will mean that "all restraint will be blown to the winds." He then stressed the key to his psychological arms control strategy: "We are prepared to engage in radical cut backs in nuclear weapons provided the door to unleashing an arms race in outer space is firmly slammed shut."

Mr. Gorbachev heatedly denied that American advanced technology would give the United States an edge in shifting to space weapons. The program the Soviet Union would mount in response, he said, "will be effective, though less expensive, and quicker to produce."

On October 26, 1985, *Pravda* devoted nearly seven pages to the draft of a new party program outlining the course that Gorbachev will follow as he leads the Soviet Union toward the twenty-first century. Since the party has had only three programs in its history, Gorbachev's Geneva press conference must be analyzed in terms of this 4th CPSU program bearing his imprimatur. With regard to foreign policy and strategy, the Gorbachev program makes these points: "The international policy of the CPSU," it says, "proceeds from the humane nature of socialist society, which is free from exploitation and oppression and has no classes or social groups with an interest in unleashing war."

The document singles out the following main goals and directions of the international policy of the CPSU:

- Provision of auspicious external conditions for refinement of socialist society and for advance to communism in the USSR, removal of the threat of world war and achievement of universal security and disarmament;
- Constant development and expansion of cooperation between the USSR and the fraternal socialist countries and all-round promotion of consolidation and progress in the world socialist system;
- Development of relations of equality and friendship with newly-free countries;
- Maintenance and development of relations between the USSR and capitalist states on a basis of peaceful coexistence and businesslike mutually beneficial cooperation;
- Internationalist solidarity with communist and revolutionary-democratic parties, with the international working class movement and with the national-liberation struggle of the peoples.

"There is no loftier or more responsible mission than that of safeguarding and strengthening peace and curbing the forces of aggression and militarism for the cause of life for the present and future generations," the draft new edition f the CPSU's Programme says. "A world without wars, without weapons is the ideal of socialism."[27]

By matching Gorbachev's Geneva press conference with the CPSU party's program, the Soviet post-summit arms control strategy becomes quite clear. Gorbachev's strategy rests on three foundations. The first is that he will have to deal with President Reagan for less than two years, while the United States will probably have to deal with Gorbachev for the remainder of this century. Consequently, he has plenty of time to whittle away at public support for Reagan's SDI. The man who succeeds Reagan may be more pliable or even opposed to the SDI.

Secondly, Gorbachev is aware that many opinion makers in the West believe that superpower arms control provides the surest way toward global peace and security. He appeals to such people by volunteering radical cuts in offensive nuclear weapons provided the U.S. abandons its SDI program; the comparable Soviet Anti Missile program will of course continue. The campaign to scuttle Reagan's SDI will be relentless and will involve well-orchestrated peace campaigns in Europe, the United States, and Japan. That intellectual support for Gorbachev's anti-SDI campaign already exists can be seen from this pre-1985 summit editorial in the British newspaper, *Guardian:*

> . . . the Russians appear to many in the West to be right and the Americans wrong. SDI is not what Mr. Reagan thinks it is: the alchemist's stone which transmutes plutonium to dust. It is an instrument of instability. Opponents of SDI seem in American eyes to stand accused of indifferentism between East and West, of regarding the superpowers as much of a muchness. That is not the case at all. It is simply that on the conceptual and technical question of whether SDI is a good idea or a bad one the Kremlin is right and the White House is wrong.[28]

The Soviets will treat human rights and regional conflicts as peripheral issues which must not interfere with the main question of arms control. In this the Soviets will be aided by those in the West who deliberately close their eyes to Soviet-supported terrorism or the genocidal Soviet campaign against the freedom fighters in Afghanistan. There are legions of moral cowards in the West who ignore Soviet atrocities since they do not wish to face up to the realities of the Soviet challenge to peace with freedom.

Rather than being "a fresh start" the first Reagan-Gorbachev summit was another stage in a long, tough struggle with no end in sight. Despite his savoir-faire and charm, Gorbachev was cast in the same mold as Lenin, Stalin, Khrushchev, and Brezhnev. As long as Gorbachev and men like him are at the top of the Soviet pinnacle of power, the mistrust that President Reagan mused upon at the eye of the summit cannot disappear.

The failure of the 1985 Geneva summit to achieve any significant arms control program was passed over by plans for Gorbachev to visit Washington in 1986. Surprisingly the second Reagan-Gorbachev summit took place in Reykjavik, Iceland in October 1986. In protracted negotiations between the Soviet police state and the United States the Kremlin has a built-in advantage in not having to deal with a free press, public opinion, or allies. Under Gorbachev, Soviet diplomacy will dangle the prospects of major nuclear arms cuts provided the U.S. abandons its allegedly misguided and dangerous SDI program. The pressure to do so, aided by the vast KGB-supported Soviet propaganda machine, will be enormous. Gorbachev's focus on peace as the driving force of his anti-SDI campaign is not new.

According to a resolution of the 1928 Sixth World Congress of the Communist International, the peace policy of the USSR is of a kind which 'provides the best basis for taking advantage of the antagonisms among the imperialist states.' The Soviet Union's program for peace is in reality a form of war. 'The peace policy of the proletarian state does not imply that the Soviet State has become reconciled with capitalism,' continued this resolution. 'It is merely a more advantageous form of fighting capitalism, a form which the USSR had consistently employed since the October revolution.'[29]

Toward the close of 1985 Gorbachev underscored his own personal peace campaign by arranging to publish a collection of statements made between March and October 1985. "Since my election as general secretary of the Communist party central committee"[30] This collection was published under the title of, "A Time For Peace".

In the forward to this book Gorbachev wrote:

The vital need for peace and ways of achieving it are a major theme of this book. In addressing the American reader, let me say that our country has never instigated or initiated an arms race. We have not been the first to start manufacturing any type of weapon. The Soviet Union has pledged not to deploy weapons in space if other nations do not do so. We shall not conduct nuclear tests and explosions if the United States joins the moratorium we have declared. We would like this moratorium to be the first step on the road towards reducing and eventually eliminating nuclear weapons.[31]

Although the theme of peace runs through this collection so does the vehemence of a dyed-in-the-wool Leninist against the United States. A most notable inclusion was his speech given at a meeting in Moscow to mark the 113th anniversary of Lenin's birth, April 22, 1983.[32]

According to Gorbachev:

Lenin said: ". . . An issue . . . of war and peace cannot properly be posed if the class antagonisms of modern society are lost sight of . . ." Imperialist reaction can hide behind many masks, but it cannot hide the fact that its foreign course is dictated, even today, by narrowly selfish class interests.

The striving for maximum profits, for the perpetuation of a society of oppression and exploitation, for world domination is the real basis of imperialism. Lenin's characterization of imperialism and of the forces that motivate its policy retains all its significance in our time.

Comrades! The U.S. imperial ambitions, the arms race, the cult of force, war propaganda—all that makes the imperialist approach to international problems a universal danger. As we know, the aggressive stand of the ruling circles of the Western camp is opposed by a more realistic, sober stand whose advocates favor detente and cooperation.[33]

The United States, according to Gorbachev, is the sole obstacle to peace and peaceful solutions. At the end of November 1985 Gorbachev told the Soviet parliament that the Soviet Union wanted a political solution to end its bloody aggression against Afghanistan, but that the U.S. was preventing such a move.

Gorbachev told the Soviet parliament:

"If there is somebody who prevents the immediate solution of the problem, that is the United States, which finances and supports and arms the bands of counterrevolutionaries and jeopardizes the efforts to normalize the situation."[34]

While condemning U.S. support for freedom fighters in Afghanistan the Soviet Union, under Gorbachev, strongly supported pro-communist groups seeking to take over power in most areas of the globe. But Gorbachev's "peace" drum beats the loudest when he attacks the U.S. SDI program as the main obstacle to improve U.S.-Soviet relations.

The Soviet Union's campaign against U.S. Strategic defenses belies its own commitment to balanced offensive-defensive forces. As Mose Harvey has written:

> Soviet military strategy requires force capabilities not only to destroy the opponent but also to protect the Soviet Union. While strategic offensive weapons might to a considerable degree perform the first task, strategic defense together with civil defense is deemed essential for the latter. Consequently, the Soviets do not view strategic offense and strategic defense/civil defense as conflicting components, but rather as complementary components of the modern nuclear arsenal. In the words of one Soviet spokesman, "offense and defense constitute a dialectical unity of opposites, which simultaneously both exclude and assume one another. They not only are interconnected, but also mutually penetrate one another and cannot exist separately."[35]

Recognizing the flagrant dichotomy between Soviet propaganda and strategic doctrine, the State Department has rejected the Soviet Campaign against the U.S. SDI as sheer hypocrisy. Paul Nitze the Chief U.S. Advisor on Arms Control has written that the Soviets have long funded at high levels their own SDI research program and are ahead of the U.S. in several exotic missile defense areas.[36]

Gorbachev's energetic criticisms of the U.S. SDI program before and after the 1985 and 1986 summit meetings should be seen as an effort to derail the SDI program while obscuring Soviet bids for mastery in space. The Soviets are well on their way to achieving the kind of ABM defense the President is seeking. In fact, the Soviets are making their own ballistic nuclear-defense program an operational reality, in defiance of treaty and entreaty.

The SDI, or Star Wars, represents the first real challenge to the most ominous strategic development of the decade; a growing Soviet nuclear first-strike capability combined with its own "Red Shield", a ballistic-missile-defense system covering the entire USSR. While Star Wars remains largely theory, with experimental testing, Red Shield is an emerging operational reality. Its main elements:

> Completion by next year of a modernized 100-launcher ABM system around Moscow.
> Production of a new generation of ABM interceptor rockets and associated radars.
> Continued upgrading of and new construction on a nationwide network of long-range detection and battle-management radars of unparalleled size and power.
> Intensive work on "beam weapons" and other advanced technologies, including testing of laser weapons.[37]

Soviet leaders and military planners are profound students of Clausewitz, the great German military theoretician. Bernard Brodie, one of the
leading American strategic thinkers once described Clausewitz's book,
"On War", as "not simply the greatest but the only truly great book on war".
Lenin was an avid student of Clausewitz and kept a copy of "On War" by his
bedside. The key issue Clausewitz addressed was the relation between the
political object and the military aim of war. A serious American student of
strategy has summed up the contribution of Clausewitz this way:

> Clausewitz's solution, in theory, to this problem is grounded ultimately upon the
> premise that offensive and defensive forms of fighting can be combined in such a way as
> to make the defense the stronger form of war.[38]

In total contrast McNamara, a strategic babe compared to Clausewitz, in
1966 stated; "If we had to spend the entire budget of the Defense Department, $50 billion, on the strategic offensive, we would prepare to do so to
insure that the Soviets do not develop an effective counter." (McNamara
Says Soviets Err on ABMs, Missiles and Rockets, May 2, 1966, p.2) The
difference between Soviet and U.S. concepts of strategy and arms control
are profound. Many United States citizens view the future in terms of peace
or nuclear war. The Soviets, in contrast still view war as an instrument of
policy and arms control talks an arena of diplomatic conflict as became
evident once more at the 1986 Reykjavik summit.

Gorbachev; Year Two, 1986

The 1986 events that were most revealing about Soviet strategy were the
unveiling of a plan to rid the world of all nuclear weapons by the end of the
century, the program adopted by February 1986 27th party congress, the
Soviet handling of the Chernobyl nuclear disaster, the Soviet frame up of
the American journalist Nicholas Daniloff, and Gorbachev's determined
effort to torpedo President Reagan's SDI program at their Reykjavik summit meeting.

On January 15, Gorbachev shifted his "peace campaign" into high gear
by unveiling a plan to rid the world of all nuclear weapons by the year
2000.[39]Gorbachev's planned process for doing this was highly publicized in
the Soviet Union on the eve of the resumption of the Geneva arms talks.
The Soviet leader declared that his disarmament process could begin only if
the U.S. gave up its SDI which Gorbachev called "space strike weapons."
President Reagan stated he was "gratified" for the Soviet plan which he
called "different." In essence the Gorbachev package is an innovative
combination of some old and new proposals containing many ambiguities.
U.S. negotiations at Geneva will have to probe deeply into Gorbachev's
proposal to see whether it is a serious package or an artfully designed
booby trap. For one thing they will have to find out what Gorbachev means

by saying on-site inspections can be allowed "whenever necessary." For another, the British, the French and the Chinese will have to be somehow drawn into the process. Sweeping demands for "universal and complete disarmament" have been made many times by the Soviet Union. In 1946 Stalin called for a ban on the production and use of nuclear weapons while secretly ordering a colossal Soviet program for acquiring atomic bombs. Even if the Soviet plan is adopted and the world is rid of nuclear weapons, the Soviet Union would still retain massive conventional superiority over its neighbors in Europe and Asia. In sum, the Gorbachev proposal could be a two-edge sword designed to put the U.S. on the defensive in the battle over "peace."

The program adopted by the 27th party congress was notable for its strict adherence to Marxism-Leninism concerning the source and character of the world struggle. A few excerpts follow:

The arms race started by imperialism has resulted in the 20th century in world politics ending with the question of whether humanity will manage to elude the nuclear danger or if the policy of confrontation will take precedence, increasing the probability of nuclear conflict. The capitalist world has not abandoned the ideology and policy of hegemonism, its rulers have not yet lost the hope of taking social revenge, and continue to indulge themselves with illusions of superior strength. The sober view of what is going on is hewing its way forward with great difficulty through a dense thicket of prejudices and preconceptions in the thinking of the ruling class. But the complexity and acuteness of this moment in history makes it increasingly vital to outlaw nuclear weapons, destroy them and other weapons of mass annihilation completely, and improve international relations.

World developments confirm the fundamental Marxist-Leninist conclusion that the history of society is not a sum of fortuitous elements, that it is not a disorderly Brownian motion, but a law-governed onward process. Not only do its contradictions pass sentence on the old world, on everything that impedes the advance; they are also the source, the motive force behind the progress of society, progress that is taking place in the context of the struggle that is inevitable as long as exploitation and exploiting classes still exist.

Here we can speak of a whole complex of impelling motives: the predatory appetites of the arms manufacturers and the influential military-bureaucratic groups, the selfish interest of the monopolies in sources of raw materials and sales markets, the bourgeoisie's fear of the ongoing changes, and, lastly, the attempts to resolve its own, worsening problems at socialism's expense.

The latter are especially typical of U.S. imperialism. It was nothing but imperial ideology and policy, the wish to create the most unfavorable external conditions for socialism and for the USSR that prompted the start of the race of nuclear and other arms after 1945, just when the crushing defeat of fascism and militarism was, it would seem, offering a realistic opportunity for building a world without wars, and a mechanism of international cooperation—the United Nations—had been created for this purpose. But imperialism's nature asserted itself that time again.

Today, too, the right wing of the U.S. monopolistic bourgeoisie regards the stoking up of international tensions as something that justifies military allocations, claims to global supremacy, interference in the affairs of other states, and an offensive against the interests and rights of the American working people. No small role seems to be played by the calculation of using tension to exercise pressure on the allies, to make them completely obedient, to subordinate them to Washington's dictation.

Will the ruling centres of the capitalist world manage to embark on the path of sober, constructive assessments of what is going on? The easiest thing is to say: maybe yes and maybe no. But history denies us the right to make such predictions. We cannot take "no" for an answer to the question: Will mankind survive or not? We say: The progress of society, the life of civilization, must and will continue. (**prolonged applause**)

The United States and its military-industrial machine, which so far does not intend to slow its pace, remain the locomotive of militarism. This must of course be taken into account. But we understand very well that the interests and goals of the military-industrial complex are by no means the same as the interests and goals of the U.S. people and genuine national interests of that great country.

The first of them can be described as the lesson of truth. A responsible analysis of the past clears the path to the future, while half-truths, shamefully avoiding sharp angles, slow down the working out of realistic policies and hinders our progress.

"Our strength," Vladimir Ilich Lenin used to say, "lies in stating the truth." (**prolonged applause**) That is why the Central Committee considered it necessary in the new edition of the party program to once again speak of the negative processes which emerged in the seventies and the beginning of the eighties, and that is why we are also talking about them today at the congress."[40]

This appeal for openness was to be severely tested in the Soviet information policy following the April 1986 Chernobyl disaster. Soviet public silence in the aftermath of the calamity sparked a negative reaction toward the Soviet Union in the west, particularly among the countries directly affected by the nuclear fall-out.

The Soviet Chernobyl Nuclear Calamity

On April 25, 1986, a series of events occurred at the Chernobyl nuclear facility near Kiev in the Soviet Union, leading to a fire, explosion and continuing meltdown. The explosion and fire released a plume of radioactive materials into the air. The radioactive plume traveled west, then northwest toward East European and Scandinavian countries. The Soviet Union did not warn her neighbors to the west and north of the accident and the approach of radioactive clouds. Only after excessive radiation (100 times higher than normal) was detected in Sweden did the Soviets in fact admit that the catastrophe had taken place.

The Soviet delay in releasing detailed information on the Chernobyl accident contrasts sharply with the handling of industrial accidents in other countries. The accidents at Three Mile Island and in Bhopal, India, were followed by immediate and detailed reporting of what happened and full public investigation.

The secrecy surrounding Chernobyl is also in sharp contrast with Soviet General Secretary Gorbachev's call for "glasnost"—more public discussion of problems in the USSR. As "Die Welt" of West Germany editorialized: "Soviet references to international cooperation, confidence-building measures, 'security partnership' between Moscow and the West as well as Gorbachev's thesis of the 'common European house' have proved to be nothing but empty phrases. The Soviets have frivolously contaminated the 'common house.' (Die Welt, May 2, 1986)

It took the Soviets one full day after Sweden recorded heightened radiation readings to acknowledge the accident. Five days later, they had still not fully explained what happened, when, why and with what potential consequences. Soviet television showed only a snapshot of the damaged reactor, made by a worker and said, "as you can see for yourself, there was no gigantic destruction or fire."

If the official approach divulged little about the accident, it spoke volumes about the Soviet system, about the relationship of the state to the individual. Since taking power Mikhail S. Gorbachev, the Soviet leader, had been preaching greater openness in the press and greater candor about failings. But when Chernobyl struck, the Kremlin reverted to its time honored pattern of rationing information and castigating the West.

It was an approach rooted in a view that information is a tool of the state, and that domestic disasters must not be allowed to spread alarm or to raise questions about the wisdom of Soviet leaders.

On May 14, three weeks after the nuclear disaster, Mikhail Gorbachev candidly described what had happened at Chernobyl. "The new Soviet leader, facing his first international crisis, finally stood erect in disclosing the toll, in virtually apologizing for the anxiety caused in other nations by the radiation cloud from Chernobyl and in acknowledging the assistance swiftly offered from abroad. That part of his speech was only a sample of how enlightened governments ought to address a common danger in the nuclear age.[41]

In a paradoxical way the Soviets may gain from their mode of commenting on the Chernobyl calamity. Rather than blaming Soviet incompetence they blamed the "inherent instability of nuclear reactors." In the West a negative reaction against nuclear power has been blown up perhaps beyond repair.

For example, Sweden's Prime Minister Ingvar Carlsson assailed nuclear power, particularly stressing the Chernobyl disaster, which has forced many Swedes to change their eating habits. "Nuclear power is one of the greatest threats to our environment," Mr. Carlsson told a labor rally in Stockholm, adding that the Chernobyl accident had strengthened Sweden's conviction that nuclear power must be eliminated.

Influential groups within Mr. Carlsson's ruling Social Democratic Party want an immediate abolition of nuclear power, which provides more than 40 percent of Sweden's energy. Sweden says its nuclear program is the safest in the world. Mr. Carlsson's position up to now has been that the reactors will be closed down ahead of schedule only if experts appointed by the Government say nuclear power is dangerous.[42]

In the not too distant future both western nations and the Soviets will become increasingly dependent on electricity generated by nuclear reactors. In the West nuclear energy requires acceptance by public opinion.

Whether they like it or not Soviet citizens will have nuclear energy. On June 18, 1986 Prime Minister Nikolai I. Ryzhkov affirmed Soviet plans to expand nuclear power production despite the Chernobyl disaster.

The Daniloff Affair and Reykjavik

The Soviet handling of the Chernobyl nuclear disaster revealed the hollowness of Gorbachev's pledge of "openness" on the part of the Soviet Union. The subsequent KGB frame up of a U.S. reporter, Nicholas S. Daniloff, on trumped up spying charges revealed a pattern of malignant Soviet behaviour reminiscent of the Stalin era.

The KGB made a hostage out of Daniloff in retaliation for the FBI seizure of Soviet physicist and UN employee, Gennadi F. Zakarov who was caught red-handed purchasing military secrets from a double agent. After intense U.S.-Soviet negotiations, personally handled by Secretary of State Shultz, the two men were initially released to their respective national embassies while still subject to trial.

> "These actions agreed to by the United States and the Soviet Union are an interim step," Mr. Shultz said. "In taking this step, the United States Government had prominently in mind the well-being of Mr. Daniloff.
>
> "There can be no question of equating the cases of Mr. Daniloff and Zakharov. Mr. Daniloff is not a spy.[43]

A New York Times editorial summarized the American outrage over this kind of brazen, brutal Soviet behavior.

> Nicholas Daniloff remains a hostage in Moscow and the United States has been forced for the moment to equate his status with that of an accused Soviet spy in New York. Their simultaneous release from jail, under identical terms, so far ratifies an obvious Soviet extortion. But at least Mr. Daniloff is relieved of grueling daily interrogations and life in a tiny cell.[44]

Finally a swap was made of the American reporter and the Soviet spy with the latter flying out of the United States a few hours before Daniloff set foot on American soil. During the process of making this swap President Reagan accepted Gorbachev's proposal for the two of them to meet in Reykjavik, Iceland on the weekend of October 11–12.

The willingness of President Reagan to meet with the Soviet leader in Iceland rather than in the United States was due to a significant foreign policy shift in the second Reagan administration from an initial apparent indifference toward the significance of the role of arms control in U.S.-Soviet relations to a 1986 momentum that arms control might be the door to a more stable world. An example of this shift was the announcement on August 7 by the Reagan administration that it was going to send its top arms control team to Moscow to explore with Soviet counterparts, areas where progress could be made before a possible Reagan-Gorbachev summit meeting.

In part the decision to send a top team to Moscow was made to counter arms control moves in Congress that were opposed by the administration. In part it was in response to Gorbachev's clever campaign to shift attention from Soviet political warfare activities to arms control negotiations. From Reagan's decision to send the top U.S. Arms control team to Moscow the Reykjavik summit eventually emerged.

At Reykjavik sweeping proposals were made by both sides for drastic reductions in offensive nuclear weapons. There was even talk about their eventual elimination.

The two sides disagreed over what precisely Mr. Reagan said in Reykjavik about the possible elimination of strategic, or long-range, offensive forces by 1996 and about the broader issue of abolishing all nuclear arms.

At a Moscow briefing on Oct. 25, 1986, Aleksandr A. Bessmertnykh, a Deputy Foreign Minister, said, "The President made the following statement, and again I quote:

'If we agree that by the end of the 10-year period, all nuclear arms are to be eliminated, we can refer this to our delegations in Geneva to prepare an agreement that you could sign during your visit to the United States.'"[45]

Although unhappy about the Soviet disclosure the White House did not quarrel with the Soviet statement in order to preserve its credibility with Moscow.

The Reykjavik talks broke up after President Reagan refused to consider Gorbachev's demands that the U.S. put the SDI program on ice. There is much evidence that the Soviet aim at Reykjavik was to stop the U.S. SDI while going full speed ahead with their own "star wars" R&D, testing in space and deployment.

In a TV speech to the Soviet people on October 14, 1986 Gorbachev stated:

"After Reykjavik, the S.D.I. has become an even more sore spot in everybody's eyes, as a thorn, as a stumbling block, which does not allow us to find a way out of the threat that hangs over the heads of mankind. There is no other way of looking at it after the meeting in Reykjavik, and in summing up what has happened in these days, I would say that this was an important event. It has been a reassessment and has created a qualitatively new situation. And nobody is now in a position to act the way he was able to act before.[46]"

Soviet military strategy which ungirds the Soviet aim of defeating the United States without war demands that the Soviet Union obtain offensive and defensive nuclear superiority over the U.S. This goal can be reached by simultaneously pursuing a "foreign policy in the streets" designed to frustrate effective U.S.defense efforts.

Within a few days of the collapse of the Reykjavik summit both sides were talking about making new arms control progress. Mr. Reagan and Mr. Shultz, believe that Mr. Gorbachev was negotiating in good faith and that the concessions put on the table cannot be withdrawn so easily.

"They believe there are grounds for some hope that they can make progress with the Russians in coming months. From what was said by Mr. Gorbachev, it looks as if Moscow also believes there is room for additional bargaining, particularly on reducing the number of medium range missiles."

According to Richard Pipes, "The shift of the Reagan administration toward making arms control the dominant focus of U.S.-Soviet relations can be traced to the bureaucratic ascending of Mr. Shultz. Mr. Reagan now receives his advice on policy toward Moscow from a single source, Secretary of State George P. Shultz. The National Security Council has been reduced to near impotence and the White House staff lacks the expertise to offer alternative views. Mr. Shultz seems as firmly in control of American foreign policy as Henry A. Kissinger was at the height of his powers, and he has used this authority quietly to turn the President's Soviet policy around by 180 degrees.

The rationale behind the Administration's shift and its sense of urgency is the belief that Mikhail S. Gorbachev faces a profound internal crisis and is therefore genuinely eager for some sort of "deal."[47]

Gorbachev does want a deal but not the kind sought by Mr. Shultz. Gorbachev's principle advisor on how to deal with the U.S. is Anatoly Dobrynin who was the Kremlin's Ambassador to Washington for 25 years. Dobrynin advises Gorbachev on how to manipulate American and congressional public opinion with proposals and gestures that can trap the U.S. with little cost to the Soviets. "Peace" via arms control has become the focus of Soviet diplomacy and the struggle for peace has become the new label for the class struggle aimed at defeating capitalism. Neither Mr. Shultz nor anyone in his immediate entourage has anywhere near the insight into the Soviet system, as Dobrynin has about ours.

Not surprisingly Secretary of State George P. Shultz had this to say about the Iceland meeting:

> The Reykjavik meeting between President Reagan and General Secretary Mikhail S. Gorbachev was an extraordinary event. Far more was achieved than anyone had considered possible. If the Soviets are as prepared as we to follow through on the work done last week, Reykjavik could set the stage for a major advance in United States-Soviet relations, one that could potentially transform the international security landscape.[48]

This assertion verges on the utopian as can be seen from the sorry record of western negotiations with the Soviets. The aim of Soviet negotiators ever since Lenin seized power in 1917 has been to divert western attention from what they are really doing while the west is nourishing the hope that the Soviets will come to terms with their opponents.

Suppose we fall into the Soviet trap and postpone the U.S. SDI until the Soviets have their version of SDI operational. In the process we might even agree to give up all nuclear weapons. Such a mutual agreement to disarm, if actually carried out, would probably give rise to new means of conflict, which could ultimately be as destructive to political institutions and human values as the outlawed weapons systems. In fact, many strategists contend that the existence of nuclear weapons has forced the superpowers to proceed with great caution and to conduct their competition with limited violence. Such analysts fear that if nuclear weapons should be done away with, the tendency toward the full-scale use of force might very well reappear. This could lead to conditions of grave instability and, sooner or later, to general war, which, paradoxically, would be likely to become nuclear.

The goal of the communists is peace—but for their kind of peace, the precondition is the elimination or conversion of non-communist political systems. Practically all persons who seek an alternative to the present armed truce share the belief that evolutionary changes will have to take place within the Soviet system if the basis for a more peaceful world is to be created. The issue dividing the advocates of differing paths toward peace is really one of means. There is no guarantee against war, but there is almost a moral certainty that if we remain strong, there will be no nuclear holocaust in the indefinite future.

President Reagan has fully endorsed serious arms control negotiations with the Soviet Union. Some arms control advocates believe that President Reagan has the opportunity to conclude the most comprehensive arms limitations in history. For him to do so, we are told that the President must take charge and personally establish the contours of a plausible U.S.-Soviet agreement. Perhaps such contours can be found but not at the expense of U.S. security.

The Nature of the Soviet Regime

In 1986 a Soviet soldier who deserted in Afghanistan went to the United States and later decided to return to his homeland:

> "Upon his return Nikilai Ryzhkov was tried, convicted of high treason and sentenced to a labor camp in Moldavia for twelve years. What makes this case particularly poignant is that Ryzhkov returned home voluntarily. Anatoly Dobrynin, then the Soviet Ambassador in Washington and now a major foreign policy official for the Communist Party, *guaranteed* Ryzhkov that he would not be prosecuted. So much for one's word and the rule of law in the Soviet Union. If one of the highest ranking officials in the state can lie, it is clearly an approach to the law countenenced by every political figure."[49]

Would Dobrynin advise Gorbachev to always tell the truth in negotiating with the U.S.?

It is difficult for most westerners to really believe the true character of the Soviet regime—to accept the fact that our opponents do not act on principle but only on expediency. President Reagan once called the Soviet Union "an evil empire" and was castigated for so doing. Perhaps the President had once read Reinhold Niebuhr's profound essay, "Why is Communism so Evil?"[50] What makes communism so evil and what are the sources of its malignancy? We are bound to ask the question because we are fated as a generation to live in the insecurity which this universal evil of commnunism creates for our world. The timid spirits ask another question: is communism really as evil as we now think; or are we tempted by the tensions of our conflict with it to exaggerate our negative judgements about it.

Niebuhr answers this question in several ways:

"If we seek to isolate the various causes of an organized evil which spreads terror and cruelty throughout the world and confronts us everywhere with faceless men who are immune to every form of moral and political suasion, we must inevitably begin with the monopoly of power which communism establishes. Disproportions of power anywhere in the human community are fruitful of injustice, but a system which gives some men absolute power over other men results in evils which are worse than injustice.

"Another reason for the excessive concentration of power is that the Marxist theory wrongly assumes that economic power inheres solely in the ownership of property and obscures the power of the manager of property. It therefore wrongly concludes that the socialization of property causes economic power to evaporate when in fact it merely gives a single oligarchy a monopal of both economic and political power.

"The Marxist dogmatism, coupled wth its pretensions of scientific rationality, is an additional source of evil. The dogmas are the more questionable because the tyrannical organization prevents a re-examination of the dogmas when the facts refute them.

"Niebuhr summed up his analysis of why communism is so evil in this fashion."

"The evil of communism flows from a combination of political and "spiritual" factors, which prove that the combination of power and pride is responsible for turning the illusory dreams of yesterday into the present nightmare that disturbs the ease of millions of men in our generation."

All Marxist dogmatism is based on philosophical materialism. Both Marx and Lenin held to a materialistic philosophy which rejects any higher force than the earths and waters from which the body of a man and the body of a fly are made. In materialist morality there is no difference between swatting a fly or killing a man as exemplified by the genocidal Soviet war against the Afghan freedom fighters.

The major reason why the West is retreating in the face of the Soviet assault on freedom is that many Western intellectuals are unable or unwilling to see what Niebuhr so starkly described. A typical example of illusory thinking is the following rejoinder to Richard Pipes's contention that arms control negotiations should not be the core activity of U.S.-Soviet relations.

Richard Pipes's thesis (Op-Ed, Oct. 10) that arms control enables the Kremlin to preserve the Stalinist system should not go unchallenged. The contrary contention comes closer to the truth: arms control helps the Kremlin to dismantle the Stalinist heritage. General Secretary Mikhail S. Gorbachev is the least Stalinist among the post-Stalin leaders; he tries to introduce a new openness and tolerance, over the protest of the old-time Stalinists. In addition, as Professor Pipes states, he faces a crisis: his Government cannot live up to its promise of improving living standards and at the same time match the pace set by the United States in the arms race.[51]

How much more realistic is the testimony of a man who has experienced the evil of communism first-hand. This man is Eugene Loebl[52] a former Czech Communist who was tortured and tried in 1952 and spent 14 years in prison at least 5 of which were in solitary confinement. Loebl described the human dilemma in dealing with communism this way:

To apply to the world a theory developed before 1850, even if it were correct at that time, when all societal problems have changed all of us who advocated that theory in *this* century bear a grave moral responsibility, even though we have suffered terribly for our mistakes. To face this fact, to question this dream, is a painful experience, and some can go through the pain and some cannot.[53]

The malignant dream fashioned by Marx and subsequently developed by Lenin has created the most vicious form of totalitarianism ever known by man. The Soviet Union is not a normal state but the headquarters of a conspiracy determined to eradicate human freedom throughout the globe. Stefan Possony summed up the strategic dichotomy that exists between Communists and their opponents succinctly:

The political victory of communism requires the moral destruction and the physical defeat of the bourgeoisie. The strength of communism must be increased physically and morally, while the weaknesses of the burgbeoisie are to be accentuated, physically and morally. To their own defeat, the bourgeoisie must contribute partial self-destruction. Bourgeois self-destruction will result from demoralization. Demoralization will be stimulated by "pacifism." The war for communism must use peace as one of its most powerful weapons. The idea is simple indeed: degeneratvie peace for the bourgeoisie and a strong war for the communists.[54]

In dealing with Gobvachev we must not forget that he is a protégé of Andropov, former head of the KGB. Gorbachev served in that notorious organization as did many of his closest associates. The one god they worship is power. Before the Soviet onslaught against freedom can be checked, Soviet leaders will have to abandon the Marxism-Leninism on which their edifice of power rests.

Many will assert that this description of the Soviet regime is both too harsh and unrealistic. The almost simultaneous December 1986 release of Sakhorov from internal exile and the reporting on Soviet TV of anti-Soviet rioting in Kazakhstan demonstrated Gorbachev's ability to pursue his policy of openness designed to give Moscow's diplomacy a new look. During his December meeting with possible presidential candidate Gary Hart, he downplayed the U.S.-Iranian weapons deal crisis and stressed his desire to reach a major arms control agreement with the U.S. Simultaneously, Moscow announced resumption of underground nuclear testing after the first American explosion in 1987. This indicated the end of Moscow unilateral testing moratorium, an exercise in Gorbachev-style diplomacy. The Reagan Administration regarded the test ban as a public relations ploy, but the moratorium gave Moscow the high ground on a symbolic arms-control issue and contributed to anxiety in Congress about American arms policy. 57 members of the 1987 Senate have urged President Reagan to reverse his decision to exceed weapons ceilings set in the unratified 1979 strategic arms limitation treaty. Obvisously Gorbachev will continue to press arms control as the center piece of his "peace" offensive.

Writing in the Winter 1986/87 issue of "Foreign Affairs", Robert G. Kaiser noted the, "substantial qualitative change that Gobachev has brought to Soviet political discourse," He argued that official confidence in the certain victory of socialism over capitalism which might be called the Great Pretense (the title of his article) is collapsing under Mikhail Gorbachev. This may enable the West to "achieve a new, more sensible consensus on the Soviet problem and how best to deal with it." Kaiser conceded, however, that Gorbachev (or a successor) "could revert to a deliberate policy of an artificial cold war as a cover for the country's shortcomings."

Senator Daniel Moynihan in a December 21, 1986 N.Y. times Op Ed article entitled: "Reagan's Doctrine and the Iran Issue" argued that "we are obsessed with the false belief that communism is expanding." He cited "the near complete collapse of Marxism as an ideogical force," while asserting, "we do not extend that proposition to Leninism." In fact, with respect to Marxist-Leninist insurgencies in the Third World, "we may predict that between now and the year two thousand between four and eleven such regimes will come to power. I would put Haiti on a list of candidates, if we don't act."

There is no unanimity among seasoned Soviet observers as to how Gorbachev's Soviet Empire will march into the future. It is still not time to accept that Gorbachev believes that the inevitable "triumph of socialism is no longer possible.

This book has sought to demonstrate that the Soviet Union inspired by Marxism-Leninism is expanionist by nature, brutally repressive and in Niebuhr's view, an evil and malignant empire.

What Is To Be Done

None of the policies the U.S. has pursued during the past 40 years toward the Soviet Union have been effective. NSC 68 submitted to President Truman, in April 1950, was the most ambitious. It called for a defensive military political policy of containment combined with an offensive ideological policy of planting and nurturing "the seeds of destruction within the Soviet system." The NSC 68 enemy was not the Soviet people but the leaders of the Soviet system. Unfortunately, the Soviet Union was never contained. Paul Nitze, the principal architect of NSC 68 advocated in a 1985 *Foreign Affairs* article a policy of "live and let live." This makes sense if the Soviets would reciprocate. This they will not do as long as their march toward world domination appears to them increasingly attainable.

During the early 70s, President Nixon and Henry Kissinger tried detente to tame the Soviet bear. The alleged aim of the detente strategy was to create an inter-locking web of relationships with the Soviet Union. Through such a web, "vested interests" would be created within the Soviet Union which would inhibit Soviet leaders to reverting to aggression. This theory was exploded by the Soviet-backed 1973 Egyptian-Israeli War.

Jimmy Carter asked us to abandon our "inordinate fear of communism" and to focus on building up the Third World and expanding human rights. This idyllic dream was punctured by the December 1979 Soviet invasion of Afghanistan.

President Reagan began his first term by becoming the first western leader to tell the world that the Soviet Union was in fact an "Evil Empire." Later in a speech before British parliament on June 8, 1982, President Reagan urged the West to begin "a crusade for freedom that will engage the faith and fortitude of the next generation. For the sake of peace and justice, let us move toward a world in which all people are at last free to determine their own destiny."

Unfortunately, the U.S. and its democratic allies have had little stomach to wage a crusade for freedom against the Soviet Union. So once again, negotiations and possible arms control agreements have become the magic formula for curbing aggressive Soviet behavior.

Every possible effort should be made to obtain an equitable and verifiable strategic arms reduction agreement with the Soviet Union. But do the Soviets want to bargain away their politically important strategic advantage which they built up at tremendous costs over the past 20 years? I think not.

Exceptionally well-informed, Henry S. Rowen, who has served at high levels in both Democratic and Republican administrations, believes that the "Soviet leaders have not shared our views" on arms control.

> "They built up as we built down for 20 years, almost eliminating our air defense, dropping civil defense, and reducing spending on offensive forces and their megatonnage. Moscow has never shared the peculiar American view of arms control. To Moscow, the functions of arms control are to show us where we have a technical advantage (e.g. ballistic-missile defenses in the early 1970s) or are behind and are about to move out (anti-satellite weapons and ballistic-missile defenses today); to prevent deployments intended to strengthen U.S. ties to Europe (block NATO's intermediate-range missiles); to try to preserve a Soviet advantage ("heavy" missiles in SALT-I) and so on.[55]

After observing that when we try to limit forces by agreement "we get mostly self-restraint and the illusion of Soviet restraint," Rowen concluded:

Notwithstanding the potential for agreements on selected issues, there is no important U.S. objective related to the balance of nuclear forces, or the role of these forces in discouraging Soviet moves abroad, which is obtainable through any remotely feasible arms-control *agreement*. Nor will the Soviets agree to anything that entails abandoning their aim of splitting our alliance or hindering them in coercing the democracies. If we want a better protected and more discriminate nuclear force—and, if possible, a less costly one—we will have to get it on our own.[56]

As the U.S. moves toward acceptance of Gorbachev's March 1987 gambit for removing all medium range missiles from Central Europe, Rowen's appraisal should be kept in mind. Andre Giraud, the French Minister of Defense, called acceptance of Gorbachev's missile ploy a "Munich" of nuclear appeasement.

Despite accumulating evidence that Soviet society, organized in accordance with the precepts and practices of Marxism-Leninism, is grieviously flawed, there has been no sustained and systematic effort made to expose the root cause of the massive human failure of Lenin's experiment. This root cause is, simply, the Communist philosophy as created by Marx and subsequently developed by Lenin which claims to rest on objective, "scientific" analysis. There is no basis for this spurious claim.

Soviet rulers claim to have ended all forms of exploitation of man by man, which the Soviet Union asserts is endemic in capitalist societies. Yet the Soviet hierarchial system, dominated by its nomenklatura is one of the most oppressive and exploitive systems ever designed by man.

According to Milovan Djilas, Michael Voslensky's "Nomenklatura—The Soviet Ruling Class—an Insider's Report," (Doubleday & Company, 1984) "indisputably belongs to the best that has ever been written about the Soviet system."

Voslensky asserts:

"Lenin and Stalin created a new class, the nucleus of which was Lenin's organization of professional revolutionaries. After the seizure of power by that organization, Stalin's nomenklatura arose and became the ruling class in the Soviet Union.

The nomenklatura is a class of privileged exploiters. It acquired wealth from power, not power from wealth. The domestic policy of the nomenklatura class is to consolidate its dictatorial power, and its foreign policy is to extend it to the whole world."

The Communists are fighting with great skill, determination and conviction. But Communism can be defeated, once Western societies really understand their enemy and wage the kind of struggle the situation demands.

The last thing to go when the Soviet Union rejoins the world community of pluralism and freedom, will be the cruel utopian dreams of Marx and Lenin. But eventually they too will be abandoned by future leaders in Moscow.

The pre-condition of such an outcome will be the realization by the Soviet leadership that the Soviet drive for world domination is unattainable. This recognition will take a long time in coming and will come only if the U.S. and its allies are able to block further Soviet expansionism.

Beyond that the United States and its allies must work to help bring about a fundamental change in the reactionary Soviet political system. There will be no real peace for the world unless such a transformation of the Soviet political system takes place.

At a conference held in Washington late in 1985, sponsored by the Committee for the Free World, Irving Kristol said:

> "We are not going to achieve any stability in this world or reach any level of satisfaction, or attainment, in American foreign policy until the Soviet Union has been pushed into an ideological reformation—that is to say, until the Soviet Union ceases being a political regime with an established religion called Marxist Leninism imposed on the Soviet people."[57]

Richard Pipes, a Harvard history professor and National Security Council member in 1981–1982, agreed. The Soviet regime, he said, depends on "the notion of invincibility." A Russian defeat abroad, he stated, would mean that the Soviets "would immediately suffer domestic consequences."[58]

The average citizen of the Soviet Union knows the flaws of the Soviet society far better than any outsider. Except in the leadership group, there are no real Marxists, let alone communists, in the Soviet Union. The time has come for the United States to encourage the domestic Soviet forces which could bring about a fundamental transformation in the Soviet system of internal rule and could thus disarm the power which the Soviets use to threaten the West.

Some believe nothing should be done to destabilize the Soviet system for fear of triggering a nuclear war. Actually, the Soviet system already appears to be disintegrating due to the internal contradictions of Marxism—a process which will continue come what may. It is difficult to believe that spreading more realistic accounts of what is happening within the Soviet Empire than are officially available, can make the process more dangerous. It could conceivably have the reverse effect, since it would aid those Soviet citizens, such as Sakharov, who wish to change their society, unfetter their economy, and stop Soviet expansion. The fact that the Kremlin leadership goes to great lengths to prevent "subversive" literature and radio programs from reaching the Soviet people shows how fearsome they are of the spoken and written truth. The hunger for Western books in the Soviet bloc, particularly those presenting a critical view of Soviet society, is insatiable: worn copies of "Animal Farm," Solzhenitsyn's works, and Robert Conquest's "The Great Terror" change hands on the black market at high prices.

The Soviet propaganda campaign sends the West massive barrages of left-wing tracts, subsidizes left-wing journals, plants false rumors among sympathetic western journalists, and cultivates Free-World politicians, academics and others who can serve Soviet purposes. In the Third World, the USSR supports "wars of national liberation" by spreading false accounts of Western ambitions and provides counterfeit documents as supporting evidence.

It is time for the West to undertake a systematic campaign of exposing the philosophical, political, and operational vulnerabilities of Soviet communism. The crisis of communism in Poland is but the most recent demonstration of the failure of Marxism-Leninism to create a humane existence for people living under its oppressive tenets. Soviet vulnerabilities are legion, but we must have the wit, develop the means, and have the will to exploit them. Helping the Soviet people transform their system is the only alternative to a costly unending struggle to maintain military equilibrium and check Soviet forays into every part of the globe.

The Soviets pursue military superiority while simultaneously waging a campaign of subversion against free societies everywhere.

If we are to reverse this struggle, we must change our strategy and battle for the ideas of freedom as vigorously as the Soviet Union conducts its campaign for fictitious peace. The Soviet definition of peaceful co-existence permits them to employ unlimited subversion against all free societies. Free people have the right and the obligation to fight by the same rules against the Soviet nomenklatura.

The rationale and imperative for helping to bring about a transformation in the Soviet political system was set forth in a short book entitled, *A Strategy for Peace Through Strength*. This study described why and how the world is at a cross-road.

The world is going to have peace through strength. What is being decided now is whose strength and whose peace.

The leaders of the Soviet Union want a peace in which they dominate all other nations. Americans and most of the people of the world want peace with freedom.[59]

NOTES

1. *The New York Times,* March 15, 1985, p. A.7.
2. Simes, Dimitri K., "Gorbachev's Hardball with a Soft Touch" *New York Times,* April 19, 1985, p. A31.
3. Goldman, Marshall I., "The Kremlin's Grain Disaster," *New York Times,* September 23, 1981, p. 31.
4. Lochau, Miriam and Lee, Ta-Ling et al. "Bread, Rice, and Freedom", *Freedom at Issue,* May–June 1983, p. 3.
5. *Ibid,* p. 5.
6. *New York Times,* August 5, 1983.
7. *Soviet Military Power,* (op. cit.), p. 71.

8. Education and Employment of Scientists and Engineers in U.S. and U.S.S.R. Summary Report and Commentary in *Implications for U.S. National Security Policy,* Stanford Research Institute, May 1981.
9. Labedez, Leopold, "Ideology and Soviet Foreign Policy", *Philadelphia Papers,* No. 151, Summer 1979, page 92.
10. Krasin, Victor, "How I was Broken by the KGB", *New York Times Magazine,* March 18, 1984.
11. *Philadelphia Inquirer,* April 11, 1985, p. 3A.
12. Elegant, Robert, "How to Lose a War", *Encounter,* August 1981, p. 88.
13. Revel, Jean-Francois, *How Democracies Perish,* Doubleday, NY, 1984, p. 3-4.
14. Tass Accuses State Department of 'New Falsehood' on Nicaragua LD042059 Moscow Tass in English 1515 GMT 4 Sep 85 ("Falsehood"—Tass Headline)
15. Sir James Goldsmith, publisher of L'Express news magazine, Paris, Wall Street Journal, Aug. 22, 1984, p. 24.
16. Andrei Gromyko, "Lenin's Peace Policy," *Moscow News,* 22 April 1984.
17. *New York Times,* April 29, 1985, p. A6. (Moscow, April 23 AP). Following are the excerpts from Mikhail S. Gorbachev's speech to the Communist Party Central Committee, as distributed in translation by the Soviet press agency Tass)
18. The *New York Times,* Nov. 22, 1985, p. 2.
19. *Ibid.*
20. *New York Times,* Nov. 23, 1985, p. 6.
21. *Ibid.*
22. *Ibid.*
23. Nixon, Richard, Superpower Summitry, Foreign Affairs, 1985, p. 1.
24. *U.S. News and World Report,* Inc. Nov. 18, 1985.
25. *Ibid.* 31
26. Excerpts from Gorbachev's news conference 'All have a Stake' Geneva, Nov. 21 (AP)— Following are excerpts from Mikhail S. Gorbachev's news conference in Geneva today, as translated by the Swiss organizers of the summit meeting.) In the *New York Times,* Nov. 22, 1985, A-10. Subsequent references to his news conference will be from this same source.
27. FBIS. LD251438 Moscow TASS in English 1433 GMT 25 Oct. 85 ["Draft New Edition of the CPSU's Programme"—TASS headline]
28. Why Moscow has the Best Argument, The Guardian, Nov. 14, 1985, p. 12.
29. "The Struggle Against Imperialist War and the Tasks of the Communists, 33
30. Gorbachev, Mikhail, *"A Time For Peace",* Richardson and Steinman, New York, 1985, p. 3.
31. *Ibid,* p. 4.
32. *Ibid,* p. 23
33. *Ibid,* p. 26
34. *The Philadephia Inquirer*
35. *Deane, Michael J. Strategic Defense in Soviet Strategy,* Monographs in International Affairs, Advanced International Studies Institute, from the foreword by Mose L. Harvey, Director, p. III, IV
36. Nitze, Paul, SDI: Soviet Program, United States Department of State, current policy, No. 717, 1985.
37. Ralph K. Bennet, "Russia's Secret Red Shield", *Reader's Digest,* July 1986, p. 14c.
38. (Wendell J. Coats, "Clausewitz's Theory on War; An Alternative View Comparitive Strategy, Vol. 5, No. 4, Crane, Russek and Co. 1986, p. 370)
39. *New York Times,* Jan. 15, 1986, p. 1.
40. Current Digest of the Soviet Union, March 28, 1986. [Political Report of the CPSU Central Committee delivered on 25 February by M.S. Gorbachev, general secretary of the CPSU Central Committee, to the 27th CPSU Congress at the Kremlin Palace of Congresses— differences between *PRAVDA* and Moscow Television version noted within brackets; the

Moscow Television version was originally published in the 26 and 27 February Soviet Union *DAILY REPORT* National Affairs Supplement Nos 038 and 039; this authoritative *PRAVDA* version is being published for archival purposes]

41. (New York Times Editorial, May 16, 1986, p. A-34)
42. *New York Times,* Aug. 18, 1986, p. A-6
43. *New York Times,* Sept. 13, 1986, p. 4
44. *New York Times* Editorial, Sept. 13, 1986, p. 26
45. *New York Times,* October 26, 1986, p. 1
46. *New York Times,* Oct. 15, 1986, p. A2
47. Richard Pipes, *New York Times,* Oct. 14, 1986, p. A39
48. George P. Shultz, op to *New York Times,* Oct. 19, 1986, E-23
49. Herbert London, "The USSR is Still a Regime of Liars" *New York Tribune,* Oct. 7, 1986. Dr. Herbert I. London is dean of the Gallatin Division of New York University and director of the Hudson Institute's Visions of the Future division.
50. Reinhold, Niebuhr, "Why Is Communism So Evil?" published in the New Leader, June 8, 1953, republished in "The World Crisis and American Response" nine essays edited by Ernest W. Lefever, *Association Press,* 1958
51. Letter to the Editor, "Its in Our Power to Ease East-West Tensions, *New York Times,* Oct. 26, 1986, E, 22. Theodore H. Von Laue, Prof. of European History Emeritus, Clark University, Worcester, Mass.
52. The author had several long discussions with Loebl after he fled from Czechoslovakia 1968.
53. Methvin, Eugene, Hitler, Stalin, Superkillers, National Review, May 31st, 1985, p. 29
54. Stefen Possony, "A Century of Conflict" Henry Regency Co., 1953, p. 418
55. Henry S. Rowen, "Potholes on the Road to Geneva," *The Wall Street Journal,* Dec. 17, 1984.
56. *Ibid.*
57. Push the Russians, Intellectuals Ask, *New York Times,* Oct. 25, 1985, A-9
58. *Ibid*
59. *A Strategy for Peace Through Strength,* published by the American Security Council, Boston, VA, 1984, p. VIII. The content of this study is the sole responsibility of the Strategy Board of the ASC Foundation. The Strategy Board Co-Chairman of the ASC Foundation are: Dr. Ray Cline, John M. Fisher, Ambassador William Kintner, Dr. William Van Cleave, Rear Admiral Robert H. Sprio, Jr. USNR (Ret.)

Index